CW00825715

The Travel Journals of

Robert Hyde Greg

THE TRAVEL JOURNALS OF
ROBERT HYDE GREG
OF QUARRY BANK MILL

TRAVELS IN SCOTLAND,
SPAIN AND PORTUGAL,
FRANCE, ITALY, AND THE
OTTOMAN EMPIRE
1814–17

EDITED BY

BERYL AND ALLEN FREER

For Ann —
with love and every
good wish from
Beryl + Allen

SHAUN TYAS
DONINGTON
2007

Published from the discs of the editors by
SHAUN TYAS
1 High Street
Donington
PE11 4TA

ISBN
978-1900289-887

Printed and bound in the United Kingdom by Biddles of King's Lynn

CONTENTS

For Adam and Gaby
with gratitude and affection

PREFACE

Shaw's Bookshop in Police Street, Manchester now no longer exists, but when I knew it in the seventies and eighties of the last century, it was a place of bibliophilic serendipity, for you never knew what you would discover – anything from a seventeenth-century Herbal to a modern first edition in its original book jacket. So it came as no surprise that I made a chance discovery in the summer of 1983 when I went to the bookshop during a mid-week lunch break. On the bookseller's desk was a large manilla envelope, roughly opened, out of which spilled half a dozen pocket-sized notebooks written in elegant copperplate on hand-made paper. Three of them were bound in calf, as if ready for a gentleman's library. The others were shabby, quarter-bound books with rather battered marbled covers. The dates written on the flyleaves intrigued me – 1814, 1815, 1817. Fascinated, I asked the bookseller what they were and was told that they were travel journals of Robert Hyde Greg, a member of the family of Samuel Greg who had established one of the first textile factories in England – Quarry Bank Mill at Styal near Wilmslow, Cheshire. I knew the mill well, having visited it several times since the National Trust opened it to the public in 1978. Here was an opportunity to hear a son of Samuel Greg speak 'in his own voice'. I asked if the books were for sale, was told they were, and as an inveterate book collector could not resist buying them for their historical interest. My wife and I eagerly began to read them as soon as I took them home. Our interest grew as page succeeded page: but we both realised that if the books were ever to reach a wider audience, they would have to be transcribed from this neat, but faint copperplate handwriting. This task would need time and concentration. In the meantime the demands of work and the needs of the family had to come first and we had to postpone the transcription.

From time to time we fetched the journals out to show them to friends, who all expressed interest in them and urged us to do something with them, before we put them away and all but forgot about them.

It was only when we visited Andalucia in the 1990s that we realised that we were travelling over the same terrain that Robert Hyde Greg had travelled – in very different circumstances – nearly two hundred years before. On a subsequent tour of 'off beat Andalucia' with Adam Hopkins, the distinguished travel writer and authority on Spain and all things Spanish, we produced the sections of the Spanish journal that we had already transcribed, together with the volume relating to Andalucia, and it was he who in the first place, seriously urged us to complete the transcription of the journals so that hopefully they could be published.

So we began the work that would take months to complete. The account of the 1814 tour of the Highlands of Scotland was the shortest of the journals and so we tackled this first. Once this was done, we completed the transcription of the longest and most detailed account of Robert Hyde Greg's travels abroad. The tour of the Iberian Peninsula took eleven months – from September 1814 to August 1815 – and the description of this fills three closely written volumes. Finally, after a considerable pause, we transcribed the account of Greg's Grand Tour of 1817, which fortunately was not as long as the previous one.

The journals that surfaced in the Manchester bookshop must presumably have been part of a library, at some time disbanded, belonging to a member of the Greg family. How they came to be sold we shall never know. What we realised soon after we acquired the notebooks, was that their existence was unknown at Quarry Bank. Dr Mary Rose, the authority on the Greg commercial enterprises, with unrivalled knowledge of the Greg archive, both at Quarry Bank and Manchester Central Library which houses the bulk of it, was most surprised to see them, being totally unaware that such documentary material existed.

It was known that Robert Hyde Greg had travelled extensively on the continent of Europe before joining the family firm, from unpublished letters written to his father, mother, and other members of his family, which are in the archive of Quarry Bank Mill. But these letters refer to the 1817 Grand Tour to France, Italy and the Ottoman Empire. Nothing apparently was known of his Highland tour in Scotland of 1814 and the only previous evidence of his extensive travels in Portugal and Spain in 1814 and 1815 was the drawings he made of places in those countries.

The journals therefore provide valuable source material about a period of Robert Hyde Greg's early life before he became one of Manchester's most important textile manufacturers until his death in 1875.

It must be emphasised that the journals are the work of a young man. Greg was 19 when he went to Spain and 21 when he undertook the more conventional Grand Tour of 1817. They were written to provide a record of what he had seen for the entertainment and interest of his family. They could have been the raw material for a more polished version to be published later, but this is unlikely, since Greg was not a professional writer and the business, which he joined formally in 1817, became his priority. As it is, they provide the reader with a sense of immediacy and authenticity. They were a perfect aide-memoire for the writer and they give the modern reader a first-hand account of travelling conditions in post-Napoleonic Europe.

A.F. 2005

ACKNOWLEDGEMENTS

We are very grateful to all those who have helped and encouraged us to prepare these travel journals for publication. Though David Sekers, the first director of the Quarry Bank Mill Museum, showed enormous interest in the journals when we first acquired them, and encouraged us to prepare them for publication, it was not possible for us to devote the time to the project until many years later. At this point, our thanks must go to three people without whom the journals would not have seen the light of day: Adam Hopkins, who inspired us with his profound knowledge of Spain and persuaded us to consider publishing the Iberian tour volumes; Professor Andor Gomme, who introduced us to our publisher; and finally Dr Shaun Tyas himself, who urged us to tackle the 1817 journal in order to complete the trilogy and gave us valuable advice on editorial matters.

We were greatly heartened by the interest shown in the project by Dr Mary Rose of Lancaster University, the leading authority on the manufacturing and commercial interests of the Greg family. At Quarry Bank Mill, Adam Daber, Josselin Hill and Caroline Hill could not have been more helpful when we consulted them for information about the Greg family and the drawings of Robert Hyde Greg, some of which were expertly scanned by Caroline Hill so that they could be reproduced in the book. Carol Burrows of the John Rylands University of Manchester Library was most assiduous in researching material relevant to the journals, and Dorothy Clayton sympathetically dealt with our request for permission to reproduce our chosen illustrations from the Special Collections of the Library. David Morris, Keeper of Prints at the Whitworth Art Gallery, University of Manchester, produced a facsimile of a Goya etching for us.

Thanks to Charmaine Dean, we spent a memorable afternoon in the Skilliter Centre for Ottoman Studies at Newnham College Cambridge in order to select contemporary illustrations for the 1817 journal which Dr Kate Fleet, Director of the Centre, kindly allowed us to reproduce. Ian Robertson generously shared with us his unrivalled knowledge of early British travellers to Spain and allowed us to reproduce prints from his personal collection.

We received valuable information on matters geographical, classical, biographical and illustrative from Angus Beaton, Dr Catharine Davies, Nigel Hurst, Dr Jarl Kremeier, the late Joan Livesey, Martin Randall and Ian Ray, and practical help from Eleanor McGann and Michael Pollard. Mary Freer helped us to retrace the footsteps of Robert Hyde Greg and his friends in Scotland. Louise Baylis drew maps of admirable clarity which will assist readers to find their way around Robert Hyde Greg's journeys. Catharine, Jonathan and Thomas Davies helped us to check the transcriptions at a crucial time. Our heartfelt thanks must go to Jane Lindo, who with care and genuine interest, typed our handwritten transcriptions and editorial material and dealt patiently with alterations and revisions.

At a late stage in our project, we were very pleased to meet, at Quarry Bank, three members of the Greg family. Mr Michael James, Mrs Katharine Gore, and Mrs Katharine Walker. Not only did they greatly encourage us by their enthusiasm and keen interest in our work, but also to our delight and excitement, produced important illustrative material. Mrs Katharine Walker, the Great, Great, Great Granddaughter of Robert Hyde Greg, revealed that she owned a miniature of him made in 1824 at the time of his marriage. Mrs Katharine Gore, his Great, Great Granddaughter, showed us a sketchbook which included drawings made by him in 1817 during his travels in the Ottoman Empire. We much appreciated their willingness for us to reproduce these pictures in the book, thus providing it with its frontispiece and valuable additional images of Robert Hyde Greg's travels. This meeting was for us a special occasion, and it brought about a most memorable and satisfying conclusion to our work.

Illustration Acknowledgements
Each illustration is separately acknowledged, but this is our collected list of the sources of illustrations:

Falmouth Art Gallery: plate 4.
Mrs Katherine Gore: plates 27, 39, 45, 48, 50, 52, 53, 54, 55, 56, 57 and 59.
National Trust / Caroline Hill, plates 1 and 61.
National Trust, Quarry Bank Mill Museum: plates 7, 10, 13, 15, 16, 18, 19, 33, 34, 37 and 38.
Ian Robertson: plates 8 and 23.
John Rylands Library, University of Manchester: plates 2, 3, 5, 6, 20, 21, 24, 25, 26, 28, 29, 30, 31, 32, 33, 35, 40, 41 and 60.
Skilliter Centre for Ottoman Studies, Newnham College, Cambridge: plates 42, 43, 44, 46, 47, 49, 51 and 58.
Mrs Katharine Walker: plate 62.
Whitworth Art Gallery, University of Manchester: plate 22.
And, finally, plates 9, 11, 12, 14 and 17 are illustrations from the journals themselves.
We are also indebted to the National Trust for permission to quote from two letters from Robert Hyde Greg to his mother.

INTRODUCTION

The writer of these journals, Robert Hyde Greg, was the second son of Samuel Greg from Belfast, one of the most successful entrepreneurs in the cotton industry in the late eighteenth and early nineteenth centuries. In 1784 he established Quarry Bank Mill at Styal, near Wilmslow in Cheshire, to produce cotton yarn. Powered originally by the waters of the River Bollin, it was enlarged several times over the years, during which weaving, as well as spinning, was introduced. The mill was powered by steam from 1833. Besides Quarry Bank Mill, Samuel Greg acquired several spinning and weaving mills in the Manchester area and became wealthy and influential. He built an elegant Regency house for himself and his family next to the mill. Like other early manufacturers, he liked to keep a close watch on the work being done there. This became the family home in preference to the house in King Street, Manchester, in which Robert Hyde Greg was born on 24th September 1795. He spent most of his childhood there, and it was to Quarry Bank House that he returned, with evident relief, at the end of his long tour of Spain in 1815.

The Gregs were Unitarian in religious belief and Robert was most likely educated at Dissenting Academies in Nottingham and Bristol. Such schools offered a much broader education than that of the famous public schools of the time with their unrelieved diet of Latin and Greek. As he had a wealthy father, he might well have been expected to go to Oxford or Cambridge, but his Nonconformist background precluded this. He apparently spent some time at Edinburgh University but did not take a degree.

It was from Edinburgh that he set out on May 7th 1814 with two friends, Tom and Sam Robinson, on a tour of the Scottish Highlands. The Robinson brothers most probably came from the Manchester area and were friends of the family and equally probably were fellow undergraduates of Robert's at Edinburgh University.

Greg's first trip had an element of student adventure about it, but his second and third journeys were more in the tradition of the Grand Tour, but with a difference.

Like most of his brothers, Robert Hyde Greg was destined to enter the family firm, but his father wanted him to travel abroad before he settled down to regular work. As a son of the new entrepreneurial class, however, his Grand Tour of Europe would have a commercial as well as a cultural purpose, unlike that of his aristocratic predecessors in the eighteenth century who went for cultural and social reasons alone. He was to travel as the representative of the firm, to meet customers and investigate the current state of the market for English textiles. Armed with letters of introduction to English merchants and other persons of influence, together with letters of credit and bills of exchange with which to finance his journeys, he was to have a form of work experience rather than an opportunity to collect antique statues and paintings with which to decorate the family mansion.

However, he was to have the chance to do some sightseeing. His mother, Hannah, was a highly educated, cultivated woman who was most concerned that her sons should not only have a training in commercial skills but the widest possible cultural education as well. So in Spain he would visit the Alhambra, the Escorial, Cathedrals in Seville, Segovia and Toledo and the palaces and gardens of Aranjuez and St Ildefonso (la Granja) and museums in Madrid. In France, the Louvre and Versailles were to be visited and in Italy there was the Renaissance art of Florence to be enjoyed and the wonderful classical remains of Rome and Naples.

EDITORIAL PRINCIPLES

We have retained most of the original spelling, capitalisation, punctuation and underlining throughout the text, indicating most obvious mistakes or variant spellings with '[sic]'.

The 'long s', which looks confusingly like 'f' to the modern reader, has been altered to 's'.

Any unusual editorial insertions to restore omitted words or letters are inserted in square brackets.

The author often used ampersands (&), but not always, and we decided to standardise these as 'and' throughout, except for '&c.' which has been standardised as 'etc.'. Other contractions (e.g. y^e, wh^c), which were rarely encountered, have been retained. Superscripts on numbers, such as 4th, have been normalised (as 4th).

We have standardised the presentation of dates in bold type and as a heading, for the sake of clarity, though it was Greg's normal style to underline the date and continue the text on the same line.

Words which are hyphenated in the manuscript because they cross two lines, have been rejoined.

Editorial footnotes have been kept to a minimum. We have concentrated on providing information about people, places, events, words and phrases that may be unfamiliar to readers.

We wish to say that we accept full responsibility for any errors or omissions in either the transcription or the editorial material.

TRAVELS IN SCOTLAND, 1814

Introduction

People travelling for pleasure did not go to Scotland, or more specifically, the Scottish Highlands, before the 1770s. The country was regarded as dangerous and uninviting before this time. The inhabitants were thought to be wild, and the mountainous terrain full of terrors. So the land was virtually unknown to the English and even the Lowland Scots. By the 1770s, however, attitudes were changing. Jacobitism was a spent force after the Battle of Culloden in 1746, and the power of the clans in the Highlands was broken, so that the Scots who lived there were no longer feared. The Cult of the Picturesque provided a strong incentive for travel in a previously unexplored area. The Reverend William Gilpin, author of *Three Essays on Picturesque Beauty*, *Picturesque Travel* and *Sketching Landscape*, was one of those responsible for encouraging people to really look at, and appreciate, landscape.

People who had been on the Grand Tour in Europe and seen the wonders of the Alps, and probably seen and admired the paintings of Salvator Rosa, were beginning to realise that mountainous scenery in Wales, the Lake District and Scotland, albeit on a smaller scale than the Alps, was worthy of their attention, especially when Europe was closed to them during the Napoleonic Wars. The whole Romantic movement, in literature and painting, persuaded people not only to look and appreciate natural beauty in all its forms, but also to give their feelings full rein when enjoying it.

The famous jaunt to Scotland made by Dr Samuel Johnson and James Boswell in 1773, and Thomas Pennant's *Tour in Scotland* of 1771 to 1775, started to arouse general interest. William and Dorothy Wordsworth went on a tour of Scotland in a 'jaunting car' with Coleridge in 1803. William Gilpin himself published a book on *The Highlands* in 1800, and Alexander Campbell produced *A Journey from Edinburgh through Parts of North Britain* in 1811. These and other accounts provided would-be travellers with useful information and could very well have been known to Robert Hyde Greg and his friends Tom and Sam Robinson. In the Spring of 1814 when Greg was eighteen, and his friends presumably were about the same age, they decided to make a journey into the Highlands and then across to the Western Isles.

One can imagine the three of them setting off in high spirits from Edinburgh on May 7th 1814, in a carriage which carried them to Linlithgow, Falkirk, Stirling, Dunkeld, Aberfeldy and Taymour. Here they found that it was not possible to hire a chaise to take them to Inverary on Loch Fyne as they had apparently planned. They realised that it was a question of walking, or failing to reach their destination. But they were all three hardy, vigorous and determined young men so they set out, packs on backs, to walk to Inverness and then make their way down the Great Glen to the west coast. The way over the rugged Highland landscape was hard. Only rarely did they encounter an acceptable inn, for, not surprisingly, such places were in short supply in view of the limited demand for them before the days of mass tourism. Greg and his friends were forced to seek shelter from the elements wherever they could, and be grateful for what they found, even if it meant the three of them "being stowed like biscuits upon our sides as close as we could squeeze" in one small bed, and having a hen coming to roost on top of their sleeping forms in one poor house. Food was plain and hard to eat; hard oatcakes, harder cheese and milk curds, formed the greater part of their diet. A dull, hard diet indeed, but it gave them the necessary sustenance for their trek across mountains and boggy valleys. Here they encountered poor peasants who shared what they had with them with grace and dignity.

Then, as now, few could encounter the grandeur and extraordinary beauty of Highland scenery and remain unmoved. The wild romantic hills, the high mountains, the great lochs, and wondrous waterfalls, are sights that lift the spirits and Greg responded to them all. We do not know if he had read Gilpin's essays on the Picturesque, but the spirit of the reverend gentleman seems to lurk behind his estimate of each prospect. There is an air of loftiness in his appraisals, and his judgement seems to be based on Gilpin's principles. One wishes that Greg had taken a sketch book with him on this tour, but alas, if he did so, nothing survives of his drawings.

The account of the tour has its memorable moments, and they burst upon the reader with a freshness and immediacy that is very appealing. Greg described with amazement the unexpected sight of ragged children in school studying their copies of Livy, Horace and Caesar and one is reminded of Dr Johnson's astonishment at finding that his hosts in the farthest Hebrides had a working knowledge of classical authors. Then there was the encounter with the poor old woman in a lonely part of the Highlands, who offered the three young men some milk (curds and whey) to be eaten with the help of horn spoons "very thick and fully a foot long".

Having tramped across mountains for thirty seven miles before they reached Aviemore, the three travellers decided to hire ponies to take them part of the way to Inverness. Their encounter with three mangy animals, with decrepit trappings, and their unsuccessful attempts to ride them, clearly caused them much hilarity, and is described in comic detail.

After a dangerous trip across the sea from Mull, they arrived in Oban to find that they had to rub away the crystallised salt that had formed on their faces

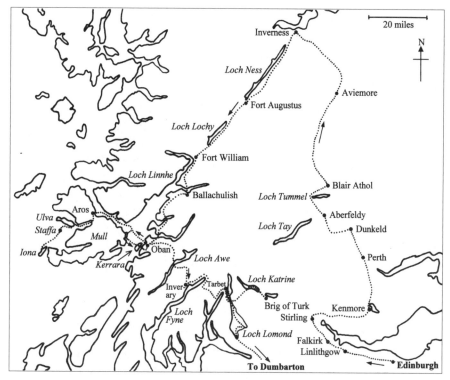

Robert Hyde Greg's Travels through Scotland, May 1814.

through constant wetting with salt water and subsequent rapid evaporation. Meeting a funeral party after leaving Oban, they were persuaded to drink a glass of whisky for "it was the custom", and several days later were shown a secret distillery on an island in Loch Katrine and sworn to secrecy on a dram of illicit liquor. These were all episodes that could easily have been described more elaborately, but the very brevity with which Greg depicted them is probably more effective in making them memorable.

It would be a mistake to make large claims for Robert Hyde Greg's Scottish journal. It was, after all, the work of an eighteen year old, but it has a freshness, directness and honesty of response that deserves fair and just recognition. The journal comes to an abrupt end. Why Greg failed to complete it, we shall never know.

To have undertaken such an enterprise as the Scottish tour as early as 1814 betokened a determination on the part of the three friends to push it through to a satisfactory conclusion. The experience was to stand Greg in good stead when he went to the Iberian Peninsula in September 1814, to spend, as it turned out, eleven months travelling through another strange land.

5

Text of the Scottish Journal

May 7th 1814

Thos. Robinson, Sam Robinson and myself set out upon our Highland Tour. We left Edinburgh in the morning in a chaise, each provided with a knapsack and a Plaid. The day being rainy we had no opportunity of judging of the surrounding country which however we understood presented nothing worthy of attention. To Linlithgow 16 miles, a small place distinguished only by the remains of the ancient Palace of the James'. The ruins are extensive, the walls of most of the rooms standing and some of the staircases entire, but the architecture is very plain, not to say inelegant. The apartment is shown in which it is said that Queen Mary was born. The Cathedral has been lately refitted in a neat and elegant manner.*

A note here directs the reader to the back of the book (and the following poem)

Written in the ruins of Linlithgow

1

Alas how changed since days of old
Linlithgow's turrets grey
Since royal James and Barons bold
Spent here the festal day.
Those walls so thick with Ivy hung
With Mirth's loud voice have often rung
And hollow winds sweep thro' the tower
Where Minstrel erst beguil'd the hour

2

No more is heard the maiden's prayer
At Evening's dewy fall
Nor princes now the Banquet share
Within the stately hall
But the hoarse Raven builds her nest
Where Scotland's Monarchs used to rest
And low born swains unconscious tread
The sod that wraps the Mighty Dead

3

Yet beauties still those towers appear
By Eve's uncertain light
Or from the Lake reflected clear
In yellow Moonbeam bright
And still at midnight hour ('tis said)
Rise from their graves the honour'd Dead

By rustic seen with figures princely tall
Pacing along their ancient hall.

1814

To Falkirk 8 miles. An insignificant little town, famous only for being the place where Wallace suffered his last and total defeat.

To Stirling 11 miles. From what we were able to discover of the country, it must be fine amid the distant views very beautiful. We arrived at Stirling in the evening; the approach to it with the distant view of the castle and mountains is truly magnificent. The castle rock is very high and on the west, perpendicular, resembling in almost every particular that of Edinburgh. The Barracks deface the rock with their plain walls and batteries, but the ancient Palace, though not extensive, is perfect, built in good style and makes a handsome appearance. The most striking object however is the wide and beautiful prospect of the surrounding country. The junction of the Forth and the Firth and the Annan takes place at a small distance and the former is seen meandering in a singularly beautiful manner through an immense extent of country. Ben Lomond and Ben Ledi make a distinguishing feature in this landscape but they were so enveloped in clouds as to be quite invisible to us.

May 8th

Rose early and the morning being fine, immediately proceeded to the Castle walk. The view was equal to anything of the kind I ever saw and the infinite variety of tints caused by the bright sunshine and the shadows of the clouds added greatly to the beauty of the scene. The clouds now rolling away from the lofty summits of Ben Lomond and Ben Ledi, which with an extensive range of mountains gave to the surrounding flat country the appearance of a vast and magnificent amphitheatre.

To Dollart 12 miles, the former part of the road very beautiful along the foot of the mountains but afterwards becomes rather uninteresting. Dollart is only a single house, whilst the horses rested, we walked to see the Caldron Lin, a waterfall which runs into a very deep cleft in the rock, which it has hollowed out into a polished bason [sic], whence it receives its name. It is well worth visiting. The distance from Dollart about 3 miles. We then walked on a mile farther to the rumbling Brig, a small bridge over the same river, the Devon, where it is precipitated down a narrow but immensely deep cleft. We descended with some difficulty to the bottom, where we were amply repaid for our trouble by singularly romantic and stupendous spectacle which presented itself to our eyes. Near this place the chaise overtook us, and we proceeded to Kinross.

From Dollart to Kinross 13 miles. The town of Kinross is a small and insignificant place, Loch Leven on which it stands is extensive and pretty. About the centre of it is a small Island with the remains of the Castle in which Mary Queen of Scots was confined and from which she made her escape. From Kinross to Perth 17 miles. The road runs for a long way through a romantic ravine and at last breaks out into the open country. The view of Perth and the wanderings of the river Tay as seen from the hill above the town make a pleasing appearance. We arrived just in time to see little of the town[;] it seems to present nothing worthy of the attention of an English traveller.

May 9th

After procuring a few necessaries which cannot be found in the Highlands we proceeded still in chaises to Dunkeld 15 miles.

The road is through a rather uninteresting country, though the valley of Perth which lay behind us was still pretty. The descent into the valley of Dunkeld is very pleasing. Whilst dinner was preparing we procured a guide to show us the place. The grounds which belong to the Duke of Athol lie entirely on the banks of the river (this is a mountain torrent running in a rough and deep channel making numerous waterfalls). The principal path is close upon the side of this stream, and conducts the traveller to the great cascade. Just above this fall is an elegant summerhouse. On entering it a painting of Osian presents itself which being suddenly withdrawn, a small saloon is seen with the waterfall rushing down the rocks. Mirrors are attached to the sides and the top of the room and the scene on every direction running upwards or downwards according to the mirror in which it is seen, the whole producing an effect novel and amusing. After walking a mile or two farther we came to the rumbling brig resembling much the one we had seen on the road to Kinross, but the river somewhat larger.

Dunkeld is a small village. The Tay on which it stands is of considerable breadth, the Duke has lately built a bridge over it at his own expence which cost it is said £30,000.

To Aberfeldy 18 miles. The road all the way on the banks of the river and in general well wooded. Whilst the horses rested we went with a guide to look at the waterfall which is distant from the inn about a mile. The fall is buried in a deep glen, it is not perpendicular, but very elegant and on the whole superior to any we had seen before.

To Kenmore 6 miles, the road still on the banks of the Tay and very beautiful especially on approaching Kenmore when we came in view at the Loch.

May 10th

At the inn at Kenmore we found tolerably comfortable accommodations. The village consists of a few neat white cottages and a church well appropriated to the place. Before setting out to examine the grounds of Lord Bredalben to whom the place belongs, we went into a school which is situated near the Church. Most of the boys had some Latin book before them, and the Master informed us that

some of his ragged pupils were reading Livy, Horace, Caesar etc. Before breakfast we walked about two miles along the lake which appears to present nothing
worthy of attention farther on. The view is closed by Ben Lawers a mountain
4015 feet high. The summit of the hill was still covered with snow which generally remains till July. The Gaelic meaning of the term is Mountain of Flames and
the old people of the country say that it was once a volcano. There is near the
summit a hollow much resembling a crater, in which is a considerable pool of
water. On our return the view of the lake, a woodland island with the ruins of a
priory, the bridge, Church, village etc was extremely beautiful. After breakfast
the Earl's gardener attended us to show us the grounds. The walk above the
North bank of the river presents many pretty peeps. The house itself is but lately
erected, and is an elegant building in the Castle style. We now ascended a hill
across the river, to battery – 18 cannon; from this spot the view is by much the
finest of any about the place. The lake, mountains, woods and the numerous
meanderings of the Tay form a very striking and romantic picture. Though not
so much visited, I should certainly pronounce Taymour more beautiful than
Dunkeld, or indeed anything we had yet seen. After a little refreshment at the inn
we prepared for our departure. We had no longer to order the chaise and com-
posedly walk into it: no more chaises were to be had until we reached Inverary;
we therefore without complaining philosophically strapped our knapsacks and
plaids on our backs, and after a hearty laugh at the strange and novel figures
which we made, we set out trudging along the road to Tumal Bridge: 10 or 11
miles. We had been told that the inn at this place afforded good sleeping accommodations we determined to stay there all night. The first two miles of the
road was tolerably pretty along the glens, but we soon came to a hill the ascent
of which is fully 3 miles, the sun full on our backs, was rather trying for novices
loaded as we were. From the top of the hill a very desolate scene presented itself, a very great extent of heath with[out] any sign of cultivation and the mountains rising one behind another to an immense distance. We arrived somewhat
fatigued at Tumal Bridge and after having been looking forward for some time to
the pleasure of resting ourselves, how great was our disappointment when we
found the inn so dirty and uncomfortable that we were compelled to make our
way to Athol 8 miles further over the mountains. After the refreshment which
some hard cheese and very coarse oat cake could furnish we set out at about 6½
o'clock after very narrowly taking the wrong road which instead of taking us 8
miles would have made it 18. The road was very galling to the feet, in winter serving for the channel of a torrent; by some mistake we got out of road and coming
to some huts we procured a guide. We soon reached the top of the hills and
began to cross a wide heath. There we found that missing our way was the most
fortunate thing which could have happened, for this moor had scarcely any path
and we should have had to have returned to ask our way or have gone on to the

danger of spending the night on the heather as the sun was by this time setting. We pursued our way along this dreadfully rough road till descending at last we reached a riverside. A boy of whom we asked the way, gave a very expressive answer, saying "that we must go along and we should hardly ken that it was a road".

After crossing the river we joined the high road again and after two miles more we arrived at Blair Athol, not a little fatigued having walked near thirty miles, 20 of which were over steep mountains and rough roads with the knapsacks on our backs. At Blair we learnt that had we pursued the road we were on when we discovered our error we should have gone 7 or 8 miles round and had two more rivers to cross. At Blair we found good accommodations.

May 11th

Rose in good time and after breakfast we set out to visit the falls of the Brewer water distant about 4 miles. There was so little water in the river that the appearance was not particularly striking. Like all the others we had seen its charm is a deep glen in the mountainside. After our return we went to examine the grounds of the Duke of Athol. The situation is fine, upon the river Garey and surrounded with hills, the only thing however which deserves particular attention is scenery upon the small river which falls into the Garey where the rocks and waterfalls are beautiful. The evening we spent in the inn preparing our feet for a walk of 32 miles over the mountains.

The Gaelic language first saluted our ears at Dunkeld, at Aberfeldy and Kenmore it is the common language though most can speak English; at Tumal the English has been introduced within a few years and our guide there told us that he understood the English spoken in his turn better than ours. At Athol both languages are spoken almost indifferently, though our guide at Brewer falls could not speak a word of English. The Highlands generally speak very well, much better than in many of the counties of England, for learning it from books and travellers, they have it in all its purity. The education is much attended to, the boys being taught English, Latin and sometimes I believe a little French, the girls English, writing etc. The people have all much curiosity to know how far you are going, how far you have travelled that day, and where you live when you are at home. As might be expected from their education, they are generally well informed and intelligent, seemingly well acquainted with the history of their country though by no means anxious to show their knowledge, always supposing you well versed in history. The dress of the ancient Highlanders is much laid aside in these parts and is only worn by the children and some of the shepherds.

As to the Agriculture of this part of the country, not much need be said. There seems to be little or no meadow ground; on the arable ground is grown some little wheat but principally oats, barley, potatoes and Oat Cakes seem to be giving way to the potatoes for food. The men of middling stature, rather broad faces, the women short, thickset, fat and many extremely ugly to an Englishman's eye.

May 12th

Rose at 6 o'clock and before setting [off] drank a bason of milk and eat a few slices of bread and butter, the tailor of the village was our guide whom we understood to be the best acquainted with [the] country over which we were to travel. We had the choice either of going along the high road, and reaching the inn of Avamore in two stages one of 23 miles, the other of 27, or of reaching the same place in one day by this mountain path which we understood would exceed 32 miles. We therefore determined to take the latter and about 7 o'clock we departed from Athol. The first nine miles we found a tolerable road which leads to a small lodge of the Duke's. After leaving this we saw nothing more of any path and we soon ascended to the summit of some of the highest of the mountains and found large patches of snow in various places. Here the road became extremely fatiguing, the moss and bog sinking continually under our feet, and we had to cross many of the small glens covered with snow with brooks running under them, which were not only unpleasant to pass, but even dangerous and our guide fell through one of them but fortunately he escaped unhurt the hollow being so small that he reached the bottom with his feet. When we had advanced about 16 miles from Athol we sat down by the side of a well between two great patches of snow, to rest for a quarter or half an hour and eat a little meat and bread which we had brought with us. We rose again and pursued our way over hills much resembling those we had already past, and on descending from them our guide took his leave. We now entered a wild and romantic Glen with a river running through it, and thinly scattered with Firs and birch. Pursuing the river for some time we at length arrived at a Herdsman's hut which our guide had mentioned to us. This was distant from Athol nearly 22 miles and this hut was the first habitation we had seen the whole way, and the old woman who lived there the first human being. We met her at the door and asked for refreshment, we entered a little hut made in the common manner of the country. The outside cannot be well distinguished from the heap of turf which stands near it, being made of that material; the inside is generally lined with split fir wood perfectly black with the constant smoke, the fire is on the floor at one end of the room, the furniture is simple enough, two or [three] shelves for the dishes which are generally wooden, a large trunk, a small rustic table, a few stools for the Children and a long bench with a back to it; the whole is dimly illuminated by the fire, by a very small aperture in the side of the hut and another somewhat larger in the roof to carry off the smoke. Such is the only kind of building in these parts, and such the one we entered. The old woman set before us a large wooden bowl of sour milk, some oat cake at least one inch thick, some highland cheese which resisted almost every effort of the knife; she also gave each a horn spoon very thick and fully a foot long to help ourselves to the milk. Coarse and frugal the fare was we devoured it with great relish and taking leave of the old woman pursued our way along the valley. The scenery was very wild and beautiful, but notwithstanding the miles appeared extremely long. We had been told that it was only 6 miles to a ferry which we had to pass; when we arrived there we discovered that on one side of the river they reckoned in Scotch and on the opposite side in English miles; and that instead of having walked 6 miles it was upwards of nine, and that instead of having 4 more to go we had 6 along the high road before reaching Avamore. Getting therefore some refreshment we proceeded and arrived at Ava-more about 8 o'clock, considerably fatigued, having walked nearly 37 miles, 22 of which was over the mountains, with paths very steep and rugged. The ac-commodations at Avamore though not particularly good were as well as we could expect in that part of the country. Being only 30 miles from Inverness we deter-mined to reach it on the following day and afraid that our legs would fail us we engaged 3 ponies to take us a part of the way.

May 13th
We did not take our departure from Avamore till near 11 o'clock. The ponies were to meet us about ½ a mile upon the way and the owner of them was to walk by our sides to bring them back. It was some time before we could even make an attempt to mount so great was our laughter at the sight of them. Sam seized upon the best,which though nothing to boast of, was certainly of a much superior rank to the other two. Thos Robinson's was the most miserable thing it is possible to conceive of, very small, all skin and bone, scarcely any hair except-ing the mane which covered both neck and head. Its trappings were very well adapted to such a singular body, a bridle or rather halter of twisted osier so con-trived that if the poney turned any way it was necessary to turn it completely round to bring it to a proper direction again. The saddle was much in the same style, the remains of the leather of the upper part floating loosely upon a heap of carpet plaid wool and bits of old sack. My horse was much of the same make as T.R.'s but had large quantities of long hair in divers parts of its body, though others were very nearly bare, my bridle was tolerable. As for the seat on which I was to place myself, it was an old sidesaddle of which little remained but the pummels and part of the upper leather, the rest being suplied [sic] in the same manner as the saddle just described. There was only one stirrup, which breaking whilst mounting, I was nearly impaled upon the sharp iron of the pummel which stuck out as if for that very purpose. They would not go in any way but one after another, and we found the caution of the guide quite unnecessary that we should go any faster than a man could walk for we found no little difficulty in making [them] go at all unless he himself went first. Add to this, they were frequently

turning out of the road to some house where they had been accustomed to stop and here the only remedy was to whip one another's ponies. Sam's being the best stood first, he whipped it before and Tom behind. Tom beat mine before and I his behind as well as my own and by this continued application on all sides they were once more put in motion. T.R. at last dismounted and finding it easier walking, relinquished his horse to the man. Mine kept stopping every nine or ten steps and was so difficult to get going again that I took to my feet as well to rest as to get forward a little, which in the present state of things was impossible. Sam also joined us, and thus after riding 7 or 8 miles we dismissed the ponies, and proceeded to perform the remaining 23 miles on foot. The country rather uninteresting, we passed a few woods of stunted birch, but saw more of heather than anything else. We got some bread and butter at a small house about 14 miles from Inverness called Fryburn, and then pursued our journey. The road is very good, the country presents nothing particularly worthy of attention, except a small Loch romantically situated to the right hand side. About 3 or 4 miles from Inverness we crossed over a moor which is near to the spot where the battle of Culloden was fought, and from there had a fine view of the Frith [sic] of Moray, the hills of Ross shire and many mountains in every direction. We arrived rather late at Inverness but found and enjoyed an admirable accommodations at Bennets Hotel.

May 14th

Looked about the town, which is small, part of it consisting of decent looking houses, part of miserable huts, the port is small and we only saw 3 or 4 vessels. The grand Canal[1] to connect the Eastern and Western seas is carrying on with vigour. It will admit ships of all sizes.

May 15th Sunday

In the morning we went to look at the remains of one of the ancient vitrified Forts[2] situated on a hill to the west of Inverness and distant about a mile and a half, called Craigphartick. No part of the fort can be seen without close examination, none of the walls being now above ground, and they can only be seen where some excavations have been made. It must have been some hundred yards round; the line of the outside and inside walls are visible and there appears

---

[1]   This was the Caledonian Canal, constructed by Thomas Telford between 1803 and 1822.

[2]   There are the remains of about fifty vitrified forts in Scotland. The origin of them is a mystery, but it is generally thought that they date from the Iron Age. The walls were built of stones with a high content of silica which was fused to form a hard glass-like substance as the result of intense heat – apparently made by wood being packed around the walls and between the stones and then fired.

to have been a deep and wide trench between them. The walls in the small places where they are visible have a singular and curious appearance. At first it appears as if the stones were cemented together by a substance exactly like the slag of a glasshouse; on breaking the stones however, which are principally Gneiss, Mica, Slate etc they themselves seem to have undergone a partial vitrification in a manner totally unaccountable. We therefore carried away several specimens to examine at home at our leisure. In the afternoon we went to the Gaelic Chapel, but were soon tired of hearing guttural sounds which we could not understand, and so being near the door we came out in the course of half an hour. In the evening we took a walk down the river to Cromwels [sic] Fort which itself is not worth looking at though the view of the Frith [sic] and surrounding hills is tolerably pleasing.

May 16th Monday
Notwithstanding our comfortable accommodations at Inverness we were impatient to recommence our journey. There being no kind of conveyance between this place and Inverary we engaged a chaise to take us forward and after so much walking we found it a great luxury. The distance to Fort Augustus 32 miles. The first 10 miles of road is along the riverside and in parts pretty, we then for the first time got a view of Loch Ness and saw distinctly the Mountains at the further end a distance of 24 miles. This view is striking and magnificent, the Loch being enclosed on both sides by steep rugged hills and its shores generally thickly lined with the weeping birch. The road is narrow and as it were hangs over the lake, whilst on the other side the rocks rise almost perpendicular to a great elevation. The Loch has a very picturesque appearance the whole way. At the distance of 16 miles from Inverness we alighted to examine the remains of a vitrified Fort on the summit of the hill of Doonaduie. The ascent to this is a difficult undertaking owing to the height and steepness of the hill, but we were amply repaid for our exertions by the extensive and magnificent prospect which presented itself at the summit, of the Loch beneath and of wooded glens and rocky hills on every side. For the [fort] itself it does not at all repay the trouble of ascending, the shape is similar to that of Craigphartick, but much smaller and standing on the summit of an almost inaccessible rock, there has been neither fosse nor outer wall. No part of the wall is to be seen, and few of the vitrified parts are discernable. We now joined the chaise at the Generals Hut,[3] a wretched little inn where the horses were to rest. After a frugal meal, we set out to view the fall of Fyres,[4] the most celebrated fall in Scotland, and distant from this place about a mile. We saw it to great disadvantage the water being very low, but we saw enough to picture to ourselves what it must have been had the river been as it sometimes is, 8 or 10 feet above its present level. The water is first precipitated down a fall of 70 f into deep and gloomy bason over which is thrown a small bridge. It then

rushes through [a] wide and profound vent in the mountain till it reaches a precipice of between 150 and 200 feet where it falls perpendicularly down a black rock into a chasm dismal, of immense depth and extent and which terrifies the boldest eye to look down.

We now took leave [of] the shores of Loch Ness and proceeded by a rather precipitous road through a wild but very romantic and interesting country to Fort Augustus.[5]

The descent from the hills is particularly striking and magnificent. The Fort is small, not very ornamental to the scenery, the village consists of 5 or 6 small houses, and at the inn we found but poor accommodations, the fire is made on the ground and all wears somewhat an air of desolation.

May 17th Tuesday

We found our beds tolerably comfortable, and after breakfast proceeded along a narrow and precipitous road, undulating like the waves of a stormy sea. The scenery on the lakes in many parts sufficiently grand though much inferior to Loch Ness, being almost destitute of wood. We got some refreshment, if such miserable fare deserves the name at a house much like the Generals hut, and again continued our way along Loch Lochy. When within a few miles of Fort William[6] we came in sight of Ben Nevis, the highest mountain in Great Britain being about 4250 feet above the level of the sea. Its summit was lost in the clouds, but it made a very striking appearance, rising almost immediately from the road. Fort William is distant from Fort Augustus about 30 miles; from the hills above the appearance is by no means as fine as that of Fort Augustus. The Fort itself is a little larger and but out of repair and worth examining. It contains at present

[3] The General's Hut was so called because General Wade lodged there when he commanded the English army in the North of Scotland. Dr Johnson and James Boswell
dined there on Monday 30th August 1773.

[4] Falls of Fyres, i.e. Foyers, is one of the most spectacular waterfalls in Scotland. Christopher North reckoned it was the most magnificent cataract in Britain while Dr Johnson
complained about the dangers of approaching its depth. The waters have been har-
nessed to produce hydro-electric power since 1896. The consultant engineer was Lord
Kelvin and it was the first hydro-electric power station in Scotland.

[5] In 1730 General Wade replaced the barracks built after the 1715 Jacobite Rising by
this fort called after William Augustus, Duke of Cumberland, then aged 9 (he was better known as 'Butcher' Cumberland). He used it from 1746 as a base from which to
hunt down fugitive Jacobites after the Battle of Culloden. It was still garrisoned when
Robert Hyde Greg saw it.

[6] Originally built by General Monck in 1654, Fort William was repaired in 1690, and renamed after King William III. The adjacent village of Maryburgh was called after the
King's wife, Queen Mary II. Both fort and village have now disappeared since the railway was built on the site.

30 or 40 veterans. The village of Maryburgh near which it stands is, of considerable extent and the inn is some little better than that at Fort Augustus though very far from having anything to boast of.

May 18th: Wednesday

Set off in good time from Fort William to Ballyhulish 13 miles. The road lies along the side of Loch Eil and the views are very beautiful of the water and distant mountains. The approach to Ballyhulish is uncommonly fine, and for Mountain scenery cannot well be excelled; the ferry is over a narrow part of Loch Linn there is a small house for the accommodation of travellers and as we were unwilling to pass by the celebrated pass of Glencoe we determined to remain here during the day. After breakfast therefore we procured a boat and rowed up the Loch for 3 miles and then landed to walk through the Glen. The scenery on every side of this Loch is uncommonly magnificent, the mountains which encompass it lofty, and of the boldest outlines that can be conceived. We advanced 3 or 4 miles through the pass which certainly is grand, and well deserving of a visit but having heard so much of it, we all suffered some disappointment. It is very far inferior to Dunloe Gap at Killarny [sic], and a person who has seen that will not be particularly struck with this. We returned hungry, and found the first dinner which we had yet met with in Scotland, which hunger could not make us enjoy. The houses in these parts of the country are smaller and if possible more miserable than those we had seen and the spots of cultivated ground before them are so small as to seem totally inadequate to the support of their numerous inhabitants. We observed very few of the children who did not wear the Highland dress, though none of the grown up people continue to wear it. We saw but few cultivated fields between here and Inverness, few of the black Cattle, and the few horses we observed on the road had cruppers of wood, generally a stick a yard long and as thick as a Mop tail.

May 19th Thursday

Rose in good time, crossed the Ferry and proceeded along a very rough road by the side of Loch Linne to Portnacroish, 12 miles. Our host entertained us with the luxury of Barley instead of Oat Cakes at breakfast. The view of the Loch from this place is very fine. We were delayed at a second Ferry for nearly 3 hours and again at a third for nearly 2 hours more, which put an end to a project we had formed of sleeping in Mull, the sea being calm, and the wind favourable. This last Ferry[7] is rather dangerous, owing to the great rapidity of the stream, and a chain of rocks a short distance below. There is a fine view from it of Dunstafnage Castle, where the Duke of Argyle landed in 1685. We reached Oban a small seaport town in the evening having advanced from Ballyhulish only 27 miles. The accommodations at the inn are tolerable and we had again the felicity of tasting wheaten bread.

May 20th Friday

We were on our boat at 6 o'clock, and a gentle breeze carried us quickly across Loch Linne. On entering the Loch between Mull and that part of Argyleshire called Morven, the wind failed us, but we arrived at Arross about 12 or 1 o'clock. The boatmen call this distance 35 miles, it is probably not so much as 30, for in this part of Scotland there is a great [difference] of miles, the Scotch equal to 1¼ or 1½ English; the Mull equal to double the English, or even more the English, and what is denominated the short water mile, this is of course not only extremely inconvenient to themselves but to strangers more particularly. Our plan now was to walk over to Ulva ferry and embark immediately for Staffa, and if possible return to Arross to sleep and take the boat for Oban early the next morning. Our boatmen however advised us to walk about 3 miles over Mull to Lochnakeal, and take the boat there to Staffa and return to Arross the same way. We accordingly did so, but to our mortification found the boat repairing on shore; there was no remedy and we were obliged to walk in heat of a burning sun round the coast to Ulva Ferry; we were nearly 2½ hours in getting there and consequently too late to attempt reaching Staffa that night. The little inn at the island of Ulva was in sad confusion, but we received every possible attention from our host and hostess. In the evening at sunset we climbed a high rock to take a view of the vast Atlantic which lay stretched beneath us smooth as an inland lake, a great part of Mull was visible and the Islands of Iona, Staffa, Inch Kenneth, Tirey, Coll with a multitude of others of less note, the scene was wild and striking, but barren and desolate, for out of this wide range of country not a tree nor cornfield nor pasture was to be seen, but rocks and heaths extended in every direction. Ulva contains about 500 inhabitants.

May 21st Saturday

Slept comfortably on the ground with a chair for my pillow. We rose at 3 o'clock and had left Ulva behind us when the Sun made his first appearance. There was not a breeze on the water and we had to row which took us nearly 3½ hours; we sailed quietly into Fingals Cave, the grandest and most striking object which can be imagined: this wonderful cave is 250 feet long 50 wide and 100 high; it is formed with perfect regularity throughout, of the basaltic pillars and bears much resemblance to the interior of a Cathedral. The island has many other caves which indeed are not worth mentioning after Fingal's. The boatman's cave runs

---

[7]   The three ferries have now been replaced by bridges. A new suspension bridge crosses the Narrows of Loch Linnhe at Ballachulish, and former railway bridges cross the narrowest parts of Loch Creran and the seaward end of Loch Etive over the Falls of Lora at Connel.

quite under the island. It is said that 4 people entered this and were never after heard of. The island is about ½ a mile long and ¼ wide. It has no inhabitants at present; a herdsman lived upon it some time ago but is said to have left it because the whole island rocked so much in the storms.

From Staffa we rowed to Iona, otherwise called Icolmkill, the distance is 9 miles though, almost as far as Staffa from Iona, having the tide in our favour, we accomplished [it] in less than two hours and a half. This Island is one of the most fertile of the Hebrides, but has many rocks and not a single tree. We could not tread over the ground which covers the mouldering bones of Scotish [sic], Irish and Norwegian Kings nor stroll amidst the ruins of ancient learning piety and magnificence without mingled sensations of awe, and respect, and some moral and philosophical reflexions, but the ruins though of considerable extent are neither of elegant architecture when examined closely, nor yet do they form picturesque objects when viewed at a distance, every man of common feelings must derive much pleasure from a visit to Iona, but it must arise on reflecting what it has been, not in contemplating its present situation. Our guide was the village schoolmaster[8] and he told us that 48 Scottish, 4 Irish and 8 Norwegian Kings were interred here, and they lay now all side by side in their narrow beds. Intending if possible to return to Oban that evening, we delay'd as little as possible and were in our boat again before 12 o'clock. There not being any breeze upon the water, and the day intensely hot we got on but slowly. We landed on the shore of Mull to look at McKinnon's Cave to which travellers are generally taken; it is certainly very fine, but after having just returned from Fingals Cave and seen many of a similar kind in Ireland, I was not particularly struck with it. At the entrance of Lochnakeal we passed by the fertile little island of Inch Kenneth in the short passage between which place and Ulva was drowned the young Laird of Coll of whom Johnson[9] in his Tour makes such frequent and honourable mention.

When within a mile or two of our landing place a strong gale of wind suddenly sprung up and blew us on with some violence, one side of the boat being on a level with the water. It shortened our passage but put an end to our hopes of reaching Oban till the following day, blowing quite in a wrong direction and being indeed too late had the wind been favourable, for we had not been less than 7 hours in coming from Iona. Our boatmen were all musical and sang a number of Gaelic songs to amuse themselves; they could not tell us what the meaning of them was, and all we could make out was that one of them was about the Pretender[10] concealing himself in women's clothes. Johnson remarks that he found only one person who could translate any [of] the Gaelic compositions and it seems to be a singular fact. I found the same difficulty in Ireland. One of them drank my health in Gaelic. I answered him in Italian and directly heard from the head of the boat pronounced in a very hoarse voice, "Comment vous portez-vous Monsieur?" I looked up astonished to hear the french language from the mouth of a wild looking Gael who could not speak intelligible English. We found that he had been a soldier and lived a long time in Guernsey, where he had acquired something of the language. We now landed at the head of Lochnakeal and walked to Arross. Our boatmen told us we might be over at Oban in good time on the following day if we were off early which we resolved to do.

May 22nd – Sunday

We were in our boat by a little after 6 o'clock, and though the wind was strong and against us, we made some way by tacking. The wind however increased and the waves rose high, one side of the boat was under the water sometimes and generally on a level with it, the waves were continually breaking over the other side and wetting us. After beating about in Mull Sound in this manner for 5 or 6 hours, the sea becoming much too rough for so small a boat, we were compelled to put ashore on a little rocky island off the coast of Morven. Here we staid for a little time till the change of tide gave us hopes of a smoother sea. We again made an attempt to cross Loch Linne which was covered over with white breakers, but we instantly perceived the thing to be rash and impracticable for the part we had to cross is considered the roughest part of the western coast, three tides meeting with violence under the island of Lismore. We therefore directed our course toward a small bay in the Isle of Mull. We had not long kept this direction before a great wave, which, rushing up the side of the boat up the backs of Tom Robinson and myself and over our heads discharged the remains of its fury upon S. Robinson, warned us that this course was not much less dangerous than the one we had given up. No time was to be lost we let the boat run before the wind straight for the nearest point of Mull Having only a small fore sail up, with the wind directly astern there was now no further fear than of a little splashing, and we were able to admire the waves rolling one after another in a manner truly grand and sublime. We flew over them with astonishing velocity, or rather appeared to be bound from one to another, and in a few minutes landed safely on Mull. We left the boat and walked 6 or 7 miles to Achnacraig where there is a ferry into the island of Kerrara. We had not much hope of crossing having met a

[8]   Four years after Greg and his friends visited Iona, John Keats and Charles Brown were shown round the holy places by the very same schoolmaster. "The old schoolmaster an ignorant little man but reckoned very clever, showed me these things" (John Keats in a letter to his brother Tom, July 26th 1818).

[9]   Dr Johnson and James Boswell made their celebrated journey to Scotland and the Western Isles in 1773.

[10]   The Pretender: Charles Edward Stuart or 'Bonnie Prince Charlie'. At one stage of his flight after the defeat of the Jacobites at Culloden in 1746 he dressed up in women's clothes in order to evade capture by English troops.

gentleman who assured us the wind was too high. Finding the boat however to be considerably larger than the one we had left, and the boatmen being on the point of sailing, we again committed ourselves to the winds and waves. We accomplished the five miles in 35 minutes and landed safely in Kerrara after a second wetting by the beating in of the waves. We now scrambled over this small island to another short ferry which once more brought us to Terra Firma. After another walk of about two miles we arrived at Oban fatigued and very hungry, it now being 7 o'clock, and excepting a biscuit and bit of cheese, we had tasted nothing since a six o'clock breakfast. We now all found our faces very sore, and the skin began to peel off. The intense heat of the sun reflected from the sea had commenced this operation on our Staffa voyage the day before, and it was completed by the bitter wind we had endured all the time in returning from Arross, by the constant wetting of our faces with the salt water, and by an evaporation so rapid that when we landed we absolutely had to rub away the crystallised salt from our lips, mouths, cheeks, etc.

Monday, May 23rd

We left Oban in good time, for a few minutes our eyes were refreshed with the sight of trees now become quite a novelty. We also met a chaise, the first one we had seen except the one we travelled in since leaving Perth or if I am not mistaken Stirling. In walking up a hill we met a funeral with a large attendance. One of the principal of the mourners carried a bottle of Whiskey and insisted upon us and our driver taking a glass saying that it was the custom.

From Oban to Inverary by Loch Awe ferry is 32 miles. At the ferry we crossed and I got another wetting the waves running high. The Carriage could not be brought over till the wind was lower and so after dinner we proceeded on foot to Inverary, about 12 miles. We did not arrive until dark but again had the happiness of seeing trees taller than ourselves. Our chaise arrived soon after. We here again found ourselves in a comfortable house with a coal fire, wheaten bread, fresh butter and a thousand other luxuries. The town is neat and small consisting only of two or three streets.

Tuesday May 24th

Looked into the grounds of the Duke of Argyll. The castle is an elegantly situated building, the grounds not very striking. We proceeded in the afternoon to Cairndow thence to Arrochar through the famous pass of Glencro of which I had heard so much that I was disappointed, it is however as fine as Glencoe and might please a person who expected nothing. We arrived at Arrochar distant from Inverary 21 miles about 9 o'clock. The inn affords good accommodations, it is beautifully situated among a few trees at the head of Loch Long with the majestic Ben Arthur rising before it.

Wednesday May 25th

No traveller should think of visiting Loch Katrine from this side of the country there being no place to stay at between Arrochar and Callender a distance of above 30 miles without including sailing about Loch Katrine which cannot be done in a very short time. We had omitted seeing it when at Stirling as we understood that the trees would not be out so early, we had therefore made up our minds to endure any fatigue, rather than see so renowned a place to any disadvantage. We accordingly rose early, buckled on our Knapsacks and proceeded to Tarbet, about 2 miles. Here we were delay[ed] for a long time before a boat could be procured, we at last crossed to a place called the Garrison, this distance might be 4 or 5 miles. We had now 4 or 5 more to walk to the nearest point of Loch Katrine, on approaching it however we lost our way, and got too far to the South. We now sat down by a brook side to consider what must be done and to eat a piece of coarse oat cake and a bit of cheese with which we had provided ourselves. We now struck off in the path we thought lay most in the direction. I climbed to the top of a hill and saw the lake at [the] foot, we descended and enquired at a hut if we could have a boat to carry us across, or take us down the water. The boat was out and did not return till evening; we then rowed down. The upper part for a distance of 7 or 8 miles presents nothing worthy of regard. The Lonely Isle is covered with a thin brush wood and disappointed me much; but nothing can exceed the Goblins Cave, where a bold craggy rock, covered to its summit with weeping birch, rises from the lake in a manner beautiful and sublime. We landed and with some labour and fatigue reached the highest peak. The view from this point is infinitely superior to anything we saw below. On one side a very deep wooded glen with Benvenue rising to the clouds, on the other, Loch Katrine, Loch Achray and Loch Vennachar half seen, half hidden by the light birch trees and behind them the Trossachs and a chain of high mountains. The whole made a view perhaps not to be excelled by any scenery of similar kind in this country. We rowed down the remaining part of the lake which was about half a mile, this though very beautiful was far inferior to the scenery we had just left. I certainly was disappointed with Loch Katrine even making every allowance for our seeing it fatigued and hungry with little hope of rest or food before us for that night or the following day. There is only about 1 mile of it which has any pretence at all to singular beauty, and this part is very narrow and confined. The foliage is in many places scanty, and excepting some of the birches which hung from almost inaccessible cliffs, I did not see a tree that could be above 15 or 20 years old at the most. We were now landed at the bottom of the lake about a mile from which we had heard was some little inn where people coming from Callender sometimes eat their lunch. We arrived much fatigued and found nothing more than a mud cabin, receiving as we got to the door that there was only one room in the house which contained 3 beds occupied by 8 men and that there was not room even to sit down. We now expected little less than to sleep all night upon the heather, being told however we might possibly find a whisky shop or public house at the Brig of Turk we proceeded. When we got there we could barely distinguish in the dusk that there was a house, we made up to it and entered. The scanty light of a few dying embers was just sufficient to distinguish the figures of a man and woman, we told them our distress and they said they would do the best for us in their power. They made up the fire, boiled some eggs and gave us a bason of milk, all very acceptable. As to beds, the woman wished us to sleep in a large bed she had which would hold 3 or 4 persons well. We would much rather have slept over the fire, as it was our hosts bed chamber as well as kitchen, the thing was impossible. We went therefore into another apartment with a cold damp mud floor. In it were two small beds in one of which were the children, and in the other one we three were to sleep. We wrapt ourselves up in our plaids and stowed like biscuits upon our sides as close as we could squeeze, even then the bed would not quite hold us. We were sadly tormented with fleas as we expected.

In the morning **May 26th Thursday** our host came in to take a hen away which had roosted on the top of our bed. We rose, of course early and after a scanty breakfast proceeded to the lakeside. Owing to the diminution of travellers there is now only one boat, the owner was digging turf. It was in vain to think of rowing up the lake as we wished, we could barely prevail upon him to row us past the Trossachs w[h]ere we landed and walked along the side of the lake, it was raining a little and very unpleasant scrambling through the wet heather. In about 2 hours we arrived at the hut we had stopped at the day before. The clouds which threatened us behind, joined to a heavy storm of hail, made us give up our plan of ascending Ben Lomond from this place. The men offered to row us up the lake to put us in the path we had missed the day before. As we went along they said they would show us more curious things on a little island which we had to pass than we had seen in all our travels. They took us to it, and on turning a point we first saw a barrel, then some barley sacks, and presently all the apparatus for distilling Whiskey. They said they worked here in safety without fear of the Excise men, that part of the country being seldom travelled, and never working but in the night time. They made us each drink a glass to bind us to secrecy and rowing us to shore put us on our road with a charge to say nothing about it at the ferry or Garrison. We now left the Loch and keeping the road we had come along before arrived in an hour and a half at the ferry. We crossed over and afterwards had a walk of about 3 miles to the Tarbet inn.

The views along the side of the Loch appeared superior to those on the water, for being seen through the trees, it gives the idea of a wooded country, whilst on the Loch nothing is seen but the high bare mountains the slender fringe of trees then being lost in the magnitude of the rest of the scenery. We arrived at Tarbet very much fatigued, almost knocked up, and I know not what we should have done had we ascended Ben Lomond, as the time we arrived at Tarbet was about the instant we should have been beginning the ascent of the mountain. In the evening being somewhat refreshed we sailed down the Loch to Luss, a distance of about 9 miles. The scenery is undoubtedly grand, the lofty Ben Lomond and other stupendous mountains rising immediately from the lake but it is too bare to satisfy an Englishman's eye, it has not even the boast of rocky scenery, all the hills being of gradual ascent and covered uniformly with brown heather. The ride along the road however is I believe exceedingly beautiful.

May 27th Friday

We had proposed overnight taking a boat down the lake and be landed at the farther end after visiting Inch Calliach the burying place of my ancestry the MacGregors[11] and some of the other islands and walk on to Dumbarton ...[12]

---

[11] There is apparently no proven link between the Gregs and the MacGregor clan. The Gregs, Greggs or Griegs originated in Scotland, in Ayrshire or Fife. It is not known why or when they left Scotland for Ireland. Samuel Greg (Robert Hyde Greg's father) came to England from Belfast in 1783.

[12] Here the journal ends.

23

TRAVELS IN PORTUGAL AND SPAIN, 1814–15

Introduction

> There is, Sir, a good deal of Spain that has not been perambulated. I would have
> you go thither; a man of inferior talents to yours, may furnish us with useful ob-
> servations on that country.
>
> Dr Samuel Johnson to James Boswell in 1763

September 1814 must have seemed a favourable time for a young man of nearly
nineteen to travel to the Iberian Peninsula. Napoleon Bonaparte, having at last
been defeated in the 'Battle of the Nations' at Leipzig in 1813, had been forced
to abdicate as ruler of France in April 1814 and had been exiled to the island of
Elba, where, a titular Emperor only, he was allowed to have the trappings of a little court. Europe was then at peace, and the diplomats (Metternich, Castlereagh,
with the Duke of Wellington and the Tsar Alexander I being the most prominent), were gathering in Vienna to redraw the map of Europe after twenty years
of warfare.

The French, whose troops had entered Spain in 1805, had been driven out
of the country by, on the one hand, the brilliant military leadership of Wellington and his long-suffering troops, and on the other, by the merciless and highly
effective guerrilla tactics of the Spanish peasantry under such self- proclaimed
'Generals' as the notorious Mina. Joseph Bonaparte having been forced to flee,
in 1813, Ferdinand VII, the Bourbon King, had returned to Madrid and was already ruling as a thoroughgoing autocrat.

Greg did not venture into such a land alone or unprepared. His cousin,
Isaac Hodgson, who was the business partner of his father, accompanied him,
and was to bear the main responsibility for the commercial aspects of the tour.
Before he set out, Robert took Spanish lessons and read widely in those books
of travels then available. The tour of Spain from September 1814 to August 1815,
is recorded in the journal, but unlike the journals of his other travels, this one
also includes a great deal of information taken from his reading. He conscien-
tiously acquired information about the places he visited and wrote an account of
each of the major cities and buildings based both on his own reading and conversations with local guides (who were not always accurate, but were expert in
relating local legends and beliefs). Given his commercial background, it is not
surprising that he also collected statistics wherever he went. How long? How
wide? How many? How much? What price? these were the sort of questions he
consistently asked throughout the tour.

His comments on the people and institutions of Portugal and Spain are inevitably biased. Travel may broaden the mind but it can also confirm travellers'

prejudices. Robert Hyde Greg had all the conventional ideas of his time and of the new wealthy industrial middle class. He was also self-assured, not a little disdainful, and opinionated, like many another young man.

After all, Britannia at this time really did rule the waves, thanks to Nelson and his fellow admirals and the British Navy, and on land, the Duke of Wellington had shown himself capable of defeating brilliant and experienced marshals of the army of Napoleon in the Peninsular War, and so had provided her with military glory. Her empire overseas was expanding rapidly, and her industry and commerce were making her the most formidable mercantile nation. Her institutions of Parliament and the Judiciary, however imperfect, seemed to contemporary Britons to be infinitely superior to those of other nations, and while France had fallen victim to violent revolution Britannia had survived intact (the condition of the toiling masses in the new factories and the labourers on the land – not to speak of political radical agitation – could be conveniently overlooked in the euphoria of post-war Britain at this time). Robert Hyde Greg, then, was patriotic in his views and, like most of his contemporaries, contemptuous of those people who had the misfortune to be foreigners. As a Protestant he was shocked by what he saw as the superstitious and idolatrous practices of the Roman Catholic Church, especially in Seville. He made some interesting comments, however, on the Basque people, whose love of freedom won his admiration. In short, this journal is a 'Period Piece', a tourist's view of Portugal and Spain in 1814–15.

Both of these countries were poor and backward. Their glory days had long since passed away. In the sixteenth century Spain had been the ruling power of the New World and half of Europe. She had steadily declined throughout the seventeenth century and, despite the attempts of the enlightened Charles III to modernise certain aspects of his country in the late eighteenth century, she had relapsed to become an easy prey for the French in 1808.

When Robert Hyde Greg visited Spain it was under the domination of an illiberal monarch and the newly restored Inquisition. Ferdinand VII's attempts to restrict foreign imports led Samuel Greg to dispatch Robert's companion, Isaac Hodgson, to Spain to try to negotiate more favourable terms for Samuel Greg and Co. 'the family firm'.

Tourism to Spain, as we know it, did not exist and very few people went to Spain for the sake of travel. It was not on the usual route for the Grand Tour, with its emphasis on the art of Ancient Greece and Rome, and Madrid was regarded as a rather dull inaccessible place, which could not compete with a cultured and cosmopolitan city like Paris. In short, it was an unfashionable destination. To be fair, those who did go, were generally impressed by what they saw, leaving aside the travelling conditions.

Travel to and within Spain was difficult and dangerous. To reach the Iberian Peninsula in the first place you had two alternatives. The land route was long

Robert Hyde Greg's Travels in Portugal and Spain, 1814–15.

26

and involved a passage through the Pyrenees that could be daunting, and the sea route to Lisbon involved crossing from England in a sailing ship, which was at the mercy of the weather, as Robert Hyde Greg experienced to his cost.

Travel on land had its own discomforts and perils. There were few decent roads, and journeys had to be made either on horseback or in uncomfortable conveyances such as calesas drawn by mules, or in private coaches or chaises (only the very poor went on foot). Village inns called *posadas* or *ventas* were extremely primitive and dirty and accommodation in major towns left much to be desired. As Richard Ford explained, most people did not travel: the rich stayed in their own houses or those of friends when making a journey, and monks and nuns stayed in other monasteries or convents, so there was no call for decent accommodation for travellers.

Then there was the problem of *Ladrones* (robbers) and *Banditti* who infested the countryside of Portugal and Spain. Richard Ford thought that many of the travellers' tales of robberies and roadside murders were exaggerated, and moreover, that local people secretly enjoyed playing on the fears of credulous English travellers by elaborating on the gory details. In 1814, however, the 'War of Liberation' as the Spanish called it, had only just ended. Guerilla fighters who were experienced in arranging ambushes and slitting the throats of unsuspecting French soldiers, transferred their skills, in the absence of other means of livelihood, to the business of fleecing ordinary travellers, often with dire results for their victims. So the possibility of being robbed, with or without violence, posed a very real threat to Robert Hyde Greg and Isaac Hodgson, and they showed real courage and determination in travelling along potentially dangerous routes, and at times were positively foolhardy in journeying unescorted by guards on, for instance, the route between Lisbon and the Spanish border.

Spain in 1814 was a war-ravaged country. Only two years before Greg and Hodgson visited Badajoz it had been the scene of a truly horrendous siege. They passed through Albuera, which had been virtually destroyed, and in the villages in La Mancha the starving inhabitants came out of their caves to beg for food on the road to Madrid. At the Escorial Robert Hyde Greg heard about the French pillaging the library and the art collection. It was therefore with alarm that, en route for Madrid, they heard the news of Napoleon's escape from Elba and shared the apprehension of other Europeans about the inevitable resumption of hostilities.

The social contacts that Greg had throughout the journey were chiefly with English merchants and consular officials, to whom he had letters of introduction. In Tetuan, during a brief visit to North Africa, he enjoyed Jewish hospitality of a surprising kind. When in Madrid, he had a real taste of high society through his contact with the British Ambassador, Sir Henry Wellesley, and Sir John Hunter, the English Consul General. He dutifully took daily Spanish lessons while in Seville but found little opportunity to practice the language with Spanish peo-

27

ple in extended conversations. In Granada he went regularly to *tertullias* (conversazioni) held by a Spanish lady of title, but found it difficult for various reasons to make much headway in conversations there. In spite of all this he managed to make his travel arrangements with muleteers and innkeepers and was resourceful during a complicated and lengthy tour.

Always it is his actual journeyings that afford the liveliest writing of the journal. His account of the foray that he and Isaac Hodgson made into North Africa is especially vivid. He was obviously fascinated by the people and exotic atmosphere of Tangier and Tetuan and wrote an enthusiastic impression of life in this part of the world, which he concluded by urging future travellers to visit.

The final section of the journal is also remarkable for the freshness and immediacy of the writing. Few journals could count on a culmination so grand as the arrival of the joyful news of the victory of Waterloo and the consequent splendid celebrations in Madrid which Greg and Hodgson were privileged to attend. But then there follows the most exciting conclusion the impetuous dash on horseback from the summer heat of Madrid during the hours of darkness, the near-fatal fall from his horse and then, as he and his travelling companion neared Burgos, the first breath of cool weather which gradually increased as they galloped to Bilbao. Thereafter occur the most endearing of similes when Greg noted that the Ebro was as "wide as the Trent at Nottingham". Coolness, rain, grass, rivulets offered the most delectable impressions to eyes long accustomed to a dried-out, barren landscape. But the adventures of the horse ride gave place to the terrors of a sea journey from Bilbao in a tiny Guernsey grain boat. Their worst fears were realised in the Bay of Biscay. It was a miracle that, to Greg's infinite relief, they reached Plymouth in safety. Past dangers made the journey back to Congleton, Wilmslow and eventually to Quarry Bank, especially sweet.

Text of the Journal, Volume One

"Land of Iberia! blushing read,
"In History's page, the heroic deed,
"The thirst for Honour, Virtue, Fame,
"Which once adorned thy earlier name
"Art Thou the Land, where Freedom's breath
"Inspired so oft contempt of death?
"Taught old Numantia how to fall,
"And sink in flames Saguntum's wall?
"And now of late, indignant broke
"From bloody, wasting Gallia's yoke?
"Weep, Spirit of Iberia weep!

"Thy Sons of Fame unconscious sleep:
"And Honour summons them, in vain,
"To heaven born Freedom once again.[1]

September 28th 1814

I Hodgson and myself set off in the Mail for Birmingham where we arrived at 2 o'clock on the following day. Being unwilling to pass in night thro' the fine country between that place and Bath, we determined to stay all night and proceed early on the ensuing morning. This gave us the opportunity of seeing Keane;[2] the play Hamlet; he acted most admirably and his pale countenance and hollow voice suited well the character.

Sept 30th

The Bath coach set off at 5 o'clock am. We were not called and had to post after it, but caught it the first stage. The day was fine and the views of the country round and of the Malvern hills, were extremely beautiful, which made us rejoice not having proceeded the night before. The singularly neat and beautiful vale of Rodborough attracted our particular notice and we concluded that the inhabitants must be happy and virtuous, but we learned afterwards to our surprise that they were notorious for their profligacy. We arrived at Bath at 8 o'clock pm.

October 1st

Called in good time on my aunt Jane and breakfasted with her. Afterwards we called on the Percivals and Maria accompanied us through the town and public buildings. The Town resembles Edinburgh, in the beauty of its stone buildings, fine situation and number of shops. Before leaving it we bathed with the water at the full temperature (114 Fah^r). We reached Bristol at about 9 o'clock and missed part of the beautiful country which lies between the two cities.

Oct 2nd : Sunday

We walked to Clifton and after admiring for some time the grandeur of the view and of the Cliffs we went to a little church on the hill. Crossing the ferry of the Avon, a walk of 4 or 5 miles, with a very extensive view of a richly wooded and cultivated country, we reached Ham Green, Mr Bright's, as noble a situation as can be conceived. We passed a very agreeable day and regretted much that we were not able to spend a longer time there. A chaise conveyed us back to Bristol at 12 o'clock.

---

[1]   This verse precedes the text of the first volume of the manuscript.
[2]   The famous actor, Edmund Keane.

Oct 3rd

At 6 o'clock we set off on the top of the Exeter coach. The country still continued remarkably fine. At dinner at Taunton we discovered that a Gentleman and his wife were Coach Companions – Mr and Mrs Thos Fox, to whom we had letters at Falmouth. He told us that we had no chance of meeting a packet before the 7th and we resolved to come round by Plymouth. We travelled all that night, but the Coach being full we were obliged to be forwarded in a chaise and thereby past [sic] an uncomfortable and fatiguing night. As far as might be seen by the light of the Moon, we missed some fine prospects.

October 4th

The entrance to Plymouth is altogether a beautiful and striking sight. We arrived at 7 am. After breakfast we went round the Quays and the fortifications, but one principal object was defeated, viz seeing the dockyards, for there was a sitting of the Lords of the Admiralty and the thing was impossible. A number of large vessels[3] were lying dismasted in the river, which had been paid off. The coaches were crowded with sailors and on the Bristol coach I met one who gave many curious stories of the assassinations and Intrigues of Lisbon where he had spent some time.

October 5th

Setting out from Plymouth at 10 am and crossing the harbour among all the Men of War, we joined the Falmouth Mail[4] at Tor Point. The views of the harbour are fine from the surrounding hills, and once we got a glimpse of the Eddistone lighthouse, but the country as we advanced became bleak and sterile. The hills were in some places so steep and the road so narrow that we frequently trembled for our necks. We did not arrive at Falmouth until 11 o'clock where we put up at Comyn's hotel.

October 6th

Called upon Foxes and Sons to whom we had letters and afterwards walked about. The town is small and dirty and must be a very uncomfortable place to stay at long waiting for a wind. The harbour is safe and commodious and together with the numerous vessels, forms a pleasing and picturesque object. In the afternoon the wind shifted to the west and rain came on soon after. This did not prevent us from crossing the bay to dine at Trefusis Castle, the family seat of Lord Clinton, and at present the residence of Mr G. Fox. Even here at Lands End I found myself among friends, though it must be confessed that when far from home, we consider persons as friends upon much slighter grounds than we otherwise should do. To have a friend at home you must be long in habits of intimacy with him, but abroad if you meet a man who has a single friend in common with yourself, that is quite sufficient to form a friendship with him. Thus a traveller will very often experience, and none but a traveller can tell how agreeable such meetings always are – I found at Trefusis Mr Barcley, a school fellow of my Brother Tom's and soon discovered that Mrs Robt Fox was sister to G. Barcley whom we had met at Killarney; another sister of his was likewise staying there. We met there also a Mr Gotch, a particular friend of Mr Rathbone's, and with no other claims of friendship then these slight as they may appear, I felt quite at home among old friends. We spent a very pleasant evening with their party and returned in the dark across the bay. Trefusis stands upon a hill and commands some noble and extensive views of the harbour and neighbouring coast.

October 7th

The wind which had alarmed us the day before by blowing from the West had now come round to the N.W. At breakfast we were roused by a signal gun which announced that our vessel was leaving the harbour for the roads. We could not change our Bank notes at the bank as they had no Spanish or Portuguese money and it happened to be a holiday among the Jews and persons generally applied to in these cases and they said they could have nothing to do with money that day, not even <u>touch</u> it, but they told me that Mr Fox's clerk where their doubloons and dollars were and said that "<u>he</u> might <u>take</u> them if he liked", wh^{c.} he did and we were saved the inconvenience we should otherwise have been put to had the Conscience of the Jews been as strict as they sh^{d.} have been. We afterwards passed our luggage at the Custom House and settled with our Captain who told us that he should sail in the morning. In the course of the day we walked to Pendennis Castle, one of the forts defending the harbour town of Falmouth; it is situated on a neck of rising ground running out into the sea and commands a fine view of the neighbouring coast.

October 8th : Saturday

Having received orders to be on board by 11 am we rowed two miles across the bay to our vessel the Princess Elizabeth and went on board but had to wait 3 hours for the Captain. We amused ourselves the rest of the day watching the shores of England gradually fade from our view; the bold promontory of Lizards Point was the last object which remained in sight and this disappeared about sunset. I began now to grow sick, but stood on deck to a late hour, admiring the rich purple glow which the setting sun had cast upon one side of the ocean whilst the other remained in gloomy obscurity. After it became dark an interesting and

---

[3]   The war against Napoleon was over, the sailors were discharged and ships de-commissioned from the navy.

[4]   Falmouth was the headquarters of the Royal Mail packet ships from 1688 until 1852. The trade went to Southampton in 1852.

beautiful phenomenon, though by no means a singular one, attracted my attention; this was the luminous appearance of the water, every time the spray was thrown from the prow of the vessel it seemed studded with a thousand stars and the whole much resembled a sheet of fire spread out before the ship. Whenever a wave broke, the same beautiful appearance recurred.

October 9th
Being very unwell I did not rise from my berth during the whole day, this was situated quite at the stern and consequently had much motion, another inconvenience was it being over the magazine and no light was allowed.

October 10th
I crawled upon deck and sat upon one of the cannons admiring the immense expanse of ocean; the little vessel which contained us was the only object on its surface and appeared to be the sole existing one in creation and I was more than ever astonished at the intrepidity of that man who first ventured out of sight of land; it is most probable that accident in the first instance carried his vessel from the shore. I still continued very unwell though something better.

October 11th Tuesday
In good time in the morning we came in sight of the Gallician coast; but the wind had changed to the S.W. and blown us out of our course into the Bay of Biscay. The sea however was calm and the sight of land was very refreshing; at 1 o'clock we were within 3 miles of the shore where a notable chain of jagged hills extended from Cape Finisterre to Cape Ortegal. Two hours sail would [have] brought us to Corunna, but we were now obliged to shift our course to the NWW.

October 12th
In the night it came on a strong gale of wind, with a very rough sea wh$^{c.}$ caused some anxiety on our parts. I was so ill as to be quite indifferent to the danger but I. Hodgson was very uneasy and passed a considerable part of the night trotting upon deck and back again in chemise and greatcoat. The storm continued all that day, and the following night of the day after (Thursday). I spent a good deal of the time as I have just mentioned, I was still so ill as to be indifferent to it, excepting indeed once when the vessel went down so on one side and remained in that position so long that I thought she had capsized, and sprang up in great alarm.

Friday 14th
The gale abated and we got round Cape Finisterre lying out a long way to the west. I still continued ill.

Saturday 15th

I lay in my berth all the day worse than I had been since I got on board. The weather fine.

Sunday

Mr Crawford roused us very early by entering our cabin and telling us to get up immediately as they were clearing the decks for action and that the Captain had called for the key [to] the ammunition. We jumped up and crawling up in a miserable weak state I saw a vessel in full sail at a distance of a few miles. All necessary sails were taken down and the guns got ready, but the ship, after keeping us on watch all day and approaching within 1½ miles sheered off in another direction. We had one alarm previous to this, which shows what an anxious time we should have had, if instead, or besides Americans,[5] all Europe had been our enemy. This day I began to recover – it was the first day since I got on board that I had been at table to breakfast, tea and dinner. Our company on the passage was a Mr C, a young man from Glasgow, Mr W.... [name mostly illegible] going to Oporto for his health and 3 foreigners, 2 Spaniards and a Frenchman. Had I been well enough I should have had much amusement with them, but I had neither health nor spirits for talking. Mr C had made several voyages and told some good stories, witty sayings. Mr W kept his bed almost entirely. The Spaniards spoke no English nor yet the Frenchman, but he never stopped talking a moment and was the first thing heard in the morning and the last at night. On the Thursday he kept trotting up and down with a telescope at least a yard long up to his eye, "Que voyez vous Monsieur?" said I as he was spying at the vessel. "Ah! Monsieur", said he, "Je vois le Diable". Our Captain was a very stingy old fellow, notorious for his parsimony. We never had a single delicacy of any kind though we were all more or less Invalids and he never asked any of us as to our health but bestowed all his attention on his large store of livestock. After the first few days we had nothing but coarse beef, dirty scraps of brown biscuits and bread extremely mouldy.

Monday 17th

I rose much better and on going on deck saw the Berling rocks, singular cones rising from the sea 3 or 4 miles from the rock of Lisbon. This day for the first time I opened a book and in the morning read 80 pages of Gonsalvo de Cordova.[6]

---

[5] Britain and the U.S.A. were at war between 1812 and 1815. It was during this war that British troops invaded U.S. territory and burned down the White House.

[6] Consalvo de Cordova: 'The Great Captain', captured Granada for Ferdinand and Isabella in 1492.

Thursday 18th

To our joy on coming on deck by 6 o'clock found ourselves close off the land. We soon took on board a pilot, a strange ragamuffin, his first step was to dress, putting on a decent jacket over his dirty yellow shirt, sailors breeches and boots. The Captain wanted to swear at him for something he had done, but not one on deck knew enough of the language to translate it. The pilot then began giving his instructions to the Mate, who in a true English manner said "Damn your eyes, why don't you speak English?" The sea was very calm, on the bar there were dreadful breakers. The rock of Lisbon (which is nothing more than the break of a chain of mountains running into the sea) together with a great part of the fine rocky coast, was enveloped in mist, but on passing Fort Julian, an ugly mass of buildings commanding the river, and entering the Tagus, the day cleared and discovered a beautiful view. The hills on both sides grouped together in a singular manner and of every fantastic shape were rendered doubly interesting by the immense number of country houses, villages, vineyards, olive, mango and lemon groves and the tops of most of them covered with windmills, of a size and shape which renders the delusion of Don Quixote less absurd than it appears to an English reader. The river itself was crowded with shipping of all nations, and the Portuguese fishing boats, with their large white sails, were seen in every direction. My thoughts turned to the time when the famous Vasco da Gama sailed from this river on his well known voyage of discovering the Indies. We all went on shore together at that part called Buenos Ayres, to be examined at the health office. To my astonishment on setting my foot on shore, instead of feeling perfectly well as I fully expected, my head grew dizzy, and terra firms seemed to have as much motion as the packet in the Bay of Biscay. We afterwards returned to our boat to row up to Lisbon. I then felt quite well again, but on landing the dizziness and faintness increased to such a degree that I began to be alarmed. We now loaded some Gallicians with our luggage and followed a gentleman friend of Mr W's to a Hotel at the upper part of the city. They had accommodations for one and Mr W took them. We and the 3 foreigners were now turned adrift, we went from place to place but found no room anywhere, at last, leaving me to look after the luggage, the others went to look for an inn. I was shown to one where the landlady told us in Portuguese that she had 5 beds. It was a sad, dirty house, but necessity was in the case so I.H. and I brought our things and I engaged rooms, that is bedrooms, for sitting rooms they never have. We now went out to deliver our letters and experienced the greatest difficulty in finding the persons. After showing our letters to various people and directed to wrong persons we at last found Mr Munro of the house of Munro and Burton a truly fortunate circumstance. Mr M engaged us excellent lodging[s] which were to be vacant on the following day and Mr B dined with us at an excellent ordinary dinner á l'Anglaise. With all the walking we had had, the earth felt rather quieter, and a few glasses of wine soon steadied it altogether. The dessert consisted of grapes, enormous melons and apples to which we did justice after dinner. Mr B. offered to walk with us to the celebrated acqueduct completed 1746 by John V and begun by his predecessor. By it alone Lisbon is supplied with all its water, which is brought in this manner from the mountains near Cintra, a distance of 12 miles. It is a noble stupendous work and for the indolent Portuguese a truly astonishing one, being worthy of the best days of Rome, but why the expence was not saved by bringing the water in pipes – Mr B could not tell. We visited a place where it crosses a deep ravine. The largest arch here is 220 feet high by 95 wide; the whole of the finest masonry; the stone primitive Limestone. There is a fine walk on both sides of the channel of water which is covered. Along one of these we returned home though not quite dark being much fatigued having been walking all day in our weak state – the Portuguese have a particular reverence for this acqueduct, because it withstood the shock of the earthquake,[7] here and there a stone is cracked or misplaced but no material harm done. At a coffee-house we got refreshment before returning to our bare walls in the Rua de Corps Santo. We sat till a late hour writing on a dirty little table and then retired to a hard bed.

Wednesday 19th

Rose in good time. I did not sleep well for my bed appeared to roll and pitch in such a violent manner that I expected every minute to fall out. I.H. was bit in a dreadful manner and quite disfigured. I paid my footing in Ireland[8] and escaped without damage. We made a good breakfast on strong green tea, bad salt butter and grapes. Not a being in the house could speak a word of anything but Portuguese, but by a vocabulary and by altering Spanish words with a good deal of grimace and action, I continued to make our wants known. Calling on Mr M. he took us on Change and introduced us to other persons to whom we had letters and we again had reason to be thankful that we had fallen in with Mr M. in the first instance. We spent sometime in walking through the city, got an excellent English dinner at Mr M's and spent an hour or two afterwards with some friends of his in the tea room, retiring early to finish our dispatches for England. The population of Lisbon is estimated at 500,000. It is built on a line of hills running

---

7   The Lisbon earthquake of 1755 had a devastating effect on the city itself and profoundly shocked Europe. It is probable that as many as 40,000 people died in the city as a result of the earthquake and the subsequent tidal wave which left Lisbon in ruins. It had to be almost entirely rebuilt.

8   A slang expression whose meaning is now uncertain. 'To pay one's footing' was to pay the customary fee for entrance to a trade, society, etc. The inclusion of Ireland complicates matters. Does it suggest that he had been bitten by fleas in Ireland (which he had already visited) and so believed himself now protected against future flea bites? If so, he was unlucky because he was to be badly bitten on other occasions.

along the side of the Tagus. In the whole city there is scarcely a level street. The streets are all extremely narrow and many steep to a degree that astonished us. All are dirty. Before the French were in possession of Lisbon the filth in the streets was many feet deep. Junot issued orders for keeping the streets <u>clean</u>. In vain it was represented that the people did not know the meaning of the word. He issued another order that they should be cleaned by a certain day and if they were not he would yoke a Portuguese and an ox together and make them. The streets were done by the day. In consequence of another order all the dogs were shot. The houses are built in a very large scale, the door and window frames all of large blocks of fine stone, and handsome balconies before the windows, and they would have a very fine effect if they were not daubed over with white, yellow, light red, dark and all shades of blue plaster. It looks smart at first but very soon falls off or becomes dirty and has a miserable appearance. They are all very large, a family occupying only one floor: on the ground floor is generally a court-yard, the other parts of it, even in some nobleman's house let out for shops etc. The Churches, Convent and religious buildings numberless, rather shabby looking outside, many of them are unfinished as well as other public buildings, all stopped for want of money. The streets are full of strange objects; very fat well-fed monks, miserable beggars, droves of mules and asses, carts of very rude construction and drawn by oxen, men and women of all sorts, sizes and colours. The former in cloaks called Capotas, with either the enormous slouched hat abolished by Royal edict in Spain, or a still large cocked one and the latter in cloaks with all a white handkerchief round the head which looks very becoming. The men all wear boots, the common women are all rather ugly, but their little dark eyes are very expressive. They are altogether a different race from our country women and the fine, open, generous countenance of the one forms a strong contrast to the swarthy complexions and dark suspicious looks of the other. In this however I must except the Gallicians, a fine, hardy, honest race who leave their native hills to the porters of all Spain and who, after hoarding a little money retire to their native country to enjoy it. The English, we are told, are not very popular. The natives know their own weak state and feel extremely jealous; they now call themselves the liberators of Europe. Marshal Beresford[9] is unpopular because too severe a disciplinarian. Lord W[ellesley],[10] was regarded rather as a God than anything else. During the 4 days he staid in Lisbon not a shop was open. On landing in the Praça do Commercio the friars went down on their knees and one hugged him so close about the legs that Lord W. fell to the ground. This reception was so warm that many could not refrain from tears of joy. The fruit stalls often arrested our attention, beautiful grapes, melons, figs, pomegranates, apples etc were everywhere to be seen in immense quantities. At dinner we saw people frying sardines (a fish like a herring) in oil and eating them with a fine bunch of blooming grapes or a melon. The cooking operations were generally to be carried out in the streets, the small charcoal fire being contained in an earthern jar. The jewellers' shops are the only ones which make any show; they are numerous but very small.

Thursday 20th

We rose early, breakfasted at a coffee house and then found a calash waiting at Mr Munro's door to convey us to Cintra, distant 4 or 5 leagues or 18 or 20 miles from Lisbon; famous no less for its beauties than for the convention[11] signed there with the French after the battle of Vimeiro.[12] The suburbs extend a long way in this direction. On going out of town we had a fine view of the Acqueduct and saw it in various directions most of the way to Cintra. The royal road on which we travelled was the roughest pavement I ever saw; the few hedges on the roadside were rows of aloes; the country unenclosed, all arable land without the exception of a single field and its winter dress was nothing but a barren, desolate waste. We met on the road numerous droves of mules with their drivers. Some with enormous cocked, other with enormous round hats. They were truly not men with them but hats with men under, the latter being always most prominent and striking should be placed first when both are mentioned. They were all civil to excess, taking off their hats as they said "Viva Signor" and some continuing uncovered till the carriage had passed. About halfway to Cintra is Queluz Palace which we had been desired to visit. The building is large and clumsy, the yellow and blue plaster dirty and falling to decay. Inside the taste is equally bad, nothing to be seen but guilding and mirrors, all out of repair. There are a few wretched paintings and in one room, the principal adventures of Don Quixote are painted on the roof and walls. The garden may serve as a specimen of all the Portuguese – straight walks edged with box; trees cut into all sorts of ridiculous shapes, ponds with golden fish, and a great number of spouting figures throwing water over artificial rock work. Cintra is a small town with a royal Palace, of white plaster and red tiles. It is buried in olive, orange, lemon and cork trees, stands at the foot of an immensely high jagged rock, seemingly composed of vast fragments of granite. After dinner a guide conducted us to the "Convento da

[9]   Marshal Beresford was head of the British occupying forces in Portugal. He was unpopular because of his dictatorial manner. There was a plot to assassinate him in 1814.

[10]   Lord Wellesley became the Duke of Wellington in 1814.

[11]   The Convention of Cintra (1808) allowed the French who had been defeated at Vimeiro to leave Portugal with their military equipment intact. Against his better judgement, having been overruled by officers senior to him, Wellesley signed the convention on behalf of the British Government. On returning to England he was court martialled – but duly exonerated.

[12]   In the Battle of Vimeiro (1808), the French were defeated by the British under Sir Arthur Wellesley.

Pena," a convent of the rock situated on one of the highest and most isolated peaks. The ascent is steep and laborious, but we were amply repaid at every step by the sight of some new convent rising among the trees on the side of the rock; these however were soon left far behind and continuing our course amongst the mass of antediluvian ruins, we at last reached the convent. One of the friars took us through the sacred places and then sent us to the summit for the view which was very grand, on one side the sea, on the other a long series of rugged peaks, on the two others an immense extent of country, and below the woods of Cintra. From this place the battle of Vimiero was seen. Though rather late we proceeded to an adjoining peak to examine the ruins of a Moorish Castle. It has been surrounded by two walls of vast extent, including within them all the peak, some of the gateways remaining and a vaulted building for a reservoir of water. We sat here till the moon began to have some power and whilst descending, the Convent bell began to announce the time of prayer which our guide took care not to neglect. The whole scene was so very wild and magnificent that were I to stay a month at Cintra, I think I should never be a day without visiting some part of the rock. We experienced some difficulty in clambering over the rocks by so faint a light, but we got to our inn safe at about 8 o'clock. I think I never regretted anything more than not being able to pay a second visit to the convent.

Friday 21st
Our burros or asses were ready for us in good time and we mounted with some difficulty saddles of such a size that they quite concealed the animal from our sight. The morning was fine but the convent of the rock was enveloped in clouds. After winding some time among the cork trees along the side of the hill, we began to ascend among the rocks and heaths towards the "Cork Convent", situated near the summit. Unfortunately we were completely in the clouds. I lost the magnificent view from the garden of the convent. A fat jolly old friar was showman and he displayed all the images and crucifixes without reserve, though we told him who we were. I regretted exceedingly I could not understand the language, for by his looks I am certain he would have given us abundance of good stories; he would talk, though we told him we did not understand. I made one sad mistake, whilst in one of the chapels. I asked him who that person was in the corner pointing to a decent looking figure. He told me it was Jesus Christ, and no doubt set me down for a very sad heretic. After showing everything he took us to the refectory, a sort of cell formed between two immense blocks of granite; the table was of the same stone, spread with apples, cheese and sour wine. Taking our departure we descended the other side of the rock and gradually emerged from the clouds. The village of Colares is beautifully situated at the foot of the rock and looks towards Cintra. There we visited more gardens, but being as all the rest in the same style as Queluz I need say nothing of them. On our way

back we stopped to look at Montserrat, a very fine building formerly the residence of Mr Beckford, now uninhabited and fallen to decay, and you may ride your burrow through the still beautiful though desolate chambers. On our return to Lisbon we met many people with monstrous hats, all extremely courteous; they use much form in their conversation and always address one another "Signor". The following is no bad specimen of the form they use with gentlemen. Mr Burton went into a house to ask for a glass of water for me, the man seeing him said "would you do me the favour to inform me what your respectable Highness wants".

Saturday 22nd

We called on Mr M who took us to the British consul for passports, he told us that Mina[13] had fled to France and that if we were going to Spain that we stood a good chance of getting our throats cut, and on taking leave desired us to be on the watch. On landing at Lisbon we had learnt the unpleasant intelligence that the fever was in Cadiz – the very place of our destination. We had therefore arranged our plan to go by way of Elvas and Badajos to Seville and remain there until we could enter Cadiz. On the following day another piece of news reached our ears, that General Mina at the head of a rebel army was marching upon Madrid. Thus we entered the country at a very unfortunate period. Mr M said that a Spanish family was setting out at about the time we intended, for Badajos and that if we liked we might join their party. This we determined to do as well for the sake of gaining information and improving in the language as for safety. After dinner we went out shopping with Mr M and being a fine bright moonlight evening we walked to a part of the town looking upon the Tagus, which with its numberless vessels and the distant hills, made a most striking appearance.

We wished to have gone to the theatre but was told that it would not be open until the following evening.

Sunday 23rd

I rose early and walked to the acqueduct [sic] before breakfast; on returning I met numbers going to Mass, the men variously attired and the ladies most commonly in Black gowns a white lace neckhandkerchief or shawl and black lace veil, the common women in immense cloaks like the capota of the men and with a white muslin handkerchief over their heads. I did not see one that I could call pretty. We went into several of the churches during service, the priests drest very fine and did little else than run about bobbing like so many ducks in a pond before the altar. The churches are very splendid if gilding can make them so, the paintings are not very good and they represent in many of them the Almighty and

---

[13] Mina was a self-proclaimed General of the Spanish guerilla forces. He had a fearsome reputation.

Holy Ghost as well as the Virgin and our Saviour. The Virgin however seems to be the favourite and the one to whom all prayers are addressed. In going along one street we saw a number of figures in scarlet cloaks with torches and carrying something with a kind of umbrella over it. This was the Host. In an instant every hat in the street was off, and as it passed everyone fell down on their knees. I did the same, but as they passed and I saw the poor dirty looking wretches before whom we were bowing, I felt so indignant that I think the next time this heavenly host thinks proper to parade the street I shall content myself with taking off my hat. The best was that as long as it continued in the same street no person put their hats on again.

Towards noon we rowed up the river. The western side of Lisbon is but indifferent and the eastern extremity is as bad. We dined with Mr M. After our wine we went into the drawing room, where coffee was served and, immediately after Noyan was handed round, Mr M. asked us if we had so far got over our English prejudices as to have any objection to play a game at cards, saying that it was the custom, we declined and at an early hour retired.

Monday 24th
Went to the Excise office for our passports. They described us both as having chestnut hair and the other parts of the description of our persons were about as accurate as the colour of our hair. At 1 o'clock we waited on Marshal Beresford and Colonel Arbuthnot, his secretary to whom we had letters. Lord B. was so busy he could not see us just then, but Colonel A. brought us word that his lordship was dining out that day and would have been very happy to see us to dinner and that he hoped for our company to a grand ball he was giving on Wednesday to the Portuguese. He also said that he would have given us letters, to some of the Spanish governors, but that they had behaved in a very insolent manner to some friends of his to whom he had given letters and that he did not wish any other persons to experience a similar treatment. Colonel A. added that people being out of danger had given them hints that they wished to get rid of them and had begun to throw obstacles in their way whenever they could and, that the Marshal was only waiting for the return of his R. Highness to determine what steps he should take. The ball would have been a good opportunity of seeing the Portuguese nobility but it would have detained us too long and we declined it. We learnt today that the Spanish family could not accompany us and we therefore determined to pursue our journey alone. We took coffee instead of dinner and afterwards perambulated all the eastern part of the town; the evening was fine and the views up the Tagus and the opposite side extremely beautiful. The streets in this part are excessively narrow and dirty but the houses all large and very well built. We were much disappointed in receiving no news of the state of Spain. Private letters dare not say a word.

Tuesday 25th

Spent the morning in shopping and providing utensils and provisions for our journey, but determined not to set off till Wednesday morning early. In the afternoon we went to look at the celebrated altar piece at the Church of Santa Roque. It is excessively fine and magnificent but placed in such a dark recess as scarcely to be distinguishable. The mosaic work is perhaps the finest in the world, the colours vivid and at a short distance the harmony of colouring is such that it might be taken for an admirable painting of one of the first Masters. There are two groups of figures, and a handsome floor work and these cost the King £80,000. The circular columns are of brass inlaid with Lapis Lazuli, the square ones of a kind of Sardonix of extra-ordinary size and beauty. In front of the altar is a plate of Lapis Lazuli about 3 feet long by 2 broad, surrounded by a border of amethyst. The remaining parts of the recess are filled with work of Brass and beautiful Verde Antique and precious marbles – we were told that the whole expence of the church was 3 millions of Crusados, about 425,000 £ sterling.

Wednesday 26th

"Venta de los Pregonis" Rose between 5 and 6 o'clock, finished packing and waited for the servant with whom we had made an engagement the day before to accompany us to Seville and even further if we wished. We then called upon Mr Munro who told us the tide would not serve of some time. In short, we did not leave the shore till after 9 o'clock.

Our servant did not make his appearance and living at too great a distance to send after him, we determined to take our chance rather than be detained and accordingly left him behind. As we left the shore we had an excellent view of the whole city which makes a truly magnificent appearance – The shipping, the verdure of the opposite side, a fine range of mountains behind it and another range running along the northern coast formed a scene which inclined us to give full credit to what we had heard, that in beauty and magnificence of scenery the Tagus stands unrivalled in Europe. This river derives the title of yellow from the great quantity of sand which is always mixed with its waters. I recommend to any person previous to leaving Lisbon to sail 5 or 10 miles up the Tagus and also across en route to the Aldea Gallega. This place is distant from Lisbon 3 leagues or 12 miles and a brisk gale carried us over in 1½ hour [sic]. Mr Munro had sent an interpreter with us but he unfortunately understood as little or less of English than we did of Portuguese and was no assistance to us. When we arrived they said the Mules were at dinner so we had to wait till they had done. Our calesa was the strangest vehicle I ever saw, but to describe it would be impossible. It was open in front, a window on each side, and a large one in the back, and the nearest part of the body of it was distant nearly a yard from the axle of the wheels, not above it, but immediately before. This was for the convenience of luggage. Presently one of the mules made its appearance, its head [and] neck totally concealed beneath a profusion of all coloured trappings, lined with goat's hair by way of a fringe. The rope traces had also a fine fringe 9 or 10 inches broad. The Mule had 3 bells under its chin. I remonstrated and wished them to be taken off, but was told – "It was the custom". But imagine how great was my dismay when they brought a band hung with 11 more bells and slung it round the neck of the mule. Notwithstanding my vexation at the tinkling of so many bells, I could not restrain my laughter on seeing another band of 16 bells buckled on to the neck of the other mule, arrayed in the same strange accoutrements as the first. They were now put to the Calesa, the whole weight of which rests upon one mule. The postilion rides the other which draws by ropes and is always about neck and shoulders before the other. Our Calesdero or driver, who was a fine tall young fellow had on a hat with a rim full eight inches broad, fustian jacket and breeches, a handsome belt round his waist and large boots; he mounted a saddle which rose at least two feet above the mule he rode, resembling a very high trunk placed upon the animal's back and with this extraordinary equipage we went out of Aldea Gallega laughing most heartily. We passed for a mile or two between extensive vineyards, with hedges of different kinds of Aloes and then entered into a forest of small pine trees. Here we lost sight of Lisbon and the fine hills of Cintra and plunged into thickets of pines with underwood of most beautiful heaths, wild thyme, lavender and a small dwarf oak which never rises above 2 feet from the ground, with a vast number of others, the names of which I do not know and have never seen many of them before. The country was a dead flat, the soil a silicious sand and the road made by the frequent passing of carts in the same track. At a small solitary house in the wood we bought some bread, grapes, chestnuts and walnuts, upon which we made a good dinner. Here we met a large cavalcade and shortly after the carriage of the Marquis de Campo – Mayor, attended with a number of carts and people on horseback. Nor long after we met a Spanish carriage drawn by 7 mules and attended by 6 or 7 armed men. We observed that all travelled in company but ourselves, but we determined to take our chance and trust to Providence as Mr Munro said we must do now that we were leaving Lisbon. The distance to Pregones 5 leagues took us 6½ hours to accomplish the mules not trotting a single inch. The road and forest here are exactly the same as on first leaving the vineyards. The venta or inn is almost a single house in this wood. The sun had set when we arrived and the Calasero, or as I shall call him Juan, drove into a sort of stable where numbers of men were standing over a small fire. We were shown into a room sufficiently desolate with 3 boards on a tile floor to serve for our bed. We got some water boiled and made some tea. Our man Juan came to know if we would have a "fronta" (a poulet) for supper. Not understanding the word, he went out and caught one to show what a "fronta" was. We said yes, and in the course of an hour a woman brought us a fowl boiled in rice with black puddings, onions and bacon, upon which we made a hearty supper.

Thursday 27th

Our bed was not the best, being nothing more than a large bag of straw laid on some board with a straw mat upon it. On this we lay down and covering ourselves with our great coats, slept quietly till 6 o'clock when Juan roused us, and we proceeded on our journey. They charged us as much for our poor accommodations as they would have done in the best Hotel in London. We had now got rid of the pine trees and instead saw quantities of Arbutuses covered with beautiful fruit, gumcistus, myrtles, lauristinus and the heaths larger than before. We could now see the fine range of hills up the Tagus, those of Lisbon and beyond, even those of Cintra. We did not arrive at "Vendas Nuevas" our breakfasting place, a distance of 3 leagues, till between 11 and 12 o'clock. After resting the mules for two hours we proceeded on the road to Montamore our sleeping place, a small town distant from Vendas Novas 4 leagues. This day's journey as well as yesterday we saw many crosses where people had been murdered. We saw also some large herds of goats which gave us some hopes of being able to procure a little milk for our tea as none of these inns can furnish any, in this, however, we were disappointed. The approach to Montamore is very striking after the flat country through which we had been travelling. Looking over an extent of wooded country on the right we saw a lofty hill crowned with the extensive ruins of an ancient castle, on the left a large convent half concealed in foliage standing on another hill, and between these two hills stood the neat whitewashed town of Montamore. Our mules as usual went at the pace of 3 miles an hour and the sun had set when we arrived. We immediately walked up to the castle. The ruins are extensive but not of Moorish origin, as I was told. At least nothing that I saw in the Architecture bespoke it Moorish. It commands a very extensive view of the flat country on this side of the Tagus and though the sun was set, yet the brightness of the sky was such that hills north of Lisbon on the opposite side of the river were perfectly visible. We returned to our venta and the hostess told us a long story about something we did not understand and we had some difficulty in making known what we wanted, and at last succeeded and made a famous meal on bread, very bad butter, tea without milk, cold eggs, ham and fine grapes. Our room resembled exactly the one we slept in last night. The desolation of the country between Montemore and Lisbon is such that between Aldea Gallega and Los Pregones (which is a single house) we saw only one house and that was a convent. Between Los Pregones and Vendas Novas we did not see one and from that place hither not above 3 houses. This is one of the grand Royal roads of the Kingdom of Portugal!

Friday 28th

Juan had us in the Calesa by sunrise, and we proceeded at our usual pace. Leaving the pretty town of Montemore, we entered on some barren plains and afterwards into some cork woods. The country however improved as we approached Arroyelos, a small hamlet situated on the side of a hill with the remains of a large Castle rising above it. The distance from Montemore is called 3 leagues, but must be more as we did not arrive till 12 o'clock. After coming this distance it may be supposed that we made a good breakfast. Before setting off again we took a look at the castle. We were told it was Moorish, the outside wall wh$^{c.}$ is perfect has some appearance of being so, but the arches are all Gothic. The country between Arruelos and Venta del Duca, another 3 league stage, bears some marks of cultivation and seemingly produces barley, though it looks rather desolate. Here and there we saw a few scattered farm houses, the first we had seen since we left Aldea Gallega. Everything looked extremely brown, and indeed I might say that since we left Falmouth we had not seen a blade of grass, such land as is cultivated is entirely arrable [sic]. The moon had risen some time before we arrived at Venta del Duque, and in passing through a wood of cork trees intersected with ravines we began to feel some fear of robbers, the crosses erected over the murdered, wh$^{c.}$ we had seen during the day before having left I suppose some impression on our minds. We however arrived safe shortly after at V. de Duque a single house situated in the middle of a wood. Hitherto we had left our large trunks behind the Calesa all night but now Juan brought them into our room, saying something about "ladrones" and "soldados", the purpose of which I could not quite understand. We met here the same accommodations as at the other ventas and as usual a straw mattrass [sic] was laid on the floor for our beds. I have said nothing of the vermin, being by no means an agreeable subject, but we have been so dreadfully plagued since our landing at Lisbon that it is impossible to be altogether silent. In Lisbon we were quite disfigured with bites either from bugs, fleas or mosquitos and we are just as badly off on our journey. If you commit a hundred murders a day it is to no purpose, they are immediately replaced by new swarms.

Saturday 29th

Orada a solitary venta. I passed but an uncomfortable night for the lamp going out suddenly, I could not find my great coat to cover me, and the night proved very cold. Juan had us up before sunrise through a large olive wood, the country being rendered rather more interesting from the view we had of a fine range of blue hills upon our right. We arrived at Estremoz a distance of 3 leagues about noon. The road winds completely round the town before reaching the gate at wh$^{c.}$ we entered. It is a neat whitewashed town surrounded with high walls, stands on a hill in a commanding situation and has been fortified, but at present has not any garrison. A man stopped us at the gates and wanted something but on telling him we were English and did not understand Portuguese he let us pass on. From Estramoz to Orada about 2 leagues the country improves greatly. We first passed through a very extensive Olive plantation and for 20 or 30 yards between two hedges and what is remarkable, saw a few square feet of green grass wh^c· was very grateful to our sight. From a Cork wood a league further we had a very fine view of a tract of undulating ground bounded by fine hills. Before reaching Orada we met a guard of soldiers on horseback, Juan said continually passed from Estramoz to Elvas for the purpose of keeping the road clear of "Ladrones" and that they had taken a considerable number of them. He was himself robbed near Venta del Duque and stripped of 12 dollars but he had more concealed about him wh^c· they did not find. We asked if there were any robbers in Spain. He said many and that all Spaniards were "ladrones and muy malos." The country through wh^c· we passed today and yesterday presents many interesting features in geology. The primary shistus [schist?] is either inclined at a very great angle, or quite perpendicular and in many places granite is seen breaking through it in veins of various thickness. At Estramoz is found handsome white marble, good for building but rather too coarse for statuary.

Sunday 30th

As no good could be got at Orada, we were in our Calesa before sunrise in order to reach Badajoz[14] before the gates were shut. We reached Elvas about noon, a distance of 4 leagues. The approach to it is very striking, situated on a hill rising out of a wood of olive trees; on each side upon two hills stands a fort wh^c· commands the town, and beyond these are visible several chains of mountains and a great Extent of the Spanish territory. Elvas, being the grand frontier town of Portugal, is strongly fortified and from its commanding situation must be a place of considerable strength. We were stopped for a long time at the gates before we were allowed to enter; we were stopped again as soon as we were within the walls and an officer examined our passports. He then sent a soldier with us to the Major General who again examined our passports and said that he would write to the Governor. There was no room for us at the inn where we wanted to dress before delivering our letters of introduction, and we were compelled to remain dirty as we were. The frenchman [sic] to whom we had letters being gone to Lisbon and thinking our Portuguese ones of no use from not knowing the language sufficiently well, we resolved upon making the best of our way to Badajoz. We got a little breakfast at a small Casa de Café; our man Juan was in distress about his mules being seized, and he was obliged before he could proceed to go to the of-

---

[14]   Greg gives a vivid account of the way in which the town of Badajoz was seized from the French in 1811. The behaviour of the British troops after they entered the town damaged the reputation of the army.

fice with his mules, and procure a passport for them as well as for himself. We were glad to get clear of the town after all the trouble we had had. A fortified town may be well enough during war, but in peace it is a great nuisance. On entering Elvas we passed under a very fine aqueduct built by the Moors. In the highest part it has 4 tiers of arches; it is built of stone but some Royal Portugeze fool has taken it into his head to whitewash it. I believe since we entered Portugal we had not seen a house wh^c was not either blue, yellow, red or whitewashed and if they had St Paul's or the ruins of ancient Greece and Italy they would do the same with them.

Badajoz is separated from Elvas by a plain of 3 leagues, and it is to Spain what Elvas is to Portugal. The two countries are divided by a petty brook which runs at about equal distance from each city. We met more people on this plain than we had done all the way from Lisbon, but Juan said that they were most of them smugglers. From its fortifications and number of towers and Convents, but most of all from the noble river Guadiana, Badajoz is rendered as striking to the eyes as Elvas, although there are no trees about it, nor is the hill on wh^c it stands so high. The stone bridge is a remarkably fine one, 28 arches and in excellent repair. Semple[15] calls it 600 yards long, but that is impossible, it may be as many feet, but I should think not more. We were not molested at entering the town, though a man was sent with us to the Custom House, where we had to leave our two trunks but allowed to take our parcels without examination. Juan has brought us to a miserable posada and we have again to sleep on the floor.

Seville – 7th of November

I have been unable to continue my journal regularly every evening since leaving Badajoz, either from want of time, inclination, table, chair or want of something necessary, but I shall set down what we saw and did, the same as if it had been written after each day's journey and if the account does nothing more it will at least give a good idea of the state of ignorance in wh^c Spaniards live, not only of what passes in their own country but in their own towns and villages.

The last day on which I wrote my journal was Sunday 30th of October, the day of our arrival in Badajoz.

Monday 31st

Called upon Señor Carbonell to whom we had letters. I made a very tame business of speaking Spanish. He sent a man to the Custom House with us and we got out our trunks without examination. On returning to S. [Señor] Carbonell's we found a young man who was to act as interpreter; he had lived in Lisbon some time, spoke English pretty well, and professed a great regard for our countrymen whom, he said, he was always ready to serve. In the Cathedral through which he took us, the only thing wh^c attracted our attention was a box for receiving money with the inscription above it, "Commutation of Oaths and Promises." S. Romero (our interpreter's name) then conducted us [to] the walls and showed us the spot where the breach was made by our batteries and where we lost such an immense number of men. The ground here is flat and the sole defence of the town on this side lay in the wall, the breach was defended in such a masterly fashion that in the opinion of the best engineers in the French army it was utterly impossible for Lord Wellington even to enter it, nor indeed to take the town otherwise than by escalade. The town I believe was taken in the following manner. L.W., thinking the breach practicable, ordered an attack to be made in the night and ordered at the same moment that a diversion should be made on the eastern side. General Picton who commanded this feigned attack, finding the walls neglected, the French having trusted to what they considered the impossibility of mischief on that side which is naturally very strong, escaladed the walls with all his men and attacked the French in the rear who were obliged immediately to submit. General Phillipon retired to a fort across the river and made his capitulation. The victorious troops immediately got to the brandy and not only murdered vast numbers of the inhabitants but also many of the Portugese and their own men. They were completely from under the control of the officers and we were informed that Lord Wellington was shot at by one of the soldiers and obliged to quit the town. At the time of the town being taken not above 600 of the inhabitants remained in it, having fled before the siege commenced. S. Romero said that 200 out of the 600 lost their lives during the pillaging of the place. At a snug corner of the wall S. Romero gave us a good deal of useful information as to the present state of Spain, the probability of civil war, etc. but as I know not whether this book may not be honoured with the perusal of some member, either of the Political or Religious Inquisition, I dare not put down any part of the conversation that passed between us.

Instead of dinner we ate 3 lbs of fine grapes and after dispatching some letters for England called again upon our guide and proceeded upon our walk. We crossed the bridge wh[c.] we measured in rough manner and concluded to be about 450 yards long. We entered Fort Napoleon, a strong place erected for the defence of the town. From this spot we had a remarkably fine view of Elvas, the chain of hills upon which it is situated and the plain which separates the two frontier towns, the river Guadiana with its noble bridge of 26 arches, the fortifications and town of Badajoz with its numerous churches and convents, and behind the immense plains of Extramadura bounded by distant chains of blue mountains. Leaving Fort Napoleon we again entered the town and went to examine the part where our troops entered. It appears impregnable from the very

[15] Robert Semple, author of *Observations on a Journey Through Spain, Italy and Naples. Comprising a Description of the Principal Places on the Route and Remarks on the Present Natural and Political State of those Countries* (1807).

47

great height of the walls, the depth of the trench and roughness of the rock and nothing less than British valour could have escaladed such a place in the dead of night. The fortifications wh$^{c.}$ the French threw up in every part of the town were admirable and are still the astonishment of the indolent Spaniards.

It being now perfectly dark we thanked S. Romero for his kindness and took our leave. The theatre being open we made our way to it and found our way in for about 15^D. The building was extremely shabby as well as the scenery, and the prompter whose head and more than half his body were seen out of a trap door in the middle of the stage made a very ridiculous appearance. The play was nothing more than a dialogue in a Coffee House. I understood nothing of the wit of it, not being able to distinguish more than 3 or 4 words. After this a fandango was danced with castanets wh$^{c.}$ was very pretty. Then an opera, then another fandango, and after that a farce. The whole was over in a very short time, not being much longer than some of our entertainments.

Thursday 1st of November
We had agreed with a calesa driver to take us to Seville for 44 dollars, and had determined to set out early in order to arrive at Santa Martha to sleep, a distance of 7 leagues, but on returning from the theatre finding a note from S. Romero saying that it would be advisable to have our passports signed by the Alcade Mayor, we called upon him but not being at home we determined to set out without further delay. On returning to our Posada we found our driver (whose name was Miguel) gone to Mass. He came at last and then we found he had no passport. We could not go without and he was not able to procure it for above two hours. He who travels in Spain must have a good stack of patience for he will meet with delays of this kind in every town. At last however we got clear into the country and had leisure to look about us and converse. Badajoz is visible to a great distance, but does not make nearly so fine an appearance as from the plain of Elvas. This side is that on which the British batteries were erected and is marked by the ruins of all the Convents and houses near the wall. Indeed there is scarcely a house which has not the mark of some cannon ball upon some part or other and balls and broken shells are to be seen in every street. Our Calesa was not nearly so convenient as our Lisbon one, it was drawn by one horse wh$^{c.}$ had round its neck a band of six and twenty bells. Our driver was a surly looking fellow who spoke so bad owing to the loss of his front teeth that we could understand but little of what he said. Having observed that all the people we met on the road between Badajoz and Lisbon were escorted by a band of soldiers, we made many enquiries as to the safety of the roads, all the answers agreed in this, the road had been very much infested with Banditti, but that owing to the vast number of troops which were constantly traversing from one town to another we might now go with perfect safety. The road between Badajoz and Albuera (4

leagues) is very good lying through an immense plain which extended almost as far as the eye can reach in every direction. In some parts it affords excellent pasture for the large flocks of sheep wh$^{c.}$ at this time continually ramble over it, in others it is covered with heaths, gumcistus and arbutus. On approaching Albuera the number of whitewashed houses which strewed the plain in every direction marked it to be the site of that famous battle in which our British heroes came off victorious. In this battle the village of Albuera suffered extremely, being battered to ruins,[16] not above half a dozen houses are now inhabited and the inhabitants of these wretchedly poor. About dark, in heavy rain, we drove up to one of these huts dignified with the name of Posada or inn. I asked for a room, they said they had none. I asked for a table, they had none, nor bread, nor eggs. The only answer I got to all my enquiries was "nada, nada" (nothing, nothing). They put us into a dirty hole where they kept oil and wine and chopped straw for their mules. It was a thoroughfare and was without doors. Whilst we were contemplating this miserable scene, a young man of genteel appearance came up to us and began to talk very loud and vehemently; for some time I did not understand a word but the sound of Ladrones and rubado (robbers and robbed) soon arrested my attention and so far quickened my wits that I made out the following account without much difficulty. He was travelling in company with a gentleman and a party of 30 muleteers when at the turn of the road near the town of Los Santos, distant 8 leagues from Albuera, about 4 o'clock of Saturday, 4 or 5 men on horseback armed with a knife and 4 muskets each, commanded them to stop. Having no arms they were obliged to stop and the robbers having tied a handkerchief over the eyes of each made him lay flat down upon his face and there they were all kept for 3 hours. When the robbers departed this gentleman found his portmanteau cut open (which he showed us) and all his linen, together with 300 dollars, was gone; before leaving him they had also stripped him of all the linen he had upon him. His friend lost 500 dollars. He told us that at S. Martha, the next town, we might procure a guard of soldiers by calling upon the Alcade[17] and that it would not be prudent to proceed without. The road to that place he said was safe because a company of soldiers was continually going backwards and forward upon it. This was the account as far as I could understand. If I made any mistake in the translation it was 30 mules instead of 30 muleteers, but I think I was quite correct. We supped as we could, eating more than a usual quantity of ham lest it sh$^{d.}$ fall into other hands before the following night. We slept upon a straw mat upon the cold floor, and were annoyed by the door into the street, wh$^{c.}$ was only of straw, blowing open during the night, and with help of a hole

[16] In 1811 the British under Beresford defeated the French under Marshal Soult at Albuera, the bloodiest battle of the Peninsula War.

[17] Mayor of a town.

in the wall just above our bed, making a constant draught of cold air. We were off very early the following morning.

Wednesday 2nd of Nov^m.

Although Miguel and another Calesero who was in our company were much alarmed about the robbers, they would not listen to my proposal of taking off their bells of wh^c. they had each 26 because they said it was not <u>usual</u> to do it in the day, had it been night they would have done it. The road to Santa Martha lies along a plain covered with evergreen oaks, and presents nothing interesting. Santa M., 3 leagues from Albuera, is but a poor little town. We had to buy what we wanted for breakfast, as at the Posada they had "Nada". We called upon a gentleman there to whom we had letters, he was not at home when we went but we were entertained by his wife, a very nice young woman, who took great pains both to understand me and to make herself understood. She said she knew England was a much finer country than Spain, and I believe paid me some compliments on speaking the language, but I was so stupid as not to understand exactly what it was she said. There was an officer in the room whom we consulted. He said he had heard nothing of the robbery we speak of, that it must all be a lie and that the road to Seville was perfectly secure on account of the great number of troops who were constantly passing from town to town. Señor Neyla now arrived. He wished us to spend the day with him and he said he would accompany us one stage on the following day. He told us that the roads were <u>not secure</u>, saying that we must take a guard of soldiers at Los Santos, the next stage, as there were none at S. [Santa] Martha. Both he and the officer said they were certain that we should find a great number of soldiers there and also that we might proceed thither with perfect safety. S^n. [Señor] Neyla also said that the man at Albuera must have told us a lie as it could not have taken place so near without their hearing of it. We should have liked very well to have spent the day with this hospitable Hidalgo[18] and his pleasant lady, but we had no time to lose. Our route to Los Santos, 4 leagues, lies aong the outskirts of the Sierra Morena. The only thing that attracts attention is the ruined castle of Leria crowning the summit of one of the mountains. It became quite dark with violent rain long before arriving at the place, and in reaching the summit of a hill our Calesero stopped in dismay at not finding the town where he expected. We however reached it at last. One of our first cares was to call upon S^n. Santiago de Lemos. We found him, his family and his servant seated in the Spanish manner round a few blazing embers placed on the floor, we joined the circle and told our story. De Lemos said there <u>were</u> soldiers in the town and sent immediately to the Alcade to request a guard, his worship was gone to bed but S^n de L^os. promised that a guard should be at the door of the posada by 6 o'clock the next morning. He said that if we had arrived there early we might have proceeded with a company of 14 muleteers who left Los Santos that morning. He also said respecting the robber of the man at Albuera, that on the Saturday we spoke of, two gentlemen with a party of Muleteers had been robbed near there much in the manner we had been told, differing principally as to the number of the company. This seemed to confirm the account we received at Albuera, the truth of which we had begun to doubt. When we returned to the inn we found the muleteers all gone to bed – that is rolled up in a mat and stretched out upon the ground, not only round the fire but in every part of the place so that we had to tread cautiously lest we sh^{d.} set our feet upon them.

Thursday 3rd

We slept upon our mattrass [sic] till 7 o'clock when we were roused by a message from S^{n.} de Lemos saying that there were no soldiers in the place and that he had sent 4 well-armed paisanos (peasants) who had been soldiers. This was another instance of Spanish information for the town of Los Santos does not consist of 500 houses and how he was so certain of there being soldiers in the place when there were none, and as we heard afterwards never had been any, I can't conceive. These men asked so high a premium for ensuring us to La Fuente de Cantós, 4 leagues, that I went to de Lemos to remonstrate but he said the men were resolute fellows and in case of attack would fight hard and, when there was any risk of that kind, men will be well paid. We accordingly set off with our guard of paisanos armed each with a musket and long knife. The road winds up a gradual ascent most of the way to Fuenté, but presents nothing worthy of notice and the rain was so violent that we could seldom look out of the Calesa. About half way we met a party of muleteers who informed our guard that the 14 muleteers who left Los Santos the day before, and whom we should have accompanied had we arrived sooner, had been robbed about half a league further on by 6 men on horseback, but then the road was clear as the banditti had fled to a wood, pointing to one along the skirts of which we had to pass. The information they gave us was not any means agreeable, nor were we certain the road was <u>clear</u> as they said, because the robbers had fled to an adjoining wood. We kept a constant lookout till we arrived safe and unmolested at La Fuenté. The next stage being long and the road very bad, Miguel said it was impossible to proceed further that day though it was not then 3 o'clock. We first called upon the Alcade and found some difficulty in telling our story as he was not quite so quick at understanding me as S^{n.} Neyla. He told us that he would call upon us in the evening. I think he expected to be feed and we made a mistake not to do it. We now thought that as we had not dined since we left Lisbon we would try to have one here and so went a shopping. We first bought 3 s. worth of a pig that had just been killed. I.H.

---

[18] A Spanish gentleman – a member of the lower nobility.

bought some cinnamon and cloves for which the man would receive nothing. I was not so handsomely treated for when I asked for ¼ lb of coffee the man weighed out 1¼ lb and made me pay for it, wilfully misunderstanding me in spite of all explanations and remonstrances. We enjoyed our pork very much and made an excellent dinner. In the evening the Alcade not coming, and two soldiers arriving who offered their services as they were proceeding to Seville to join their regiment, we went again to the Alcade who, we found, had procured two others to attend us (as to troops, there were none stationed there). The Alcade suffered us to be shamefully imposed upon for wh^c. I have little doubt he was paid handsomely, since it is very contrary to the plan of a Spanish Governor to let a person be cheated without taking a good share of the profits.

Friday 4th
We set off early with a guard of 4 soldiers and reached Monasterio, 3 leagues, about 12 o'clock. The rain had continued very violent the whole way and the street in wh^c. our posada was situated was the bed of a rapid mountain torrent. The posada c^d. not furnish a room and we went to a cabin opposite. Miguel now told us a long story which not being able to understand, he desired me to write what we wanted and he would answer it, which we did. He said he could not proceed that day as the roads were so bad they w^d. not be passable, but that in the morning he would set off very early in company with a number of muleteers who carried 5 muskets. We were obliged to submit tho very unwillingly as our quarters were miserably bad. The greater part of the time we spent round the fire with the family who were very civil and chatty. Our room was hung after the common manner here with bunches of grapes and our beds (the first we had seen since leaving Lisbon) was raised so high that we could not reach them without any trouble.

Saturday 5th
We rose very early, the rain abated, the moon shining bright and continued flashes of lightening. In setting off the Calesa getting into a hole, the horse in trying to get out jumped out of its harness. [This] being replaced we set off upon a road dreadfully cut up with the late rains and in some parts scarcely passable. At Monasterio we enter[ed] into the very heart of the Sierra Morena. How the term morena or brown came to be applied to it I cannot guess, as we saw more vegetation [at] this stage than we had done since leaving England. The heaths and gumcistus, and above all the arbutus covered at the same time with its white blossoms and blooming fruit, were very beautiful. The clouds were so low that we saw but few of the peaks and indeed the Sierra in this part does not rise to any great elevation. On approaching Santa Olalla (4 leagues from Monasterio) we had a fine view to the back of the hills and passes of the Sierra and forward

of the old castle of Santa Olalla. We met here for the first time with incivility. The woman had an apartment but [it] was a long time before she would let us in. We brought our own bread and boiled our coffee. She only furnished water and had the impudence to charge a dollar. We gave her $^2/_5$ of what she asked together with a good scolding.

Between S.O. [Santa Olalla] and Ronquillo another 4 leagues we passed through "el Puerto de los Ladrones" or Robbers' Pass – in former times much dreaded. At Ronquillo again we had to provide for ourselves but we rejoiced heartily at the thought of reaching Seville only 7 leagues further on the following evening and resting at last from our fatigues.

Sunday 6th
The mattrasses [sic] they had laid out for us swarmed to such excess with fleas, earwigs and other vermin it would have been the height of rashness to have laid down upon them, we therefore laid down on the table with the back of a chair for a pillow, but we were so dreadfully bitten even there, that it was impossible to sleep. Being cold I got up and attempted to make my way to the fire but I found such an impenetrable barrier of muleteers' bodies that I was obliged to return. At 5 o'clock I asked Miguel if he was ready, being extremely anxious to reach Seville before dark. To my extreme vexation and surprise he told me that two Muleteers had arrived that morning who said that the waters of the Guadalquivir were out, that the Bridge had risen up and that it would be impossible to reach Seville till the rains were over. I asked the Muleteers themselves who confirmed Miguel's account. We had however seen so much of the incorrectness of Spanish accounts that we determined not to stop within 28 miles of our resting place, till we had examined ourselves how things really were. We therefore insisted most positively upon proceeding and after quarreling with our man for nearly two hours we gained our point and at 7 o'clock he set off in a great passion, principally I believe with a view of punishing us for our folly and obstinacy. The company of muleteers finding we were going proceeded likewise, probably to be under the protection of our guard. The rain was very violent, but, ceasing now and then, discovered some of the finest mountain passes I ever beheld, all thickly covered with beautiful shrubs. The road was dreadfully bad and in a few days would have been impassable. We met upon the road other muleteers who told us we could not get to Seville. At a wretched posada (3 or 4 leagues) we breakfasted and I received the pleasant information that we could proceed. We had now descended from the Sierra and had only a plain to cross before arriving at Seville which was perfectly visible. At a short distance from the posada we saw a man's leg suspended on a pole. We were informed that it belonged to a robber who had murdered 16 people and that the remaining parts of his body were suspended in a similar manner in different places. This we found true for shortly

after we saw his head and approaching Seville passed by a pole with one of his arms nailed to it. About 1 league from Seville we passed through Santiponce, the Italica of the Romans. For two miles on each side, the road is made entirely of its ruins and beautiful slabs of white marble and verde Antique, fluted pillars of the same with the fragments of Corinthian Capitals which are ground to dust by the wheels of Calesas and feet of mules and Spaniards. But of Italica hereafter: I shall not leave Seville without examining its ruins. We found the waters out but not so as to stop our passing through; on entering the town our passports were examined and we were stopped at two Custom Houses but got rid of both without a moment's delay by means of a dollar. In Spain you may murder, rob or knock down the Virgin Mary if you have doubloons in your pocket; they will carry you clear out of all hands but those of Banditti. I now understood the meaning of the bridge having <u>risen up</u>; it is a platform thrown across a number of boats, and when the water rises high the platform connecting the boats with the side is torn up and it becomes impassable. Though not now quite so bad as this it was so steep that the horse fell and the Calesa ran back. No harm however ensued and we arrived safe about dark at one of the best hotels.

Monday 7th

Though one of the best hotels, we had to sleep again upon the floor which swarmed as thick with fleas as that of the worst posada. Mr Kiddel accidentally hearing of our arrival, called upon us. One of the first things he asked was if we had been stopped by robbers and he said we were perfectly right to take a guard. Two years since, he said, he and a friend had been stopt [sic] and after being stripped of everything the robbers told them to go down upon their knees to be shot, as they were sure they were Frenchmen. This he said they positively refused to do, and thus escaped being shot. About two months ago, he said, a quantity of money was going up to Ferdinand and was guarded through La Mancha by 80 dragoons, these were attacked by Banditti not superior in number but well mounted and who manoeuvred á la militaire. After an obstinate struggle the Banditti proved victorious, the dragoons fled and the money carried off. I cannot help making one remark here. From the town of Badajoz to Seville we had been informed that we sh^d. not only find troops in every town, but find the very road crowded with them. At every place at which we arrived we were told that there were no soldiers there but vast numbers in the next town and also on the road. Here we are at Seville and I can say that, excepting our own guard not a soldier have I seen from the gates of Badajoz to those of Seville and no wonder, for if we can believe accounts here, none have been stationed upon that road. A person who has never been out of England, can have no conception of such ignorance of the state of affairs, nor is it to be wondered at if he sh^d. disbelieve the account. Mr Kiddel also told us for our satisfaction that we were perfectly right in coming by way of Badajoz, as the road by Aymonto is impracticable and the passage up the Guadalquivir dangerous. Likewise he informed us that Cadiz was not yet clear of infection, though in 3 weeks or so we might possibly enter it with safety. Mr K had provided us with comfortable lodgings to wh[c.] we moved in the course of the day and most happy and thankful were we to have once more a place which for a few hours at least we might call home. The lady of the house and her two daughters as well as a servant girl are all very civil and attentive, pay us frequent visits and take great pains to make us speak correctly and understand what they say. I do not think that we c[d.] have fallen into better hands for they are none of them what in England would be called tolerably pretty and consequently we are not in much danger of falling in love with any. The advice I receive here is that I should not at present proceed to Granada on many accounts, and I shall there-fore make up my mind to remain here for the present, for reasons best known to myself. The Alcalde knows our names and where we are to be found and there-fore, no more!!

Seville : December 25th

Some of the Spanish Historians say that Seville was founded in the year 2228 by Lybian Hercules. Mendoza,[19] an historian extravagantly fond of antiquities, gives us a long dissertation upon the origin of Seville and its name stating it was the second part made by the companions of Bacchus when he came to conquer the world. What, says he, is certain is that Bacchus left in those parts names of the persons who followed him and that twice came he whom they call Hercules, or it might be that there were two Hercules in that part of Spain. The name might come to Seville from having been founded the second time that Hercules or Bac-chus or Theban Hercules came to Spain. Hispalis as he says with a slight alter-ation from the Greek signifying "that of the others time".

This is, at best, all conjecture and is of no consequence. The name Hispalis as the Romans called it became corrupted in time of the Moors to Sbilla and af-terwards to Sevilla, its present name. Muza the Saracen took it by storm soon after the defeat of Rodrigo at Xeres AD 714. It remained in possession of the Moors till the year 1248 when it was taken by the Christians under St Ferdinand III King of Castille. Mahomet Alkamar, first king of Granada, fought under the banners of his ally Ferdinand. The siege lasted above a year and after the capitu-lation 100,000 Moors left the city. Columbus sailed almost from beneath its walls in the year 1496 and the period of its greatest glory was when it was made the depot for the productions of the New World. This honor [sic] has long since been removed to Cadiz and Seville has long been in decline. In the year 1804 the Epidemy[20] carried off 36,000 people, 17,000 of whom he buried in one grave.

[19] Mendoza was author of *Guerra de Granada* (1627).

[20] An epidemic of Yellow Fever.

The infection was so great that all of the birds of which there were a great number all left the city and the animals that remained in the place almost all died. In 1808 in the month of March were riots occasioned by the hatred of the people against Godoy, the Prince of Peace.[21] The women ran in crowds through the streets with dishevelled hair crying "muera, muera" – "Let him die, let him die" brandishing at the same time their long knives. However, fortunately all the people being of one mind, not much blood was shed, and they contented themselves with pulling down his statues, paintings etc in the churches, shops and public buildings. In May of the same year broke out the revolution against the French and all the cities of Spain quickly followed the example of Seville. The French entered on the 1st of February 1810. £250,000 had been expended upon the fortifications; but so improvident had the Junta been that not a single week's provision had been provided for the siege. It surrendered without firing a shot and with the loss of only one man of the French who was killed in a drunken fray by a party of Spaniards. They made up as assassins for what they were wanting as soldiers and never lost an opportunity of stabbing a Frenchman whenever it was possible. A French Colonel told Mr Kiddel that out of his regiment, he had lost 460 men by assassination. The French behaved well to the inhabitants and the only inconveniences they suffered was having a large army quartered upon them together with the frequent and heavy contributions. In October 1812 the French were driven out by a force of Spanish and English not exceeding 2500 men.

The last revolution, if it can so be called, was on the news arriving of the King being in Valencia, the cry of the mob in Seville then was "down with the constitution,[22] Ferdinand VII forever". The few monuments which had been erected by or to the Constitution were pulled down and the friends of it obliged to fly to save themselves from the fury of the Mob.

Seville stands in the midst of a spacious plain upon the south east side of the Guadalquivir. The view is bounded on the west by a ridge of hills 2 or 3 miles from the city stretching from Santponce down to the Guadalquivir, to the North by the skirts of the Sierra Morena, to the S.East by a low ridge of hills and the mountains of Ronda at the distance of 70 or 80 miles. On the South the plain is of immense extent, the first high land that meets the sight being the southern part of the Ronda range and the mountains of Africa stretching along the coast from Tangiers to Ceuta. The town itself makes a fine appearance with its Cathedral and monumental quantity of Churches, Convents and public buildings. From its perfect freedom from smoke and the purity of the atmosphere every part of it is seen distinctly at a considerable distance. In the time of the Moors Seville is said to have contained 300,000 inhabitants. In the Epidemy of 1804 it lost 36,000 and its present population does not exceed 80,000 people; the Spaniards say 130,000 but they are always the most ignorant of the real state of things and ever ready to believe to relate anything that can redound to the honour of their country. The City is completely surrounded by walls with a square tower at the distance of every 50 or 60 yards. The whole distance round the walls may be 4 miles. These fortifications were raised by the Moors, though in many places on Roman foundations. They are composed entirely of agglutinated gravel wh$^{c.}$ has acquired the consistency of the hardest stone and might, I have no doubt, be cut and polished. There are at present 15 gates to the city. Over the gate of Xeres is this inscription rebuilt in the year 1501.

> Hercules built me
> Julius Caesar encircled me
> With walls and high towers
> The holy King gained me
> With Garci Peres de Vargas

The suburbs are not very extensive if we except that of Triana wh$^{c.}$ forms, as it were, another city on the opposite side of the River. Seville is built completely on the Moorish plan, the streets being all narrow and the houses not uniform. There are very few streets in the City where two carts can pass one another; the greater number are not wide enough to admit a person to pass a cart, and if you meet one you must either run into some Courtyard or turn back; many of them are so narrow that it is not possible to pass a loaded mule, and in some a man may stand in the middle and touch each side with his hands. I have sometimes been much squeezed by unfortunately attempting to pass a drove of mules or asses.

The houses are likewise completely Moorish, and evidently built in a manner most suitable to the heats of summer. The plan of all is much the same: you enter first into a small covered court by two folding doors wh$^{c.}$ in the daytime are always left open. By a small door you then pass into a large square court open from the bottom upwards and the house is, as it were, built round and is commonly paved with white marble having a font of marble or alabaster in the middle wh$^{c.}$ it is continually throwing up water. On three sides of this court and in large houses all the 4 sides is a covered alcove and a walk upon that covered by another alcove and supported as well as the lower one upon numerous arches and pillars. All the rooms of the first and second floor generally open upon the court. The rooms are all very long, sometimes perfect slips and the bedrooms are

[21] Godoy was the unpopular first minister of King Charles IV. The weak-willed King allowed his wife, Maria Luisa and Godoy, her favourite, to govern the country – with disastrous consequences.

[22] A liberal constitution was drawn up in Cadiz by Spanish patriots in 1812 at a special meeting of the Cortes (Spanish Parliament). It was immediately repealed by King Ferdinand VII when he was restored to the throne in 1813.

nothing more than a part taken off from the long room and open into it. All the windows that look into the street have either balconies or are completely closed in by a strong iron grating. Glass here as in other parts of Spain is rather a luxury than a necessary of life. The outsides of the houses have no elegance or beauty or regularity. Every one has been built for convenience. Nothing is to be seen of brick or stone. What the houses are built of it is hard to guess most probably of tiles but the outsides are always plastered and painted all sorts of colours and figures. Some of the public buildings are built with red tiles laid as we do bricks; this is completely a Moorish custom and the famous tower of the Giralda is built in the same manner. Seville contains 30 monasteries, 32 nunneries and 25 parish churches and the number of clergy and monks that are constantly to be seen in streets is almost incredible. When the French came, so afraid were all the inhabitants of the monasteries, that they threw off their dress and arrayed themselves in "silks and satins" of the newest fashions that they might not be known. The French however immediately issued an order commanding all to dress as Clergymen in black, forbidding them however to return to their convents which they plundered, sold or destroyed. Now, however, the blessed Ferdinand[23] is once more at the head of affairs, or rather I should say, now that the Priests govern everything, the Convents are again fast repairing and peopling again with the lazy and indigent of both sexes, though I am told and I can well believe it that thousands of those whom the French turned out have never returned to their former life. The instant that Ferdinand entered Spain, the Monks seized upon their possessions again and turned out those who had bought them from the French, and have since sent them in a charge for rent, produce of the garden etc during the time they had occupied them. A friend of Mr Beck who had bought a convent in the suburb of Triana received a few days ago a charge of 10,000 dollars for the 3 years he had occupied the grounds. He expected however to be let off at 2,000 dollars.

The principal public buildings worthy of notice are the Cathedral, Manufactory of Tobacco, Alcazar, Cannon Foundry and Mint. The Lonja or Exchange must not be omitted. As to the churches though many of them are very rich yet they do not merit a particular description.

The Cathedral wh[c.] is visible to a great distance from the surrounding country was commenced in 1401 upon the ruins of a Mosque and finished in its present state in 1529; it is however not quite complete, the two principal entrances being unfinished and have never been opened. Its length is 380 geometrical feet and 220 in breadth, the height to the roof 100 feet. In the centre of the middle aisle of which there are 5 formed by five rows of Gothic pillars stands a magnificent choir, in front is the high altar, and on both sides excellent organs. The sides are completely lined with chapels railed off from the rest of the building. Some of these have altars of extreme value and beauty and most of them contain very fine paintings principally by Murillo, the first of Spanish painters and whose works may rank with those of the first artists of Italy. He was a native of Seville and took particular pleasure in adorning the churches of his City with his finest paintings. He is particularly happy in the physiognomies of his figures wh$^{c.}$ are so pleasing, that when once you have fixed your eyes upon one, you cannot easily withdraw them again. In one of the chapels is a very celebrated painting of Pedro Campagna's before which it is said Murillo used to spend much of his leisure time without ever being able to satisfy his admiration. It was hung formerly in the Church of the Holy Cross but was carried away by the French and being retaken has since remained in the Cathedral. The subject of it is the descent from the Cross; being no connoisseur, I could not see all the excellences. I should have said the colouring was extremely rich and the figures well thrown out from the canvas but the attitudes were unnatural and the physiognomies disagreeable. In one of the vestries is a Magdalen by Murillo which took my fancy more than any paintings I ever saw. I think I could have looked at [it] for ever.

In the Cathedral are 80 altars at wh$^{c.}$ 500 Masses are said every day. The altar of the leg is so called from a painting by Luis de Varga which hangs above it, in which a leg of Adam is painted with astonishing life and nature. Near it is a painting of St Christopher of immense size being 20 or 30 feet high. When the artist of this gigantic figure saw the leg just mentioned he exclaimed, "That leg is worth all my St Christopher". The Alphonsine repository, as it is called here Los Tablas de S. Ildefonso, contains it is said, relics of 300 saints. Here is likewise a piece of the Holy Cross, a thorn of the Crown of Christ, part of the dress of the Virgin and heads, legs, arms and fingers and toes of Saints.

The furniture of this church is some of it extremely rich. Amongst other golden articles was a candlestick thickly studded with diamonds of great size and every kind of precious stones. The candlesticks used before the high altar are 4 or 5 feet high and of pure silver; they have one of extremely fine workmanship representing a tower or dome of some church of solid silver weighing nearly a ton. Likewise a very handsome one of copper made in London and weighing also a ton. The silver one is I understand carried through the town once a year as well as the Alphonsine repository to be stared at by the superstitious crowd.

The quantity of wax consumed in this church is quite incredible. I made enquiries among the priests who say that the exact quantity is not known, but that it is immense, it is indeed immense if the statement that I have approaches anything near the truth. When I mentioned it, I do not expect to gain credit from a single individual. I confess however that I who now certainly have seen a good

23 Greg was being sarcastic here. King Ferdinand VII reigned as an absolute monarch when he was restored to the throne of Spain in 1813 after the defeat of the French. He was not only illiberal in political terms, but also highly reactionary in religious matters. Greg held him in utter contempt.

deal of the Cathedral and its customs do believe the amount to be nearly correct and those who know will not accuse me of being particularly credulous. To come to the point then the amount of the consumption of wax in this building during the year is 4 or 5 thousand arrobas, that is between 50 and 60 tons, truly an almost incredible quantity.

I cannot help reflecting how foolish travellers are who relate anything very extraordinary and what is unlike anything in their own countries, at the best they are not believed by their readers and by the generality of them, they are set down if not for wilful lyars [sic] at least for credulous fools.

But what renders the foregoing statement something more probable is (and this I have from the best authority), that in the two days of Holy Thursday and Friday alone, 300 arrobas of 75 cwt of wax is consumed. Nor is it less a fact that at Easter a candle is lighted before the high altar and burns with some intermissions during 40 days, which weighs 80 or 90 arrobas or one ton. It is about 24 ft long by 6 in circumference. A man is constantly in attendance upon it. He ascends by means of an iron ladder at the top of wh$^{c.}$ is a chair; in this he seats himself with a ladle and bucket to take out the melted wax lest it should sweal [sic] over[;] he has likewise a poker to stir the wick which is as thick as a cable and the flame is proportional to the other parts of this gigantic instrument. The man receives very high wages, for the heat is so extreme that he is always very ill afterwards and sometimes even his life is in danger.

Behind the choir is the burying place of the family of the great Columbus. The first and greater part of a large marble slab is taken up in describing the many virtues of Fernando, the son of Columbus, whose bones lie beneath. He presented to the Cathedral a very valuable library and had his reward accordingly. Below upon the same stone is a globe with this inscription round it. "A 'Castilla y a' Leon muero mundo dio Colon". Columbus gave a new world to Castille and Leon. On each side are engraved two ships said to be faithful representations of those in wh$^{c.}$ Columbus sailed to discover a new world.

In this noble building are heaped together all the absurdities, and I think I may say profanities of the Catholic religion. I will mention one or two things in proof of this assertion wh$^{c.}$ have fallen under my own observation. Against the railing of almost all the chapels some writing is put, promising indulgence of a certain time from the pains of purgatory to those who shall say certain prayers before their altars. Indulgence means that they shall come out from the pains of purgatory before the time which they otherwise would have done or the time appointed them to remain there on account of their sins. I allowed myself to be locked up one day in order to copy some of these inscriptions. The following is before the statue of the Virgin holding in her arms an infant Jesus dressed in such a manner that seriously I could compare it to nothing but little red riding-hood. It was thus, "The most excellent and most illustrious Senor Don John Acciclo[?] de Vera e Delgado, Archbishop of "Laodecea, Administrator of the Spiritual and "temporal affairs of the Archbishoprick [sic] of Seville, "Titular Archdeacon and Canon of this Metropolitan" and Patriarcal Church, by the supreme" council of His Majesty elected Bishop of Cadiz "etc etc etc. Grants 80 days of Indulgence each time to all the faithful who devoutly say a "Salve or Ave Maria before this image of the most holy Mary entitled of the girdle (or ribband)" who is worshipped in the said church. Another: "80 days to those who shall say a Pater Noster "before the child which the said lady holds in her arms". Other: "80 days to those Priests who shall celebrate mass upon the altar before this most holy image". Other: "80 days to those who shall hear such mass before this most holy altar". Other: "80 days to the faithful who shall contribute to the worship of the said lady by prayer, alms or other modes asking God for the exaltation of our holy Catholic faith and happiness of the Church and state".

A money box is below with these words.

"Here are thrown in alms for the said lady".

Another runs thus and like the former has a money box attached to it. In Spain as little can be done without money in the churches as in the Courts of Justice or Custom houses!

"Our most Holy Father Pius VI has granted that the soul for whom a mass is said on the altar of the most holy Crucifix of Maracaybo [sic] shall come out of Purgatory whether the mass be said by a regular or secular Priest, by his brief given in Rome 21 of April 1777, "and by another of the same date he has granted, "that all persons who visit it on Holy Friday and the day after the invention of the Cross having confessed and communicated shall gain plenary indulgence". And by divers most holy prelates 840 days are granted to all who visit it. Besides 120 days indulgence to the effigy of St John Nepomucero [sic] who at the said altar is worshipped".

And, "It is necessary to have the Bull of the most holy crusade". This bull is a paper published first in the time of the crusades promising thousands of indulgences to all who should engage in them or assist with their money, but being found profitable from the numbers sold, it has been continued to the present time and I am told that a fresh one must be bought every year at least. Unless a person has it he cannot hope for the indulgences granted by Pius VI.

Here is another "Altar perpetually privileged". "Our most Holy Father Pius VII by his brief given in Rome 15th of May 1804 grants that always when any Priest Regular or Secular says a mass upon this altar, the soul for whom it is said shall instantly come forth from the pains of purgatory".

Again, "All persons who having confessed and communicated shall visit this chapel of St Nicholas de Bari from the 27th at the vespers of the Senors Simon and Judas until 10 o'clock of the morning of the 29th whᶜ· is when is fulfilled the 40 hours, gains plenary indulgence and remission of sins. Granted by Benedict

XIII by his brief in Rome".

"P.S. It is necessary to have the Bull of the Holy Crusade".

These inscriptions which I have copied are a few out of numbers of the same kind and I will leave all to make their own remarks.

In the Chapel of Kings situated immediately behind the high altar the body of San Fernando, the Conqueror of Seville, has been preserved for nearly 500 years in a gilt box. One of the last days of November is the anniversary of the taking of the city, observed with great respect in this Cathedral. I Hodgson and I went to see the conclusion of the ceremonies. The shrivelled body of S Ferdinand was lying before a statue of the Virgin, surrounded as usual with numerous candles of enormous size, the Archbishop in a little recess with numerous assistants singing and the whole chapel was filled with women on their knees and men and soldiers walking about crossing themselves and laughing. Presently the singing ceased, the Archbishop advanced to the altar, threw incense upon the Virgin and upon St Ferdinand and retired. A ragged drummer and fifer approached the steps of [the] altar and began to play their instruments. Immediately all the dirty shabby recruits who were present ranged out in two long rows and drew their swords; the drum sounded again and every person present fell upon his knees except the two files of soldiers, after a short time we all rose again. The word of command was given and the soldiers, some turned to the right, some to the left, and left the chapel and the Cathedral to the sound of the drum and in the same shocking order .

On the 7th of December commenced the Octave, or 8 days singing and dancing in the Cathedral. Yes dancing! I went to witness this singular ceremony, if it does not merit a harsher name. I arrived too soon for the dancing and saw 4 or 5 priests kneeling before the high altar. I approached as near as the gilt railing would permit and observed that in their praying to God they were mingling merry jests with one another, two in particular were very facetious and if I can at all judge of the words wh^c· were uttered from the looks which accompanied them their conversation was something in this style. Scene: 2 priests kneeling before the high altar praying to God at intervals.

1st Priest: "How religious you look friend".

2nd Priest: "About as religious as you, compadre, but don't laugh so the people will see us".

1st Priest: "What if they do? – Devil take the credulous fools. They may see us too and welcome if we were as well paid for our trouble as the old archbishop there".

2nd Priest: "Ha, ha, ha. Our Father who art in Heaven etc".

I say if I could judge at all from Physiognomies their conversation was something of the kind I have mentioned. I was quite shocked, but continued watching them close. One of them observed me and, when he had finished his pious devotions, approached me, nodded his head, smiled and winked his eye, as much as to say, I'm not such a fool as you take me for.

The open space at the steps of the high altar where these men had been kneeling was the spot chosen for the dance. Eight youths dressed in the ancient Spanish style danced to the solemn strains of the organ, mingled however with music of a lighter kind. I could not quite make out the figures, but amongst the rest distinguished change sides and back again, down the middle and up again and also a kind of last outsides, lead up the middle and turn your partner etc. They had all their hats on, snapped their Castanets with great vivacity and all to please the Almighty and gain his favour and protection. This farce lasted about half an hour, was repeated again in the evening and the same every day during the octave. Had I seen all this on my first arrival in Spain I should indeed have been shocked, but I had seen many farces and absurdities of a similar nature, that I had become almost hardened and insensible. This dancing is, I am told, an imitation of David dancing before the ark. The Spaniards themselves seem scarcely to know what to think upon it, and I could get no other answer from them than it was a custom "muy Antigua", and existed in no other church than that of Seville.

Before passing on to anything else I will just say a few words upon the Religion of this city. Adoration seems almost confined to the holy virgin. There are but few images which do not represent either her or St Antony. "Ave Maria" answers exactly to our "Good God", and in all conversations it is the predominant sound. On entering a house you say "Ave Maria" and the person who opens the door replies "sin pecacado concebida", that is, conceived without sin or born free from the stain of original sin. The rosaries all contain five beads of Ave Maria to one of Pater Noster, and it is the prayer they make use of when the Vesper bell rings. God himself is totally forgotten and our Saviour is seldom seen in any other character than a child richly dressed in the hands of the most holy virgin. "St Antony" is the St they invoke in case of illness or accident and with what success I shall soon have occasion to mention. His statues are generally in the streets and houses. It may not be amiss to give the "Ave Maria" a place here, as it is rarely to be met with in England, though not infrequently mentioned. It runs thus: "God save Mary, full of grace, the Lord is with thee; blessed art thou among all women and blessed is the fruit of thy womb Jesus. Holy Mary, Mother of God, intercede for us sinners, now, and in the hour of death. Amen". The creed is the same as that of the Church of England. The ten Commandments differ considerably.

1st "Love God above all things".

2nd "Not to swear by His holy name in vain". This is simply understood "Thou shalt not perjure thyself".

3rd "Sanctify the Feasts".

4th "Honour Father and Mother".

5th "Not to murder".

6th "Not commit adultery".

7th "Not steal".

8th "Not bear false witness".

9th "Not to covet a neighbour's wife".

10th "Not to covet the goods of another".

We will here take leave of the inside of the Cathedral. I must however mention one remarkable painting wh$^{c.}$ I had forgotten, it is of considerable excellence.

The subject is St. — (I forget the name)[24] carrying his head in his hands. It called to my mind the men in the moon, mentioned in Munchausen.[25]

The Giralda or famous Tower of the Cathedral is so called from the figure of a woman at the top weighting 34 cwt and which turns round with the wind. It was begun by the Moors in the year 1000 and tradition says that to make good the foundation they threw into the hole all the Roman monuments. It is 350 feet high by 50 square. The ascent in the inside is a road winding round and round the tower and it might easily be ascended in a small carriage. It is built of tiles of a light pink colour, the architecture simple and elegant, the proportions of the whole admirable; and by moonlight, or with a morning sun upon it, and a background of deep blue sky, it makes a most beautiful object and in this state I never passed it without stopping to admire. The view from the top, of Seville, the immense plains of Andalusia and the various ranges of mountains is extremely fine, and there being no coal fires, the view is never impeded by immense clouds of smoke.

The wide plains wh$^{c.}$ extend on every side are fertile in the extreme, the soil being of very great depth and without a single stone, but they are shamefully neglected or overgrown with thistles 6, 8 or 10 feet high, and liquorice roots. How different must it have been in the time of the Moors when, blush ye Spaniards, if you can blush, the single province of Andalusia contained as many inhabitants as the whole of Spain at the present time!

The Alcazar or Palace deserves next to be mentioned. In external form it presents only an ugly irregular mass of low buildings. It was begun by the Moors 67 years before the conquest by Ferdinand, and finished by the Christians, but the Moorish style well preserved. Next to the Alhambra it is the finest specimen of Moorish architecture in Spain. The carving on the walls, pillars, roofs and doors is extremely rich and minute, especially the roofs which must have taken much time and immense labor. The sides of the rooms to the height of 4 or 5 feet are lined with coloured tiles, some so small that it might almost be called Mosaic work. The rooms are now totally destitute of furniture. The gardens wh$^{c.}$ have been so much celebrated are nothing but a collection of ponds, hedges cut into letters or the arms of Spain, and spouting figures. This palace was where Don Pedro the Cruel held his court, and likewise other Christian monarchs. Philip V spent many years here, and employed himself principally in drawing figures with the smoke of a candle on deal boards, or fishing for gold fish in the ponds. Since the Revolution broke out it has been chosen by the "Junta" as the place for their sittings; and falling into the hands of the French, Joseph Bounaparte [sic] made it his court during his residence. Its governor at present, after so many changes, is a Scotchman, Brigadier-General Sir John Downie,[26] a brave man, whom I have the pleasure of being acquainted with. In the late revolution he was a commissary in the English army. He afterwards raised a regiment at his own expence and distinguished himself as a gallant officer. When Seville was taken from the French, he led the attack and charged across the bridge of boats at the head of his regiment. The sword he carried in his hand was the very one which, wielded by the famos Pizarro, had conquered Peru and which had been presented to him in great form by some of the descendants of that great man. The French had broken down one arch of the bridge, and ranged themselves on the opposite side. Sir John followed only by a single trumpeter, leaped his horse across the breach; a great gun loaded with grape shot exploded at that instant; the trumpeter and his horse fell dead on the spot, 5 men were killed and 11 wounded on the opposite side of the breach, and Sir John himself had his cheekbone and right ear shot away, and received almost at the same moment two wounds with a bayonet. He was stunned, and fell from his horse which leaped back over the breach, he was however still able to rise, the cry of Prisoner saluted his ears but he thought only of his sword the sword of Pizzaro, and collecting his little remaining strength, he made last, a noble effort, threw the sword to his men, and surrendered his mutilated body to the astonished enemy, who c^d. not help exclaiming, this is a brave man. He was ordered to be sent to the Hospitals at a place some

---

[24]   The subject was St Dyonysio, Dionysius or, in French, Denys. He was said to have been beheaded in Paris in 272 A.D. and to have carried his head in his hands for two miles and laid it on the spot where St Denys Cathedral now stands.

[25]   Baron Munchausen (1720–97) served with the Russian army against the Turks and in retirement told extraordinary, not to say preposterous, stories of his adventures. Greg would have known the English version of these, published in 1785.

[26]   A colourful, hispanophile soldier of Scots or Irish origin who was decorated by the Spanish king for his military services to Spain. During the Peninsular War he served for a time as a commissary in Wellington's army. He was allowed, despite Wellington's disapproval, to raise a legion in Extramadura to fight the French. At his own expense he initially dressed the men in sixteenth-century costume to reflect Spain's 'Golden Age'. They were apparently ill-trained and ill-disciplined and no match for the French, although the Legion Extramadura was still in existence in 1815. Downie's personal courage was not in question. The episode on the bridge that he described to Greg certainly happened.

leagues from Seville, but in the hurry and confusion of a retreat no carriage could be found to convey him. It was the middle of July, a time when the Sun had great power in these parts; he was lashed to the top of a cannon and in this manner dragged several leagues; on arriving at the place the hospitals were found deserted the French had fled, and he was left to the care of an old woman, and if he had not had the resolution to wash his wounds with vinagre, a mortification would inevitably have ensued. His wounds have of course much disfigured him and he has lost the use of his right eye and ear. Ferdinand has I understand shown him much attention, but he is not likely to grow rich in his service, for the salary attached to the "Alcazar" does not amount to £150 p.an. He had the satisfaction of recovering the sword which he so well deserves to wear, and I had it in my hands as he related the story I have just given.

The "Lonja" or Exchange deserves next to be mentioned. It stands close to the Cathedral and is an elegant, simple building of red tiles edged with stone; the inside is very handsome completely in the Doric order of architecture. Over the door is a singular inscription stating that it was built by <u>order</u> of Philip IV at the <u>expence</u> of the <u>Merchants</u>. These not making much use of it, it was appropriated by Government. It is now used for the archives, and in it are preserved all the papers respecting the Americas, with the original letters of Columbus, Cortes and Pizarro. We saw one letter of Cortes to the Emperor Charles V but they had all been carried off to Cadiz when the French were in possession of Seville, and though now returned were in such confusion we were not permitted to see them. The room in wh^{c.} they are kept extends all round the building and is where the French had their Balls.

The Royal manufactory of Tobacco[27] is a very handsome building of white stone built by Ferdinand VI. It is 200 yards square and contains 24 courts, 21 fountains, and 10 wells. It furnishes a very considerable branch of the revenue. The King buys Tobacco at 2 Reals p.lb. and sells it at 48 Reals. Any person may import tobacco by paying a duty of 48 Reals per lb. In one of the rooms <u>500</u> persons are employed in making ciggars, and I was told that each one made about <u>1000</u> in a day or <u>500,000</u> in all. Mr Kiddle knows a gentleman who pays yearly <u>8000</u> Reals, £100, duty in Tobacco which he imports for his own use.

The Cannon foundery is an extensive establishment, where only brass cannons are cast; they are not at work at present, any farther than repairing the damage done by the French, who, when they left the city threw all the cannons into the furnaces and melted them down, and every furnace has to be pulled to pieces in order to get out the metal.

The mint has not yet begun its operations but will do so soon; they have got a very handsome set of new dies. The Amphitheatre for Bull fights is large but not a very handsome building.

The Alameda is a great walk of old elms, in the heart of the city, 600 yards long by 15 broad; it is however now almost deserted, the new one on the banks of the river being justly preferred. The suburb of Triana is remarkable for nothing but the remains of a castle where in 1482 the Inquisition formed its first establishment in Spain. As this Tribunal has been so lately re-established in this country to its eternal disgrace, I will say a few words about its former and present state. It had been declining in its rigor some years before its abolishment, and though public whippings and imprisonments had been frequent there had been no one burnt for many years. The last instance of this nature occurred about 20 years since, and as the history of it is extraordinary, I write it down as it was related by a pious Catholic, and present at the execution. A Priest sent his boy one day to bring home his linen from the woman who had the washing of it; he asked the woman if it was ready, and she drew it up in a basket out of the well. The boy supposed it witchcraft, and the woman confirmed him in his belief by saying she had friends at the bottom of the well. The next time the boy went for the linen the woman was not in the way, and looking about the room he found a bottle. Finding the liquor it contained pleasant to the taste, he drank a considerable quantity, and when he got home was seized with pains in his bowels, and in a few minutes was delivered of an egg; he told the Priest all that had happened, adding that he was sure the woman was a witch. The Priest, who it is said had an illicit connection with the woman and feared that she might make it public, exhorted the boy to say nothing about the matter and gave him a dollar to ensure his secresy. But the boy who, from time to time laid eggs similar to the first, being frequently solicited by his Mother, told her all that had happened and likewise the Priests injunctions; she went straight to the Inquisition; the house of the woman was searched, many eggs were found, the same as the boy had laid; this was enough for the Inquisition; the Priest was immediately immured for not having given information, and the woman was burnt in an open space just without the walls; being first carried in triumph through the city followed by some thousand Priests and Monks crying out all the way "Long Live the Inquisition". This happened only <u>20</u> years since; and the narrator gravely observed, "that "indeed she deserved it, for having communications with the Devil". About 25 years ago, Mr Smith, a particular friend of Mrs W's the lady who related the story to me, was awoke one night, and saw two officers of the Inquisition by his bed side, who commanded him to rise that instant and follow them. He did so and on arriving at the building of the Inquisition he was thrown into a dark, narrow dungeon; he saw no person for 24 hours, during wh$^{c.}$ time he had nearly died of hunger, cold and apprehension; not having been allowed to put on all his clothes, and expecting every moment to be dragged out to the torture. At the end of that time, a man brought him a little bread and water but could not be prevailed upon to open his mouth. His friends in the meantime were much alarmed

[27] The Royal manufactory of Tobacco is now the University.

not knowing what had become of him. He was kept in this state for 5 days and then released with this satisfactory information, "You are not the person we wanted; you may go". Who would live in a country where he is liable to such mistakes as this, and not to this only, but even to be murdered in mistake, and which really did happen in Seville a short time ago.

At present it exists in the same form and power before its abolishment. The Spaniards cannot be said to have restored it; it restored itself; but they have quietly submitted to it, and for that, deserve to live exposed to its insults. If I guess right, it will soon begin to be troublesome once again. On the 13th of December I saw a proclamation pasted up at the gates of the City; and my heart beat as I observed the signature of the Inquisition – The substance of it was this, "All persons possessing books, papers, moveables, toys &c. belonging to the most holy tribunal of the Inquisition or to any of its members at the time [of] the confiscation are exhorted to restore them within the space of one month and thereby prevent the tribunal from proceeding to extremities so contrary to its characteristic benevolence and benignity but which it has so good a right to inflict, from the Bulls of several Popes, and more particularly from those of Pope Pius VII."

They some weeks ago seized some English books belonging to my friend Mr Grund and last week entered the house of Mr W. and carried a number [of books] away from him, amongst these damnable books (could an Englishman have believed it?) were "Milton's Paradise Lost" and "Thompson's Seasons". Don Francisco de Castro, a friend and fellow labourer of mine in Mr Beck's office and who has the best private Library in Seville, has furnished a month's occupation to the Inquisition in examining it. They set aside a considerable number [of books] amongst which were the work [of] one Fontaine not him whose works are prohibited. Don Francisco said to them that they were in mistake, and that was not the Fontaine whom they imagined. The Inquisitor turned to the title page and said very gravely, "Don't I see the name of Fontaine, that's enough." A few days ago in the Custom House, the officers there, very contrary to their usual nicety, were seen examining separately a parcel of 1400 dozen French fans and the answer they gave to the enquirers, was that it was the order of the Inquisition, and was done to prevent any ones not perfectly decent from being introduced. It would indeed be well if it never did anything worse than this, but even this is better left to the modesty and good sense of the people; such interferences always do more harm than good; England may be quoted as an example for in no country is there so much modesty and virtue, and yet in no country are the actions of all ranks so perfectly unfettered.

I could bring other instances of the interference of the Inquisition, but what I have given are sufficient to show that it has begun to exercise its newly restored power. I had forgot to mention that on 17th, Don Francisco de Castro was summoned to appear before the Tribunal to receive sentence; he went, but it was engaged; he was told to call again next day; it was engaged again and he was told to wait till a second summons.

With a few words upon the Trade of Seville I will return to my journal. The principal exports of Seville, are wool, fruit, oil, and manufactured silk, which latter article is sent entirely to Lima in S. America. I give here the copy of an account of a purchase of fine wool, taken from Mr Beck's books.

Account of 44 sacks of fine wool, proceeding from 1000 arrobas, in the dirty	
state at 110 Reals per arroba	110,000
Carriage to the wash house	4,000
Cost of washing &c.	10,000
Duties on 475 arrobas clean	
Proceeding from 1000 duty at 77¼ Reals	
Per arroba, clean	36,693
Carriage of 44 sacks to the C. House	176
Ditto to the Mole	44
Expences at the Quay	176
Guards, Gratification	132
Brokerage ½ p. cent	550
	161,771
Reals de Plata	85,941
Commission	2,758
Rpta	88,519

The export of oranges and lemons is not so great as it was some years ago, why the demand has been less is not known. What is singular there are here 3 kinds of Oranges the sour called by us the Seville orange; the china, and the sweet orange, wh$^{c.}$ is a medium between the two former, and possibly arises from engrafting one upon the other. As there is a sour orange so is there likewise a sweet lemon, exactly resembling one in appearance, but sweet and a little insipid; it is however much esteemed by the ladies, having the recommendation of being scarce. There is also a medium between the two. More sour than sweet oranges are exported, the latter being used for home consumption. A box holds from 5 to 7 hundred, and is worth including the dollar paid for the box 8 dollars. The freight amounts to 16 or 18 reals vellon and 10 p.cent primage. The sour oranges are rather cheaper than the sweet.

As to the Police of Seville, I could learn but little about it; I am told that there are a great many courts of judicature, independent and continually quarreling with one another; the court for criminal causes, that for civil, the Ecclesiastical and that of the Alcazar are the principal among them. If a person be taken up it frequently happens that a very long lawsuit has to be decided between some of these courts, before it can be settled which has a right to try the man, who during this dispute is languishing in a dungeon, perhaps altogether innocent, or at least ignorant of the crime he is accused of. The trials are conducted entirely in writing, the judge putting the questions and a scrivener writing down the answers. A few days ago, a man was taken up and imprisoned for having accidentally thrown a few drops of water upon an officer's new coat. The judge on his examination asked – are you married? how many children have you? what is your name? the name of your wife? that of your father? of your wife's father? etc and these, and other as pertinent questions, with the answers to each, were set down by the scrivener at full length. The man however was extremely fortunate and was released in 5 days, with no greater expence than the sum of 15 dollars.

In a law suit in which Mr Beck was engaged, the attorney brought him in a bill of which one of the items was "Given the judge <u>200</u> dollars to incline him in favour of the cause." Well, the cause was lost, and on making inquiries, he found that the Judge had been inclined in favour of the opposite side by a fee of <u>400</u> dollars, which had the desired effect. That man who trusts only in the justice of his cause, though it be as clear as a proposition of Euclid, would be looked upon as a fool and a raw Englishman. Such a thing is never thought of here. The advice I received was "if you are robbed dont mention it; and if you have the misfortune to be brought before the Judge to swear to the man who robbed you, you swear you never saw him before in your life."

The acqueduct of Seville which has been so much, and as I think, undeservedly, celebrated is scarcely worth mentioning, being low, dirty and of no great extent; it bears scarcely any sign of the Romans about it, though it is said to have been originally built by them, to appearance it is entirely Moorish, and seems to have been built at the time of raising the walls.

In the streets of Seville two things are remarkable. The first is, the great number of crosses, put up in almost every street, and which show that some person has been murdered there; and the second, the number of Glass cases containing little statues of the Virgin or of St Antony. Before these images hang in general a vast quantity of offerings; little heads, eyes, noses, bodies, legs, arms, toes, fingers &c. Before one statue of St. Antony, I counted no less than <u>350</u> of these offerings, which included not only the kind I have just mentioned but also many rude paintings, crutches, shirts, handkerchiefs, jackets, and several pigtails, queues (it is a fact). The explanation of all this is, that if anything is amiss with any part of the body, or any accident happen, St. Antony is immediately called upon; and if the person recovers within a year, the recovery is ascribed solely to St Antony, and the part which has been affected is hung up before his statue, that the miracle may be made public and the St. get the honor he so well deserves. The pictures are laughable representations of the dreadful situations from which pious individuals have been released by calling upon the aforesaid Saint. One of these paintings represents a man as having his hand fast in a piece of wood, and roaring out lustily, tugging hard at the same to get it away; the inscription below says that invoking St. Antony, he was released from his terrible situation. Another is running from the bull in the amphitheatre; and the writing informs us, that he was on the point of being gored, when giving a great leap and calling on St Antony, he cleared the barrier and escaped. A Calesa is going over the head of another, but invoking the St. he got up unhurt. In two or three, a child has fallen into the well, but its parents invoking St. Antony, it was drawn up alive, and in several a man is on his knees praying to the St. and the words below say "that a citizen of Seville had obtained what he wanted."

In all of the paintings St. Antony is made to appear with an infant Jesus in his arms; I asked a woman how this came to be done, as the Saint did not live of [sic] some hundred years after Christ; she answered that she did not know whether he lived before or after Christ; that he had an infant Jesus in his arms because it was in that state that our Lord made revelations to him. The crutches are hung up when the lame man can do without them. The articles of dress have been lost, and found only by the intervention of St. Antony. The identical shirt or handkerchief is not however hung up, but they buy a coarse one for the purpose. As to the pigtails, I am told that the women have a great value for their hair, and that in a dangerous illness they make a vow that if the St. will release them from the hands of death that he shall have their pigtails, which not withstanding their vanity, when they recover, they do not fail to fulfil.

Journal

A few days after my arrival in Seville, I was standing alone near the Cathedral when a young man of genteel appearance accosted me in English asking if I was not an Englishman, and that as I seemed to be a stranger, if he could do anything for me. I declined his offer repeatedly but he was very pressing and asked if I had yet been up the Giralda at the foot of which we stood. I had not, and I accepted his proposal to ascend it, the day being clear and favorable for the view. We now fell into conversation and he told me his name was Atkinson, that he came from Leeds and was settled there, as partner in one of the Mercantile houses of that place. He was likewise acquainted with the Gotts and Oates of Leeds, so that by this slender tie we were soon good friends, and he said he should be very happy in ~~introducing~~ [sic, deleted] showing me anything in Seville which I might wish to see. I dined with him on the following day and after dinner took a walk along the river side. We met the family of the Wetheralls to whom he introduced me and after pacing about some time, we all went into their house together. It was a "tertullia" night, and the company composed of English, Spaniards and Germans which last had fled from Cadiz on account of the fever. I found the family consisted of Mr and Mrs W., a son, a daughter, Mrs Hipkins, a young widow, Mr and Mrs Stocker and their three daughters, all English but long settled in Spain. I passed the evening agreeably enough, having tea in the English style and a good coal fire, which I had not seen since leaving Falmouth and both a particular treat to me; the amusements were cards, music, dancing and blind man's buff. The Tertullia signifies exactly the same as the conversazione of the Italians; a number of friends meet drest or not as they like and spend the evening talking, playing at cards, or dancing. At Mr W's there were two Tertullias in the week and my company was insisted upon to both, as well as to that of Mrs Hipkin's every Friday. To the next Tertullia, I. Hodgson accompanied me and during his stay we generally went twice a week. Since then as I wished to be as little as possible in English society, I have generally been not more than once a week, and that only from 8 till 11. Before I.H. left me we took an excursion to Italica or rather to Santiponce, for though we thought we had found the amphitheatre, I understand since that we were not within half a league of it. I. Hodgson left me on the last day of November and went down the river with a party of Germans to Cadiz at wh$^{c.}$ place they arrived in two days.

Since that time my life has been very uniform. I rise about 8 o'clock, breakfast on chocalate [sic], go to take a lesson in Spanish from Professor Brumenque at the College of St. Telmo, then go [to] the counting house of Cahill, White and Beck for the rest of the morning to copy letters or anything they may have for me to do. At two I dine upon a bit of fried pork and the Olla, a stew of cabbage beans, peas, beef and bacon and the only dish in Spain that is well cooked. The afternoon I generally spend in reading, and in the evening go to a tertullia, to the theatre or to drink tea at Mr Beck's The family consists of himself, an Irishman imported young, a kind, happy man, but who never in his life thought of anything but business, he is not comfortable out of the Counting-house, and consequently is always in it, not excepting a good part of Sunday, which however is the universal custom here. His wife was born in Spain, but speaks English though badly; her husband speaks one word of Spanish, and then one of English; and so on "nor I tampoco, (neither), Adios Señor Don Roberto, how do you do this morning?" Miss Beck is but just imported; his mother and two old Spanish women with Don José Guerrero, a pleasant young man, and this composes the family; they were all very kind to me, but I confess that I only visited them for the sake of speaking a little spanish, drinking tea or having a little chit chat, which I could get nowhere else. I should have wished to have gone more frequently to the theatre, being one of the best means of improving in a language, but it was sometimes shut for 10 days together, in consequence of edicts of the King, stating that the morals of the people and the holy faith having suffered much from the strangers who have been in it, and from long and cruel wars, he thinks that 8 or 10 days fasting and prayer may be no bad thing for restoring it to its original purity.

There are 3 rows of boxes, no one can go into the first two rows, without the box has been taken by them; in the top row only women can go, in the pit only men; those who pay have a seat there, if not they stand in a place railed off all round the pit and under the boxes. The admission is only 6 pence; if you have a seat you pay 1s. 6d. more. The play is generally short, the story is either historical or represents life and manners, where good acting is required it is commonly acted in an awkward unnatural manner; but where excellence is not required they are admirable. After the play the opera always comes, wh^{c.} is always very good the music and singing being excellent; some of the operas last longer than the Play. Dancing generally succeeds and this the Spaniards are pasionately fond of. All those I have seen on the stage, dance remarkably well, the dances are generally very pretty, far more so than any we have in England, but they all are danced with such extreme indecency that an Englishman cannot look at them without blushing, and we need have no farther proof of the licentiousness of the people than the fandango and Bolero danced as they are in Spain. The "entremés" or farce which succeeds the dancing is a representation of low life and manners in which the fool takes the principal part, they are generally full of low wit and humour.

In going to the Tertullias or to the theatre, and more especially returning, it is very unpleasant having no companion and being obliged to go and to return alone, for robberies are so frequent and daring that I confess I sometimes did not feel quite comfortable in passing along the dark narrow crooked streets, with the Pateo doors open, where any number of men might be concealed and spring out upon the unwary passenger. They frequently entered houses, knocking at the door and walking in when it was opened. No person stirred out at night unarmed, and, if not in company walked with his hand upon his sword; always leaving behind watch and money. In coming home one night from a Tertullia with Mr. Welsh a gentleman who has lived 20 years in Seville, I said I would take him a better way to his house than the one he was going, and I brought him through a street that I always pass through. He said on entering it: "I dont like this street, a man was stopped on this very spot a night or two ago", and when he had gone a few steps further he added, that if he was alone and to meet any person in that street that he should be afraid to pass him and would turn back. He was attacked one night in passing a patio door; a man sprung at him but he threw him off and ran back a few paces when 4 men with swords rushed out of the same court. One followed him, but giving cries of "ladrones, ladrones" they all made off. The most frightful instance of this kind happened a short time ago in Malaga. A gentleman returning home late found himself in a dark narrow street, and beginning to feel alarmed, he took a pistol in each hand and seeing a man standing alone with a torch in his hand, he approached him and asked him as a particular favour that he would accompany him to the end of the street. He said he would do it with pleasure, and as he pronounced the words, he threw the torch to the ground and drew his sword ,and before the gentleman could level his pistols both his arms were seized by some villains behind, and by a blow to the head he was brought to the ground; they did not however murder him, but robbed him of everything even to his shirt. Though encounters of this kind are not met with by all persons, yet it is not comfortable to know that everyone is subject to them. On the **11th** of this month a robber was strangled in the Plaza de St. Francisco. It was done by putting his head into an iron frame and screwing it against a stake.[28] He confessed on the scaffold, he and 3 monks throwing a cloak over their heads. He gave a long history of his innumerable robberies and said that he had expected his son to come and rescue him at the head of 2 or 3 thousand robbers. He dreamt he said at the age of 7 years, that he should one day be executed in that very Plaza and had frequently had the same dream since and yet had continued robbing. He showed great resolution, said the responses after the friar with an unfaltering voice, and gave the signal for the executioner to do his business, with perfect composure; he expired with a crucifix before him and a fat monk by his side, who after all was over gave a good discourse to the surrounding multitude.

Dec 12th

A man was murdered almost close to Mr Beck's door and a few minutes only before I passed to take a letter to his office. He had some dispute with another man and just as the man left him he was seen to fall to the ground and was found weltering in his blood; he had been stabbed to the heart and this was the second stab he had received in a month.

On the **16th** three robbers were publickly [sic] whipped, they were mounted on asses, naked from the middle upwards, in order to receive the lashes; and the knifes, muskets and pistols with which they had robbed hung about their necks. In this manner they were carried through the city. That morning I was engaged to breakfast at the Palace, but finding Sir John in bed I took a walk along the river side. Two men on the Quay, quarrelled, one knocked the other down, and then sprang upon him and began to beat him in a most savage manner; he was however taken off; but the fray began again and the same man was now knocked into the river; the instant he was taken out he continued the quarrel, the other man seized a great [c]leaver and if the friends and bystanders had not interfered, would certainly have deprived his antagonist of life. What I have seen of the Andalusians would lead me to pronounce of their character, that they are phlegmatic in the extreme, till they are roused by an injury, and then their passion knows no bounds. In general few words pass before their knives, wh^c. are of such a kind that the wound they make is almost always mortal, are drawn from their belt and plunged into the breast of their adversary. Every peasant carries one of these weapons, and if they have a cloak wrapped round their arm, a sword is but a poor defence against them.

On the **18th** returning from St. Telmo I met two files of soldiers escorting to the Quay 70 prisoners, robbers, who were going to be shipped off for Africa "to serve the King" or in plain English, going to the gallies. They marched between the two ranks of soldiers with the right leg of one shackled fast to the left leg of another, which scarcely allowed them to walk. When they arrived at the place of embarcation a very distressing scene ensued, for there were among the crowd many relations of the prisoners, Fathers, Mothers, sisters and lovers who kept breaking through the files of soldiers to get a last embrace. The men themselves furnished an excellent specimen of the phlegmatic disposition of the Andalusians, for whilst they embraced and bid farewell to their friends present and desired to be remembered to those absent, they looked perfectly unmoved, rolled up their cigars and requested the officer to light them, then smoked as coolly, and with as much indifference, as they do on common occasions. One however was instantly roused into a violent rage by being struck by the officer, his eyes flashed fire, he stamped his foot, pulled his hair and in his passion tore his very whiskers; it would have fared ill with officer if a knife had been put into the mans hands. So careful were they that the men should not carry any weapons, that before going on board all were stripped and examined, even to untying the pigtails which all the peasants wear of a great length.

On the **24th** 4 robbers were taken in women's clothes. A few days ago information arriving of 12 robbers being in a wood near Carmona. 25 soldiers were sent from Seville and took them all, but told them if they would give them (the soldiers) 4 dollars a piece they would let them go. The robbers did not refuse so cheap a bargain and recovered their liberty.

On **Christmas Day** I went to pay my respects to two English nuns, the elder one Abbess of the convent; the younger one, one of the handsomest women I ever saw with a pair of eyes far superior even to those of any Spanish lady I have seen, wh^c· is saying a great deal; she laughed heartily and her conversation was very lively. Her features are perfectly regular and her complexion beautiful, and I would forgive anyone for falling in love at first sight. I cursed a thousand times the double iron grating which concealed so much of her lovely face, as well as the laws of the country which permitted such creatures to be immured within the walls of a convent, instead of being as God intended they should be, the light and ornament of the world. The bad and vicious may be shut up in convents and welcome; there they might mend or at least the world would be benefited by their imprisonment; but to shut up the young and virtuous is indeed an absurdity, it puts it out of their power to do good to their fellow creatures and it is robbing the world of one of its richest ornaments.

[28] This was, of course, execution by garrotting.

28th

Two days ago the weather broke: during the 7 weeks that I have been in Seville there has been no rain; the sky almost continually of a beautiful blue without a single cloud, wh$^{c.}$ is generally the case for 8 months of the year. The sun has always great power, but there is a mildness a freshness and even a frostiness in the air at the same time which is truly delightful, and I am not sure if I do not injure it, by comparison with the mildest and freshest of our August mornings. Such has been the weather almost without interruption during our dreary months of November and December. Notwithstanding this, according to all I hear, our winter must be preferable to the summer of Seville, when the heat is extreme. In Spring and Autumn the climate is enchanting but the Summer is too hot and the Winter rainy. The plains are now just beginning to acquire a little verdure, the hills are covered with the green Olive, and as to the beauty of an Orange plantation no one who has not seen it can form the slightest conception of it. Indian corn is grown here in considerable quantities. The Palm tree flourishes; and the hedges are made solely of Aloes or Indian Cane, both of which make an almost impenetrable fence, the former of these acquires an astonishing size and strength, some being 8 or 10 feet high, and proportionally thick; the latter is commonly 20 feet high, and many will measure from 25 to 30 feet. These sufficiently show the warmth of the climate.

Having now been in Seville nearly two months, spending my time not exactly in the manner I wished, making but slow progress in the language from the circumstance of all my acquaintance being English, unable to get into Spanish society, having seen all worthy of attention in the city and neighbourhood, and feeling dull for want of a friend, I at last resolved to lose no more time but leave it instantly. I had no hesitation as the course I should take. Granada had been my first destination, there I sh$^{d.}$ hear nothing but Spanish spoken and should live among Spaniards; besides all I had heard, all I had read, since coming to Seville, increased to a high pitch my desire, before strong, of visiting that celebrated city. The only safe way of travelling was with the muleteers who, going always in strong parties, are seldom attacked; as to a Calesa, I had suffered too many inconveniences from that mode of travelling to attempt it again, and like poor Gil Blas[29] I put myself under the care of the head Muleteer who agreed to carry me for 10 dollars, Tuesday the 3rd of January being the day appointed for our departure. I according made all my arrangements and took leave of my friends. Mrs Beck provided me with prog[30] for the journey, a ham, a cheese, bread and good Sherry wine as well as a sack to fill with straw for a mattrass [sic], and thereby avoid the teeming beds of the Posadas. Before leaving Seville however I did not omit a second search for Italica, this time I not only discovered the foundations of a very extensive city, said to be the birthplace of Trajan, Hadrian and Theodosius, but also the Amphitheatre. The shape is oval, 100 yards long by 60 wide;

the seats on one side are tolerably perfect and visible on the other; many of the cells for the wild beasts are likewise in a good state of preservation, and the passages by which the people entered are distinguishable. These last have evidently been once cased with marble, which was I am told, pulled off by the monks to beautify the Convent of Santiponce. The city itself was destroyed by an earthquake, but the Amphitheatre was doomed to be pulled to pieces by the Spaniards, partly by the monks to build the aforementioned Convent, partly by the orders of the Seville Corporation who wanted the stone to bank up the Guadalquiver. Many valuable columns and statues have been found at Italica and were excavations to be made there is no doubt but that the richest treasures of Antiquity would be discovered: but unfortunately for lovers of the fine arts Italica was built in Spain, and these treasures will probably remain buried till they no longer have existence. Part of the statues and pillars which have been found are now to be seen tumbled about in the vaults of the Alcazar; and Gods and Goddesses some with heads, some without, and Doric, Ionic and Corinthian Pillars some with capitals some without, now supply the place of stumps in the convent yard on Santiponce. There is also to be seen a very extensive piece of Mosaic work discovered a few years ago. It remained a long time without any inclosure round it; there is now a stone wall, but all enter, who like, and carry away what they like. The execution is not particularly good, the subjects are the heads of several of the Emperors with their names, together with some dogs, foxes and birds. Some have lost half their heads, some an eye or nose, according as the colour of the stone which composed each, took the fancy of the observer. The yard may be about 20 or 25 feet square and contains an ancient well; a great part of the yard is thickly overgrown with weeds. Italica seems to have been built in imitation of Rome upon 7 hills and I think Swinburn[31] is right in his conjectures that the Guadalquiver once ran at its feet.

Tuesday 3rd

I was just setting off to join the muleteers, when to my mortification I received a message that they would not go till the following day, when I must be at their posada by mid-day.

End of Vol. 1st.

[29] The eponymous hero of the picaresque comic novel by Alain-René Lesage (1668–1747). Greg would probably know of this highly popular novel through the translation by Tobias Smollett of 1749.

[30] Prog was food for a journey.

[31] Henry Swinburne, author of *Travels through Spain in the Years 1775 and 1776. In which Several Monuments of Roman and Moorish Architecture are Illustrated by Accurate Drawings taken on the Spot*, and *The Picturesque Tour Through Spain Embellished with 20 Engravings* (1806).

Journey From Seville to Granada, Malaga, Gibraltar, Tangiers, Tetuan, Ceuta and Cadiz[1]

January 4th

At midday I repaired to the Posada del Lobo, and the main body of our Caravan I found had already departed. I and the head Muleteer were not long in following them, and we left Seville by the Gate of Carmona. The first two miles of the road lay along the acqueduct of Carmona, and soon after we entered on the great plain by which Seville is on every side surrounded. My equipment was not particular, either for expedition, or for making a great show; I had an ass provided me, which, besides an enormous pack saddle, carried a week's provision, two or three sacks and baskets, my prog and wallets, together with a number of odd things; and I seated myself as I could on the top of this heap of baggage, riding backwards, or forwards, or sideways, according to inclination, or the convenience of conversing with my companions. At a short distance from the city I saw a man's leg nailed to a piece of wood, I was told that it belonged to a man who had committed 80 robberies before 20 years of age and that like the man on the other side of Seville his limbs had been hung up in different parts of the country as a warning to the people. I had not gone very far before I recollected that I had no passport, having forgotten it entirely and I felt not a little uneasy, as at Granada, I had heard, that the police were particularly strict; but as it was then too late to think of returning, I determined to take my chance and proceed. A little before dark we fell in with 7 or 8 German Soldiers, who said that as they were going to Granada they would join our party. They detested Spain and took a fancy to me as being a "North Countryman". One of them was particularly bitter in his complaints against the Government, he and his companions were then working their way home having received their discharge on refusing to join the Expedition to America; they had served in the Spanish army during the whole of the war, having deserted from France, at first the French entered Spain. He had come over to the Spaniards, he said, with a horse, with good clothes, with money in his pocket, and well armed; he had fought for 6 years in its service and now he was sent home without receiving his pay, and not only his horse and arms, but even his clothes had been taken from him. The two last hours of riding were in the dark, the road lying for a great distance among woods of small pine trees; the frost was rather sharp and I suffered much from cold before arriving at Ervizo, a small town distant not more than 4 leagues from Seville. Our head muleteer lived at Ervizo, and I went to his house in preference to a Posada, it being rather cleaner. I found there sitting over the brazier a Gentleman of Granada one Don Miguel, who was to be of our party and finding that I did not know much of the language and customs of the country he took me under his protection. When supper came I thought that it was politer to eat with my host than by myself; I did so, not withstanding my dislike to the Spanish messes where oil onions and Garlic are the invariable ingredients. I slept in a little room with Don Miguel, as usual upon the floor, with nothing but a very thin mattrass between my body and the damp brick floor.

Thursday 5th

We did not leave Ervizo till 12 or 1 o'clock, and had, therefore, time enough to look about the place. It is a small town situated on the side of a semi circular hill which rises from an extensive plain, in front the Ronda Mountains are a grand and beautiful object. We set out to the number of 40 or 50 beasts, and 6 or 7 Muleteers, our vanguard having proceeded several hours before us. The whole of this day's journey was over a great plain where much wheat is grown; the only interesting objects to be seen in the course of it are the Ronda Mountains to the South and the City of Carmona crowning the summit of a hill to the North. From Ervizo to Marchena is only 5 leagues, yet we did not arrive above an hour after sun set, and stopped at a posada without the town. We all assembled round the fire, made as is always the case upon the hearth at one end of the posada, whilst the mules and horses occupy the other, without any division between the two. The company were all very merry, talked, laughed and smoked their Ciggars, in which I always joined them; I heard one of them tell the rest that in the morning I had washed in cold water and drank three cups of Chocolate at my breakfast, feats that appeared so extraordinary to the company that they scarcely gave credit to the relation. The Spaniards themselves seldom wash, and never on a journey of this kind, be it ever so long, and when they take chocolate never drink above one small cup of it. The same story was repeated to every newcomer, who as he heard it used to look around at me to see if I confirmed it. I was asked, If I meant to do the same on the following morning; when some of them came to confirm with their own eyes the account of the preceding evening. The Mattrass they brought me for my bed was not half as long as myself, and I was obliged to supply the deficiency by my great coat thereby depriving myself of my coverlid. I was dreadfully annoyed by vermin, as well as Don Miguel, who expressed the same thing by saying that he heard a great deal of music in his mattress, and he amused himself all night by smoking Ciggars [sic].

Friday 6th

It was some feast day, and necessary to go to Mass before setting out on our journey, they awoke me at six o'clock to accompany them, with which I complied seing them unwilling to go without me; the morning was extremely cold, and the ice thick, and we were some time wandering about the town before we could

1   The second volume begins with this heading.

find a church that was open, we at last succeeded and after performing our devotions returned to the inn. I observed a painting near the door of the Church, of St Sebastian, whom as some gilt letters below informed "tradition says to be the Patron Saint of this city" truly a strong reason why he should be worshiped there. Marchena is a small town of rather cleaner appearance than the generality: it is situated upon a hill and has the remains of a Moorish Castle and fortifications. After taking a hasty breakfast we all set out and soon joined our vanguard; together we made a very respectable caravan consisting of about 70 beasts, 10 or 12 Muleteers, an officer, 7 or 8 German soldiers, 4 Spanish, a Canonigo, his major domo and servant, a friar, two or three peasants, Don Miguel and myself.

Our journey to Ossuna, though but 5 leagues, took us the whole day, notwithstanding we never stopped an instant; the country over which we passed was a dead flat, the continuation of the plain we had crossed the preceding day, and presented nothing worthy of notice, nor, indeed nothing at all to notice. We approached Ossuna as the sun set, it is a considerable town situated on a hill and with its spires and an ancient Castle makes a good appearance from the plain below. We stopped at a posada of the usual kind as to accommodations, but formed inside a singular aspect, being divided by two long rows of pillars like the nave of a church. We soon gathered round a great blazing fire and again smoked and chatted till supper was ready which seldom happened till 2 hours after arriving, and woe to him who comes in hungry to a Spanish Posada. They all talked very loud and I suppose were very witty if I may judge by the laughter; but I could understand but little of what was said, for the common people of Andalusia, as well indeed of all the provinces of Spain excepting old Castile, speak very corrupt Castillian, almost as difficult for a foreigner to understand as the language of a Manchester carter; I could however perceive that England and Englishmen, were the subjects of many of their jests. I asked Don Miguel to explain them to me, but he, who had all the time preserved the most sullen and contemptuous silence, refused, saying that they were ill bred fellows and their wit fit only for themselves.

Saturday 7th
We started from the posada before Sunrise and ascended the hills behind Ossuna, whence the view of the turrets and spires of the city and the plain beyond was extremely beautiful and striking. The country now became very interesting, our road lying through olive groves, woods of cork and evergreen oak trees and crossing many pretty little hills and valleys. Here too we beheld for the first time the famous Sierra Nevada, rising with its snowy summits above numbers of other lofty sierras at a distance of not less than a hundred miles; and what is somewhat singular we never saw it again till within a few leagues of Granada, a circumstance which sufficiently attests its great elevation. We entered about mid day the Pass

of Roda, a solitary valley thickly covered with underwood, and oak trees, a place at all times as the Muleteers informed me, infested with banditti and where the crosses that mark the place of murder, may absolutely be said to line the road. Just as we got into the underwood we were joined by four ill-looking well armed, well mounted men, who rode leisurely along from one end of our Cavalcade to the other, eyeing us all very closely as they passed. One of them rode up alongside my ass and scowled at me from beneath his cloak in a very villainous manner, which I returned rather more boldly than I should have done, had I known what no doubt, he was, a Captain of Banditti. After riding by us for some time they dropped behind and we saw no more of them; but one of the Germans who had got drunk at Ossuna, and lagged behind the rest, joined us soon after and told us what sort of company we had been keeping, saying that all four had presented their muskets at his breast and demanded his money, questioning him very closely as to our numbers, arms, and goods we were carrying; to all which he returned such satisfactory answers, as to destroy any hope they might have had of overpowering us. We arrived about Sun set at a small town call Alameda distant 7 leagues from Ossuna, and prettily situated in the steep side of a mountain. I found seated at the fire side four surly fellows who seemed anxious to pick up a quarrel, one giving me the lie, another taking my gloves which I could not get back without a good deal of contention. I of course left them, and tho' too dark to see anything, took a stroll through the village. In returning, in a solitary place near the Church I met the same men, the one who had taken my gloves seized me by the arm and demanded my passport; I withdrew my arm, but forget what answer I made, or whether it was in English or Spanish; but he instantly said "I'll make you" and throwing aside his cloak he drew his knife. I made a step back, and felt myself seized by both arms by someone behind, which alarmed me as the affair began to look serious; there in a strange village, in a solitary place; alone with a knife held at my breast and my arms seized behind by two men, who a few minutes before had insulted me without the slightest provocation. I, therefore, thought in good earnest of defending myself, and turning round fiercely on the man who had seized me behind, I nearly knocked him down, loosed my right arm and laid my hand on my sword Cane which I had with me; he then let go my other arm and attempted to wrest my cane from me, but not succeeding in this he turned about and they all went off and I made the best of my way to the Posada. What was the object of these men I cannot guess, I confess I did not at all like my situation, for when you are in the power and need the assistance of the Spaniards, instead of finding their protection, this very circumstance is too often a sufficient cause for insult and even murder; it was evinced by too many acts of cruelty in the late revolution. I was not without some fear of seeing these men again, and was rather uneasy at not seeing any of my friends for a long while after my return to the Posada.

Sunday 8th

We were roused very early by our Muleteers to accompany them to Mass which we did about two hours before sun rise and shortly afterwards set off to Loxa where we had to sleep was called only 7 leagues, but we were told that these 7 were longer than 9, and we found them so, for though we did not stay an instant upon the road, we did not reach Loxa till nearly two hours after Sun set. A great part of the distance I walked as the day was excessively cold. The first two leagues of our road were very picturesque, and the views through the woods of the distant hills and plains interesting. I often advanced some distance before the rest to look at our long Cavalcade which made a good appearance, winding through the different passes of the rocks and mountains, in places where nature reigns undisturbed by man, and where no sound was heard but the tinkling of the mule bells and song of the Muleteer. About 3 leagues from Alameda we came in full view of a very grand and interesting, object, and particularly pleasing to the traveller who is acquainted with its history. This is the Peña de los Enamorados, an immense perpendicular rock rising from the low valley of Anteguera, and standing alone in the centre of an Amphitheatre of magnificent mountains. It received its name, rock of the Lovers, from the following story. A young Christian Knight was taken prisoner by the Moorish King of Antequera but was well treated by him and retained in his Court. The daughter of the King fell in love with him and they determined to make their escape and be united amongst the Christians. Their flight however was discovered, and finding themselves pursued they climbed up to the summit of this rock, their pursuers with the King at their head followed them thither. Escape now being hopeless, they advanced to the edge of the tremendous precipice, and declared to the King that if anyone attempted to seize them they would throw themselves down. The King began to relent but a daring soldier sprang forward and endeavoured to lay hold of one, when instantly throwing themselves into one another's arms, they jumped into the valley below, and were dashed to pieces. Antequera which is situated almost the foot of this rock, is an ancient and still a considerable city; it was built by the Moors on the site of the ancient Singilia, and was taken by Don Fernando one of the Infants of Spain, who, it is said, made use of gunpowder in the seige. After the taking of the city between 2 and 3 thousand of the Moors left it. We soon after approached Archedona another Moorish city standing in a wild and commanding situation amongst the rocks. From the summit of the hill behind Archedona we had a very fine and extensive view, on one side all over the immense plains which lay between us and Seville, the valley of Antequera and the Peña de los Enamorados, with the magnificent mountains which surround it, on the other side of the country extending almost to Granada. We now descended into the plains, and darkness soon overtook us, so that the view on approaching Loxa was entirely lost.

Monday 9th

Having only six short leagues to go to Santa Fé we did not set out very early. Loxa is like most Moorish towns built very close and has a much better appearance from a distance, standing as they all do in some commanding situation than when you approach near. It stands on the side of a steep hill, and the river Genil which rises in the Sierra Nevada runs at its foot. The country immediately in the neighbourhood is much better than that about Seville, in point of cultivation; and the state of agriculture gradually improves till we reach Granada. Our road lay for some time thro' a fine valley along the banks of the Genil, and soon after ascending some hills we once more got a view of the Sierra Nevada covered now with snow about halfway down, and crowning two majestic hills immediately at the foot of the sierra, stood the object of my search, the City of Granada.

The sun set just as we entered upon the Vega or great plain of Granada, for beauty and fertility perhaps unequalled by any in the world. It is upwards of 20 miles long and ten broad, bounded on the East by the Sierra Nevada, on the North by the Sierra Elvira, on the South by the hill of Padul, and on the west by the mountain we had crost. The cultivation here is perhaps the best in Spain,a considerable part of it is well wooded, and it contains a great number of small towns and villages. It differs from almost all the other plains we had seen in Spain by being well supplied with water; for the numerous channels with which the Moors have intersected it in every direction, being connected with the Sierra Nevada and equally full in Summer and Winter. The cold being extreme, with a bitter east wind in our face Don Miguel and I walked the last three leagues of the road and arrived at Santa Fé about an hour after dark. We assembled as usual round the fire of the Posada Soldiers, Muleteers, Canonigo, Friars all; all merry and all smoking, the incessant occupation and sometimes the only one of the Andalusians. Supper was then prepared; one mess serves for all, and the mess is generally the same every night, except on those on which fish must be eaten. They first put on the fire an enormous frying pan about half full of oil, and boil for sometime, then throw in the meat, whatever it may happen to be, with a quantity of salt, pepper onions and garlic and when this has fried some time, add a small quantity of water. The last operation is putting in rice sufficient to fill the pan, and after remaining sometime longer the whole forms into one solid mass. The pan is then set upon a small table, the handle being supported by the back of a chair, and the whole party sit round it and help themselves with their fingers and large wooden spoons. The sallad however invariably preceeds this dish; it is served up in an immense large basin, the lettuce, garlic etc chopped very small swims on the surface of a mixture of oil and water, and looks like a duckpond covered with green weed. When all the sallad is taken out, this unwieldy basin is handed round and each one raising it to his mouth drinks as much as he thinks is his share. Santa Fé is a small town with several churches and Convents; its origin forms its sole claim of interest to a traveller, having been built in the year 1491 by Ferdinand and Isabella, whose camp accidentally taking fire, whilst they were besieging Granada, replaced it by building one not liable to a similar accident. It was completed by their soldiers in 80 days. A considerable part was thrown down by an earthquake a few years ago, and the damage has not yet been entirely repaired. The Muleteers, whose information must always be received with caution tell you that S. Fé is a city of much greater antiquity than Granada.

Tuesday 10th

I passed a most miserable night, the vermin being intolerable, and I was obliged to get up in the middle of it, strip off all my clothes and after Shaking them well, dressed again, and put myself in my sack tying up head and all, but to no purpose. I could not sleep, and was glad to be up a five o'clock and get ready to proceed. The morning being extremely cold and the distance to Granada across the plain not above 2 leagues, Don Miguel and I walked thither. The view the whole way was very grand indeed and I thought surpassed far, very far, anything of the kind I had ever seen. The greater part of the City is visible from this part of the Vega, and the Cathedral, the hill of the Albaicin, the bold rock of the Alhambra, with the towers of that celebrated fortress and the palace of Charles V; the palace and gardens of the Generalife, the dark brown mountain that overhung the City, and immediately behind them the snowy peaks of the Sierra seen above the Clouds, framed a view truly magnificent and striking, and whose beauty and grandeur can seldom if ever be excelled. We entered Granada and fortunately my passport was not demanded; a couple of Shillings cleared my things at the Custom House and I made my way to the Posada. It may be supposed having neither shaved, washed or taken off my clothes for 6 days, I was impatient enough to do all three: impatient as I was however, not withstanding all my efforts, nearly two hours expired before I could get myself admitted into a room, and even then had to perform all the above operations on a dirty brick floor and at a window without a single pane of Glass in it. My first care was to call upon one of those persons I had a letter to, and who was to engage lodgings for me, which I found he had already done, bad enough indeed, but as he said the best that he could meet with. I descended into my room by half a dozen steps, it resembled a dungeon in every respect, having only one little grated window which admitted both cold and light as it was not glazed; a dirty little table was placed immediately under it, being the only place light enough to read or write, in doing either of which, or in eating my meals I was starved to a degree I never experienced in my life before. To make the matter worse I could not even call this miserable hole my own, as a Spaniard shared it with me and our beds stood hard by. However I was at Granada, and I endeavoured to bear all with fortitude, if I could not with cheerfulness. In the afternoon my friend Pizarro took me with him to deliver my letters of introduction. Two of the principal persons were then not in the city, a third procured me the common attentions of which every Spaniard is so lavish, fine words and Grand offers, but nothing more. I had also a letter to Doña Francisca Riviera, a rich widow, whose husband, I was informed, had been hung at Cadiz for his attachment to the French, and whose son was then prisoner at Madrid, for his adherence to the Constitution. Her house is the only tolerable one in point of accommodations in Granada, and she the only person who sees company and gives tertulias and dances. She received me very politely and gave me a general invitation to all her parties, which took place every Wednesday and Sunday. There were staying in her house two very gentlemanly looking officers, who, I was told were, the two deputies from King Ferdinand for the trial of the unfortunate persons lately arrested at Malaga, and then in confinement in the prisons of the Alhambra. Pizarro then took me to see the relics at the sacred mount, well known to all pious Catholics. One of the Professors of the Ecclesiastical College which stands upon the same Mountain undertook to show me all, and he went through the excavations with me, related the history of them pretty nearly in the same words as Bourgoing[2] makes use of, who very probably had it from the same Cicerone.[3] Three men went to this mount to dig in search of a treasure, but finding nothing after three days of hard labour, they were going to give up so useless a search, when one of them being in the Church of our Lady heard a voice which told him to return to the mountain and dig. He communicated the command to his companions, who continued their labour and at last came to a piece of lead 18 inches long and two inches wide, covered with characters, and was at length determined by the learned to signify as follows. The burned body of St. Mesiton, who suffered martyrdom in the reign of the Emperor Nero. The search was continued, and three more pieces of lead of similar dimensions and inscribed with the same characters were found, which mentioned the martyrdom of St. Cecil, St. Tesiphon and other saints. The Archbishop then interfered, the bodies of the martyrs were found in a calcined mass, except that of St Mesiton which was only imperfectly burnt. An assembly was summoned at which the most able divines in Spain assisted and the relics were declared genuine. April 30th 1600. Masses are said here regularly in honour of these Saints; and the grottoes in which they lived and suffered martyrdom are converted, into chapels some of extreme neatness and beauty. I saw the relics, but what they really were I could not tell. The remains of St Mesiton looked like a great brown stone, those of the others like powdered lime. They were preserved in a precious box upon one of the Altars, above them in the same box stood a small plain

[2] Author of *Travels in Spain Containing a New, Accurate and Comprehensive View of the Present State of the Country by the Chevalier de Bourgoanne* (London, 1789).
[3] Cicerone: a guide.

Birmingham casket, and on asking what it contained, my guide told me a little finger of St. Stephen. In one of the chapels are two beautiful landscapes made by inlaying pieces of coloured marbles, and a tolerably good painting of the same subject we noticed at Seville. St Dionysio with his head in his hand. The mitre and insignia of his office are still on his head, and his mouth open, crowds of people are represented as looking at him and listening to his voice with some degree of surprise and astonishment, as we probably should have done had we been in their place. The Professor who pointed out the painting gravely informed me that the people cut off his head to stop his mouth, but that notwithstanding, he walked twenty thousand pases [sic] with his head in his hand preaching the gospel of Jesus Christ; and he asked me if it did not seem to me a great miracle, to which I replied as gravely as it was asked that I most certainly thought it was. The view from this hill is particularly pleasing; it looks down upon a grove of olive trees, and on the cottages, garden and water of the river Darro; it has the palace of the Alhambra in front and commands a fine and extensive view of the Alhambra, the city, the Vega and the distant Mountains.

Granada was formerly called Illiberia founded as some say by Liberia great grand daughter of Hercules. Others, on as good a foundation, say, by Iberus, Grandson of Tubal, and was called Granada from his daughter Nata and Gar a Cave. This last is the opinion of Mendoza who wrote on the Civil war of Granada, and is a great Antiquarian; but as the date [of] its foundation is said to be upwards of 4000 years ago it matters but little, nor is it likely to be ascertained, who was the real founder whether the great grandaughter of Hercules or the great, great grandson of Noah; certain however it is that Granada can boast of some remains of the Phenicians. After the destruction of the two powerful kingdoms of Cordova and Valencia, the former by San Fernando, and the latter by Don Jayme, it appeared that nothing could resist the victorious arms of the Spaniards. Seville was the only one that remained and that was threatened by the victorious arms of Ferdinand. Mahomed Alhamar got himself proclaimed King and knowing how necessary it was that the Moors should have some Capital to take the place of Cordova, he chose Granada as best suited to his purpose. 1236 P.C. It soon rose into splendour and magnificence and during two centuries, maintained an equal contest with the Kings of Arragon and Castile, who generally at war among themselves but seldom presented an undivided force against the enemies of their country and their Faith. At last a favorable opportunity was offered for driving out the Moors entirely from their dominions in Spain no less by the union of the two crowns of Arragon and Castile by the marriage of Ferdinand and Isabella than by the dissentions which at that time existed among the first families of the Moors. On the 9th of May 1491, Ferdinand and Isabella at the head of 70,000 men laid seige to the city of Granada, after having taken possession of all the strong towns in the Kingdom. It then contained 200,000 inhabitants and was defended by Boabdil or Abdali surnamed Zogoybe or the little. The seige continued 9 months; when pressed with hunger and defeated in their frequent sallies, they were compelled at last to capitulate. Gonsalvo de Cordova surnamed the great Captain, arranged the articles, by which it was agreed that the Granadins should acknowledge for Kings Ferdinand and Isabella and their successors, should retain their laws, customs, judges and half their mosques and might sell or keep their goods and retire whether they liked without being forced to leave the country. Boabdil died in Africa. Granada was entered on the 2nd of January 1492, a day regularly celebrated there both in the Church and Theatre; and here concluded the domination of the Moors in Spain, who had possession of the whole or a considerable part of it during 782 years, the date of its conquest by Musa and his general Tarik being in 712.

The conduct of the Spaniards when they found themselves in quiet possession of Granada formed a striking contrast to the wise and generous policy of the Moors when they had conquered Spain. Every article of the capitulation was either evaded or broken. The wretched Moors were obliged to abjure their creed, to use the dress and language of the Spaniards, their women were forbidden the use of veils, and of their baths, and the children were taken from them at the age of 5 years and sent to be educated in Christian schools. A full and energetic account of the miseries they endured is to be found in the speech of Aben Humeya to the Rebel Moors, as given by Mendoza. "We are not less slaves", says he, "than if we really were so; our wives, children, estates and our own persons are at the disposal of enemies, without hope during many ages of freeing ourselves from such servitude. We have as many tyrants as neighbours; we groan under new impositions, new tributes. As Moors amongst Christians, we are despised as Christians among Moors we are neither believed nor assisted. Excluded from life and the conversation of men they command us not to use our own language, and we are ignorant of Castillian. In what language must we communicate our thoughts and ask for what we want? Without this there can be no intercourse amongst men. They call our children to their churches and schools and teach them arts which our Ancestors forbid them learning, lest they should confound the purity and render doubtful the truth of the law. Each hour they threaten to tear them from the arms of their Mothers and care of their Fathers to convey them to other lands where they will forget our way of living and become enemies to the Parents to whom they owe existence. They command us to throw off our dress and assume the Castillian! The Germans amongst them dress in one way, the French in another, the Greeks in another, the Friars in another, the young in another, the old in another; each nation, each rank, each profession has its peculiar dress, and all are Christians, but we are Moors because we dress in the Moorish manner as if religion lay in the dress and not in the heart. If we beg, no one will pity us when poor, since they scoffed at us when rich; no one will pity us because the Moors suffer this."

Grown at last desperate by so many oppressions, they flew to arms and chose for their king Aben Humeya, one of the descendants of their former Sovereigns. The rebellion broke out on Christmas night 1568. They took a cruel revenge on the Christian Priests, pulling some to pieces, boiling them in oil and putting them to the most dreadful tortures. Notwithstanding their repeated losses and defeats the war was continued with vigour for two years, and ended by the murder of the successor of Aben Humeya. Many thousand families were immediately carried off to Old Castile and the rabble of that Kingdom sent to supply their place. In 1610 Philip III commanded all of Moorish extraction to leave Spain, and this together with the long series of wars between the Moors and Christians, is sufficient to account for the great depopulation of these parts – 150,000 passed into France where they were treated with humanity by Henry IV. Some of their descendants are still to be found hidden in the mountains of the Alpuscarras. But the greater part went over to Africa where the remains of that unhappy people groan under the tyranny of the Emperor of Morrocco; they have however the satisfaction of reflecting, that their savage conquerors are now suffering under a despotism in every respect as oppressive, and far less excusable. In the year 1726, the Inquisition seized upon 360 families accused of Mahomedism, and confiscated their effects, amounting to 12 millions of crowns, a sum of which no account has ever been given. These unfortunate men had been great silk dealers and the annual produce of Silk in this province previous to 1726 amounted to 2,600,000 lbs weight. At present it falls short of 100,000. This is the last time the name of the Moors of Granada is to be found in the history to [sic] Spain.

The remains of the old walls of Granada show that it was formerly of far greater extent than it is at present. In the time of the Moors it contained a population of between 2 and 300,000; at present it does not amount to 50,000. It is situated on two hills, which are divided from each other by a very deep and narrow valley, formed by the Darro, a rapid mountain torrent, proceeding immediately from the Sierra. When Charles the V came to Granada the city presented him a crown of gold collected from the sands of this river. On the highest point of the southern of these two hills stand the fortress and Palace of the Alhambra, and on the one to the north the fortress of the Albaicin which forms a considerable part of the city, and in the time of the Moors was surrounded by walls and towers similar to those of the Alhambra, and on the northern side are still almost perfect. The rest of the city occupies the lower part of these two hills and part of a third. It can never be all seen from one point, but from every point what can be seen is grand and beautiful. The interior of the city answers but ill to the high expectations we form from its exterior appearance. The streets are narrow and very dirty; the houses large, but ill built and with a very few exceptions totally destitute of Glass, and half the windows being closed to keep out the cold with very large red shutters, gives the town a deserted and melancholy appearance. It is perhaps the healthiest city in all Spain, for standing at an elevation of two thousand feet above the sea, and at the foot of mountains eternally covered with snow the inhabitants do not experience that extreme and enervating heat in summer which is felt on the southern coast of Spain. The situation of Granada is indeed magnificent, and the eye is never fatigued, nor can ever satisfy itself, in gazing on its many beauties; the city stands upon two noble and abrupt hills divided by the woody narrow glen of the Darro. The snowy peaks of the Sierra rising immediately behind, are often seen glistening in sunshine far above the clouds whilst all around is wrapt in gloom and darkness and the fertile, beautiful Vega extends itself at its feet surrounded on every side by high ranges of peaked mountains. Were there no Alhambra, no Generalife at Granada, had the Moors never inhabited this celebrated city, the beauty the magnificence and the singularity of its situation alone would amply repay one for the troubles &inconveniences we have to undergo in arriving at it. Were I King of Spain, Granada should be my capital.

The Alhambra – This name is generally applied by us to signify merely the Palace of the Moorish Kings. It however includes the whole space contained within the walls surrounding the rock of the Alhambra, and which constituted in the Moorish time a considerable part of the city, whilst the Palace or as the Spanish call it the Casa Real, occupies but a very small portion, of what is properly denominated the Alhambra.

The grand entrance into the Alhambra is by a large square tower which a long Arabic inscription over the gateway informs us was built by Joseph Abulhaggeng in the year A.D. 1338. It is called the gate of judgement, because it was here that the Moorish sovereigns heard the complaints and received the addresses of their subjects. On the keystone of the principal arch an open hand is engraved, which is in frequent use amongst the Mahomitans [sic], as a symbol of several peculiarities of their religion and when presented open as it is in this case they thought it had power to weaken the strength of their enemies. A curious explanation of this may be found in Bourgoing Vol IV. 147. After passing some old Moorish arches you now advance into a large open space, on the left are seen a number of large square towers, called the towers of Bells, and formerly a part of the old castle, are now used for prisons, for confining those unfortunate people who have lately been arrested in various parts of Spain. On the right of this open space, the principal object that attracts the attention is the Palace of Charles V. It was in an unfinished state when that Emperor died and has continued so even since. It is a square of 220 feet. The appearance from without is simple and beautiful, and the sides are ornamented with large medallions beautifully wrought in different coloured marbles, representing the battles of the Moors and Christians. The centre is open and forms a large circle, surrounded by marble pillars of the

Ionic order. The architecture of the whole, and the minute carving of the festoons and medallions equally excellent. The plan was formed by Berruguete, a celebrated architect born near Valladolid. It was continued by Machuca, a pupil of Raphael, and after him by Siloe, who built the Cathedral, both Spaniards. The Palace was built by money obtained from the Moors under pretence of allowing them liberty of conscience. They advanced at two payments 1,600,000 ducats; what they received in return is known to all who have read their history. Near the Palace stands a church and convent of Franciscans.

The Casa Real on the outside is nothing but a mass of square towers. The Moors are invariably regardless of the exterior of their houses, which are nothing but plain bare walls; it is on the inside where they lavish all their riches and ingenuity. This is nowhere more fully exemplified than here, where without we see an irregular mass of towers, with plain walls, and within all the richness of oriental magnificence. We may describe the interior of the Alhambra, but as it is totally different from anything that is found in our own country, we can compare it to nothing, and can therefore convey no idea, much less a just one of the various singularities and beauties; we may give the number, figure and dimensions of its halls and patios; and this is all we can do; yet this is doing but little, it assists us in some measure to a knowledge of the general plan of the building but a hundred buildings may have the same dimensions, and at best it leaves us in complete ignorance of what alone the Alhambra is celebrated for, the beauty, elegance, and incredible minuteness of all its parts.

You enter from the outside by a low Gate into a court in shape a long square called by the Moors the Mesuar, by the Spaniards Pateo del Estanco or the Courtyard of the lake, there being a pond of good water which occupies the whole space, except a walk round it. At the two narrow ends of this court is a beautiful arched gallery supported on plain white marble columns, with their capitals extremely well cut and engraved with Arabic inscriptions. From the north end of this court which is 130 feet long by 30 wide, we enter into the tower of Cornares the highest and most magnificent of the Alhambra. It is said that the architect measured this tower as soon as it was completed and again a year afterwards and found that it had sunk 3 feet; I confess from the situation of the tower and from its size I suspect he must have mismeasured one of the times as it seems incredible standing as it does on the brink of a precipice and on a rock, that it should have sunk so much, or had that been possible that it should have sunk so exactly in the perpendicular. Passing from the Pateo del Estanco and through a long narrow antichamber you enter the Ambassadors hall, a square of 36 feet 36 feet high to the cornice and 18 more to the centre of the cupola. It formerly had a marble fountain in the middle of the hall but no traces of it now remain. On the north and west it has several windows, the view from which is very fine of the Albaicin, the valley of the Darro, the Vega and distant mountains. From the

Ambassadors Hall you ascend to the Toreador de la Reyna or Queens dressing room; a beautiful little chamber open on three sides and commanding a truly interesting and extensive prospect. It appears however that this was an oratory, not a dressing room. In one part, the floor is perforated to allow sweet perfumes to rise from the place they were burning them. In this part of the building there are many chambers which were modernised by Charles V and of course are not worth looking at now. The Sala de las dos hermanas or hall of the Two Sisters, so called from two very large pieces of marble, with which it is paved is extremely rich and beautiful, of a square figure and a cupula for the roof; it opens into the Court of Lions, and immediately opposite on the other side of that court is the Hall of the Abencerrages, nearly similar to that of the two Sisters.

All the halls that I have just mentioned are the same in the minutiae of their parts. To about the height of 5 feet all the walls are covered with coloured tiles, inlaied after the manner of mosaic work and so small and of such vivid colours, as make a very rich appearance. In the Hall of Ambassadors the whole floor is made of this tile work as well as that of el Tocador. In the halls of the two sisters and of the Abencerrages the floors are paved with white marble. From the tiles to the commencement of the cupula, for they all have cupulas, the walls are formed of fine white estucco, made of lime and white of eggs, of surprising consistency and which preserves the mold given to it as perfect as the hardest stone. The whole of these walls are covered over with circles, squares and every fantastic figure, extremely minute, and in every convenient place is some short Arabic inscription. It would take a good draughtsman a full hour to copy correctly a few square inches of any part of these walls. It is sufficiently evident that the composition has been regularly moulded in plates about 12 inches square and afterwards put up on the wall. Were it not for doing this the work would have been endless, and this accounts for the repetition of the same figures and same inscriptions, we so frequently meet with. It is the roofs however that astonish the observer most of all. They are composed of the most minute and delicate cell work and resemble the comb of a wasps nest bent into the form of a cupula. These cells are some guilded, some painted of a very rich blue, and others left of their original white, the whole being made of the same fine estucco. The effect produced by this, is as beautiful and striking as it is novel; and whether you look at the floor, the roof or the wall your eyes are dazzled by the richness of the colours and the minuteness of the workmanship. At the entrance of each apartment there is a beautiful little recess in the wall to leave their slippers in as the Moors always take them off at entering. What forms the greatest beauty and ornament of Alhambra is the famous court of Lions, which, as I observed, lay between and opened into the Hall of the Abencerrages and that of the Two Sisters.[4]

[4]   See the two drawings of the Alhambra by Greg in the plate section.

It is about 100 feet long by 50 wide and surrounded by a gallery; a vast number of slender elegant pillars of white marble, sometimes placed single, sometimes double or even three together, crowned with capitals of an unusual size, richly carved but all different, support arches of the Arabian order; that is, swelling out beyond the perpendicular of their column and bending inwards again to meet the capital destined to support them. At each end of the Court an extremely elegant and exquisitely contrived Cupula projects out from the gallery, supported by clusters of the same height and elegant columns with their rich capitals. The roof is form'd of the same cell work as before described, and in the centre is a marble fountain, which throws its waters into a neat plain basin sunk in the floor. The walls of this court and of the surrounding gallery are exactly the same as those of the halls and thickly scatter'd with Arabic inscriptions. In the centre of the court is a magnificent basin of white marble six feet in diameter which receives the waters of a fountain. It is supported by twelve lions of bad sculpture which give the name to the court. It is surrounded by a long inscription, as it serves as a specimen of the rest, I transcribe it. Many years ago the corporation of Granada caused all the inscriptions to be copied and faithfully translated. A considerable part of these may be found in Bourgoing IV. They all were written more or less in the extravagant style of the Arabians. That round the fountain is as follows:

O thou who examinest these lions fixed in their places, consider that they want nothing but life to be perfect; and thou who inhabitest this kingdom and this palace, receive them from the hands of thy nobles without employing violence. May God save thee for the new work with which thou has embelished me, and may thine enemy never be revenged upon thee. May the most desirable praise fall from the lips of him by whom thou art blessed, O Mahomed; our king, for thy mind is ornamented with the most amiable virtues. God forbid that this charming orchard the image of thine amiable qualities should be surpassed or equalled by any other in the world. But it is I who embellished it. It is the clear water which shines in my bosom & bubbles like melted silver. The whiteness of the stone and that of the water it contains are unrivalled. Examine well this cup if thou wilt distinguish the water which runs from it, for it will seem to thee either that they both run together or that they remain unmoveable. Like one of loves Captives whose face is bathed with the tears which the envious have caused him to shed, so the water seems to be jealous of the stone by which it is contained and the cup in its twin appears to be jealous of the limpid stream. Nothing but the generous hand of Mahomed can be compared to that which rushes from my bosom and flies impetuously into the air. A lion is not so strong and courageous as Mahomed is liberal.

The most frequently repeated of the short inscriptions are. "God only is the conqueror," Honour and happiness to our Lord Abdalla," There is but one God and Mahomet is his prophet, "Glory to God" with many others of a similar nature. In the centre of the hall of the Abencerrages, is a very large fountain, the basin of which has many reddish stains. This is said to have been caused by the blood of the six and thirty noble Chevaliers of the tribe of the Abencerrages who fell victim to the treachery of a rival tribe, and the hasty revenge of their monarch. The two tribes of the Gomelies and Zegries had long borne secret hatred against the noble Abencerrages. They accused Aben Hamet, the chief of the latter of having an illicit connection with the Queen and swore to their King Abdali that they had seen her in the arms of Aben Hamet in the gardens of the Generalife. The King vowed terrible revenge upon the whole tribe of the Abencerrages; he sent for them to attend him one by one in the hall which now bears their name, and having guards and an executioner ready, had them beheaded as they entered at the edge of the basin. Thirty six had been in this manner murdered, when a page who had attended his master, happened to peep through a hole in the wall which is still shown, and saw what was going forward, descended instantly into the city and warned the rest of the tribe. These immediately assembled their friends in arms and ran through the streets crying "treason, treason, let the King die!" The people who loved the Abencerrages immediately joined them and fourteen thousand rushed to the Alhambra. Abdali commanded the gates to be closed, but the people set fire to them and proclaimed Muley Hassem King, who some years before had been obliged to resign his crown in favour of his son. They rushed into the palace and finding the King in the Court of Lions, defended by the Gomeles and Zegris, in a short time killed above two hundred. The King escaped, and his brother Muza found means of appeasing the tumult. Those however who had accused the Queen, persisted in their accusations, and offered to maintain, by force of arms, their statement, against all who should contradict them. The Queen was imprisoned [sic] and the day of her execution arriving without any Moors daring to defend her, she trusted her cause to some Christian knights who appeared at the appointed time and vanquished her accusers.

Semple is wrong in stating that this story does not rest upon one single authority, and probably never would have had existence or at least been long since forgotten, had it not been laid hold of by superstition, it being said that the unfortunate sufferers were secretly attached to Christianity, and were heard at the time of their execution exhorting each other to die in the faith of Jesus. I never met with this part of the story elsewhere, and Semple is mistaken in saying that it rests on no good authority, for the whole account almost exactly as it is commonly related, is found in an Arabic manuscript written the year after the event took place, its date being 1492, that is the very year in which Granada was taken. This MS. Adds that "the Christians were in danger of being taken but that God delivered them" At one end of the Court of Lions a Cross has been painted on the wall to mark the Spot where Mass was first said in the Alhambra. Near it are four paintings in the ceiling of the Gallery which Bourgoing calls Moorish, the Cicerone however says that they were painted after the time of the Moors, and he is probably right for they represent the murder of the Abencerrages, the trial of the Queen and her deliverance by the Christian knights, subjects which reflected so little honour upon Abdali that it is not likely that he caused them to be put there, and he was the last Moorish inhabitant of the Alhambra. The interest which a stranger must take in beholding this celebrated court is very great whether he reflects on its past history, or regards only the astonishing combination of beauties and singularities which it presents, what then are his sensations when as he sees the one, he thinks upon the other. Let those who have been there answer, if they can find language to express what they felt.

There are several other chambers in the Palace, that present nothing particularly worthy of remark, such as the whispering gallery, the Royal baths and the chamber for reposing after coming out of the baths. It is a square room the walls are like those I have described; on two of [the] sides, is a recess raised about three feet above the floor and lined with fine tile work, these were, I supposed covered with silk cushions for the Monarch and his ladies to rest upon after leaving the baths which adjoin this room, the floor is of white marble and in the centre of it is a beautiful basin and fountain of the same; at a considerable height is a covered orchestra for the Musicians and you cant look upon this apartment without confessing that the Monarchs of Granada well understood what was luxury.

The Hall of Nymphs is so called from two female figures beautifully wrought in white marble, they are generally supposed to be of Arabian sculpture, but this appears to me to be extremely doubtful. The Moors are forbidden by their religion to imitate any living creatures in their sculpture and though they sometimes break this law as in the instance of the Lions supporting the great basin, yet they did this so seldom that they could not have attained such excellence with so little practice, but rather where they did attempt anything of the kind, would bring forth such ill formed productions as the said Lions. What confirms me in this opinion is that over the door, at the side of which the nymphs are placed, is a small piece of sculpture representing one of the amours of Jupiter. Very probably these three pieces of sculpture are Roman and have either been found amongst other Roman remains in Africa, or have formed a part of the splendid presents sent by the Greek Emperor to the Moors.

Would any one suppose that amongst such scenes as those of the Alhambra, any person going as I did, not only with the desire, but the determination of being pleased with everything, could have found objects to excite his pity, his indignation and even his disgust? Yet so it is and as he beholds these objects, his feelings rise high against the hand that causes them, and allows them to remain in their present state. The Towers of bells, are prisons crowded with unfortunate victims accused of the unpardonable crime of being friends of the liberties of man and lovers of their country. Swarms of fat greasy Monks, are seen in every direction upon that noble rock, strolling up and down, whispering pretty compliments to the women, or stretching their indolent carcases upon the walls, praising French cookery or damning the English because they are Heretics. The beautiful tile work of the Moors in the Gate of Judgement has been broken through to make room for a large wooden image of the Virgin Mary; the same offence has been committed in another part of the same tower to make room for paintings of St. Antonio, Santiago and many other Sts together with one of the Virgin which has under it the following inscription in gilt letters. "A hundred days indulgence is granted to all who shall devoutly say an Ave Maria before this picture of the Virgin, being the second likeness taken by the Evangelist Luke of our Lady." The admirably wrought medallions in the palace of Charles V of a stone that would have lasted to eternity, have been most wantonly abused and broke to piece, and the very Palace of the Alhambra itself destroyed in the inside by vermin and moisture and shattered on the outside by repeated earthquakes, is fast falling to decay, and if not repaired, will, in a few years, no longer exist, to gratify the curiosity of the traveller and the researches of the antiquarian. The Spaniards, indeed, boast of Granada but it is absurd to do so; for everything there beautiful, magnificent and singular has been the work of Nature or of the Moors, everything that excites an unpleasant feeling has been the work of the Spaniards, and these are by no means few: in short it seems as if the only object of that nation after taking Granada had been to destroy all the good done and blessings lavished by the beneficent hand of Nature and the labour of their enlightened Conquerors ...

We enter the gardens of the Generalife from the rock of the Alhambra, by the Torre de picos, through a small gate, which favoured the escape of Abdali when the Spaniards took Granada. Generalife is a word said to signify the house of Love, dance and pleasure; and it was built by Omar who was passionately fond of Music and used to spend here almost all his time. The gardens of the Generalife do not exist at all in their former state. The Palace is nearly as it was, as far as respects the outside; there is just enough remaining in the inside to show that it was once the same as the Alhambra in the style of workmanship; at present all the plaster having fallen from the walls, it has been replaced by simple white washing. In two of the rooms are several paintings: a Moorish one of Abdali or el Reychico, the last King is tolerably well done, the rest I know not whether or not they are originals but they are very indifferent paintings, they are portraits of all the Christians who distinguished themselves at the seige of Granada. The most remarkable however is, one of the Queen of the same Abdali, in the dress of a Carmelite Nun. My Cicerone said that after the Christian knights had vanquished her accusers, she refused to have anything more to say to her husband and flying from Granada, retired to a Convent; that she refused again to live with Abdali is sanctioned by history, but what is the foundation of so strange a conceit it is not easy to guess.

Within the walls of this Palace, are two beautiful little gardens with borders and hedges of myrtles and a clear stream of water running through them. In the higher of the two, are a couple of ancient Cypresses, whose thick trunks and white bark show that they must have existed for centuries. They are called Cypresses of the Queen, and tradition says that it was under these trees, that the perfidious Gomel swore that he saw the Queen in the arms of Abenhamet. The Generalife stands in one of the finest situations about Granada, it overlooks the rock of the Alhambra, a great part of the city and commands a delicious view of the whole Vega and the distant mountains. When in the time of its glory it must truly have been a delicious summer residence; with its impenetrable shade, fountains, and running streams …

So much for the Alhambra and Generalife. The Cathedral which was never finished, is the only other building in Granada that deserves mentioning. It is inferior in grandeur and magnificence to that of Seville and has not so many rich chapels attached to it, but the beauty and elegance of the whole cannot fail to please all eyes. It has attached to it a Parochial Church and the Ancient Mosque of Moors, the latter is remarkable for nothing but the extreme simplicity and freedom from all ornament in the inside. The outside is handsome, with a good deal of tracery work, and very large Arabic characters all round the building; before the high Altar of this ancient mosque are two magnificent mausoleums beneath which are interred the bodies of Ferdinand and Isabella, Philip IV[5] and Gonzalos de Cordova the great Captain. The latter was buried in a fine convent of the Monks of St. Jerome, endowed by himself, but being pulled down by the French his body was removed to the Royal vault. The great dome of this Cathedral is a noble specimen of Architecture, and it is said that many people of science visit Granada solely for the purpose of seeing this. There are some good paintings, and two or three splendid altars of Santiago and St. Michael. On every other pillar of the cathedral is written in large letters the following singular exhortation, which shows that the Priests never omit getting a penny where they can do it. "Nadie se paseé; hable con las Mugeres; ni esté en corillos en estas naves, pena de ex communion y dos ducados por obras pias". That is "nobody shall walk about, talk with the women or form parties in these naves, under pain of <u>excommunication and two ducats</u> for pious purposes." What can be more absurd than to put the greatest curse the Church can bestow on a level with a trivial fine.

Under one of the Chapels of the Cathedral, stands the foundation of the famous Torre Turpiana, discovered in the year 1588. The form and style of building, left no doubt that it was originally a work of the Phoenicians. Don Juan

Mendes de Salvatierra was then Archbishop of Granada; when the workmen who were then employed in digging in the foundation discovered a long square case of lead; it was opened, and found to contain a bone, a triangular bit of linen, and a scroll of parchment filled with characters of different languages. So long ago as the reign of Nero this tower was called a very ancient one. Antiquarians declared the parchment to be very ancient and that it was not made of the skin of any animal now used for that purpose. At the top was a cross formed by five little crosses; after which came a long writing in Arabic, on the subject of which the Pope under pain of excommunication commanded the most rigorous silence. Under the writing was a long figure formed of several squares in each of which was a Roman character, the rest were Greek. When the Roman letters were united, they formed a prophecy in Spanish, concerning the end of the world; and the language was as pure as that spoken at Court at present. Each of the Greek letters were followed by two Arabic characters, but the signification of this could not be made out. Afterwards came the signature of St. Cecil, Bishop of Granada. The parchment concludes with the declaration of Patricius the Priest as follows. "The servant of God Cecil being in Iberia and seeing the end of his days approach, said to me in secret that he was assured of Martyrdom. But as he was extremely fond of his treasure of Relics he commended it to me and besought me to conceal it, that it might not fall into the hands of Infidels; he observed that he had travelled both by sea and land to procure it and that this treasure would remain hidden until it please God to make it manifest; and I, to do what I thought was best, concealed it in the place where it is deposited, having supplicated God to take it under his protection. These relics are; a prophecy of St John the Evangelist concerning the end of the world, the half of the linen with which the Virgin Mary wiped away her tears at the passion of her son, and a bone of St Stephen, the first martyr" The bone and linen are still present in the Cathedral, and on particular days are exposed to the veneration of the pious. Philip II wished to see these rarities. A Canon was deputed to convey them. The King having fallen ill did not neglect so good an opportunity of curing himself. He applied the linen to the part affected, and finding it effectual, he stole a thread of it caused it to be enshrined, and placed it amongst the relics of the Escorial.

Granada is at present in a sad state of decline, its sole manufactures are in silk, but these once so famous are at present of no consideration, and their machinery despicable. The silk however produced here still maintains its reputation and is considered the best in Spain. If it were not for the number of people you see in street you would think Granada an uninhabited place, and that it had

---

5   This is an error on Greg's part. King Philip IV was buried in the Escorial. Greg probably confused him with Philip the Fair, husband of Juana the Mad and father of Charles V, whose tomb is in the Capilla Real alongside Juana's parents – Ferdinand and Isabella, the Catholic monarchs.

remained so ever since the expulsion of the Moors. The Moors on the opposite coast of Africa offer up prayers every friday for the recovery of Granada, which is said to be the only part of Spain which they regret. The last Moorish Ambassador who came to Spain obtained permission of the Court to visit Granada; as he entered the Alhambra, overcome by his feelings he could not refrain from tears, and exclaimed "by the folly of our Ancestors we have been deprived of this delightful Paradise."

Journal

The excessive cold and want of every comfort and accommodation, deprived me in some degree of the complete satisfaction, I should otherwise have enjoyed during my short residence in this celebrated city. I always left my horrid dungeon, after washing and shaving in the open air, and swallowing a hasty breakfast at an open window and wandered up and down, with my pencil and paper in my hand, every spot in the neighbourhood of Granada. Sometimes I spent the morning in the palace of the Alhambra or the gardens of the Generalife, or strolling through the Albaicin to try to discover the features of the Moors in any of its present inhabitants; sometimes climbing to the top of the lofty hills behind the city and looking down on the Alhambra and the wide extended Vega, or gazing on the towering peaks of the Sierra; and sometimes to vary the walk rambled on the Vega to look at those imposing objects from below. My "Olla"[6] was generally ready at 3 o'clock, after which I walked till it was dark then went to a Coffee house, and afterwards to the theatre. The theatre is large and handsome, finished during the stay of the French; the actors were all indifferent except one who having fallen under the displeasure of the Inquisition, only made his appearance on particular occasions. The routine of the plays, operas and farces, was the same as at Seville. The dancing such as no modest man or woman could look at without a blush of shame and indignation. Doña Francisca's parties never commenced till after the theatre closed, consequently were extremely late, and the misery of dressing for them, not trifling. The company there was always very miscellaneous and like all other Spanish tertullias, not pleasant to a foreigner, or indeed to any stranger; for every lady having her "cortego" from whom she expects exclusive attention, and every gentleman having a particular lady to whom likewise he wishes to pay his exclusive attention, and neither of them, sufficient delicacy or good breeding, to know how uncomfortable a stranger must necessarily feel in such a situation, he seldom gets half a dozen words from anybody, and though he is capable and willing to begin and maintain a conversation, it is impossible for him to make the attempt when he sees all the company divided into tête a tête parties. This is an observation that almost every foreigner must make on going for the first time into a Spanish tertulia. We always had to go armed after dark, as the robberies were frequent and daring, and besides robbing they sometimes stripped the person to his shirt and sent him home in that state. It was curious enough to see the whole party turn out from Doña Francisca's, some armed with pikes, and some with swords almost as long. On the evening of the **19th** when I went to my lodgings to get my sword, before going to the theatre, to my no small surprise I found I. Hodgson who had been arrived about two hours; his letter, written from Cadiz 10 days or a fortnight before, never having come to hand. Intending to visit Malaga, Gibraltar, and if possible, part of Africa before returning to Cadiz, we determined to leave Granada, as soon as we had seen everything there, or rather as soon as I. Hodgson had, for there was not a place within two miles, that I had not visited many times. When we had done this, we agreed with some Muleteers to take us to Malaga for 5 dollars each. On **Tuesday 24th of January**, after having waited till two o'clock, to receive our letters we set out, each mounted on a good mule, in company with the head Muleteers; the loaded beasts and the rest having departed at break of day. We set off much later than we ought to have done, having nine leagues to go and the greater part the distance the road being bad, and dangerous. The weather had broken and rain began to fall, two days before leaving Granada; it did not rain when we set out, but the view as we crossed the Vega was very different from what it was when we first approached it. The Sierra Nevada was no longer visible and clouds of the blackest and most stormy hue being heavy upon the lower Sierras, and spread a deep gloom over the City and surrounding Country. As we passed along the Vega, to the left of us lay the hill of Padul, where Abdali stopped, and turned to bid a last adieu to Granada. As he gazed upon it, he could not help bursting into tears, and bewailing the bitterness of his fate; when his mother thus reproached him: "Thou dost well my son to weep like a woman for the loss of that kingdom, which thou knewest not how to defend and to die for, like a man." To our right at a considerable distance, and extending almost to the foot of the Sierra Elvira, lay the Soto de Roma formerly a Royal domain, but now belonging to one who well deserves such a gift from Spain; that is, our gallant General Wellington. It is about 6 miles long by 4 broad, and includes the finest part of the Vega, being well wooded and containing many populous villages. It is said to bring him in very considerable rents. It is at present under the care of General O Lawlor, Governor-General of the City and Kingdom of Granada, a gentleman to whom we had letters, and by whom we were most kindly and politely received. It was from him that I got a passport, replacing the one that I had forgotten at Seville.

At the top of the hills which bound the Vega, we stopped a while to breathe our mules, and take a last farewell look at the city and plain we were leaving behind, and which probably it would never be our fate to see again. These consid-

---

[6] Olla podrida is a Spanish stew.

erations caused us both some pain; but descending the hill to a place more sheltered from the wind, we stopped again to take some refreshment and soon forgot our feelings by repeated visits to our leathern wine bottle ...[7]

We now got amongst the mountains, and had to descend some such steep
and dangerous passes, that we were obliged to walk, not liking to trust our necks
even to such safe creatures as the Spanish mules generally are. To add to our
distress, darkness and heavy rain overtook us, before we had advanced much
more than halfway to Alhama; my mule got so tired I could hardly make it go; and
as misfortunes never come alone, I contrived to tear my Lisbon Capote,[8] and
lose a new pair of Gloves that cost me near 2 dollars. We arrived at last wet, fatigued and out of humour at Alhama, the wind being in our faces, and cutting in
the extreme. The posada was of the usual kind; for it is very rare indeed to meet
with better than the generality, and it is almost impossible to imagine one worse
– I had to cover myself with my wet Capote, and manage, as I could, but happen
what might, I never lost my sleep, and I awoke next morning, after having enjoyed a comfortable night's rest. Before setting off in the morning we took a walk
through the town, which is most nobly situated on the summit of a perpendicular rock of 300 feet high; at the bottom of which rushes an impetuous torrent;
part of the old walls and citadel still exist, though in ruins, but the aqueduct is still
in good preservation. In the time of the Moors it must have been a place of considerable strength and was I believe one of the last places which fell into the
hands of the Christians, before Granada was taken. We set off about 8 o'clock
from Alhama, the wind bitter and so strong I could with great difficulty keep my
seat on the mule; in the very streets of the town the ice was several inches thick.
We kept along the foot of the Sierra Texada, covered halfway down the side with
snow, and passing one hill after another about mid-day we came in sight of the
Mediterranean sea, stretching its blue waters over the tops of the hills we had still
to pass. The greater part of this days journey lay through wild and romantic hills;
at one time we kept along the bottom of some deep cleft among the rocks, at another we kept winding round the sides of a number of successive hills or descending very steep and rocky declivities and frequently the narrow path hung
over some rapid torrent. Towards evening, we descended into the vallies, and experienced very remarkable and sudden change of climate. At the summit of the
hills we had just crossed, we left everything buried in frost and snow and ourselves perishing with a sharp wind; in short the climate there was severe winter.
But as we approached Velez Malaga, the air was as mild as a summer evening's,
the people thinly clad, and the immense size of the aloes and reeds, and the extensive plantations of the Sugar cane sufficiently attested to the warmth of the climate. In the vallies were orange and Lemon trees; on the hills' Vineyards and Fig
trees; and the whole formed a pleasant variegated appearance. We passed two or
3 Sugar mills, erected here for the purpose of boiling the cane produced in the

neighbourhood. This year the proprietor, it is said, will make money, but the business instead of being encouraged by Government, has been almost ruined by the heavy duties imposed on the sugar thus made and at present not half the number of mills work as formerly. Velez contains about 8,000 inhabitants; it is a neat white town with the ruins of a Moorish castle situated on a small hill at the foot of a snow Sierra. We stopped at a posada just without the town, unquestionably the best we had seen in Spain; but even here they could give us nothing to eat.

Thursday 26th

We set off from Velez in good time, the view on leaving it was very pretty, the town having a very good appearance. Our road lay for some distance through low muddy lanes with hedges of high Canes on both sides; in one of these my mule unfortunately fell and tumbled me over its head. It was not the first time this had happened, for in coming down a rocky hill the day before I got an awkward fall over its head, and thought myself fortunate in coming off with a cut hand and very much dirtied. After going about one league of the five we had to go before reaching Malaga, we found ourselves upon the shore of the mediterranean and continued close on the edge of the water till we arrived at Malaga. The views of the different headlands, the water and Martello towers with which this coast is thickly lined for the prevention of smuggling, were generally very fine. In winding round some of these headlands, we were obliged to dismount, the path being so narrow and the precipice so great, that a single false step of the mules would have hurried us to instant destruction. Malaga as we approach it from this side has a very fine appearance, its Cathedral the slender spires of the churches, its old Castle, mole, and shipping, all being striking objects. We stopped at a very good Hotel with everything in the English style and a waiter who spoke English; all which was very agreeable to me who had seen nothing of the kind since leaving Lisbon.

We went that night to the theatre a small building and miserable performers. The play was called Othello and I suppose was taken from Shakespear, but so disguised that we could not exactly determine. The love affairs not being sufficiently intricate, it was altered to the Spanish taste. The Doge's son is introduced instead of Castro [i.e. Cassio], and he is made to be desperately in love with Desdemona and the whole rendered as complicated as possible. To heighten the effect of the last scene the Moor and Desdemona wandering in a forest in a dreadful storm of thunder and lightening, take refuge in a wretched hovel, the window of which to excite the feelings of the audience still more, is

[7] There follows a heavily crossed-out sentence which may well be of a confessional nature!

[8] A Capote is a cloak.

shattered by the lightning and falls to pieces in the clumsiest and most laughable manner that can be imagined.

The Cathedral of Malaga[9] is a handsome building, something on the plan of the one at Granada like it, never finished; and and its inside also like it, not so crowded with grants of indulgences to sinners as that of Seville. The Custom House is a very noble building, but like all other such buildings in Spain, it is on an immense scale, and quite unfinished. There are numberless remains of the Moors in old walls, towers, and castles. In the old Castle at the top of the hill which overhangs Malaga, the French erected a strong fort which commands the harbour and country round to a considerable extent; in the same spot they also built excellent barracks capable of containing a strong force. As soon as the French evacuated the place, the Spaniards as a sort of revenge for the miseries they had been forced to endure most absurdly pulled the whole to the ground; whereas if instead of doing this, they had placed a force there and defended it like men, they might have prevented the intrusion of any enemy. A short time ago many marble stones with Roman inscriptions upon them were dug up near the Alameda, and they still stand upon the same spot where they were discovered, acting the part of stumps, like the Gods and Goddesses in the Convent garden at Santiponce. Malaga is undoubtedly a very ancient city, and its claim to antiquity rests on rather better foundation than that of many other cities of Spain. The name is said to be derived from a Phoenician word signifying salt, and that they had formerly a large settlement here for salting fish. It is mentioned by Pliny and Strabo under the name of Malaca, and the latter states it to be about the same distance from Calpé or Gibraltar, as Calpé from Cadiz, which is the case.

We were anxious to proceed almost immediately to Gibraltar[10] by sea, not liking 3 days tedious and expensive journey, and liable to be robbed by the numerous smugglers who infest that coast, but the wind was contrary and not a vessel could move out of the bay, and the rain was so incessant and the rivers so swelled that it was impossible to proceed by land, and we were therefore compelled to wait, thankful that we have over our heads a comfortable hotel instead of a wretched Venta.

Malaga was taken from the Moors in 1487, that is 4 or 5 years, before Granada. The Cathedral was begun in 1528 and never will be finished. On the Alameda is a handsome fountain of white marble, said to have been sent as a present from Charles V to the republic of Venice to have been taken at sea by the famous Corsair Barbarossa; and retaken by Spanish galleys, and carried into Malaga where it has been suffered to remain. The new part of the town about the Alameda is open and well built, the old part quite the contrary.

Malaga suffered extremely in the Epidemies [sic] of 1800 and 1804; and vast numbers of the inhabitants were starved to death during the time the French held the town, for they seized on all provisions for themselves, and three or four miserable wretches were found dead in the streets every morning. Its present population may be estimated at 40,000. The principal exports of Malaga, are wines and fruit, which are carried to all parts of the world. The best wines of Malaga are said to be made from vines originally brought from the Rhine. A great number of Greeks frequent this port; the principal article they bring is wheat; the generality of them are fine looking men and the dress picturesque.

At length the rains having in some degree abated, and the wind still continuing contrary, we determined to set out by land, and hired horses for the purpose. As we had some fear of the smugglers who are very numerous on this coast we thought it well to make as good an appearance of defence as we could and therefore both of us carried a brace of pistols in our breast, and a long sword by our sides. After having to send back the horses twice in consequence of the rain coming on, we at last set out on the **31st** about one o'clock, intending to sleep that night at Fuengirola a small place 5 leagues from Malaga. I.H. and myself were mounted on tolerable horses, our guide, portmanteaus and a considerable number of loose parcels on a fine mule. We proceeded along a broad plain for about a league, and the view of Malaga and the hills behind was very pleasing. We now began to ascend a steep [hill] nearly knee deep in stiff white clay, when about half way up the mule fell and the man and all our luggage were rolled in the dirt; I had to dismount and to help the beast to rise, which we did after unloading it completely. We loaded again, and set off; but before it had proceeded 5 yards fell again, and in the shocking dirty state in which I then was, I had to ride back to Malaga to bring another horse. This misfortune delayed us two or three hours which made us rather uneasy, as the road we had to go was rather a dangerous one. Beyond this hill, we crossed another fine rich plain, which a few days ago had been flooded. A river of some breadth ran through the middle in summer however, it has little or no water in it. This river has changed its bed in a very remarkable manner within the last century; 70 or 80 years since they attempted to throw over it a very magnificent bridge, but just as they completed a few piers and arches, the river moved a little farther off; they continued building after it as fast as possible but in vain for the river completely gave them the slip, and now you cross it on a wooden platform thrown across three or four low piers. This singular bridge is of very great extent; some of the arches are completed, others half done, and an immense number of piers where they have not commenced throwing the arch. It has now been discontinued many years, and is not likely to be taken in hand again. Several gentlemen of Malaga purchased this plain a short time ago

[9] Malaga Cathedral is still incomplete. The south tower lacks its full elevation and is known locally as *la Manquita* (the missing one).

[10] The British captured Gibraltar from the Spanish in 1704 during the War of the Spanish Succession. The Treaty of Utrecht (1713) at the end of this war confirmed their possession of it.

for the purpose of growing Cotton; the first crop had just paid expences, a second failed from some accident or other, and the French then taking possession of Malaga the Partnership was dissolved and the experiment has not since been made. After ascending a small hill we passed through a little village called Churiana where is made the greater part of the bread consumed in Malaga; and soon after entered a barren and uncultivated tract of country, furrowed Sierras on our right and at a short distance on our left, the Mediterranean. The road was both bad and dangerous having to pass many ravines formed by the rapid torrents which descend from these Sierras, and darkness had now completely closed in upon us; we expected every instant that our own horses would get out of the narrow track and fall; and our fears were yet greater lest any accident should happen to the horse carrying the luggage. At last however we arrived at a small village a league short of Fuengirolo, the place we had intended to have slept at. The posada was a wretched little hovel and as there was no room we were obliged to sit round the embers with the dirty inmates. When we had finished our supper of the prog we had brought with us, our beds were laid on the floor one on each side of the fire, and we lay down without in any way breaking up the family circle which did not move till an hour or two afterwards. Our host was one of the most dirty, idle and insolent of the dirtiest, idlest and most insolent of all the classes of men that Spain can boast of, that is the Posaderos or Innkeepers; we consequently did not find our situation particularly agreeable. In the night the children cried, and were brought to the fire to be cleared of vermin; which as soon as laid hold of, was thrown on the fire for our benefit, though we had ourselves been so badly bitten before that it was scarcely possible to get a moments sleep.

Wednesday 1st February
We got up very early, alike impatient to leave the filthy Posada and to proceed upon our journey. To our extreme mortification it rained very hard, but it was impossible to stay longer and we set out; meaning to reach Estepona before night, distant from where we slept about 10 leagues. The weather happily cleared up a little, though it continued showery; the road lay mostly upon the sand of the beach; some of the views of the Sierras fine but the shore was rather uninteresting. It is said that there is no ebb and flow of the Mediterranean in these parts; and from the appearance of this coast and the observations we made at Malaga we were convinced that if there is any tide here, it is very inconsiderable, or indeed scarcely perceptible. We reached Marbella, about one o'clock, and were about to proceed when the people at the posada said it would be impossible to cross the "rio verde" or green river; and that a gentleman had been waiting there four days, stopped by the same cause. We did not rely much upon the accuracy of Spanish information but having in the course of the morning crossed 12 or 14

torrents some very broad and of considerable depth we were inclined to credit what we heard and alighted not a little mortified at having to spend another day upon the road, and an additional night at a posada.

Marbella is a small neat fishing town and has the remains of an old Castle which the style of building shows to be Moorish.

Thursday 2nd

We set out from Marbella in company with Mr Devereux, a Malaga gentleman, and so extremely deaf as almost to prove an unsurmountable bar to conversation. After going about a league through the same kind of country we had passed through the day before, entirely overgrown with the palmeta or dwarf palm, we arrived at the rio Verde; it proved indeed deep and broad but we crossed it without difficulty; had we come the preceding day we should have been unable to get over, and so upon the whole it happened well that we did not leave Malaga, as we should undoubtedly have had to keep Mr D company in the little Posada of Marbella.

We passed in the course of the morning the remains of an aqueduct, which we could not determine at the moment to be Moorish or Roman, but our men informed us, that there stood near the place in which we then were, a great city of the Moors.[11]

We reached Estepona, another small fishing town like Marbella and distant from it but five leagues, about 2 o'clock in the afternoon and again to our mortification we were stopped short by hearing the ferry boat over the river Guadaro had been carried away; as it was distant 4 leagues and no venta was to be found on that side of the river we were compelled to stay at Estepona.

Estepona used to carry on an extensive trade in Anchovies which are caught in great abundance on this coast. Here too like Marbella, we find the remains of an old Moorish building which seems to have been the Citadel; from the top of it we had a good view of Gibraltar, which we already had for a glimpse of in the course of the day. All along this coast it presents the same appearance that is one perpendicular face of rock rising out of the sea, with two peaks, considerably above the elevation of the rest of the rock.

Friday 3rd

We now set out with full expectation of reaching Gibraltar in good time in the afternoon and we were not disappointed – The four leagues we had to go before reaching the Guadaro, lay entirely over flat alluvial ground washed down from the Sierras, and overgrown with the palmeta. The Sierras here are dark lofty and cut into a thousand shapes by the fury of the winter torrents. They afford shelter for

[11]   A marginal note reads "It was the remains of the Roman Carteia."

the numerous bands of smugglers who inhabit this coast, and who are sometimes so powerful that it would be in vain for the military to attempt to pursue them to their huts and caves among the mountains. We met a strong force between Estepona and Marbella who were coming to be stationed along the coast for the purpose of repressing these smugglers.

We crossed the Guadaro in the ferry boat and might have done so the evening before had we come forward. The views of Gibraltar become more and more interesting the nearer you approach and shortly put on an appearance truly grand and magnificent; and our admiration was increased on reflecting that this stupendous rock rising so boldly from the shores of Spain, belonged to our Countrymen, that it was a little spot where freedom had found an asylum, whilst all the surrounding kingdoms were groaning under the scourge of tyranny and despotism. After riding for some time along the low sandy istmus which connects Gibraltar with the shores of Spain we arrived at the Spanish lines, which are nothing more than a few small dirty huts, where some soldiers reside; our companion, as being a subject of Spain, had to pay 3 shillings, but this is a fine which the English are not subject to.

The former Spanish lines erected immediately after the siege, were a fine and noble piece of work, and in case of a second attack might have annoyed our garrison much; and when the late revolution broke out, we obtained the unwilling consent of the Cortes to destroy them, for fear of their falling into the hands of the French. In making the necessary excavations for blowing up these works, 1000 barrels of gunpowder were discovered which the Spaniards knew nothing of; had this immense quantity exploded it is difficult to say what might have been the consequences. After crossing a very narrow artificial causeway we entered the town by 3 tremendous lines of batteries, each commanded by an infinity of others. We seemed to have entered all at once, into a different country, if not into another world; the neatness, cleanliness and elegance of the streets and buildings, the noise of carts and carriages, the bustle and activity of the inhabitants, formed indeed a striking contrast to the gloomy solitudes, and filthy huts to which we had been so long accustomed, and which we had just left.

We had passed through no medium to prepare us for such a change, but in one instant, we were in the deserts of Spain, and in the next we found ourselves in the centre of the luxuries and splendour of an English city, where as there is no room to spare, everything has been laid out with the utmost attention. But nothing struck us so much as the appearance of our countrymen, all clean, neat, shaved and well dressed with handsome, open, generous countenances and liberty stamped upon their foreheads whilst the people we had just left are far from being any one of these; always dirty, ill-looking and rolled up in a dirty brown cloak from under which nothing can be seen but a dark scowling pair of eyes. What is particularly striking to all new comers to Gibraltar is the strange mixture of people of every nation which are seen in all the streets. You may frequently see standing together, Jews, Turks, Moors, Algerines, Greeks, Spaniards and English, all in their peculiar dress and speaking their own language. The numbers of Jews are very great and the present governor is anxious to get rid of some of them, being Jews in character as well as name.

We took up our lodgings at a good Hotel, where we could refresh ourselves comfortably after the fatigues of a troublesome journey. We met with all the politeness and warm hospitality from our friends, which characterises our nation. From Mr Stedman and his lady, Miss Myers, that was, from Mr Dugaild and Mr Lee we received particular attention; the latter fixed the following morning for a visit to the celebrated excavations in the rock, made for the purpose of placing cannon for the defence of that part of the istmus not commanded by the other batteries.

Saturday 4th

Mr Lee had provided a sergeant of the artillery to accompany us and we set out. These excavations are indeed a most wonderful work, and will for ever remain a monument of British industry and ingenuity. They are very capacious and extend for a long way round the perpendicular side of the rock. In one part which projects out beyond the rest, the rock has been cut away so as to form a great chamber, called St George's hall; cannon are placed all round except on the side on which you enter. Some years ago the Governor gave a grand ball in this place, it must indeed have been well worth seeing, for the handsome dresses of the company, the cannon and the sound of the fine band of music in this lofty rugged hall, must have been a new and striking spectacle. The rock is of a limestone extremely hard and durable and the expence of making the excavations must have been enormous. It may be doubted if this expence, has been repaid by the advantage derived from these new batteries; it is said they could not be fired above two or three times in succession as the smoke would be sufficient to suffocate all those who might be in the excavations; and it might be asked, was not Gibraltar sufficiently strong before? These works were commenced soon after the siege, and only lately completed; they might at least be a place of security for the inhabitants or wounded, in case of another bombardment, a thing however never likely to take place again; for it is considerably stronger now than at the time of the late siege, and then all that human ingenuity and perseverance could do, was attempted. We afterwards ascended to the light house situated at the centre of the three summits, it is not the highest point of all but is built here because it is in sight of the town which the highest is not. At this moment a few Soldiers reside who have the care of the signals.

From this point is a view, for beauty and extent perhaps not excelled by any in the world. To the South you see the shores of Africa extending for an immense distance to the East, and as far as Cape Espartil towards the West; on this coast you distinguish the high promontory of Tetuan, the Promontory, istmus [sic] and City of Ceuta, the city Tangiers; above all, rising to a height far greater than Gibraltar, the rugged mountain or rather rock of Calpeshill one of the Two Pillars of Hercules, and far inland stretch a long and lofty ridge of snow capped Sierras, probably a branch of the Atlas Mountains. To the east the blue waters of the Mediterranean extend further than the eye can reach. To the North East you see the beautiful line of the Spanish coast as far as Fuenriolo [sic, for Fuengirolo] and almost as far as Malaga, with the snowy sierras of Velez Malaga and Granada. To the north, you see far into the interior of Spain. To the west the beautiful bay of Gibraltar covered with shipping beyond the handsome town of Algeciris the neighbouring coast, and behind it lofty hills, and to the left, the straights of Gibraltar. To conclude, you are standing on the sharp ridge of a rock 1200 feet high, whilst on one side immediately below you is the town of Gibraltar, and on the other side at the bottom of a perfectly perpendicular precipice dash the waves of the Mediterranean. The extent of this view, even on a map astonishes us, but to see each object in its peculiar form and colouring is indeed striking. We were not fortunate enough to see any of the monkies which abound on the perpendicular side of the rock, which is to the east, they informed us that 30, or 40 had passed over to the west side in the morning, but though we returned the way which we were told they had gone we did not meet any. In the evening we took a walk to Europa point, the most Southerly part of Gibraltar, and being a beautiful evening and near sunset we enjoyed one of the most enchanting views that can be imagined, of the coast of Africa and the straights and bay of Gibraltar.

Sunday 5th

We breakfasted with Mr Dugaild and went with him to the Governor's Chapel, a small neat building adjoining his house; we unfortunately sat so far from the pulpit that we could not hear much, but not having been in a place of worship for three or four months, it was a great pleasure to be even present, and one which those only know how to apreciate who have been in similar circumstances.

After Church we commenced a long ramble upon the rock, Mr D. being our guide. We walked nearly as far as Europa point, and and then began to ascend by an angular road, the descent here being too steep to ascend in a straight line. About halfway up, is situated St Michael's Cave, a very large hollow in the rock covered with stalactitical incrustations. These however are smoked by the illuminations, so frequently kept there, that they have lost all there [sic] lustre and are become perfectly brown. They say that the effect is very fine when the cavern is well lighted up; the same may be said of any cave of similar size and form, but owing to the aforesaid cause it differs but little from other caves which are not stalactitic. You cannot proceed without ladders and torches as you shortly arrive at a steep descent where the passage becomes extremely narrow. On the whole it does not bear a moment's comparison with the wonderful but little known, subterranean Palace of Skepewrinky in Ireland, where you may wander about [for] hours, nay days, your guide assures you, through galleries and domes 40 or 50 feet high, adorned with the most fantastic columns arches and festoons of Calcareous matter, whose perfect whiteness and delicate forms have never been injured by the hand of man, or sullied by the smoke of torches.

Having arrived within 150 or 200 feet of the summit we entered a passage cut through the rock from side to side; it was done by order and under the direction of General O'Hara,[12] and always goes by the name of "O'Hara's Folly." Having passed through this we found ourselves on the edge of the great precipice, washed by the sea; above us was another precipice not quite perpendicular but nearly so. Mr D. told us to follow him, which we did, though had we known where he was going to take us we should certainly not have attempted it. After keeping for a few yards along a narrow ledge of the rock he began to ascend by some rude half formed steps, formed out of the projecting points of the rock, made also by the orders of the same O'Hara. After advancing up two or three steps we wished to return, but this was next to impossible, for independantly [sic] of the difficulty of descending the high rugged steps; it was unavoidable to turn our faces round towards the sea and the height was so great as instantly to make us giddy. We were therefore compelled to proceed, and arrived in a few minutes at the top, and were then ever more alarmed at looking down upon the path we had just ascended than we had been whilst accomplishing it. The part on which we now stood was nothing more than a narrow ridge of rocks, with the precipice to the east, and an extremely rapid descent towards the west. It is the highest point of the rock being very near 1500 feet above the sea. We went then to the southerly point of the rock where stand the ruins of St Georges Tower built by O'Hara for the signal post or light House, and destroyed as soon as completed by lightening or, as the Spaniards say, by the hand of God to punish the presumption of the general in building so high a tower upon such a point. We descended by the Mediterranean stairs, on the Eastern side of the rock, but where the declivity is not so great as more to the N. being cut angularly and defended by a strong wall they can be descended without difficulty or danger. We returned to the town by way of Europa Point and arrived about 5 o'clock, some little fatigued with our excursion.

[12] General Charles O'Hara (1740–1802) joined the Coldstream Guards as a Cornet at the age of 12. Steadily promoted through his service, he fought in the American War of Independence. He was the general who surrended the sword of the British Commander-in-Chief Lord Cornwallis at Yorktown in 1781, thus ending the war. As Governor of Gibraltar (1795–7) he was very popular, being famous for his lavish hospitality and was known as 'The Old Cock of the Rock' by the men.

We dined and spent the evening at Mr D's.

Monday 6th

Ever since leaving Granada, we had determined, if the weather permitted, and if we did not find letters at Gibraltar hastening our return to Cadiz, to visit some part of the African Coast; to set our feet if only for a few minutes in another quarter of the world. Prudence and the facility of the voyage suggested Ceuta; nor, until arriving at Gibraltar, until seeing the beautiful outline of the opposite coast, and conversing with those who had travelled in Barbary, did our ambition rise higher than to visit the Spanish colony.

But imagining ourselves already set down in Ceuta, that fortress seen and the first sensations on touching African ground over; our desire became extreme to see something of the interior of the country, and of a nation differing entirely in Religion, Manners, Customs and dress from those of Europe. We made the necessary inquiries. Our friend Mr Stedman the Civil Secretary, told us that we should have our throats cut if we attempted it; but the best informed assuring us that us [sic], that the journey from Tangiers to Tetuan was not only safe but perfectly easy and pleasant; we determined most firmly to put it in execution. Taking a boat to Ceuta; thence to Tetuan, crossing the country to Tangiers, and sailing thence to Tarifa or Gibraltar according as we should find vessels going; seemed to be the best plan and was the one fixed upon.

We accordingly employed this morning in engaging a boat, but could not agree with any about the prices, whilst still busy in inquiring, Mr Lee sent us word that the Commissioner's Yacht would sail on the following Morning to Tangiers, and if we chose to change our plans we might have a place in it. This we instantly did, and arranged our plans accordingly. We employed our time before dinner in a walk to the sandy istmus, and round the edge of the rock to Catalan Bay, which is far as can be gone on the Eastern side of the rock.

It was on this side where the French were employed in making a deep mine with the intention of blowing up a great piece of the rock, this was however prevented by peace. People do not agree as to the effects which would have resulted from this explosion – General Elliot said that had he known of this mine he would not have been so easy as he was. The enemy approached this mine unobserved by the garrison having hollowed out a path at the foot of the rock, on the north side all round to the place where they were digging the mine. There is on this side of the rock a very considerable debris of silicious sand, originating from the sand stone on which the limestone rests; the latter it is, which forms the great mass of the rock; the former only appearing on this side, low down and disposed in regular strata inclined upwards at a small angle.

We dined with Mr Stedman, and went with him in the evening to a mask Ball at Mr Arengo's being the last night of Carnival.

Thursday 7th

We were almost distracted with the number of things we had to do before 10 o'clock the hour fixed by the Captain of the yacht for meeting us upon the new mole distant from our inn upwards of a mile. As our clothes were not returned from the washerwoman we could not pack our portmanteaus; at 7 o'clock we went to breakfast with Mr Stedman, who would not leave us afterwards till he had shown us the public Library. We had then to call upon our friends to bid them goodbye, get money and provisions for the journey, pack up, pay bills etc. We however contrived to make our appearance on the mole at the appointed time. The Captain shortly made his appearance and we got under weigh between 11 and 12 o'clock, leaving Gibraltar behind with a fine gale of wind.

Gibraltar

[Gibraltar] is the famous Mount Calpe of the Ancients and one of the Pillars of Hercules. By it the Moors made their entrance into Spain in the year 714. It was called by them Ghiblaltath or the mountain of entrance, whence comes the present name of Gibraltar. It was one of the last places held by the Moors in Spain being taken by the Spaniards only in the year 1462 or 30 years before the fall of Granada. In 1704 Gibraltar was taken by the English, in the following manner. Our fleet then lying off the rock had made some slight attacks but in vain, when one day a number of sailors being half drunk, thought it would be a fine thing to say they had set their feet on shore. They made the attempt, and finding nobody to oppose them landed on the part where the Tumpers Battery is now erected. Finding themselves still unmolested, they hoisted a red jacket for a signal to the fleet, which came to their assistance. The sailors were attacked by the Garrison but maintained their post till succors arrived when they immediately made themselves master of the whole rock. It was beseiged by the Spaniards the following year and again in 1727, equally without success. Every means that human ingenuity could suggest, was tried by the combined forces of France and Spain both by sea and land, in that ever memorable siege which lasted from the year 1779 till the Peace of Utrecht in 1783. It may however be considered as terminated in September 1782 when the famous floating Batteries of D'Arçon were burnt by red hot balls from the English artillery. The Court of Spain wearied by a fruitless blockade, resolved to take the fortress by some extraordinary expedient, against which the natural strength of the place, and the skill of General Elliot should prove unavailing. Plans poured in from all quarters, some bold to extravagance, some so whimsical it was scarcely possible to look upon them as serious. One of these sent to Ministers formally proposed to throw up in front of the lines of St Rockea a prodigious mount higher than Gibraltar which would consequently deprive that fortress of its principal means of defence. The author had calculated the quantity of cubic fathoms of earth, the number of hands and the time that would be required by this enormous undertaking and proved that it would be less expensive and less destructive than the prolongation of the siege upon the plan on which it had been begun. Another plan proposed to fill the bombs with a substance so strongly mephitic than on bursting in the fortress, they would either put to flight, or poison the besieged with their exhalations.

The plan of D'Arçon was at length presented, and engaged the more serious attention of the Spanish Government. Scarcely anything is generally known respecting it, except what relates to the ten floating batteries which on the 13th September 1782 foolishly exposed themselves to the fire of Gibraltar and were reduced to ashes by the red hot shot from the English Batteries. Don Ventura Moreno who had the command of the floating Batteries in consequence of a letter of General Crillon, hastened their departure and placed them in an order contrary to that which should have been adopted. In consequence of this mistake only two could place themselves at the concerted distance. These were the Pastora commanded by Moreno himself, and the Tallapiedra, on board of which were the Prince of Nassau and d'Arçon but they were exposed to the fire of the most formidable battery that of the Royal Bastion instead of all ten being drawn up round the old Mole and receiving only sideways the fire of that battery. The only two batteries which occupied this dangerous post made great havoc and sustained dreadful loss. The Tallapiedra received a fatal shot. In spite of all precautions a red hot ball penetrated to the dry part of the vessel. The T.piedra had opened her fire about ten in the morning the ball struck her between 3 and 5. The mischief did not appear immediate until midnight. The St. Juan shared the same fate. It appears certain that the 8 others remained untouched. But what was still more distressing, everything was wanting at once; cables to tow off the batteries in case of accident and boats to receive the wounded. The attack was to have been supported by ten ships and upwards of sixty gunboats. Neither boats, ships, nor gunboats, made their appearance. Lastly according to the projected position the gunboats were to have been seconded by 180 pieces of Cannon at the lines of St Rocke. Nearly 400 pieces of artillery were to have opened at once upon the North Battery, Montagu Bastion and Orange Bastion. With a superiority of near 300 pieces, D'Arçon flattered himself that he should be able to silence the artillery of the fortress. What was his Consternation when he found that the Besiegers had no more than sixty or seventy pieces to oppose to more that 280 belonging to the Besieged.[13]

The combined squadrons remained quiet spectators of this tremendous scene. Guichen who commanded the French ships, sent to offer assistance to Moreno who replied that he had no occasion for any. Matters continued to grow worse and no remedy could be devised. Eight of the ten batteries were at too great a distance to do or sustain much injury. The other two bore in their bosoms the elements of destruction. Moreno dispairing of being able to save any of them and resolving not to let any of them fall into the hands of the English, directed that those that were already on fire should be suffered to burn and the rest committed to the flames. Such was the result of this day on which were annihilated ten vessels, the masterpieces of human industry and ingenuity, the building of which had cost three millions of livres and whose artillery anchors rigging etc. amounted to near two millions and a half more.

Such is the account which Bourgoing gives of the destruction of the floating Batteries. It is impossible to say what would have been the issue of an attack carried on under so many disadvantages, had it been executed on the plan intended, and laid out by D'Arcon. It seems however highly probable, that the result would have been little different from what really happened. All the artillery from the istmus, the ships and gunboats had completely failed in their vigorous &repeated attacks. The same would have happened again had they again been brought into action. Bourgoing says that of the ten floating batteries only two were near enough to do or sustain any injury; those two were burned; and had the other eight taken up their appointed position a position much nearer our batteries than that of the two which were burned; we have reason to suppose that they would have shared a similar fate. It is true that the batteries from the position they took, were exposed to the full, instead of the oblique fire of the Royal Battery; the one however which did the principal mischief, that is, the one that threw the red hot balls was Willis's Battery, situated higher up the rock; and to the fire of this, they would have been much more exposed in the projected position, than in the real one. Probably the only difference in the result of the day would have been the destruction of all the ten batteries by the red hot balls, instead of only two being destroyed by them, and the other eight by the torches of their owners. The place has been made much stronger since the siege by new batteries of every description, new works are still carrying on, and in the opinion of most engineers it is impregnable. It is not probable that it will ever have to endure another siege.

The complement of men for the defence of the place is estimated at 12,000. The number of Cannon now mounted exceeds eight hundred, and by means of excavations in the rock, batteries run completely round with the exception of a small distance. The fortifications towards the istmus are tremendous and you enter the town by three or four immense batteries one above another, separated by deep trenches, and every battery is commanded by two or three, sometimes by eight or ten, others. The istmus itself has been cut through by a wide and deep trench into which the sea flows; it is passable only along a very narrow

---

[13]   This page of the manuscript has a diagram of the floating batteries, reproduced in the plate section.

causeway and this is commanded by half the artillery of the Garrison. The town of Gibraltar owing to the unevenness of the ground is very irregularly built, but nevertheless with English neatness and cleanliness. Towards the South end of the town are many neat pretty gardens, and as extensive as the nature of the place will allow. The number of large trees is considerable, they had just put out their leaves when we were there, and the beautiful light green of their foliage, the fine dark blue of the sea below with the brown rugged rock above, made together a scene singular and enchanting. The climate of Gibraltar was fine and very healthy before it was infested with the Epidemic Fever introduced into Spain from the West Indies in the year 1800. In the year 1804 it made dreadful ravages in Gibraltar; during the month of October 120 persons died daily. It has been visited several times since by this scourge, though not with the same violence, there being fewer subjects for it. During the last year 1814 it made considerable ravages, but it is hoped this will not occur again, as the present Governor, General Don, is making the most vigorous exertions for preventing its return. From the situation of Gibraltar it is necessarily exposed to great heats in summer, and the inhabitants complain still more of the influence of the Levant wind. An old Moorish wall of astonishing height runs almost from the bottom to the top of the rock dividing it into two parts. In the northern of these two parts stands the old town, containing from 8 to 10,000 inhabitants, in the southern part, stands the south, or new town, which consists principally of public buildings, barracks, stone houses etc. The society of Gibraltar is said to be not very good, owing to feuds subsisting between the inhabitants themselves, and still more so between the inhabitants and the military, who often abuse the power placed in their hands by the circumstance of Gibraltar being a garrisoned town. There is always kept in the magazines provisions for three years, and in time of war for six or seven years. The meat for the supply of the place is brought over from Barbary, the Emperor of Morocco permitting the export of 2,000 head of Cattle annually. The Contractor is bound to supply the Garrison with beef at 2 pence, half penny per pound, and with the overplus he supplies the inhabitants with what they want at 10d. It has often been a question whether Gibraltar in any way repays us for the enormous expence we are at in maintaining an establishment there. There seems to be little doubt but that it has done, by the facilities it has aforded [sic] to our commerce during the late war. In time of war with Spain it certainly is of the utmost importance, as a depot, and the protection which it affords to our shipping. Besides which it prevents the command which Spain would otherwise have over the commerce of the Mediterranean by stationing a fleet in the ports of Ceuta and Gibraltar; or their vessels being allowed to pass in safety from Ceuta to Algeziras.

The following are the measurements of the different parts of the rock, given me by one of the Engineers:

	Feet
Height of the rock from St George's tower to the level of the sea	1470
Height of the rock mortar	1330
of the Signal House	1276
of the Grand Battery	30
of the Old Mole or Devil's tongue	3
New Mortar battery above the istmus	580
Queen's battery ditto	440

	Yards
Distance from the Spanish lines to the rock	750
Length of the rock from the Waterport to Europa point	4700
or nearly 2¾ miles	
Distance of the old and new Mole head to Algeziris.	8752
From the old Mole to Algeziris. by the istmus	16,000
Breadth of the istmus at the Spanish lines	1750
Breadth over the rock	950
Breadth of the istmus at the advance huts	1200
Distance from the King's lines to the extremity of the istmus	3000
Thus the circumference of the rock is 7 miles and ¼	
The length of it not quite 2¾ miles	
The distance across the bay from the town of Gibraltar to Algeziras.	5 miles
The distance from the same to the same round by the istmus	9 miles
The breadth of the istmus at the Spanish lines	1 mile
Ditto at the shortest part a little more than ½ mile.	

Our company on board the yatch [sic] was but small, consisting only of one of the contractors for Cattle, and an officer of Dillon's regiment lately disbanded. The wind which had been strong and favourable all the morning had carried out a great number of vessels, some of which had been wind bound upwards of a month or five weeks, and their white sails gliding along the blue coast of Africa formed a lively and beautiful scene, from which however our attention was continually called off, to gaze upon the magnificent rock of Gibraltar, now rapidly sinking in the background. The whole coast of the bay with the towns of St Roque and Algeziras were perfectly seen and added much to the beauty of the prospect. In doubling Cabrita point, the western extremity of Gibraltar bay, the wind unfortunately changed, and we saw all the vessels which had sailed that morning successively put back again into the Bay.

By means however of the lightness of our vessel and the quantity of sail she carried, we were enabled to reach a little after dark the point of Tarifa, the southern extremity of Europe. About ten oclock we found ourselves immediately off

115

the long rocky promontory on which the Lighthouse stands; and we went on deck to see it. I seldom recollect to have witnessed a more enchanting spectacle. There was not the slightest breeze and our little vessel was quite still and stationary; but high breakers were falling upon the rocks scattering their white spray over the dark body of the lighthouse, and making a gentle and melancholic music; whilst a bright moon lighted the tops of the neighbouring hills, gave to the breakers the appearance of clouds of silver, or was clearly reflected from the smooth water which surrounded the vessel. The sailors informed us that however calm the straights might be, breakers were always to be seen on these rocks. After enjoying this delightful scene for some time we retired to our beds. Mine was formed of a number of wet flags and pennants, and the rest, of what the Captain had on board.

Wednesday 8th

When we went on deck in the morning we found ourselves some miles nearer Gibraltar than on the preceding evening and the wind still continued unfavourable. By means of the tide and of tacking as close under the Spanish coast as possible, we were enabled to get a little to the westward of Tangiers,[14] and then crossed over with a side wind, the current carrying us a little to the eastward. The singular fact is well known that in the Straights of Gibraltar, although there is a regular tide flowing eastward and westward alternately, near the sides, yet that in the middle the current always runs to the eastward, and that too, with considerable rapidity, at the rate of 3 or four knots an hour. This current is many miles in breadth. Hence it has been a question often agitated, what becomes of so immense body of water, there being no outlet in the eastern part of the Mediterranean, on the contrary, receiving the waters of the Black Sea and of many large rivers. As Evaporation alone does not satisfactorily account for so immense consumption of water, though to some indeed this does appear a sufficient cause, many have imagined that there must be an under current, which carried off the water again; this supposition seems to have arisen rather from not being able to think of a probable cause which might account for the phenomenon, than from any actual experiment. Captain Lewes told us that he had been employed in sounding in the Straights by Admiral Duckworth; and he assured us that near the middle he had found bottom at 357 fathoms and that the line after being carried sometime by the current to the eastward, began to be carried with considerable rapidity towards the West. He said there could be no deception and that he was perfectly convinced that there really existed an under current. The central current extends to within a mile and a half of each side.

Towards evening we began to approach the African Coast. The ideas of Africa and sand, are so intimately connected that it is difficult to separate them, and we of course expected to find if not the whole coast at least a considerable part sandy and barren. We were however agreeably disappointed to find shrubs and a beautiful verdure, even to the water edge, a remarkable contrast to the opposite coast of Spain, where the hills are brown and barren in the extreme. The coast in this part is not steep or rocky, but a line of hills slant gently into the sea. On one of the lowest of these is situated the town of Tangiers, which reaches from near the top of the ridge of the hill to the beach. To the left of the town is a sand hill thrown up from the sea but to the right and above it, are green fields, hedge rows and trees which make a truly agreeable and refreshing sight. The only objects in Tangiers which attract the eye of him who approaches it, are houses of the Consuls, built in the European style, the extensive ruins of an old Castle, the old wall surrounding the town and the handsome slender towers of several Mosques. As for the great mass of the town, look at it from where you will, nothing is distinguishable but a confused heap of white walls, which is owing to the Moorish style of building houses. We were still at a considerable distance from Tangiers when the tide changed, and we had now no chance of reaching shore that night except in the boat, for nobody is permitted to land after sunset.

We all were quite wearied with the length of our passage and preferred the boat to remaining another night on board, and accordingly set off immediately. Fortunately for us the Governor himself was on the beach, and we were permitted to land without delay. He and two or three others were seated on their hams after the Arab fashion, and as we bowed to him in passing he said through his interpreter "Gentlemen welcome to Tangiers". As we got out of the boat, a number of Jews, preceded by one or two Europeans, rushed forward to enquire for letters and news from Gibraltar. Pacing up and down the shore were a number of Moors some in the dress of higher classes, some in that of the slaves. After some bustle at the Custom House, we passed our portmanteaus etc by the help of a dollar, and then sending them to the posada, proceeded ourselves to the house of the English Consul Mr Green to whom we had letters of introduction.

He gave us a kind reception, and inviting us to breakfast with him on the following morning, we took our leave. The posada is kept by a Genoese, who speaks English, Spanish and Moorish; he lives in one of the Moorish built houses, and having spent some time in Gibraltar, and frequently having English in his house, has some idea of comfort and cleanliness, and is able to give the traveller tolerable accommodations. His servants are a young Moor and a handsome Jewish girl. Our host made us a good dinner, with a dessert of oranges and dates, the excellence of which cannot be judged of from those eaten in England; and being somewhat fatigued we retired early to bed.

[14] Tangiers was ceded to Britain in 1662 by Portugal. Together with Bombay it was part of the dowry of Catherine of Braganza when she married King Charles II. It was abandoned by the British in 1684 because Parliament considered it was too expensive to defend.

Thursday 9th

It not yet being time for Mr Green's breakfast we took a walk into the market place, and being market day we saw many grotesque figures who came in from the Country; the immense straw hats of the women prevented us from seeing their faces. We walked from stall to stall to examine all the articles of sale, which were generally very simple and principally provisions of some kind. But what attracted our attention most was the Camels. Their tractability is astonishing; on receiving a slight rap on the legs they double them in an extraordinary manner, and resting on the knees of their fore legs and the thigh bones of their hind legs they remain in this manner to be loaded or unloaded.

From the frequent intercourse with Europeans and the residence of the Consuls there, the people of Tangiers are seldom uncivil to strangers. The streets are narrow and rather dirty, which I believe is the case in all Moorish towns. The principal street is lined with shops, which are in fact nothing more than large boxes in the walls big enough to hold two or three men sitting on their hams, but not standing upright. The principal articles displayed in them for sale are Silks, Slippers, Otto of Roses and some English Cotton Goods. The houses are all upon the same plan; square, without any external opening except a low door; a flat top, and a square open court in the centre, from which proceeds all the light for the rooms, which are built round it. This plan is well suited to Moorish jealousy, and to a hot climate, and is still continued by the Spaniards throughout the Kingdom of Andalusia.

We found everything at Mr Green's in the most elegant English style, and we can say that we never sat down to a more excellent breakfast than we did in Tangiers.

Mr Green then sent an old Moorish servant with us to call upon the Governor, to ask permission to see the old Castle. We found him and his interpreter sitting upon a mat in a little room that opened into the street, where he was giving audience to a number of people. He received us very graciously, and sent his brother in law one of Cadies or magistrates to attend upon us, this we were told he did, to show us more "grandity" but Mr G. said the real motive was to put his brother in the way of gaining a dollar in which very probably he would himself go shares; so we had no reason to flatter ourselves as having so illustrious a conductor appointed to attend us.

He took us first to look at a couple of Lions kept in a large den; they were feeding when we went, and looking incautiously through the grate one of them sprang up and nearly laid hold of me. We then went to the castle a very large deserted building which has for many years been uninhabited. It belongs we were told to some Bashaw. The whole is much in the same style as the Alhambra of Granada but infinitely inferior in magnificence, beauty, delicacy and excellence of execution. It contains a great number of high open courts, with gardens, orange trees etc. where the women might spend their time secure and unobserved. One of these courts is surrounded with an arched gallery supported by a vast number of high marble pillars with Corinthian Capitals. In the castle yard we observed a great number of similar Capitals ranged along the bottom of a wall, and half covered with grass. Our guide knew nothing about them except that they had lain there for a long time. From what I have seen of the Moorish pillars I should be inclined to think that they cannot be the work of that nation and from the excellent state of preservation they are in, they can scarcely be Roman.

In passing by one of the porticoes of the Castle we saw two men, to all appearance Moors, and were passing on without taking any notice, when in perfectly good English they entreated us for God's sake to stop. We were a good deal astonished and still more so when one told us that he was an Englishman and a native of Liverpool, and that the other that he was an American from Philadelphia. The former said that his vessel had been wrecked four years ago on the coast of Guinea, that all his companions had been murdered, and that he had saved his life only by turning Moor. He had been sent up to Morocco and had come to Tangiers in the hopes of escaping. The story of the American is a similar one but he had only been in the country two years and a half. Where he was shipwrecked or how the two met together I either did not hear or do not recollect. The American, we were afterwards told had some time ago, many good opportunities of escape, but his companion being then ill of a fever he would not leave him. Arrived at Tangiers they declared their wish to leave the country and return to their old religion, for which they were imprisoned and they are not without fears of being burnt to death, the punishment of apostacy among the Moors. The guards would not let us converse longer with them, and we were obliged to take our departure. We spoke to Mr G about them and he said that he had written to the Emperor and shortly expected an answer ordering their release. Money had been given them to buy clothes and fit themselves out as Europeans, but this they spent in drink, a crime surely pardonable in a sailor who during four years has tasted nothing stronger than water.

On returning to the posada we found horses and a guard to attend us, ready for an excursion into the country. We rode upon great clumsy pack saddles which seem intended for carrying half a dozen persons instead of one. We ascended the hill beyond the town and taking a sweep through the fields to the left, returned by a narrow lane or rather ditch bordered with Indian Cane, and across the sand hill before mentioned to the town. The view from the top of the hill is of considerable extent, but not interesting, owing to a want of trees, not known in the immediate vicinity of the town. The face of the country is prettily variegated with hill and dale covered at this season of the year with beautiful verdure. We dined and spent the evening with the Consul. Our party was increased by the Sweedish [sic] consul and a French Emigrant, who form almost all the society Mr Green

THE TRAVEL JOURNALS OF ROBERT HYDE GREG

has and we passed away the evening at the card table.

The yatch [sic] returned to Gibraltar the same afternoon with the Commissioner; Captain Brombie remained with us, having persuaded him to accompany us to <u>Tetuan</u>, for finding ourselves in the country we determined to see something more of it, and resolved to proceed to that city on the following morning very early and endeavour to reach it the same night. Had time and opportunity allowed, we should certainly have extended our journey still further and gone to Fez, the Capital, and residence of the Emperor of Morocco, but as we were situated, this was impossible.

Friday 10th

Our guard was with us at an early hour but as the horses did not make their appearance, we were obliged to defer our departure. About ten o'clock a gentleman of the name of Sullivan, an American, arrived at the posada. He had come from Mogador, a distance of 4 or 500 miles; having been detained by the rains and swelling of the different torrents, this journey took him seventeen days. He had been attended only by a single soldier of the Emperor's, one of the handsomest men I ever saw; his complexion was considerably darker than that of the Moors of the coast, his person tall, handsome and majestic, his features regular, his teeth exquisitely white, his eyes large, dark and expressive, and his hair black and curly. He had on a white turban, his light cloak was thrown around him with an elegant negligence, in an ornamented leathern belt was stuck his dirk, and a long sabre hung at his side. I would have given a good deal for a picture of him, for I think that he was without exception the most striking figure I have ever seen. Mr S. spoke very highly of his conduct and Fidelity. We learnt from him that the roads were in such a state it would be impossible to reach Tetuan in one day; he advised our setting out immediately and offered us his own tent and cloaks in such good earnest that we took both his advice and his offer and made immediate preparations for our journey. As to the safety of travelling, he assured us that he would rather travel in any part of Barbary with one soldier than in Spain with six. The Christians in Mogador he said were extremely well treated; if anyone was insulted he had only to complain to the Governor and say what he thought the Culprit deserved and he was sure to be punished accordingly. The city was divided into three portions, one allotted for the Governor the principal Moors and the Christians; the second to the inferior Moors, and the third to the Jews.

By two o'clock we were ready to set off, and our horses and guard all waiting. Our soldier was a good looking man, and of rather benevolent countenance; he could not speak half a dozen words of Spanish or English, and we of course had to converse by signs when we wanted anything. The soldier we had the former day was a sharp, noisy fellow who understood a little Spanish, talked a great deal, and amused us with some of the Martial manoeuvres of the Moors, charging sometimes at full gallop, cutting on each side with his sabre, and uttering the shrill cries, a general and ancient custom of this people; and then after going for a while at full speed, suddenly reined up his horse. The bridle is a very strong curb, the saddle not inelegant, the stirrups are hung very short, and the spurs are spikes with a round guard placed about four inches from the point to prevent it, I suppose, from penetrating deep into the horse's side. The dress of the soldier is not at first distinguishable from that of another man, as it consists of a light blue undergarment, generally concealed beneath the white cloak. The Moorish soldiery consists principally of Cavalry, it is raised by billet; a man provides his own horse and arms; and I believe they are free after serving a certain time and being engaged in a certain number of actions. When the Christians make their appearance on the coast every man is obliged to be a soldier and instantly takes the field. The arms of the Moorish Cavalry are a musket of immense length the use of which they well understand, a long sabre not more crooked than that used by our soldiers, and a knife or dirk in their belts, which serves the same purpose as in Spain, either to stab an enemy or eat a dinner with. We were told that Tangiers had a regular force of 3,000 men which seems a great number for a population of 10, or 15,000 souls.

Besides our soldier we had a young Moor to attend us and bring back the horses. Having bid adieu to Mr Green, who gave us on taking leave a letter to the Vice-Consul in Tetuan, we set out and took the direction of the sand hill, and soon got into the open country. After going for about 2 miles, we met with a small plain which had been completely flooded with the late rains; the Country people all took a circuitous route by some hills on the left, but our soldier took us through the very middle, thinking it a straighter road than the other. The consequence was that we were all very nearly set fast in the mud and I.H.'s mule falling, he came down in the midst of it, and stood sometime over boot tops in mud and water; he mounted again, but his mule after tottering on for a short distance fell a second time, and he was obliged to walk till we once more found ourselves on firm ground. We soon saw the cause of the mule's falling; it had half trodden off one of its fore shoes, and on the edge of this at every step it placed its hind foot thus throwing itself down. After wasting the best part of an hour in attempting to remedy this, our soldier dismounted, gave his horse to I.H. and pulling off his slippers walked for a while and then mounted the mule. The country through which we passed was divided into small rounded hills and small plains and vallies destitute of trees but with good pasturage. We saw to the right and left as we passed along two or three hamlets of miserable huts such as are to be met with in some parts of Ireland and the north of Scotland, and here and there herds of Cattle were feeding. As it grew near the time of sunset we arrived at a small green hillock well adapted for pitching our tent and passing the night. The soldier signified this to us by leaning his head in his hand and shutting his eyes, but wishing to go on as far as possible that evening, we replied by pointing to the sun which had not yet set, and then to the road along which we had to go. He unfortunately consented and we proceeded a little farther but were unable to find a suitable spot for our tent as the late heavy rains had left the ground wet and dirty; darkness came on and we were compelled to stop in a place very ill suited to our purpose being at the bottom of a hill and consequently very wet. To add to our distress we could not for a long time understand the mechanism of the tent and we had to put it up by candlelight; when up, the curtain on one side would not meet the ground and it had to be done over again. Our soldier had left us as soon as we stopped and gone to some village to get corn for his horse, another man had joined us in the bog, but he did not speak any language but his own, and our muleteer only a few words of Spanish so that they could not give us much assistance. At length all was completed, our tent was pitched, our baggage brought inside, and shortly after our soldier returned which we were glad of, as we had not felt quite comfortable without him. We now thought only of settling for the night, our men cut a great quantity of the palmetta or dwarf palm and spread it on the ground to secure us from the moisture, on this we spread our cloaks, and saddlebags etc, and made a very tolerable bed. Supper was our next care, and we drew from our basket a plentiful store of fowls, partridges, bread, oranges and dates with a bottle of rum and the old leathern bottle well furnished with wine. We made a merry and hearty meal drinking the healths of all our dear friends in Europe and Old England, and offered a bumper of rum to our Soldier to do the same, an offer which he by no means refused. He would not lie under cover of the tent but stretched himself across the entrance as a warrant for our security. The other two men when I last peeped out of the tent were sitting quietly on their hams on the wet ground. They probably lay down soon after but I should imagine that none of them spent the time very comfortably as it rained hard during the night. For my own part I slept quite well, much better than in a Spanish posada.

We were off next morning, our tent struck and baggage mule loaded before sunrise. Before starting our Soldier came for another draught of rum, and in the fullness of his heart he exclaimed as soon as he had swallowed it "viva drinka bono" – a strange jumble of words and which included almost all the knowledge he had of the English and Spanish languages. This days journey proved much more interesting than the former a considerable part of it being well wooded. The number of Cattle of kinds was very great and in some of the distant hills, the ground was enclosed. After ascending a very long and tedious hill and turning the corner of another, we came in sight of the white buildings of Tetuan, still at a considerable distance. As we approached that city, the country gradually became more variegated, better cultivated, and more interesting, and we could not help bursting out into expressions of pleasure and astonishment at the extreme beauty of its immediate vicinities. We now entered the principal gate and passed along to the great market place. In crossing it a Moor who was riding bye struck me a violent blow on my breast, that nearly brought me to the ground and he was gone before I could inform our guard of the offender. We went first to the Governor's, and were then conducted to the Jewish quarter of the town, appropriated to them alone. Though we had seldom seen a more rascally set of faces than those of the crowd of Jews who greeted us at the gate, yet we were not sorry to get amongst them, for the Moors here seemed to have more savage and uncivilised looks than those of Tangiers and I had some fear of receiving a second compliment similar to that I had just met with, in the Market place. They showed us the way to the house of the English vice consul, that of Mr Levi the Jew, who, we found, was ignorant of a single word of the English language; he went out to find lodgings for us, and till he returned we sat in his court surrounded by half the synagogue, who had come to stare at us. Mr Levi now took us to the house of his brother-in-law, Mr Torri, where we found very good accommodations, eating, drinking etc and all <u>free of expence</u>, which we did not expect in the house of a <u>Jew</u> [sic]. We now dismissed our men; the soldier shook hands with us very heartily, and bid us farewell, but, the rascally muleteer imposed upon us shamefully, and when we gave the money agreed upon, he threw it down on the table and left the room, a thing which the Moors always do when not satisfied with what is given them; he refused, at the same time, to take the tent belonging to Mr Sullivan, and on that account we, at last, were obliged to give him what he demanded.

Our Host made many apologies, that for the present he could neither let us have a candle nor anything to eat, as it was the Jewish Sabbath, on which the law prohibits them from touching <u>fire</u>. We were rather alarmed at the idea of staying till Sunday morning without light and supper. But they quieted our alarm by informing us that the Sabbath concluded at 7 or 8 o'clock, and that night it should be over rather sooner. We begged that it might not be hurried on our account, as we could wait till the time appointed for its expiration. In the meantime, however, the servant David had for a <u>Moor</u> to light the fire, boil the water and hold a candle for him whilst he got everything ready. So the instant Sunday [sic] was over, candles and tea were immediately put on the table, and we began to eat and make merry, thanking fortune for having been so kind to us, where we had so little reason to expect it, in a foreign land and amongst a people differing widely in religion, language and manners from our own. The house we were in was one of the best belonging to the Jews; on the same plan exactly as the Moorish, with a patio or courtyard in the middle, and the rooms built round. These, as is still the case in Andalusia, are very long and narrow with the bed at one end, divided from the rest of the room only by a curtain or thin partition.

Sunday 12th of February

Having a letter to Ben Taleb, one of the first Moors of this place or even in Barbary, we sent it to him and he called upon us whilst we were at breakfast, accompanied by an Algerine friend. After travelling through most of the countries of Europe, Ben Taleb was foolish enough to return to his own, where riches are sure to bring suffering upon the possessor; it is said that he has already been robbed of above half his fortune by the Emperor, and that he knows not how soon the other half may go, and his life along with it. He could not speak English, consequently we conversed in Spanish; he spoke with pleasure of the wonders of London, the beauty of the fields of England, and neatness and elegance of the new town of Edinburgh. But what he mentioned with the greatest admiration was Vauxhall[15] and he turned aside to his friend to give him a long description of it, but as he spoke in Arabic it was of course lost upon us, though by his actions and gestures we could judge how much he had been delighted with the spectacle. After asking us if we should like to see his country house and gardens and promising to send a servant there to meet us, he took his leave, and we ordered horses to take us there. Our attendant or guard, was the Moor who has the care of the gate leading to the Jews' quarter, and the person to whom they appeal when insulted by a Moor. We found our horses waiting for us on the outside of the town, as they do not like a Christian to ride through the gate when they can possibly avoid it, although they have the privilege of doing it. We now descended from the hill on which Tetuan is situated, into the beautiful valley which lies at its feet; we had then to be ferried across a small river; twenty or thirty women just landed as we reached the side, but they were so covered with their immense straw hats, with rims of a foot broad bent downwards, that we could scarcely see any of their faces. After giving some time on the opposite side of the river, along narrow dirty lanes lined with hedges of the Indian Cane we arrived at Ben Taleb's garden, or rather it should be called an orange grove, with a number of straight walks; some covered with lattice work; some open, and every here and there an arbour or alcove, the whole neat, pretty and kept in very good order. The house was more in the European than Moorish style, having no Court or patio; two or three good rooms with glazed lattice windows, which his servant pointed out to our particular attention. From the top of the house we had a fine view of the surrounding country, the scenery is indeed truly beautiful, scarcely surpassed by any I have seen. To the north, on the ridge of a low hill branching out from the Sierra behind, and jutting out to the centre of the valley, stood the City of Tetuan, its white buildings, towers and minarets glittering in the sun; to the east extended a beautifully verdant plain of many miles in extent and beyond the waters of the Mediterranean, to the west we traced the windings of the river till it was lost amongst the hills; whilst behind us rose a noble and magnificent mountain, near the bottom enclosed and cultivated, but higher up divided by deep ravines, and adorned with steep craggy rocks, as thickly covered with shrubs, as the lower parts were with trees. Over the southern summit of this mountain were visible the ridges of some snow capped sierras, and on some of these we were told the snow remained all the year round. The Moors might here build a city, the rival of their beloved Granada in beauty, magnificence and fame, they might here select rocks worthy of being crowned with another Alhambra, and might find many situations superior to that of the Palace and Gardens of the Generalife. It was indeed a magnificent scene and the extensive groves of orange trees covered with their golden fruit which surrounded us in every direction added not a little to the beauty of it. After continuing our ride for some miles along the riverside, we returned and had some difficulty in persuading the guards to let us enter the city on horseback, as they made some signs for us to dismount, however after a long parley in which our Jew servant served as interpreter they let us pass; he, however, was obliged to go on foot, as, on no account is a Jew ever suffered to enter the gate of the city without dismounting, or pass the door of a Mosque without taking off his shoes.

Whilst at Tangiers we could not walk about on the top of the house where we lodged for fear of being shot at by the Moors, who think you are looking down into their patios. This actually happened some time ago. But in Tetuan the Jewish quarter being quite distinct and separated from the Moorish, we had liberty to walk up and down as far as we liked wand'ring from one house top to another, to any distance. This we often did both from the singularity of the scene, the beauty of the distant mountains, and because it was pleasanter than in the dirty narrow streets, where we were stared at like wild beasts. In one of these excursions in looking down into a patio we saw three very handsome Jewish girls, and to our surprise a girl in a French dress. We immediately accosted her and she said she was from Bordeaux, that she had lived in Tetuan above three years and that her Father had been settled there a still longer time. She wished much to return to France as she said all the people in Tetuan with the exception of that family in which we saw her, were great brutes, perfectly uncivilised. The Father of these Jewish ladies, proved to be the Spanish consul, who we found knew more of the Spanish language, than our Consul did of English. The consequence of this interview was that the old Jew sent us an invitation, and we went to his house the same evening. Our party was surely the most extraordinary mixture of people that ever met together; and we sat in a circle so that everyone could see all the company at one glance. Next to me sat this little French girl, a very pretty lively creature, then a Jewess, then the Mother of the French girl, next to her sat I.H. at his left hand side another of the young Jewesses, then came the Consul,

[15] Vauxhall was the site of the famous pleasure gardens in London, renowned for its entertainments and brilliant lighting at night.

next to him a Moor, then the Consul's wife, then the third daughter and lastly Captain Brombie. I could not help laughing heartily to see so strange and motley a group ranged out in this manner. After the first compliments were over conversation began to lag, partly for want of having subjects in common, on which to converse, partly for want of language; for I spoke Spanish very little, I.H. still less and Captain Brombie not at all, but he spoke French, of which I.H. and I could only speak a few words. The young Jewish ladies were shy, and had never in their lives been out of Tetuan, and could neither read nor write, consequently it was not an easy matter to know what to say to them, and from one of the aforementioned causes, whatever subject we started, it was certain soon to be dropped; and if had not another ready, a dead silence ensued. At length conversation beginning to be a task on both sides, we took our leave. On the following day we renewed our visit, and once or twice more before leaving the place. The Jewish women are in general fine-looking, with beautiful complexions; from the largeness and regularity of their features, there are scarcely any of them which can be called pretty, though many are handsome. Their dress is becoming, splendid and expensive, costing from 80, or 100 to 200 dollars. About the breast it is of fine linen or muslin, the rest of broadcloth bordered with silk, gold and silver lace etc. Over the forehead is a broad band ornamented with gold, silver and false stones. On their hands and feet are silver bracelets an inch or more in breadth, and some of them wear earrings which hang down to the shoulder. They say that there are no forced marriages among them; the man, I believe, must be worth 300, or 400 dollars before he can marry. In the marriage ceremony there are many curious rites. The evening before it is to take place the woman is carried about the streets, in a singular dress, her face so painted that her best friends would not know her, and during the whole time she keeps her eyes close shut; the next morning she is raised on a kind of throne, just in the same state as the night before and with her eyes still shut, the Rabbi reads the service, the attendants sing and the whole is concluded, by the Bridegroom putting a ring on the lady's finger. When the Jewish women go out of the house they cover their faces almost as close as the Moorish women, which they say they consider decent and proper to do. Very few of the Jewish men are handsome, they stoop a good deal which makes them appear rather hump backed, and the chin is very long. The expression of their countenance is extremely disagreeable, and sly cunning and sordid avarice is strongly painted on almost all their faces. Our dealings with them gave us no reason to suppose that their physiognomy did them injustice, but rather the contrary. Their dress is handsome, but not so magnificent as that of the women. The exterior and only visible garment is a small dark blue great coat, with a good deal of ornament and tassels about the button holes, and closed by a beautiful silk sash.

They suffer the greatest indignities and affronts from the Moors, and if they complain, get little redress, the Moor being reprimanded for striking the Jew, without sufficient cause, but the Jew being ordered to pay 2, or 3 dollars for the expences [sic] of the suit. They cannot ride into the city, and in passing by any of the numerous mosques, are obliged to go barefoot, and in Tetuan these are so numerous that their shoes are more off than on. They are not allowed to wear hats, the place of which is supplied by a little black cap. The little Moors are allowed to whip, kick or spit at the young Jews, as often as they like, and make frequent use of this liberty. There is a tax on the Jews of 7, or 8 dollars a head per an. and they pay 4 dollars whenever they go out of the country though only for a few days; the exportation of a Jewish woman is much more, the duty amounting to three hundred dollars. These Jews being descended from those expelled from Spain, their common language is Spanish a good deal corrupted; but living amongst the Moors they almost all speak Arabic.

Monday 13th
We employed ourselves in going through the different manufactures. We went first to a place where they were making earthen jars, which a man shaped and turned very expertly, telling us that we could not make such things in England. We went next to a tanner's and leather dyer where they prepare the material for the Morocco slippers, giving the leather a very fine colour. Afterwards we were taken to the mat manufacture, made of dyed rushes; they are handsome and better suited to the floor in a hot climate than carpet, they are made with hand, and you may get them of any size and at a very low rate. The silk manufacturers in which the Moors were formerly so celebrated, we found most deserving of attention. The machines for spinning were very simple, but superior to those we had seen in Granada. The looms were much the same as ours and we found them making very handsome handkerchiefs, though rather slight. One man told us he could make 2 of these a day and that for weaving one he received 4 pesetas or shillings. Some of these handkerchiefs we brought away with us as specimens. We then went to a place where they were making gun barrels and saw the whole of the process. They are of an extraordinary length, very thin, of small bore and very light; it is said that the Moors scarcely ever miss their aim with these guns. Wishing to take one home with us, we enquired the price, which was not above 4, or 5 dollars, but, they said we could not take one away without permission of the Governor, so, to him we went. He was not in his room when we arrived, but, shortly made his appearance, and as soon as he had settled himself on his hams to his complete satisfaction, I told him in Spanish, (which he understood) what we had come for. He gravely replied, that he could not grant our request, as the Emperor had strictly forbid him to allow the exportation of anything; but that he would send to Morocco to ask permission of his Majesty, and that he should receive an answer in three weeks. We of course thanked him for his civility, and said

as were leaving the country immediately it would be unnecessary to trouble the Emperor on the subject.

We had engaged with the Master of a Gibraltar Felucca, then fortunately for us lying at the mouth of the river to take us to Gibraltar, stopping half a day on the way at Ceuta.[16] He was to sail when we wished, and we fixed the following morning for our departure; but he came to us over night with some idle pretences that he should not be able to sail till the day after; the real reason was that his cargo was not yet got in, which he promised when we made the bargain, should not detain us, as he would sail without if it we were ready. As we were quite in his hands we could say nothing.

Tuesday 14th

We spent the greater part of this day in rambling through the streets, and enjoying the lovely view from the top of the houses.

It is now time to say a few words about the Moors as by this [time] we had seen a good deal of them. The Moors in their persons are very cleanly, having in this particular a remarkable superiority over their neighbours on the opposite Coast. They are in general, tall, handsome, and well made, except about the legs which are, in the greater part, thick and swollen, arising, probably, from the Elephantiasis a disease very common among them. They all wear the hair on the upper lip, many on the lower lip, and some likewise the beard. The head is always shaved for the accommodation of the turban. The dress is the turban, and a white woollen cloth wrapt in a confused manner round the body and thrown over the left shoulder, leaving the leg bare from the knee downwards. The servants and slaves generally dress differently, without a turban, etc, instead of the woollen cloth, have a kind of smock frock, with a hood for the head. Their manners are courteous and polished; when they address you they incline the body forward, smile and modulate the tone of their voice as the most finished gentleman would do in addressing a lady. This is what the Spaniards are extremely deficient in; when they speak to you they shout as though they believed you deaf, and this in a very unpleasant tone of voice; you may often look at a Spanish woman and think her handsome, but, if she begins to speak, instead of listening to the words with pleasure as would happen in any other case, you feel strongly inclined to stop your ears, and leave her. The Moors whom we met in the street were generally very well behaved, both here and in Tangiers; most of them could speak a few words of English and Spanish, for the Moors are remarkably good linguists, and acquire a language with great rapidity and correctness. They always asked us immediately, if we were English, and on answering in the affirmative seemed pleased, and said, "good", "English good" or "I am very glad" or "I am quite delighted" or something of that kind, and then always appeared glad to do anything for us. One man accosted me in good English, and gave us his address in

London, he was a trader in ostrich feathers, etc. His son, who was just going to be married, took us to show us the house he was fitting up. The ceilings were beautifully painted and gilded, the floors done in coloured tiles in the Moorish manner. Another handsome, civil fellow who spoke both English and Spanish perfectly, said the Moors were a savage jealous people; that for his own part he should like to walk in the streets arm in arm with his wives and daughters but that he should be called Christian. In short, from the men we met with scarcely anything but civility, the boys were now and then troublesome, throwing pebbles or trying to pick our pockets. As for the women, as we saw but few, we can say but little. The ladies in the city never leave their houses; those who come in from the country are drest the same as the men, except having an immense straw hat instead of a turban; the flap or rim of this is bent over the face; a band of linen is tied round the chin and mouth, another over the forehead, so in this way it is impossible to see more than the nose and eyes. This is the case when they enter the town; when you meet them in the country they are not so particularly careful, or rather there are not so many people to watch them; and curiosity prevailing, they even raise their hat, to take a peep at you and you in return get a peep at them. But the most we saw of them was in passing by the open doors of the houses, and giving a glance into the patios where we caught them employed in their household occupations. From always keeping themselves covered their complexions are preserved uninjured, and are remarkably light, their cheeks are rather plump and the languishing melancholy expression of their dark eyes is particularly interesting. From what I saw, I should imagine that many of them are handsome, and our Jewish friends assured us that many of them are extremely beautiful. They must lead a strange life, rather vegitating [sic] than living, as they only go out of the house once a year. This is to Mosque, and in the night time, and when there, as a Moor told me, they did not spend much of their time in devotion. Before hand, they prepare a little billet, saying that their Father or Brother or Uncle, or somebody, is very cruel to them, and that they wish much to be freed from his tyranny. When in the Mosque they watch their opportunity and slip the billet into the hand of the first handsome young man they see, and the next morning, if he is gallant, he asks her in marriage from the cruel Father or Brother. The day following the famous night, the Moor said an immense number of marriages always take place. Being a handsome man he very probably spoke from experience.

The Mosques have nothing at all to distinguish them on the outside; the principal ones have a light, elegant square tower like that of the Giralda at Seville, with a minaret, crowned by a crescent or half moon, the same as our steeples with a cross. We should have been killed instantly had we attempted to enter, but

[16] Ceuta has been a Spanish enclave in Morocco from 1580. It still belongs to Spain.

there is nothing to see in them, being only a number of arched walks like cloisters, into which we could see as we passed along the streets.

Tetuan is built exactly in the same manner as Tangiers, the streets narrow and extremely dirty; it has a castle upon a hill behind the city, but, we did not find our way to it. Tetuan may contain some 40, or 50,000 souls. Fez, we were told, contained about 100,000, Morocco about 150,000. The number of Jews included here is very considerable. In Tetuan they amount to 5 or 6,000.

I might have said, when speaking of Tangiers, that, it primarily belonged to the Portugeze, and was ceded to England in the year [1662] as a marriage dowry with Catherine [of Braganza], married to Charles the Second; who abandoned it in 1683.

Tetuan was formerly the residence of the Consuls and Tangiers is a bad exchange; it was made through the caprice of one of the late Emperors who commanded that no European should set his feet within the walls of Tetuan.

No one who visits Gibraltar should omit making the little trip which I have just made a confused and hasty sketch. It is an opportunity of seeing something of a nation, differing in many essential particulars from those of Europe, and which once made a figure in history. If he has travelled through Andalusia, and is acquainted with the magnificent remains of the Moors at Granada, he cannot fail being highly gratified in tracing the same persons, dress, manners, customs, and religion amongst the descendants of that people, which formerly characterised that very people themselves. It is a journey soon made, vessels are continually going from Gibraltar; and others may generally be found to bring you back. With common prudence it may be performed not only without danger, but, without inconvenience, and with a great deal of pleasure. He who has the opportunity and does not make use of it, may be, with justice, charged of having a want of proper curiosity. The advantage and pleasure of the journey is worth paying for at the expence of much trouble and inconvenience, and there is scarcely any, either of one, or the other. For my own part, I would not have missed it on any account. The amusement and gratification I received at the time, was great, and is renewed whenever those days present themselves to my recollection.

Wednesday 15th

At 11 o'clock we were at the city gate and mounted on our horses, having previously had a long dispute with the owner who wanted to impose upon us. We took the way to the Custom House situated on the shore 7 miles distant from Tetuan, accompanied by a crowd of Moors and Jews. We found our Captain on the shore, and having dispatched our luggage we went on board our little vessel. We found the deck almost covered with live stock, which costs but little in Tetuan. Of the price of different articles there, some judgement may be formed by the following list.

	Dollars
A Horse is worth from	50 to 150
A Mule	" "
A Camel	40–50
A Bullock	14
12 Fowls	1–
Wheat per quarter	5–7
1000 oranges	2
Ditto with dates	5
A lb of spun silk	5–
Ditto of raw cotton	½

I have already observed Cattle are almost the only thing allowed to be exported, and these only in a limited number. The Emperor as a particular favour to some individual, sometimes allows the export of a horse, and then he pays a duty of about 100 dollars.

In bringing merchandise into the country, Christians and Jews pay a duty of 10 p.c. Moors only 2½ per cent.

We got under weigh at 1, or 2 o'clock, but, being too heavily laden, we struck on a bar, the water being perfectly calm, there was no danger and our only remedy was to wait, till the tide came in, during which time we had leisure to admire the lovely scene, which we were now leaving behind, the beautiful plain, the white city of the Moors, and the magnificent mountains, which closed the view.

Finis[17]

---

[17] End of the second volume of the manuscript.

Continuation of the journey to Cadiz, thence to Madrid, the Escorial,
St Ildefonso, Segovia etc, Toledo, Burgos, Bilboa, and Plymouth[1]

The sun had already sunk behind the hills of Tetuan, before we got clear of the
bar, and had hoisted the long angular sail of our little vessel. The wind was strong
and favourable and bore us rapidly along the high rocky coast of Africa the bold
promontories of which we distinctly saw by the bright light of the moon.

Our crew was one of the strangest mixtures possible, being formed of
Spaniards, Greeks and Italians and including the Captain were only 7 in number.
Though the vessel sailed under the English colours not one of them could speak
a word of the English language. Our company was still more extraordinary than
our crew. We were five and twenty or thirty in number, including eight Turckish
deserters from the Dey of Algiers, eight or nine Barbary Jews, a Rabbi with very
long white beard and a number [of] Moors. There being no accommodations
below we were all obliged to remain on deck, and it was truly amusing to watch
the extraordinary collection of people in their various dresses and attitudes; more
or less distinctly seen accordingly as the Moon or the blaze of a bright fire shone
upon them. Beginning to feel hungry, as soon as the Turks had done with the fire
and pot we put in it a savoury mess, of Rabbits, onions and pepper and waited
with some impatience till it was ready and then sat down with great relish to eat,
putting the dish in the middle as we sat round it, but unluckily as we were raising the first morsel to our mouths, the dish from some unknown cause upset,
and the rich gravy and all was spread on the dirty deck. It was however too good
to be lost and, picking up what we could the dog devoured the rest. The Captain
had left a little narrow space in the hold, where there was just room enough between the packages and the deck for a person to lie down; and we crept to sleep.
I past the night very uncomfortably for, finding all the room occupied as I went
in last, I was obliged to lie across my two companions, with my head against the
sharp corner of a trunk.

Thursday 16th
Not being very comfortable below, we were on deck long before day and witnessed one of the most splendid sights that can be imagined, the sun rising out
of the sea, when perfectly calm. The first rays of golden light which shot across
the water was indeed magnificent. We now found ourselves immediately under
the rock of Ceuta, but on the opposite from that on which the town is built. The
wind having dropped we were obliged to row round the promontory which gave
us an opportunity of observing it leisurely; it is truly a second Gibraltar, differing
from it only in the height and steepness of the rock, which is much lower, and
though very rocky towards the sea, is not so steep but that landings might be

made in many parts, and once landed the ascent to the summit is easy. It is entirely surrounded by a small wall, and defended by a number of small batteries, the citadel at the top is defended by a greater wall, though this not very high nor properly built for the planting of artillery. We were two hours in rowing round the rock and then had to wait some time before a boat would put off to take us ashore, and we were obliged to go to the Governor to ask permission to see the town before we could go to the posada. This being done we breakfasted and then took a guide to show us about the place. The view from the citadel is remarkable [sic] fine, commanding a view of the town and fortifications the Moorish camp and the green hills behind; the beautiful bay formed by the headlands of Ceuta and Tetuan, the African coast towards the south to a great extent, and the snow mountains behind; the Mediterranean to the east, the straights to the west, the stupendous rock of Gibraltar, the line of the Spanish coast almost as far as Malaga and the high Sierras behind Granada and Velez Malaga. We found here the graves of about a hundred of our countrymen who died here during the time they held the place in the late revolution. We found everything bearing the marks of ruin and desolation, as generally is the case in everything where the Spaniards are concerned. Not even a Cannon is mounted, they were all taken away when the place was given up to our troops by way of showing their confidence in English honour. The fortifications on the land side are extremely strong; the istmus having been cut through, and surmounted by a wall of immense height and thickness, with a battery at the top. The sea flows through this channel and vessels of considerable size can enter it, beyond this are three or four other ranges of batteries which render the place extremely strong at least against any attacks of the Moors; it was once besieged by an immense army of them, some say 500,000, assisted by some English Engineers but without effect. The ground rises gradually on the Moorish side from the outermost battery, and at a distance of quarter of a mile, the whole town and istmus are completely commanded. Whilst standing in the last battery we were fortunate enough to see a party between the Moors and Spaniards. The former advanced on horseback, the latter on foot being a few companies of infantery [sic]. They drew up in two lines opposite each other, planted a white flag, and one or two persons advanced from each line into the open space between to converse. The reason of the Conference was that a Spaniard on guard, the night before had fled to the Camp of the Moors, and the Spaniards demanded that he should be given up. The man was brought forward but said that he wished to renounce his religion and live amongst the Moors, they refused to give him up and both parties returned.

Ceuta is one of the better sort of Spanish towns and built in a more regular plan than the generality of them judging from the size of it, the number of in-

---

[1]   The third volume of the Iberian Journey begins with this heading.

habitants may be some little inferior to that of Gibraltar. The garrison is estimated at about ... During the revolution they were almost starved to death and were provisioned for three years from Gibraltar; the officers absolutely coming to beg for bread and a few shillings from Admiral Heming and others. Ceuta is principally used by the Spaniards as a place for sending the convicts; at the time we were there many of rank, fortune and respectability, were numbered amongst the Criminals. They compel these to work at all the laborious, slavish occupations, the same as the most notorious villains, making no distinction whatever. Not being on good terms with the Moors, Ceuta has to receive everything from Spain, as the rock produces nothing. The bay is not good for shipping as the water is shallow and the bottom rocky. We went on board again about 2 o'clock, and as the wind was now fresh and favourable we calculated on reaching Gibraltar long before sunset. But in this we were doomed to be disappointed. In the meantime we employed ourselves in repairing the loss we had sustained the night before; the sailors after skinning a rabbit laid it on the deck and chopped the bones with a rusty hatchet, and then pulled it to pieces with their tarry hands, putting it in the same pot which the Turks had just drawn out their mess. The same accident did not happen again, and notwithstanding having seen the delicate way of cooking it, we made a hearty meal. We now began to draw near Gibraltar, which has a more noble and imposing aspect on this side than on any other. Unfortunately as the sun declined the wind failed us; we reached the new mole the place whence we sailed just as the gun from the signal post was fired, and with that all the hopes of landing till the following morning at once vanished. We, however, hailed a boat and sent it for wine, oranges and refreshments and then composed ourselves as well as we could in our miserable hole, for the night.

Friday 17th of February

The health boat came to us at an early hour, and we went on shore in it, the rest of the company remaining on board for farther examination. We made the best of our way to the hotel, and after breakfast went immediately to enquire for some vessel going to Cadiz. The wind had changed to the east, the day before, and from the citadel of Ceuta we had seen all the ships so long windbound, sailing through the straights. During the night it had again come round to the west. We found a small vessel which was to sail for Cadiz on the following morning if the wind proved favourable but as this was doubtful we determined to proceed by land without delay, and go to Algeziras that same evening. As we went to the pier head to enquire when the packet sailed, we were stopped by the guard at the gate and asked if we had not arrived that morning in a vessel with a number of Jews and Moors. On answering in the infirmative [sic, for affirmative] he said he had orders to send us to the town Major, and gave us in care of a Serjeant. The Major was not at home which was provoking enough, as we were in such haste to be off. After waiting some time we were let off on availing ourselves of Mr Stedman's name. Having taken leave of all our friends, and this wonderful little spot, the possession of our Countrymen, we embarked in one of the Algeziras packet boats. Everybody on board but ourselves was employed in smuggling cotton goods. An army and navy officer was amongst the number; the one said he had not received a farthing of pay during 5 years, and the other not for two or three. We asked them how they could get through the Custom House, and they replied they had friends there. The sailors had got a great quantity of printed Calicoes etc and when about halfway across, they stripped to their shirts, lapped the goods round their bodies, and then put on their jackets again. At the Custom House I was going to open my trunk, but the officer nudged my elbow, and at the same time held out his hand for a shilling in which we did not disappoint him. He had at the same time seized upon a poor woman who had brought over a teapot in the same boat with us.

The Custom Houses in Spain are not only to be found in the seaport towns, every one however small, has one of them; they are the trouble and annoyance of the traveller, who must either bribe, or submit to have his portmanteau searched by dirty rascally, scoundrels, half a dozen times a day. And if a smuggler comes and says here are a couple of dollars, will you permit a thousand pounds worth of Contraband goods to pass, he would not hesitate a moment in saying, yes. Such is the miserable ill-judged policy of the Spanish government!

Algeciras is a neat clean town, and its inhabitants are somewhat civilized with their constant intercourse with Gibraltar.

Saturday 18th

Having hired horses to take us to Cadiz, we set out at an early hour and ascended a high sierra which lies behind Algeciras and whence is a most magnificent view. The horse with our baggage fell three or four times and we were greatly delayed by these accidents. Some parts of the sierra being well wooded, presents many interesting views, and after descending from it the country is romantic and variegated. We staid half an hour at a small venta and then proceeded to Vijez without stopping, again; it was dusk long before we arrived and including this short stop we had been on horseback 14 hours. Vijez is an old Moorish town situated on the summit of a steep hill, a river of considerable size runs at the bottom, crossed by an old Roman bridge. The posada stands at the foot of the hill.

Sunday 19.

We rode to Chiclana 5 leagues to breakfast, crossing on the way the famous field of Barrosa. The whole distance from Vejez to Chiclana is a perfect desert, totally uninhabited. Chiclana is a considerable town, the summer residence of the Cadiz gentry. In neatness and Cleanliness it is the rival of Cadiz. From it is a very extensive view of the bay of Cadiz, the Isla de Leon, and all the flat low land where the salt is procured. Descending the hill on which Chiclana is situated, you enter on a low boggy plain, often flooded by the sea, and so intersected by deep trenches in every direction as to be utterly impassable; you can cross it only by a straight wide road, or causeway, which has been through it at much expence. After keeping along this for some time you arrive at a wide, and deep river or arm of the sea across which you are ferried. Immediately on the opposite side is [a] strong fort which guards the passage of the river and commands the causeway just mentioned. You then pass along another causeway, made through a still more impassable country than the former, being completely covered with salt pits; this road is likewise defended by several strong forts, which, [i.e. the road] being perfectly straight, would sweep it from end to end, rendering all approach impossible. Behind these forts is the old Roman Bridge of Suazo, thrown over the river Santi Petri, which running from the Bay of Cadiz into the sea, forms the isle of Leon. The French never advanced beyond this bridge, retiring on the first discharge of the few guns posted here; it was fortunate for the cause of Spain that they did so, for the Spaniards only had ammunition for two more rounds, and had they advanced that instant Cadiz in all probability would have fallen into their hands. The Town which bears the name of the Island, though begun only in the middle of the seventeenth century, contained in 1790, 40,000 communicants. The principal street is above a mile in length, the houses are neat and whitewashed, and the whole presents an air [of] cleanliness and prosperity rarely to be met with in a Spanish town. Leaving the Isla, as the Spanish call it, you continue your route still amongst salt pits, with the bay on the right hand and the open sea on the left. This istmus here pursues a westerly direction, and keeps continually growing narrower till you reach the Torre gorda, where the sea almost washes the causeway on both sides. Here the English had erected a fine fort which commanded the causeway and flat land in all directions,but for what reason it is not easy to guess, the Spaniards have completely destroyed it, and scarcely a trace is left of its existence. The istmus now turns off suddenly to the right and continually keeps narrowing until you reach a large fort distant about 2 miles from Cadiz, where it again widens. The fortifications of the City on this side [are] strong and kept in good repair. On entering the gate we were stopped to enquire about our luggage; this was the third time we had been robbed on the same pretence since leaving Algeçiras. At Vijez a dirty fellow entered our room at five o'clock in the morning, for this purpose; and after quitting Chiclana, another crept out of a clod cabin on the rode [sic] side to fleece us again. The one on the Bridge of Suazo we past without being observed.

The approach to Cadiz on the land side presents nothing remarkable, but from the bay the appearance of the City is singularly beautiful, the high white houses with their numerous turrets seeming to spring out of the bosom of the

Ocean. On a fine day when the water is of a deep blue and the sun glistening on the buildings, you can scarcely believe of the existence of what you see, the whole appears to be magic.

We made the best of our way to Mr Beeslow's, where we found once more a good house and English accommodations. The month we passed there presented not a single thing worth relating; being Lent, all amusements, gaiety and tertulias had given way to fasting and Catholic devotion in neither of which we could take a very active part. Before breakfast we had a Spanish Master, till noon we were in the Counting house, before dinner we took a walk in the great square, the Exchange of Cadiz, in the evening we walked[2] on the Alameda, to see the humours and fashions of the place. The walk continues very crowded till the vesper bell rings, the moment this is heard they all stand and cease talking, muttering a short prayer; the men take off their hats; as soon as it is over they generally retire. With the greater part this is letter [i.e. little] better than a mockery. In the other provinces of Spain, they do not observe this ceremony so strictly as Andalusia.

Cadiz, the Gades of the Ancients is undoubtedly one of the oldest, and most famous of Spain, and has at all times carried on an extensive commerce, and has particularly flourished since the trade of South America and Mexico has fallen into its hands. It was under the active administration of O'Reilly[3] that this city received its greatest embellishments. Old houses were pulled down and others built in their place on a regular plan. The streets were paved and kept constantly clean; and new buildings erected on the vacant places. He even endeavoured to gain land from the sea. The space occupied by the Custom House had been obtained from that element but at a period anterior to his administration. He paid much attention to the embellishment of the approach on the land side, and gardens and houses extended a mile from the land gate. But [since] his time they have been neglected and this space is at present little better than a sandy desert. Cadiz is perhaps the cleanest and most beautiful city in Europe. The streets are all narrow, but well paved and kept in excellent order. The houses are high whitewashed from top to bottom, and have all one or more handsome balconies, some of which being glazed make a part of the room. They have all flat roofs called azoteas, some houses have several of these azoteas, of varios [sic] heights owing

---

2   The next page is the map of the Bay of Cadiz, reproduced in the plate section.

3   Count Alexander O'Reilly (c.1722–94) was of Irish origin. He served in the armies of Austria, France and Spain, settled in Spain and was highly thought of by King Charles III, whose life he saved during a popular uprising in Madrid. He held several prestigious offices in Spain and in overseas Spanish possessions and despite being humiliated by his failure to take Algiers for Spain in 1775, he was made Governor of Cadiz and Captain-General of Andalusia. His rule was regarded as liberal and enlightened, but he was forced out of office (by a jealous rival?) in 1786.

to some parts of the house being raised a story higher than the rest. They have all a small wall round them, and from these reasons you cannot walk from house to house as in Tetuan. Most of the houses have a high turret for look[ing] over the town and ocean. They still preserve the Moorish style of building, that is with large square patios and a corridor or gallery round it on the second and third floors. These patios are paved with handsome square pieces of marble, and the staircaise likewise is commonly of marble. The rooms open into the Corridor, and also into one another; they are divided only by a thin partition of paper or canvass, and in this way you may walk into every room in the same floor passing from one to another without being obliged to go into the Corridor. The doors are often half glass and notwithstanding a muslin curtain you may see what passes in the adjoining room.

Cadiz has scarcely a single public building worthy of notice. The Cathedral begun near a hundred years ago was never finished and probably never will, as they have long since ceased working at it.[4] Cadiz is entirely surrounded by a fine wall, but the sea is committing such ravages, that if great efforts are not speedily made the city will fall a prey to the waves; a great part of this wall having already fallen in the sea advancing behind it, and the rest undermined in every part will soon be washed away. The expence of repairing will be enormous, now that the evil has proceeded to such an extent. Cadiz is said to be full of life and gaiety in the season, and that a person may spend his time there very agreeably; it must be confessed however that it is like living on board a ship, being shut in by the ocean, and subject to the inconvenience of being confined to one walk, and being cut off from everything like country. The nearest to Cadiz is Port St. Mary, across the bay; or Chiclana the road to which is along the sandy istmus; nor indeed does this deserve the name of country but rather desert, for it is so uncultivated that the traveller finds it difficult to imagine how so great a population is supported, for this is in fact one of the most populous parts of Spain, from the number of towns situated near one another, namely Cadiz, the Isla, Chiclana, the Caraccas, Puerto Real, Puerto de Sta Maria and Rota. All the water of Cadiz came formerly from Port St. Mary for which the inhabitants paid one year with another 90,000 dollars. They are now sufficiently supplied from the water which falls upon the azoteas and is collected in a cistern below the patio. This water though not very good is yet ill tasted. O'Reilly began an aqueduct which he meant should supply Cadiz with water from the hills of Medina Sidonia, but it was discontinued at his disgrace. The Commerce of Cadiz is very extensive. In the year 1776, the number of ships that entered its port amounted to 949 of which 265 were French. In the year 1791, the whole number which entered was 1010 ships. Of these 180 were English, 176 from the Spanish Dominions in America, 162 from the Spanish Dominions in Europe, 116 French, 104 Portugueze, 90 from the United States, 80 Dutch, 41 Danish, 25 Swedish, 22 Ragusan, 6 Genoese, 2 Venetian, 1 Hamburgher, 1 Russian, 1 Imperial and one Spanish ship from the Manilla. The 177 ships from the Spanish Colonies brought gold and silver to the amount of 25,778,175 dollars.

The entrance to the bay of Cadiz is but ill defended by the fort of St Sebastian situated on a narrow neck of land running out from the city, and another fort on the opposite site of the water. The inner bay however is completely secured by the two forts of the Puntales and Matagorda immediately opposed to one another, in a part where the bay is much contracted. It was this fort of the puntales which saved Cadiz in the late siege for, the fort of Matagorda having been destroyed, the French unable to advance to the point of that neck of land, on account of the fire from the Puntales, could not establish their batteries near enough to Cadiz to do any material injury by a bombardment. They made in the Cannon Foundery of Seville 14 enormous bombs, some of them weighing upwards of four tons, and brought them down by machines made for the purpose. When the wind was contrary and strong a charge of 36 or 40 pounds of powder was necessary to throw the shells, 15 inches in diameter. To give these shells sufficient weight it was necessary to load them so heavily with lead, that they could not find enough powder to burst them; it was owing in a great measure to the number that fell without bursting that so few lives were lost during so long a bombardment. The siege lasted two years and a half. The distance which these shells were thrown is almost incredible; being little short of four miles; the time they were in coming was about thirty six seconds. In the night they were distinctly seen from the light of their fusees, and the inhabitants used to amuse themselves with watching them; all fourteen were fired at the same time, and these every three hours day and night, so that people always knew where they were coming and might put themselves in a place of safety. One fell in the great square, but that did not burst, most fortunately as it was full of people. It is said that they took so long to cool that the bombs could not be fired oftener than once in three hours. Before the end of the siege three or four had been quite worn out and become totally useless.

In the year 1799 Cadiz contained a population [of] 75,000 souls. It was considerably diminished the following year by the yellow fever or as the Spaniards call it the Epidemy. This was not known in Europe till the year 1800, when it was introduced from the West Indies by a Captain who broke quarantine and came ashore. I believe he himself died of the desease a day or two after. It shortly committed the most terrible ravages amongst the inhabitants of Cadiz. It was observed that those born in the West Indies and South America escaped its influence, that it was not quite so destructive among the old inhabitants as those recently settled in Cadiz, and that the majority of Foreigners fell victim to its fury.

---

[4]   Cadiz Cathedral was completed in 1838.

It was likewise observed to rage with greatest violence amongst the men than the women. This difference is said to have been as great as 48 to one. It was between the 12th of August and the 31st of October that the contagion made the greatest ravages. During this interval it attacked 47,350 persons and carried off 7195 of that number exclusive of the troops who had recently arrived for the defence of the coast who alone lost 3000 men. It was not wholly free till the end of April 1801. When the contagion was at its height in September and October from 140 to 170 people died daily. The fever made similar ravages in the neighbouring towns, and extended to Xeres, Seville, Malaga and all Andalusia. In the year 1804 it broke out again in a dreadful way at Malaga. Cadiz did not escape this new scourge, but it was not so dreadful as the first. The greatest mortality amounted to 70 in a day and this only during a short time. It is singular almost the only years Cadiz has been completely free from the Epidemy, was during the siege, a most providential circumstance, as it would have proved a dreadful scourge,in its then crowded population. In 1804 the population was estimated at 70,000, and this has not decreased in late years.

The quantity of salt made in the neighbourhood of Cadiz is immense, but it is coarse and extremely dirty. It is exported by the Swedes, Danes, Dutch and English, and especially the Portugeze. Everyone that pleases is at liberty to make these artificial salt pits in his own ground. He may dispose of the produce to foreigners, but not to natives as salt in Spain is exclusively for the King's account.

The females of Cadiz are generally reputed the handsomest in Spain. There certainly are many handsome women amongst them, but by far the greatest part of them are more remarkable for the expression of their dark eyes and their majestic manner of walking than for their beauty. Their dress too is so becoming, and sits so well upon their small delicately shaped figures that, if a woman is not absolutely ugly, you think her pretty. This dress is the saya, or frock of black silk or bombazine, extremely well made, and weighted with lead at the bottom to make it hang better; over the bosom is a neck handkerchief of richly coloured silk, and over the head is thrown a mantilla, a long black or white lace veil which falls gracefully on each side of the head, crosses on the neck, and is commonly passed under the arm; the face is thus discoverd and the olive complexion suits well with the simple dress in which it is seen. The Cadiz ladies say they are the only women in the world that know how to walk well; they certainly walk different from any body else with a great air and grace which is in fact nothing more than a majestic strut, and for which a woman in England would be stared at, and get the character of consummate haughtiness and conceit if not of something worse. If one may believe one half of what is related of the Cadiz ladies, their reputation does not stand very high, nor is it fit that it should, if half of the things alledged against them is true.

The late Governor of Cadiz, [the] Marquis of Solano made some neat gardens, and erected public paths on an open space at one end of the Alameda; but the populace, whose practice it is here when a man falls out of favour to undo whatever good he may have done; when they murdered him destroyed his baths and gardens, the remains of which are still to be seen; numberless similar instances might be quoted.

Cadiz has two theatres and an amphitheatre where are exhibited the best Bull Fights in Spain.

We said adieu to Cadiz on the **20th of March** happy in the prospect of Speedily visiting France, and perhaps part of Switzerland and Holland, and still more in the idea that we were now on the way home having our faces once more turned towards England. Our views then were to hasten to Madrid where business might probably detain us a month or three weeks, then going to Barcelona and passing to Paris either by way of Narbonne, Lyons etc or by Genoa, Turin, Geneva etc. We little thought then of the changes which had already taken place in France, and which were about to involve all Europe once more in a bloody war.

We had bought a carriage in Cadiz with the intention of posting up to Madrid; we at the same time hired a servant, whom we first met in the hotel in Gibraltar. We sent him with the carriage by land to Port St Mary, and crossed the bay ourselves in company with two Cadiz friends who were going to see the festivals of the holy week in Seville. We were only an hour and a quarter on the voyage and arrived at about five o'clock in the evening. Port St Mary is a small neat white town, and like all others in the neighbourhood of Cadiz seems to have taken example from the cleanliness of that city. Only vessels of the smallest size can enter the port and these only at high tide, on account of the bar formed by the sands of the Guadalete, the famous river Lethe of the Ancients, and which here discharges itself into the sea. In crossing this bar the sailors do not fail to make a collection to be said in masses for the souls of those who have perished there which if you may believe them, have been very numerous. We found horses ready for us when we reached the posada; the harness is of the most clumsy contrivance and made of ropes as indeed is almost all [the harness] in the kingdom with the exception of the Kings. When once set off the horses go well and are kept at full speed the greatest part of the way. The driver has not any peculiar dress, drives on the boot, and has often two whips a long one and a short one, which he uses according as he whips the first horses, or the nearest for, in these carriages you have always 4 horses. The stages are generally short, from 2 to 3 leagues each, and never exceed four. You might travel exceedingly quick on this road if they were not so exceeding slow and tiresome at the post houses; if you tell to be quick for you are in a hurry, he is sure to say "poco a poco" that is literally "little by little", or "gently".

It is only since the year 1785 that a post chaise could travel from Madrid to

Cadiz, this kind of travelling being formerly quite unknown in Spain except between the capital and the Royal residences. There are at present only two or three roads on which you can post at present. In leaving Port St Mary, whisked along in a carriage on a good road, and under the shade of a long and beautiful Alameda, I could not help but fancying myself in England, at least that I was no longer in Spain, for this kind of travelling I had not yet seen there.

The whole distance from Cadiz to Madrid is ... From Cadiz to Xeres 5, we arrived about 9 o'clock in the evening, and put up at a large posada. Xeres is one of the most flourishing towns in Spain, it commands a fine view of the bay of Cadiz and a great extent of flat uncultivated ground, where was fought the battle in which Rodrigo the Gothic King lost his crown and his life, and which delivered into the hands of the Moors the whole of Spain.[5] It is in the neighbourhood of this town that some people have placed the Elysian Fields; they are indeed much altered and their old inhabitants I am sure would not yet recognise them.

From this town is exported the well known wine which we call Sherry. The vineyards though badly managed produce one year with another 360,000 arrobas of wine of which 200,000 is exported principally to England and France. The arroba is a weight of 25 pounds, as I mentioned before. From the olive plantations proceed annually 32,000 arrobas. The breed of horses once famous has lost its reputation.

We left Xeres at 12 o'clock the same night and travelled till we reached Seville, which we did about 3 o'clock the following evening. The only place worth remarking this distance is Alcala two leagues from Seville, a small place with the extensive remains of a Moorish Castle on the hill. In coming out of Alcala the front wheel of the carriage came of[f], and so damaged the axle tree that at Seville we were obliged to get a new one.

Wednesday 22nd
We devoted this morning to visiting the ruins of Italica, of which I have already spoken. We went likewise to see the veil rent in the Cathedral, which is done on this day, though not the proper one, that is it may not interfere with other ceremonies. Whilst it is rent noises are made above as of thunder and we only regretted that to heighten the effect, we could not likewise have an earthquake. We devoted the evening of this day to our old friends and it was then we first received the astonishing and almost incredible news of the landing of Bonaparte.[6]
Thursday the greater part of this morning we spent on top of the Giralda and were inclined to think that we had been mistaken in supposing the distant mountains, those of Africa. Probably they are those we crossed immediately on leaving Algiziras, which however are not situated very far from Africa, the straits there being only 15 miles wide. We afterwards spent some time in the Alcazar, the gar-

dens and apartments of which there are good specimens of the Moorish work. In the afternoon we took care to be present at the processions. A description of one of these will suffice for all. First marches a long line of Soldiers to clear the way, after these comes a whole regiment of Friars of all colours, black, white and blue, instead of muskets carrying wax candles long, thick and heavy. What follows next is really shocking; it is the whole scene of the crucifixion, represented in figures as large as life and splendidly drest. Two men on ladders are letting Christ down from the cross, the virgin is on her knees with a white handkerchief in her hand, drest in flowing robes of black velvet and with several steel daggers in her heart to show the anguish she is suffering. Standing near her are likewise similarly drest other women. The whole is on a large platform and carried along on men's shoulders. After this come files of common people with the same long candles as the monks. Porters carry large baskets full of these and anyone that likes can join the train. Amongst the rest are seen a number of people in long black dresses, and high conical pasteboard caps, like boys fools'caps. These we were told were playing the part of penitents, but were not so in reality, as anyone that chose might put on the same dress and join the procession. Some of these have whips to beat themselves with, but it is not observed that they strike hard. As to the numerous bystanders, it is easy to see these puppet shows of Priesthood are rapidly losing their effect upon the minds of the public, for superstition can not reign for ever, it is supported only by ignorance, and men must be enlightened sometime. There was [no] kissing the ground, nor even any kneeling at which I was surprised. At Cadiz these processions were ordered to be discontinued for five years, as the people had begun to laugh at them.

We drank tea at Mrs H's. and afterwards sallied out, a very large party of us ladies and gentlemen, to visit the principal churches. We began with the Cathedral. There we found a brilliant and magnificent spectacle; the famous Monument of which the Sevillians make so much boast, had been erecting for three weeks, was now complete and lighted up with upwards of three tons weight of wax candles. This monument is meant to signify the tomb of Christ and the candles remain lighted during the time our Saviour lay in the grave. It is a magnificent temple made of wood admirably painted, and gold ornaments, and by the light of so many candles the whole is wonderfully resplendent. It consists of three or four floors or stories, each supported by beautiful columns. The first floor is approached on four sides by steps, from the ground floor of the Cathedral. In the

---

[5]   Marginal note: AD 702.

[6]   The landing of Bonaparte: Napoleon escaped from Elba in February 1815, landed near Cannes and advanced on Paris. From 20th March to 22nd June 1815 he again ruled as Emperor. The period is always known as "The Hundred Days" and was brought to an end by the Battle of Waterloo.

centre of this first floor is placed the custodia, made in the shape of a temple, and of pure silver, it weighs a ton, and the workmanship is excellent and delicate. The beauty and brilliancy of this mass of silver placed in the center of such a blaze of light is inconceivable, and the effect of the whole monument raised in the center of the great nave of a dark, and majestic Gothic Cathedral is to a stranger particularly striking. The number of strange figures at their devotion, likewise attracts the attention; some are kneeling, gazing on the monument and crossing themselves, some striking their breasts and groaning; some kissing the ground; and others walking on their knees from the door to the monument, repeating this several times. Bidding adieu, perhaps a lasting one, to this Cathedral we proceeded to many other churches, likewise with monuments but infinite inferior to that just mentioned. I may just observe that the great Candle weighing near a ton was not to be lighted till the following day good Friday. We saw it through the key hole of the house where it was kept, or rather I should say a part of it, as part passed through the floor into the room above. From the further observations we made on the place w[h]ere it is erected, we concluded it must be about five feet in circumference and near thirty in height. We rambled about with the ladies till near 12 o'clock, then went home, packed up and got into the carriage, which we had ordered for that hour.

From Seville to Carmona is six leagues. We arrived about six o'clock in the morning, Carmona once famous is still a considerable town. It is situated on an eminence and overlooks a great extent of level country towards the south; on this plain I could easily trace the road on which I travelled during two days in my journey to Granada; I was then on the back of an ass, trudging along at a slow walk. I was now lolling at my ease in a commodious carriage, rattling over the ground as fast as 4 horses could gallop. To the east of the town is the ancient castle, which now presents little more to the eye than a monstrous mass of ruins, of great extent. Don Pedro the cruel held his court here for a long time, and after him it became the residence of his brother Henry of Transtamare. Carmona still exhibits many remains of the Romans; among the principal of this the gateway of the city which has been in some places absurdly retouched in the modern style.

To Ecija 9½ leagues; the country from Carmona to this place is extremely uninteresting, the road lying principally through a dull barren plain. Three leagues before arriving at Ecija you pass the small neat town of Luisiana one of the colonies of the Sierra Morena; it has of late years declined much, as well as the other colonies; they extend from this place to the other side of the sierra, comprising a space of upwards of 40 leagues. In the year 1791 Luisiana contained only 240 inhabitants and at present some of the houses seem to be unoccupied. At Ecija I once more found myself on the banks of my beloved Xenil the waters of which are considerably greater than when I saw them last washing the walls of Granada. Ecija is a large town containing about 6000 houses and an immense number of churches, both one and the other painted in the strangest and most ridiculous manner, some red, some yellow and some all the colours of the rainbow. The houses and streets are much upon the plan of the Seville ones. The plaza major or great square is quite Moorish, and seems scarcely to have altered since their time. Ecija was famous in the time of the Moors, and judging from the marble pillars and statues which are often dug up we may infer that it was not an inconsiderable place in the time of the Romans. From its situation between two hills it is dreadfully hot in summer and is esteemed to be the hottest place in Spain. The banks of the Xenil are as fruitful here as in the Vega of Granada, it is said that corn yields forty fold. The posada here is one of the best we have met with in Spain.

From Ecija to Cordova [Cordoba] is a distance of 10 leagues; changing horses at the venta of Mango Negro you arrive after a considerable and tedious ascent to Carlotta, a neat, pretty town regularly built, situated on an eminence and command[ing] a view of the plains to the south and the hills to the north. It is surrounded with gardens and has some pleasant and extensive alamedas. This is the principal of the second colonies of the Sierra Morena; in the year 1791 it contained only 60 inhabitants but the district contained 600. Leaving Carlotta you are exceeding pleased with the neat white farmhouses, placed at regular distances on each side of the road, each with its portion of ground for corn and gardens. They extend along this road for some miles and have an appearance of neatness and comfort, but seldom seen in Spain, and the surrounding woods tend not a little to refresh the eye of the traveller who has passed the barren country between Alcala and this place.

It was nearly dark when we entered Cor[dova] and we were awoke [sic] out of our sleep to pay the fees at the gate and Custom House. We found then a tolerable posada immediately opposite the great Mosque.

Saturday 25th of March
We now found ourselves in the Corduba of the Romans, the famous Colonia Patricia, and the still more celebrated capital of the Moors, the native city of the two Senecas, and of Lucan, of Averroes and many learned Arabians and of the great Captain Gonsalvo de Cordova.

Cordova was the first or almost the first colony which the Romans planted in Spain, and the first that had a right to coin money; it received the name of Patricia from having been founded by Patrician families. It is a question and a difficult one to answer, whether we must receive as truths the wonderful accounts of the population and magnificence of Cordova under its Moorish Sovereigns, or regard them only as the exaggerations of its Arabian historians, a fault too common amongst the Orientals. I confess for my own part that after having been at Granada and seen the monuments of the Moors in that city which became their capital only in the decline of their empire, power and magnificence I can give credit to the seemingly extravagant relations of the grandeur of Cordova their capital, their holy city, in the era of their glory. The accounts the Moors themselves have left us of Granada are metaphorical, but not exaggerated, and judging from them, we have reason to suppose that neither are the relations they have left us of Cordova, much exaggerated and certainly not to the extent which many persons imagine. It is said that Cordova in the time of its glory contained within the walls two hundred thousand houses, six hundred Mosques and nine hundred public baths. The population then must have exceeded that of London in the present day. Abdoulrahman III, the greatest Caliph Cordova ever had was enamoured all his life of a beautiful slave called Zehra; in honour of her he built a city[7] two miles distance from Cordova, situated at the foot of the mountains. In the palace of this new city, beside 40 columns of Granite, a present from the Emperor of Constantinople, were 1200 of the marble of Spain and Italy. Historians add that in the pavillon where he passed the siesta with his favourite, the ceiling was of gold and steel incrusted with precious stones, and amid the splendour of lights reflected from a hundred mirrors, a stream of quicksilver rose up out [of] a basin of Alabaster.

I cannot for my own part imagine that this ceiling could be superior to those of the Alhambra when uninjured by the hand of time, nor do I conceive that the stream of quicksilver could be more beautiful than the transparent waters which rise from the marble fountains of that palace. The building the City and Palace of Zehra cost annually three hundred thousand dinars of gold, equal to seventy five million of livres, and it took 25 years to complete this work. To this immense expence was added that of his seraglio of women, his slaves and household amounted to six thousand, three hundred persons. His bodyguard was 12,000 men. Being in continual war with the Spaniards he had to keep on foot immense armies, a fleet, and often to hire troops from Africa. His revenues to defray these enormous expences amounted to *12,045,000 dinars of gold, besides a great part of the taxes paid in the fruits of the earth. He had mines of Gold and Silver. The commerce of the country was immense. *130,000,000 of Livres.

And lastly, on the coasts of Catalonia were fisheries of Coral and of Pearls.

Such riches as these, appear almost incredible but less so when we consider that Abdoulrhaman possessed Portugal, Andalusia, the Kingdoms of Granada, of Murcia, of Valencia and a great part of New Castile, that is the most beautiful provinces of Spain. These provinces were then extremely populous and the Moors had carried agriculture to the highest pitch of perfection. Historians assure us that on the banks of the Guadalquiver were 12,000 villages, that the traveller could not walk a quarter of an hour without meeting with some hamlet. They reckoned in the states of the Caliph 80 great cities, 300, of the second order and an infinite number of towns.

In short, all accounts we have of the immense wealth and power of the Caliphs of Cordova are consistent with one another and the sources whence these proceeded seem adequate to furnish them so that we may receive with some confidence in their correctness, the relations given by the Arab historians.

Whatever has been our confidence in these accounts before, belief is however when you look at Cordova in its present state. Of the immense population what now remains 35,000 souls can scarcely support themselves. Of its astonishing commerce, and manufactures all has vanished, except a trifling trade in ribbands, hats and baize. Of the Palaces of the Caliphs not a vestige remains; and of the famous city of Zehra not even the situation can be discovered. Of its 600 mosques the great one still remains and certainly is one of the most curious monuments of antiquity. Cordova however has suffered less in its religious establishments than with commerce extent and magnificence. Besides a Cathedral and Collegiate church it contains 15 parish churches, forty Convents and a great number of pious institutions.

The mosque is a low quadrangular building of 620 feet in length by 440 in breadth. The architecture on the outside is uniform on two sides, and very simple; as is the case in their fortifications, there is a square tower at the distance of every 50, or 60, feet. Between each of these is a door of the same as those of the Alhambra, with the arch an ornament peculiar to the Moors. The inside presents to the eye nothing but an immense forest of pillars being upwards of 600 in number, low, of different colored marble, and crowned with the capitals of very different sizes some being as high again as their neighbours. From one pillar to another is thrown a couple of arches one above another. These pillars divide the mosque into 30 naves in its length and 19 in its breadth. The effect of the whole is singular and surprising, but not either imposing or pleasing owing to the insignificant height of the pillars. Cordova was conquered in the year 1236, by San Ferdinand but preserved in its ancient form till the time of Charles V when a light, elegant, gothic Cathedral was erected near the centre of the mosque; you walk immediate from one to the other and the effect produced by sudden change from the low dark forest of pillars into a beautiful and lofty Gothic Cathedral, and no one can help remarking the infinite superiority of the latter style of Architecture to the Moorish. The Sanctum Sanctorum of the Moors is still presented in its ancient form and presents very many curious specimens of the Moorish arches and ornaments, besides some beautiful inscriptions, as perfect as

7   Medina Ahazara: this vast, wonderful palace complex had a glorious but short existence. Started in 936, it was sacked in 1010 by Berber troops from Morocco whose strict religious beliefs were oppposed to luxury. Only in 1944 did excavations to rediscover the site begin, and they still continue.

the day they were made. A person showed us on two of the pillars a crucifix which he said had been cut by a nail by two Christians whom the Moors kept chained there. His story seems improbable enough as the Moors on no account whatever permit a Christian to enter their mosques. At one end of this building is a large Court containing many fountains an orange grove and two immense palm trees. The entrance to the Mosque from this court displays the good taste of somebody; the two pillars of the doorway are Roman mile stones of Granite, with Moorish capitals of marble, and these are surmounted by a great wooden ball painted yellow. I forget what is the inscription on these milestones but some-one has added in the same character, "this year was born the saviour of the world" and on the other "this is the year of the Passion". This Court was used by the Moors for ablutions. What surprised me most about the Mosque was the cap-itals of the pillars these are not only of different sizes, but in a totally different style from all those I had seen in Granada; they are all in imitation of the Corinthian capitals; some better than others but all of them very indifferently ex-ecuted. The Guadalquivir washes the walls of Cordova and an ancient and mag-nificent bridge is still in a good state of preservation. It is defended on one side by a fine Moorish tower now converted into a Guard House, on the other you enter the town by a handsome Gateway of the time of Charles V.

There is not one good street in Cordova and scarcely one good house. To what are we to attribute this? To the negligence of St Raphael the patron and guardian of this chosen city? Were its inhabitants consistent they would certainly attribute [it] to this; they tell you that God has entrusted this city solely to his care; they tell of the good he has done, the miracles he has wrought, the fires and pestilences from which he has delivered them. In gratitude for all this he is wor-shiped in all the churches. Images are erected to him in every street and there is one of wonderful height before the Bishops Palace; the gilt statue is placed on a lofty pillar, resting on artificial rock. On the shield of the Saint is the following inscription "Yo juro que yo soy Rafael a quien Diostiene puesto por guardia de esta ciudad". And if you were to ask one of the people how he knew that Raphael was the guardian of the city, he would reply pointing to the statue "Como! no lo jura il Santo mismo"! That is "How! Does not the Saint himself swear it?".

In wandering through the streets we saw in a courtyard a number of broken heads and bodies of marble. We went in and counted no less than 120 antiques, heads, bodies and inscriptions, amongst which was a Greek inscription well cut on a piece of white marble, and extremely beautiful Arabic inscriptions. There was an old servant in the Court and we asked him for the owner of these antiq-uities. He said his young master was in Cadiz and his old one, 90 years of age ill in bed; he added they had a fine collection of Coins, that neither of his masters knew or cared anything about them, but, that all had been collected by the Fa-ther of the old man. He only knew that they had been found at some little distance in the mountains.

We did not leave Cordova without seeing the fountain of the Poltro mentioned in 'Don Quixote'.

Having run through all Cordova and its environs, which are pleasant enough, by two o'clock in the afternoon we set out again on the road for Madrid, and skirting along the foot of the Sierra Morena for 9 leagues, reached Aldea del Rio about 9, or 10 o'clock. We here rested for a few hours and at one oclock next morning, proceeded again upon our journey. At daybreak we entered Andujar, a city famous in the time of the Moors, but sunk even lower than Cordova which might be expected for the churches and Convents seem to be five times as numerous as in that city: every other building is either a church or a Convent and have no doubt that if we had not arrived there so early, every other person we met in the street would be either a priest or monk. It stands on the Guadalquivir, and its situation is exactly similar to that of Cordova.

On leaving Andujar you begin to ascend the Sierra Morena by a rough broken road lying through groves of olives and gumcistus.

We breakfasted at Baylin, a small town 5 leagues from Andujar. In the neighbourhood of this place was performed almost the only great action of the Spaniards during the late revolution where Dupont with an army that might have conquered anything that Spain could have opposed to him, surrendered to a numerous but ill-clad, ill-armed and undisciplined mob.

Four leagues more brought us to Carolina, the Capital of the Colonies of the Sierra Morena and containing upwards of 5000 inhabitants. The approach to it is very pretty along an extensive Alameda lined with gardens. It is situated on an eminence commanding a fine view on both sides; like the rest of the Colonies it is built on a regular plan, and like the rest has declined since the disgrace of its illustrious Founder, Olavidé.[8] The sentence pronounced on this eminent man by that Institution, whose very name cannot be pronounced without causing horror still lives in the memory of most people that I cannot forbear making a few extracts on the subject from Bourgoing in which may be found all the particulars of Olavidé's condemnation.

"The times of sacred rigour appeared to have passed away; the Holy Office in a word appeared asleep when suddenly it gave signs of wakefulness in 1777, at the expence of an illustrious victim; and with it awakened in Spain terror and

---

[8] Pablo Olavidé (1725–1803) was born in Lima, Peru. He was a writer, dramatist, jurist and politician, a friend of Voltaire and Diderot and a respected figure of the Enlightenment in Europe. Despite holding prestigious positions in Andalucia, his views made him a natural target for the Inquisition. Charged with heresy, he was condemned to imprisonment from which he escaped to France. He returned to Spain in 1798, shocked by the excesses of the French Revolution. A new university in Seville named after Olavidé was founded in 1997.

false zeal and without its frontiers the indignation of the apostles of a wise toleration.

"Don Pablo Olavidé, a native of Peru, had risen by his talents to one of the highest places in the administration, that of Intendant of the four kingdoms of Andalusia and Assistente de Sevilla. The King conceived the idea of clearing and peopling that part of the Sierra Morena traversed by the route from Cadiz to Madrid, a district formerly inhabited and cultivated but which had since become covered with wood, and was the haunt of the banditti and of wild beasts. This commission was entrusted to Olavidé. He executed it in a most distinguished manner; but he was not able to avoid the common splitting rock of great enterprise. He made enemies; he drew upon him above all the aversion of Father Romuald, a German Capuchin who, armed with a patent from his chief declaring him prefect of the new missions, affected an unlimited authority in all things he had to do with, even those not relating to religion. He experienced opposition above all on the part of Olavidé who however admitted him to his intimacy. The disappointed ambition of the monk was irritated; some discourse let slip by Olavidé increased his resentment. He nourished the ill-will of some colonists, his companions, and made use of them to discredit the new establishment and its chief. Memorials were remitted to the Counsel of Castile containing very heavy accusations against Olavidé, who was suddenly recalled to court in the month of November 1775, to treat there on certain subjects relative to his mission."

"Whilst he lived tranquilly in Madrid chance discovered to him the plot which had been laid against him. Some intercepted letters informed him that Father Romuald conspired his distruction and even flattered himself with the support of a great court.

"He knew by another channel that the vindictive monk had the year before [found] the minister in being wanting in proper respect for religion, of having prohibited books, and that recently he had been denounced to the Inquisition.

"These discoveries did not as yet trouble his security. He sought protectors near the throne. He went to the Grand Inquisitor protests the purety of his faith and offers to retract any assertions with which they reproached him. During more than a year that he had lived at Madrid he had conducted himself in the most exemplary manner, but nothing could dissipate the storm that hung over his head.

"On the 14th of November 1776 a grandee of Spain in quality of Alguazil, Mayor of the Inquisition, accompanied by officers of Justice went to arrest him and conduct him to the prisons of the Inquisition, whilst at Carolina where his wife was living and at Seville his common residence his effects, his books his papers were seized. From this moment he was lost to his wife his parents and his friends. During two years they were ignorant of what part of the earth he inhabited, or if he still breathed, and all had renounced the idea of seeing him again.

"At length on the 21st of November 1778 there was held in the Casa de la

Inquision an assembly to which were invited 40 people of different ranks, amongst whom were found many Grandees of Spain, General officers, Priests and monks.

"The culprit appeared dressed in yellow with a green taper in his hand and attended by officers of the Inquisition. They read all the details of the proceedure [sic]. The most interesting part was a circumstantial relation which he himself had made of his whole life. He avowed in it that in the course of his travels he had frequented the Esprits forts, namely Voltaire and Rousseau; that he had returned to Spain imbued with prejudices against the clergy and persuaded that the privileges and opinions of the Church of Rome are opposed to the prosperity of States; and that since he had been at the head of the Colonies of the Sierra Morena, he had expressed himself rashly and without reflexion on the obstacles which retarded their progress, on the infallibility of the Pope and the Tribunal of the Inquisition.

Then followed the depositions of 78 witnesses who accused him of having foften [i.e. often] spoken the language of the Esprits Forts, of having cast ridicule on the Fathers, the Church etc.

The accused acknowledged some of these changes and denied others, assuring them that the assertions they imputed to him, proceeded from the purest source; that some had for their object to encourage to work the the [sic] Colonists confided to his care, and whose insolence took for a mask the exterior forms of religion; and that when he spoke of the inconveniences of Celibacy he had only in view to encourage population so necessary for the prosperity of the country.

"The tribunal judged him guilty of all the crimes imputed to him and pronounced the sentence of heretic in form, He interrupted the reading to repulse this epithet. This was the last effort of his constancy. He fainted on the bench where he was seated. As soon as he recovered his senses, they continued the reading of the sentences. It confiscated all his goods, declared him incapable of holding any office, banished him to the distance of 20 leagues from Madrid, the Royal residences, from Seville, the theatre of his past authority, from Lima his country; t condemned him to be during eight years in a monastery, where he should read the works which piety dictated, and confess every month"…

"This was the fate of Olavidé; thus did the Inquisition crush one of the few great men which Spain has had to boast of in latter ages, and thus did the Spanish government admit the persecution of its greatest Patriots…"

The rest of the history of Olavidé is short; he shortly found means to escape to France. The Spanish government demanded that he should be given up, but it was refused. He lived in Paris in the first society till the revolution broke out, when he retired to the banks of the Loire; At length, wishing to visit Spain, and having returned sincerely to his old religion, he received permission to enter

Spain and in 1798, made his appearance in that capital which 20 years before had witnessed his condemnation. He soon retired to Andalusia, and died in 1803.

St Helana [sic] is distant 2 leagues from Carolina and is the highest point to which the road ascends; from it is a fine view of the Pass of Despeñaperros, a complete rent in the Sierra and through which we had to go; this is the only pass of any kind you meet with between Cadiz and Madrid. Leaving St. Helena you begin to descend by an excellent new road made by Le Maur a French Engineer and equal to any over the mountains in England; through the craggy rock just mentioned it is particularly well executed and excites the wonder of the traveller. Having passed this you very soon find yourself in the immense plains of La Mancha, which extend from this place to Aranjuez a distance of above 150 miles with the slightest rise in the ground, and where as far as the eye can reach on every side not a single hillock can be discovered. We therefore determined to travel on all that night which was then beginning to close upon us, and endeavour to reach Aranjuez by the following evening. This we accomplished never stopping but to change horses. The country the whole distance is the most uninteresting that can be conceived of, perfectly flat, perfectly uninclosed, completely brown and without a single shrub or tree. Between the towns is not a single house, and you rarely meet with a human being. The towns we passed through were all in ruins, the French having pulled off all the roofs for firewood, the few wretched inhabitants who have escaped fire sword and famine live in caves or without any shelter and when a stranger arrives he has the whole population about him immediately to ask charity. These towns have however been but in a miserable state before the French destroyed them, for I see Ponz remarks in his Viage de España that all the towns in La Mancha appear as if they had just suffered a bombardment, which is just a description of them.

The principal places through which we passed were Valdepeñas, Manzanares, Villata, Puerto La Piche, Madrilejos, Tembleque, La Guadia and Ocaña. Valdepeñas and Manzanares are famous for their wines. These wines are all good enough when drunk on the spot, but as it can only be carried about in skins, these give it a very unpleasant taste. Puerto La Piche is a small village near which Don Quixote armed himself on entering on his career.

A little on leaving Villalta you cross a long narrow stone bridge, which crosses a large fen this the river Guadiana which near here sinks underground, afterwards reappearing in a place called Los ojos de Guadiana, that is the eyes of the Guadiana.

About 9 o'clock on Monday night we reached Aranjuez.

Tuesday 28th March
We employed this morning in seeing the wonders of Aranjuez which are nothing very particular. The town is modern, built on a regular plan, the houses only

two stories, the streets wide. When the Court resides here, it contains a population of 10,000, but no one that can avoid it stays longer than June, as the air then becomes unhealthy. The Palace is a large brick building with an immense dome, and does not make a pleasing appearance. It was begun by Charles V, and added to by Ferdinand VI and Charles III. No particular splendour is displayed in the interior; but it contains an excellent collection of paintings principally the spoils of St. Ildefonso. The country house here, called the Casa del Labrador, or farmhouse, is better worth seeing; it consists of a number of small low rooms delicately and beautifully fitted up with rich marbles, paintings in oil and fresco, embroidered silk etc, the whole executed with extreme taste and excellence. The gardens consist of long, shady walks with handsome marble fountains which the French have entirely destroyed. The whole is little more than a wood of fine trees in a valley surrounded by bare naked hills. Through this valley flows the Tagus, a very different river from what it is where it washes the walls of Lisbon.

Having seen Aranjuez in this hasty manner, because there seemed to be nothing to detain us longer there, we proceeded the same evening to Madrid. Excepting a single row of trees on each side of the road the eight leagues between Aranjuez and Madrid is uninteresting brown and desert a scene as that just described, almost to the very gates of Madrid, in some parts quite; for there is more than one part where you may lean your back against the walls of Madrid and look over an extent of country of 20 or 30 miles without seeing a tree a shrub, a house, cottage, human being, and I think I may say a blade of grass. We found a great illumination in the City it being the anniversary of Ferdinand's return to his country and crown. Making our way through the crowd with some difficulty, and to our mutual inconvenience, we stopped at the Cruz de Malta, a large but dirty Posada. The next day we moved into lodgings, which we changed again the next day for others much better.

Sir John Hunter the English Consul General had written to us when at Cadiz to say that if we came to Madrid he should be happy to show us every attention. This he certainly did and to the kindness of him and his family, that is Lady Hunter and two very agreeable daughters, we owe the pleasantness of our long stay in Madrid. Their house was quite open to us at all hours, and when no other engagement called us another way we spent all our evenings in their company. We brought a letter of Introduction to the Chevalier de Souza the Portugueze Minister; Sir John introduced us to Sir H. Wellesley, to Count La Gardie the Swedish Minister, and Mons. Cambier the Dutch Minister; from all of whom we experienced every possible attention. We were likewise introduced to some of the other Ministers, but visited only with those mentioned.

At the end of 5 weeks, the Hunters going to spend some weeks in Aranjuez set us completely at liberty to make any little excursion we thought proper, and on the **sixth of May** I.H., Mr Kinder and I set off for the famous monastery of the Escorial. They left me in two days; I remained there 8 or 10 days to examine leisurely the paintings etc. and to converse with the friars; and then returned to Madrid by way of St. Ildefonso and Segovia.

If a stranger forms his expectations of the Escorial from what Spanish authors have written on the subject he will in all probability be disappointed. Padre Santos in his history of the Escorial calls it the only wonder of the world, the most famous building known in the whole globe, the miracle of the idea of perfection. Such praises are not only extravagant but injudicious, for a person is disappointed if on beholding it for the first time he is not struck dumb with astonishment; which is far from being the case, as on the out side it presents nothing to the eye but an immense square building of the simplest and most unadorned architecture, quite too plain and too destitute of embellishments for so great a building. What surprised me most, was the great superiority beauty and accuracy of the masonry work within, the turning of the arches, vaulted roofs, and the joining of the stones.

The principal front is towards the west and immediately faces a high mountain; this seems ill judged, for you cannot see it except when close under the building. The only ornaments or pillars about the outside of the Monastery are some simple ones of the doric order, placed about the principal door. This side is 740 feet long, with three doors and 200 windows.

The Eastern side is the same length as the western but the parts of the church and Palace forming the handle of the Gridiron, for such is the shape of the building standing out from the right line, is computed at 11000 feet; it has 366 windows.

The Southern front is 580 feet long and the number of windows 306; that towards the north is the same length but has much fewer windows, on account of the north wind which is very much felt in this situation.

On the north and west, the height to the cornice is 70 feet, on the other two 75. In each corner is a square tower 200 feet high, and the great dome of the church towers far above the rest.

The situation of the Monastery is very agreeable; behind rise a lofty chain of mountains, before is an extensive plain belonging to the friars, covered with wood and beautifully green, and there are abundance of trees in its immediate vicinity. The view it commands is rather extensive than interesting; you see Madrid and the barren country beyond, with the immense arid plains of La Mancha; the view however towards the hills is fine.

Italy, France and Spain all dispute the honour of having given birth to the architect of the Monastery of the Escorial, and all mention the name of one of their countrymen as the original planner and director of it; much has been written on the subject, but very unnecessarily as the dispute might have been settled at once by referring to the foundation stone of the building itself which gives the names of the founder, the architect and the date; namely Philip the Second, Juan Bautista de Toledo and 23rd of April 1563. Juan Bautista dying was succeeded by Juan de Herrera.

It was built by Philip 2nd in consequence of a vow made at the battle of St. Quentin and dedicated to San Lorenzo, the battle being fought on the anniversary of the martyrdom of that saint. And as he was roasted to death on a gridiron, the Pious monarch in celebration of the event gave this form to the Monastery; this has been done by means of a great number of square courts on the inside. The whole cost was about 6,000,000 of ducats or £825,000 and it was completed in the surprisingly short period of 6 years, an expedition perhaps almost unequalled, considering the immense size of the building.

Entering at the principal door you advance into the Pateo de los Reyes; and see before you the principal front of the church which is very handsome; in niches stand six statues of the Kings of Israel which give the name to the pateo. These statues are of granite with marble heads, are all 17 feet in height. The church is singularly elegant and majestic, and is as beautiful a specimen of architecture of the Doric order as can well be imagined. It consists of three naves, the largest 50 feet wide, the smaller ones 30. The height from the bottom to the spring of the arch is 110 feet. The pillars are distant from each other at the base 53 feet, their circumference is 30 feet. The diameter of the great dome is 66 feet. On the needle of the dome is [a] ball of gilt brass which weighs 136 arrobas or 3400 lbs and the iron cross by which it is surmounted weighs 73 arrobas or 1825 lbs. The ceilings of the church are made after the manner of the Vatican, and admirably painted by Jordan. The Choir, as in many churches is not placed in the great nave where it always takes off much from the grandeur of the whole, but is in one of the recesses formed by the horizontal part of the cross. The ceiling is a monstrous representation of the interior of heaven with all the great personages as large as life painted by Cambiaso. From the roof hangs a magnificent chandelier of rock chrystal with the figures of a peacock dove and other birds admirably wrought. It weighs 35 arrobas or 875 pounds, and is as beautiful as curious.

Before the Paris collection was formed and before the French banditti pillaged Spain, the Monastery of the Escorial was reputed to possess the best collection of paintings in the world except that of Dresden. It has however suffered extremely, the French having sold or carried off the most valuable. Of the six original paintings of the Divine Raphael, one alone remains, two of them, viz. the pearl of Rafael, as it was called by way of excellence, and the Madonna del Pesce two of the most famous in the world, are I hear in Paris; though some say that one of them, together with many other extremely valuable, were taken by Lord Wellington at Vittoria, in Joseph's baggage. The pearl was once in the collection of King Charles the first of England and when all his effects were put up to auction, it and many others were bought by the Spanish ambassador; its value seems to have been well understood then as now, for the Ambassador paid £2,000 for it even at that time. There are two good copies of these paintings done by the Padre Santos, one of the friars and a very good painter. The best paintings which remain are that of Rafael, 2 of Leonardi da Vinci, a copy by Titian of the famous painting of the supper by Leonardi, a virgin by Rubens, Peter and Paul by Guido, an annunciation by Corregio, the coronation of Charles 2nd by Coello, a dead Christ by Titian and two paintings by the same of Charles V and Philip 2nd. The best painting Jordan ever did is the Battle of St Quintin and St Lorenzo pleading before the Holy Trinity, both in fresco on the ceiling above the grand staircase. Of Titian, Paul Veronese and Jordan there remains a great number of admirable performances as well as of Elmudo, a dumb friar and good painter and of some others. El Jacobo, the most esteemed work of Velasques is now in London.

The Library of the Escorial though it never consisted of above 30,000 volumes, was always considered as of great value and excellence. Of what books it can boast at the present moment it is impossible to say, as the French carried off a great number to Madrid and many to France; those which they left at Madrid are returning daily, so that at present the Librarian cannot tell how far they have suffered. Before the revolution there were in this library above 4300 Manuscripts, viz. 567 greek, 67 Hebrew, above 1800 Arabic, and 1820 Latin and other languages. The Mss of the Bible which are preserved here are of very great antiquity, written as well in Hebrew, as in Gothic characters, Longobardic etc. There is likewise a greek one of the Emperor Cantacucenus which is considered to agree very closely with the Septuagint version, printed at Rome by the solicitude of Cardinal Carrafa.

The number of Mss was much greater before the great fire which took place, [in] 1671 and during 15 days consumed a great portion of the rooms of the monastery. Before the accident the Arabic manuscripts amounted to 3,000; these were principally taken by Admiral Don Luis Faxedo from the Moors who were carrying them from one city of Africa to another. An account of the greater part of these has been published by Casiri, Librarian to his Majesty Charles III.

But what the pious Catholic upholds with greater pleasure than either library or paintings, is the monstrous collection of relics preserved in the monastery. An Englishman starts on reading the sum total of these relics, in a printed list hung up near the Choir, he can scarcely believe his eyes when he sees the figures, 7422; of these says the list, 462 are famous; 255, almost famous; 1006, smaller ones, and 4168 little ones. The list farther states that amongst these are 12 whole bodies, 144 entire heads and 306 great leg bones. I saw the heads which are ranged out on shelves like books. One puzzles his memory and ingenuity not a little to divine what can all those be the relics of, but the following list of a few will enable us to guess what kind of relics are the rest.

"Relics of Christ, the 12 Apostles and upwards of a thousand saints.

The whole body of one of the children killed by order of Herod.

One of the jars in which our Saviour turned the water into wine.

The thigh bone of Lazarus.

A bit of the tomb of Christ.

A tooth of Santa Margarita.

A bit of the skin of John the Baptist.

Two pieces of the Holy Cross which grow

One of the offerings of the Magi. ["]

It is not difficult to mention many more but it may be easily guessed what they are.

In the collection of relics is one of the pieces of silver which Judas received to betray his master, and a coin with the head of our Saviour and the inscription Jesus Nazarenus rex Judaeorum. After this one is not astonished at hearing of a feather of the Holy Ghost being preserved at the Cathedral of Seville, and some milk of the Virgin in that of Toledo.

The Pantheon to which you descend by a beautiful staircase the steps sides and roof of which are of polished marble, is an octagonal vault likewise of polished marble with rich ornaments of brass and gold; the gloom of this place scarcely broken in upon by the scanty light of a small candle is particularly impressive. Around you in niches one above the other, are seen six and twenty beautiful urns of fine marble with ornaments of bronze. Fourteen of these already are occupied, and the names of the Kings and queens whose bodies they contain are written on the side in letters of gold. They are as follows: Charles V, Philip II, Philip III, Philip IV, Charles II, Luis 1st, Charles III. The Empress Doña Isabel, and the Queens Anna, Margaret of Austria, Doña Isabel de Bourbon, Marianne of Austria, Luisa de Savoya and Maria Amalia of Saxony. On a plain but elegant altar is a large cross of Black marble, a beautiful chandelier hangs from the lofty dome and the whole is executed with simplicity and good taste.

Mass is said in the Pantheon once a year. The Friars of the Escorial are of the order of St Jerome; before the revolution there were about 200, of them, and 70 have already returned to the Monastery; 48 died during the revolution, and a few have fled to France. In order to enter this community it is necessary to deliver a memorial to the Prelate stating yourself to be of good family, and that you understand the Latin language and music. The business of the Prelate is to enquire if the person has these qualifications, and then calling an assembly of the friars, it is decided by the black and white ball whether he shall be admitted. If the number of white balls exceed that of the black the person takes the habit the following day. If he brings any money the Prelate takes possession of it but gives it him as he requires it; it does not belong to the community, till after his death.

The riches of the Friars of the Escorial were immense, arising partly from the immense donations of the Founder, from donations of private individuals and from Tythes. Their possessions in land are very great, and they have estates even in America; they had, we were told, above 40,000 of the best Merino sheep, and adjoining the monastery they have manufactures of cloth linen, leather, earthenware and everything they require for their own consumption and the surplus they sell.

Masses. In the course of the year when the place had its full complement of Friars, upwards of 24,000 masses were regularly said, including 220 annually for the soul of Charles V, 220 for Philip II, 220 for Philip III, 220 for Philip IV, etc. It made on average 180 a day; but at present from the small number of Friars only 70 are said each day. I was told that to say a mass well, you should be above half an hour nor less than 20 minutes.

I was not intimately acquainted with more than one of the Friars, namely Father Isidro, a well informed, benevolent and liberal old man with whom I could speak with more freedom on religion and other topics than with any Spaniard I have met with; and it is generally the case that a stranger and especially an Englishman may indulge in a greater freedom of conversation with the friars and Clergy than with any other class of people in Spain, for whatever state of ignorance and bigotry they may keep the people, they are often liberal themselves.

I lodged all the time in the Posada, generally got a good long walk before breakfast and before the heat of the day; after breakfast I generally went to chat an hour or two with Father Isidro and did the same again in the afternoon. The weather being fine, I spent the time pleasantly enough, and not unprofitably.

Having a wish to see the famous gardens of St. Ildefonso,[9] and the ancient city of Segovia, I determined to return to Madrid by those places and hiring a mule to carry myself and my portmanteau, a good stout lad taking hold of the halter and walking before, I left the Escorial at 5 o'clock in the morning **May 17th**.

There is an excellent high road to St Ildefonso, a distance of 7 leagues or 28 miles, it carries you nearly in a straight line to the summit of the Guadarama chain of mountains and you descend on the other side by an angular road, the hills on that part being extremely steep. I have never met with any statement of the height of the Guadarama sierra, but it certainly is above 6, if not 7 thousand feet above the sea. The Escorial which stands at its feet is about 3000 feet above the sea, and the hills behind are undoubtedly upwards of 3000 feet higher. The snow remains upon them all the year round. The greater part of this sierra is thickly covered with woods of Pines, which afford shelter to a great number of wolves and wild boars, as well as to an infinity of game of all species. Near the summit we staid half an hour in a little venta to wait for a party of muleteers, and accompanied them the rest of the journey, as there had been some robberies a day or two before; they pointed out the spot where one had taken place and where signs still remained that such a thing had taken place. From the summit we had a very extensive view towards both north and south, at the same instant; towards the south you see the Escorial, the hills of Toledo and the immense plains of La Mancha extending almost to the Sierra Morena; to the north are the still great plains of Old Castille.

The situation of St Ildefonso is like that of the Escorial, but neither so magnificent nor picturesque. It is situated at the foot of the Guadarama mountains but it is not much elevated above the high plains of Old Castille and as it is completely an artificial place, the very soil having been brought from a distance, everything without the walls of the grounds is a barren wilderness. The Palace is a handsome building, superior in point of appearance to that of Aranjuez. The inside presents nothing very remarkable. There [are] some paintings but not very excellent ones as Charles the 4th removed 400 of the best to adorn his palace at Aranjuez. In a long gallery are some fine specimens of ancient sculpture, formerly in the possession of Christina of Sweden, and purchased in Rome by order of Philip V. The gardens are perhaps the finest of their kind in Europe, that is where the beauty consists in straight walks straight rows of trees and elegant fountains. The latter have been very justly celebrated. Many of them are very large indeed, of delicate white marble and figures of bronze, the two of the most famous, are that of La Fama which throws up water to the height of 70 feet and that of Daños de Diana, where Diana and a number of nymphs of the natural size are bathing whilst the water is shooting out from a thousand parts and falling from the top of a Grotto of coral into shells and beautifully wrought basins of white Alabaster. The King was so delighted with this work when he first saw it play that he ordered a thousand dollars be given to the architects. These gardens have not suffered so much as many other things from the wanton destruction of the French, as Joseph took a fancy to the place and frequently visited it. I was shown the palace and gardens by one of the Canons of the Collegiate Church to whom Father Isidro had given me letter.

On the following morning at an early hour he sent his nephew to carry me through the glass manufactures, the only ones in Spain. These, as well as the palace and gardens, were the work of Philip 5th, they were begun in 1728, and completed under his successor Ferdinand 6th. There are four manufactures of the glass articles, namely that of mirrors, of window Glass, of bottles and of engraving the glass. The first only of these can be put in competition with those of England and the continent and the famous mirrors, like many other things in Spain, are more extraordinary in size than excellence. The largest size they make is upwards of four yards long by above 2 yards wide (quarto baras de largo por dos y tercia de ancho). The brass plate on which these immense mirrors are cast,

<hr/>

[9]   St. Ildefonso: better known now as La Granja.

weighs nineteen thousand and eight hundred pounds and the cylinder of the same metal, which rolls the liquid matter, weighs twelve hundred. This manufacture is not able to support itself, but is carried out at the King's expence whom it costs annually at least 8000 dollars, deducting all the profits which arise from the sale of the glass. The building in which these mirrors are made is spacious and handsome, and contains 20 furnaces where the glass is tempered; it remains in them hermetically sealed during from 15 to 25 days. They are polished with Emery and black lead and the operation requires 8, or 10 days. When finished they are sent to adorn the Royal Palaces, or as presents to different Sovereigns. Charles the third sent 13 to Naples and 15 of them amongst others presents to the Ottoman Porte.

Segovia. From St Ildefonso to Segovia is only 2 leagues, the road is good and level, lined on each side by [a] row of small trees, the only ones that can be seen in the immense tract of country which they [sic] eye embraces. The appearance of Segovia approaching it from any side is grand and imposing. It is situated on a high rock surrounded by a deep ravine, and two rivers, which have worn a deep and narrow channel in the rock. At the summit of a high sharp ridge formed by the junction of these two rivers stands the Alcazar or ancient castle, an extraordinary and confused mass of buildings once the residence of the Gothic kings and afterwards the Moorish Princes. The interior is fitted up in the modern style and is now converted into a military College.

The Cathedral, which stands on the highest point of the rock, is one of the finest Gothic buildings in Spain. It is nearly destitute of all ornaments inside, nor are there any paintings of note, but the height, elegance and lightness of the pillars, the beauty of the arches and majestic simplicity [of] the whole is pleasing and striking. It consists of 3 naves of which the middle one is much the highest; were the divisions between the chapels thrown down it would consist of five naves. It is much inferior in size and grandeur to that of Seville, but I have never seen its equal in elegance and lightness. But the most venerable monument which Segovia and perhaps Spain has to boast of is its acqueduct, almost in a perfect state of preservation, and uninjured by the hand of time or modern patchwork. It stretches over the valley from the valley [sic] from the opposite hill to the highest part of the city, a distance of 2400 feet; at its greatest height it is 102 feet above the ground. The arches are in two rows, one above another, the pillars on which these are supported are only 8 feet wide in front, and 11 in thickness; the lightness of its appearance from such proportions is almost inconceivable, and it appears a very thin wall as of only a single brick rising to this astonishing height and stretching its delicate arches over the valley and a part of the city. The Spanish historians, who do not think this acqueduct to be the work of Hercules and the Phenicians, maintain it to be a work of the Grecians. There is little reason to doubt and the most intelligent Travellers seem to be of the same opinion that it was built by the Romans, and they generally give it to the reign of the Emperor Trajan. It is undoubtedly the best preserved of all the Roman remains in Spain.

Segovia, and the same may be said of almost all the great cities of Spain, has been famous once, has once contained a great population, has had great manufactures, and has carried on an extensive trade, none of these things can be said of it in the present day; its fame exists only in the pages of history, its population has dwindled to 2,000 citizens and its manufactures are confined to the making of a few coarse cloths. Ponz in his "Viage de España" observes that "Segovia does not contain 10,000 inhabitants men, women and children, a number very disproportioned to its twenty five Parishes." "The number too," says he, "of twenty one convents appears out of proportion for so small a number of people, for although Segovia contained six times as many people, (as in former times very probably it did) yet it might be abundantly served by so many churches." As I remarked before, the decline of a city and the increase of convents always seem to keep pace with each other.

Segovia has a mint where copper money is struck off. It had just begun to issue some new Fernandos. It had the privilege of coining money in the Roman times of which I have a specimen, such coins however are extremely rare.

Segovia has more signs about it of being an ancient city than any I ever saw; the whole place is an antiquity for the houses and streets look as if they had neither been repaired nor cleaned since the time of the Moors, I and doubt if they ever have. You might amuse yourself for hours in every street in examining the remains of former magnificence. The second story of almost all the houses, like some of our old buildings in England, project out far beyond the lower one, and are supported by pillars; some of these are very handsome, of black or white marble, granite or other stone, well cut, fanciful capitals and scarcely two of them alike, from which I conclude them to be Moorish. Every doorway has two of these curious pillars, which support arches of every description, Roman, Gothic, Saxon, Moorish and mixtures of all these, especially of the Moorish and Gothic which have naturally a strong resemblance. Some of the Saxon arches are well made and handsome, but what brought them there I could not imagine, being the only ones of the kind I had met with or heard of in Spain.

Having seen the principal curiosities of Segovia, and not having time to hunt about for the less important ones, I set off at 4 o'clock A.M. **May 19th** in company with three or four Muleteers, and after proceeding over two leagues of barren arid country we began once more to ascend the Guadarama sierra by a pass more to the west and considerably higher than the one we had taken on our former route. We continued ascending for some hours among thick forests of pines, having occasionally fine news of the flat land of Old Castille. Having reached the summit we had a complete view on both sides [of] the ridge of mountains and being so sharp that you [look] down both sides without moving from the spot; both views are magnificent. The descent on the other side was very rapid for a considerable distance, but then became gradual. Near the village of Guadarama we got onto the high road from the Escorial to St. Ildefonso, but soon branched off on to the royal road to Madrid. We reached La Torre, a miserable village situated amongst some barren rocks, long before sunset, though I came on my mule only at a walk and the distance was full 40 miles. Here I had to spend the evening sitting over a fire of straw and rubbish, making my tea in a frying pan and having my ears annoyed by a number of squawling children. After comforting myself with smoking 15, or 20 cigaritos, I lay down for a few hours on a miserable bed.

May 20th

I was off and out of sight of La Torre before sunrise and happily accomplishing the five leagues which remained in 6 hours, I arrived in Madrid to breakfast; after having been away a fortnight. I took I.H. by surprise as he had received no news of me during that time as the letter I had written some days before never arrived.

Toledo was now the only place in the neighbourhood of Madrid of any consequence which I had not seen, and a visit to it had been previously resolved on. The weather having now become very warm we determined to travel during the night.

Toledo is distant from Madrid only 12 leagues but as we had attractions at Aranjuez we went there on our way, which made a 2 days journey of seven leagues or 28 miles each.

May 28th

We set out from Madrid in a Calesa at 1 o'clock in the morning accompanied by Mr Kinder on horseback. We reached Aranjuez by about 10 o'clock and after breakfast went to the Hunters with whom we spent the rest of the day and the evening very agreeably. At 5 o'clock the next morning we left Aranjuez. The road, after leaving the shady avenues of that place, is very bad and lies through a country sterile and uninteresting until reaching Toledo, the view of which as you approach is very fine. It stands upon a large rock or hill surrounded on every side except the north by the Tagus which flows through a deep and rugged ravine. It is crossed by two fine bridges, that of Alcantara is of two arches and of very great height, being thrown not only over the river but the Ravine. Toledo very much resembles Segovia both in situation and in history. It must have been a great city in the time of the Romans, as is sufficiently attested by the coins struck there, the remains of a great acqueduct, and the ruins of an immense amphitheatre. In the time of the Goths it was the capital of Spain, the residence [of] her monarchs. It did not cease to be a capital in the time of the Moors, being the court of the Kings of the province of the same name. It was likewise for some time the residence of the Emperor Charles V. It is now the seat of the Primate of all Spain. It was taken from the Moors after they had kept possession 376 years by Alphonso VI in the year 1090. This monarch, having been driven from his own dominions, was kindly received at the court of the Moorish King of Toledo. One day the King was conversing with his friends about the strength of his Capital which he said was absolutely impregnable, but that it might be taken by a 9 months siege. Alphonso happened to be taking his siesta in an adjoining room and overheard the conversation, and when circumstances once more recalled him to his kingdom; he besieged Toledo and took it in the time mentioned.

Half of the city is now in ruins, half of what remains is churches and convents. The streets are narrow and crooked, with scarcely a single good house. The population has declined proportionally; three centuries ago it contained two hundred thousand inhabitants, these do not amount at present to 25,000; the increase of Madrid has partly contributed to this depopulation, but not altogether for Madrid, does not contain a number of inhabitants which added to the 25000 would make up the former population of Toledo. But this decay is not confined to the city of Toledo "for the Province which little more than a century ago contained 551 villages of considerable importance, does not now contain above 349, and the greater part of these almost destitute of manufactures and commerce and even of inhabitants." This is speaking of it as it was before the revolution, at present the state of the province is much worse as it has suffered as much or even more than any other part of Spain.

The Cathedral of Toledo is deserving of the first mention. It was originally built in the reign of the Gothic King Recaredo and consecrated in the year 587. In 714 it fell into the hands of the Moors who used it for their principal mosque. It preserved the form given it by the Moors till the time of San Fernando, when it was rebuilt in the way it now exists. The Tower is exceeding light, elegant and richly ornamented to the summit. The rest of the building makes no show from without on account of other buildings being connected with it, but the doorways are very magnificent and highly ornamented. The interior is on the same plan precisely as that of Segovia with three naves, or including the chapels with 5, and with the head of the cross circular, but this is very inferior in lightness, height and elegant simplicity. A row of arches and pillars placed two and two in the upper part of the second nave are unquestionably Moorish. The Moorish stucco work on the walls still exists in one or two of the chapels and the chapters hall. In the Muzarabic Chapel is a painting of ancient date representing some battle between the Moors and Christians and a Virgin in mosaic work admirably executed. There are only a very few of the paintings worthy of notice; those painted in fresco on the walls of the beautiful Cloisters, by Francisco Bayen are very good as well as five small ones in oil by Maella, in one of the rooms of the Cathedral. The valuable custodium and all the rich garments belonging to this place were sent to

Cadiz during the revolution, and by this means escaped the fate of the still more valuable ones of the Escorial, that is being melted down, and sold. Amongst the relics they show a great stone with the mark of a foot upon it, which they say was made by the Virgin Mary, when she descended to invest St. Ildefonso with the cloak of Office. An antiquarian may amuse himself well here in reading the old Latin and Gothic Inscriptions, which are very numerous. It is a building deservedly considered as worthy of a visit from the curious traveller; but the lowness of the pillars detracts as much from the majesty of its appearance, as the superabundance of ornaments do from its simplicity.

The cloisters of the hospital of Saint Juan Bautista built by the famous architect of the Escorial are generally allowed to [be] very well worth seeing, but this building is now the house of the Inquisition and we were told it would be in vain to solicit admission. Four or five of the churches we observed to have small square towers exactly similar to the windows of which were completely in the Moorish style of architecture. We went into one of these and to our surprise found that it had been a mosque and preserved the ancient form little altered by giving it that of the cross. It consisted of three naves made by rows of Moorish arches such as we had seen in the mosques of Barbary. Could we have found our way into some of the others we might probably have found other mosques still existing in Toledo. From this and other circumstances, such as the good repair of some of the Gateways, houses built on arches unquestionably Moorish, which do not seem of older date than the rest of the town, and the similarity of these to those of Granada, Ecija and other Moorish towns, inclines me to suppose that the greater part of the present buildings of Toledo are of Moorish construction, and shows still more clearly what I was pretty well convinced of at Granada, that the style of building among the Moors of Spain was in many respects different from what is now, and probably then was in use among the Moors of Africa. None of the houses of Granada nor the palaces of the Alhambra and Generalife have flat roofs, a practice universal in Barbary.

The Church of Saint Juan de los Reyes, is a very handsome Gothic building with many rich ornaments inside, but completely spoiled by the French who made use of it for a stable. On the outside are hung a great number of chains which were taken off the Christian captives at the conquest of Granada. It is called Saint John of the Kings because it is built on the site of the ancient Palace of the Gothic Kings.

The Alcazar or castle was begun in the time of Alphonso VI and completed under the direction of the famous architect Covarrubias and Herrera in the time of Charles V. The northern front is of Doric order and extremely handsome.

It suffered dreadfully from a fire which took place from accident or malice, the night the Portugueze troops, allies of the Emperor, evacuated the place. It remained in this state till about thirty years ago when it was repaired by the archbishop and appropriated to silk manufactures for the employment of the poor children of Toledo. The French, when they quitted it, wantonly set it on fire, and it is now perhaps in a more dilapidated state than before it was repaired by the archbishop. The court is very beautiful, from the elegance and admirable proportion of the Doric pillars and arches by which it is surrounded. The great staircase, which has been much celebrated for its beauty and grandeur is now covered with a heap of ruins.

Near the bridge of Alcantara are seen the remains of the famous machine of the Italian mechanic Juanelo, constructed for throwing up the waters of the Tagus to the highest part of the Alcazar.

Little is known of Juanelo except that he was born in Cremona in Lombardy, made excellent watches in the time of Charles V and Philip II and threw water from the Tagus to the Alcazar by means of some extraordinary machine of his invention. He died in Toledo in 1585. If we may judge by the ruins of the building this machine must have been rather an unwieldy one. It was all carried away by a flood. It is said to have been of the nature of a batting machine; the water being struck by powerful hammers was forced up pipes placed for the purpose, but it is said the violence of the water was such that no pipes could be made strong enough to resist it.

A little farther down the river are the small remains of the ancient Roman acqueduct, which when perfect must have been a noble object stretching across the river and deep ravine to the highest part of the city.

Juanelo and the Romans seem to have been the only ones who succeeded in thus raising water for the supply of Toledo; it was attempted before the time of Juanelo by a servant of the Count of Nassau in 1528, but without success. Towards the beginning of the last century, a company of English entered into an agreement with the inhabitants to supply the city with water, and for this purpose brought a number of great iron pipes but not being able to effect their purpose they left the pipes, which may be seen to this day; and some 30, or 40 years ago it was again attempted by some individuals but with as little success as all the former ones.

The temper of the swords of Toledo was celebrated during many ages, but the art was totally lost above a hundred years ago. Charles III took great pains to restore this art, with considerable success, though the blades now made are still inferior to the ancient both in elegance of shape and temper. One of the first specimens of this new manufacture, and one of the handsomest I have seen, I purchased in Madrid. They are made in a large spacious and handsome building, situated on the banks of the river about a quarter of a league below the town. About 40, or 50 workmen are the whole number employed in this building, large enough for 200 persons at least. The iron they use is of Biscay. The following is the manner they make the blades; they put between two pieces of steel of a foot long, a piece of iron of about the same thickness but not quite so long. By hammering the pieces when at a white heat they unite into one piece. It is then beat out to the requisite shape. It is having all the centre part of the sword of iron that makes the stiff temper of the Toledo blades, which in general have little tendency to bend; it likewise makes them much less brittle than when entirely composed of steel, and this too accounts for one defect which these blades have of not coming perfectly straight again after being much bent; their excellency by no means consists in elasticity, and a person fond of trying how far his sword will bent [sic] would in a few minutes spoil the best Toledo blade in the world. Their merit consists in extreme hardness, a stiff unyielding temper which, though it renders the blade not perfectly elastic ensures it from breaking in any proof you make upon it. The severest of all proofs is striking the blade sideways upon a flat table, which throws it into an extreme state of vibration; this is what few of our English blades will stand. They generally shiver like a piece of glass, but those of Toledo very seldom fail.

After the proper shape is given to the blade it is heated red hot and plunged in this state into cold water, this hardens it. It is then held over a charcoal fire for a few minutes till it becomes of a blue colour, and then being once more plunged in the water, the temper is complete. It is then ground and sent to be proved, a simple operation confined merely to ascertaining whether it be free from all defect; without any reference to the temper of the blade. This is the plan now pursued in the sword manufactory of Toledo, whether it is in conformity to that anciently practiced I do not know, nor can it I suppose be ascertained. Notwithstanding all our enquiries we could not learn how many swords they could make in a week, month or year, but from what we saw I should think that if the building were in Birmingham, they would turn out 50 or a hundred to one that is made now.

Returning through the vega we found ourselves amongst the ruins of the Roman Amphitheatre. These are just sufficient to show the line of the outside wall and little more, from this it appears to have been much greater than the one of Italica of which I have spoken before.

Near these ruins is a low square solid building on which it is said the Inquisition used to burn their victims.

The Tagus at Toledo is about as large as the Mersey before reaching Warrington; the water is of a dirty green colour, occasioned by the clayey country through which it flows. After great floods it is said that gold and silver coins and ornaments are frequently found amongst the sand, as well of the Moors as of the Goths and Romans. It is supposed, and perhaps with good foundation, that when these different people were obliged to quit Toledo, or saw themselves on the point of falling into the power of their enemies, they threw their treasures into the Tagus, in hopes of returning once more to the place, or of fishing them up again when the pillage of the place was over. I enquired at all the most likely places for meeting with such antiquities but was not able to find any. I was told that some Canonigo bought them all up for some museum he was making.

Having seen the principal things which can be seen in Toledo in so short a time we quitted it in our Calesa at 2 o'clock in the morning. It was bright moonlight and I never shall forget the view we had on descending from the city, of the Tagus, the lofty bridge of Alcantara, the Moorish tower gateway and fortifications, the Alcazar, the antique houses, the dark ravine through which the river flows, and the double tier of ruined arches, the small remains of the ingenuity of Juanelo. The beauty, grandeur and singularity of the scene, joined with the reflections which rose in my mind of its past glories and present state of decline made an impression on my memory which will not soon be erased. It was one of the three most interesting moonlight scenes I have witnessed since leaving England, or I may say in my life. The first of the three I allude to was on the rock of Lisbon descending of [i.e. from] the heights of the Peña Convent which, situated on the summit of a lofty, isolated and almost inaccessible peak, was still in view, whilst the most perfect silence reigned all around. The second time was whilst sailing between the shores of Europe and Africa, off the point of Tarifa where the murmuring of the breakers was music as pleasant to the ear as their silvery spray upon the rocks was to our eye. But those were interesting only from their beauty, this independant of the grandeur of the scene was doubly interesting from the reflections to which it gave me.

The lines which Quevede applied to Rome, might be said of Toledo, changing the word Tiber into Tajo.

"Solo el Tajo quedo caya corriente

"Si eiudad la rege ya sepultada

"La mira con confuso son doliente"

Like all poetry it suffers much from translation. The meaning is this:-

"The Tagus alone remains, whose current which watered the city once, now buried in its ruins, gazes on it with a confused and doleful sound".

May 31st

We reached Aranjuez by the same dull road we had crossed two days before, and arrived at 9, or 10 o'clock in the morning. After breakfast we went for a second time through the Palace and received much pleasure from looking at the paintings; we afterwards took a walk in the gardens and then called upon the Hunters with whom we spent the rest of the day, and in the evening we went out in the carriage with the ladies. We had ordered the Calesa to be at the door at 10 o'clock when we were compelled to take our leave and bidding as we thought a final adieu to our hospitable friends, we set off. At Valdemoro halfway to Madrid we got an hour or two's sleep. Next morning **June 1st** I. Hodgson and Mr Kinder rode into Madrid and left me to come in the Calesa. My patience was wearied with being 4 hours in coming the 15 miles. I was rather cross for want of my breakfast, when on arriving at the gates of the city I had the vexation of being arrested for having no passport, and was carried to a guard house to give an account of myself, which I did satisfactorily and giving my address got off. I had the still farther annoyance of being taken to the Custom house to have a few dirty clothes examined, and to save farther trouble and waste of time was obliged to fee the officer.

Madrid

The Spanish Historians who seem anxious to ascribe a Greek or Phoenician origin to every city and every antiquity of their country have not omitted to do the same for their capital. Madrid is however most probably of Moorish origin, and some of the Moorish walls may yet be seen on the western side of the city. The first mention made of it in history is in the year 939 about 225 years after the invasion of the Moors, and then it is called by the name of Majorit. The occasion on which it is mentioned is the taking it by Don Ramond II who plundered it and dismantled the walls. It was taken by Alphonso VI in 1085, but once more fell into the momentary possession of the Moors.

In the year 1329 Alonso IX assembled the Cortes in Madrid.

Henry III was the first king proclaimed in Madrid; it did not however become the permanent residence of the Spanish Monarchs till after the time of Charles V. Since that time it has been gradually increasing in size and opulence. It is still however an unworthy residence for so great a monarch as the King of Spain ought to be, and it must have been a very disagreeable residence before the time of Charles III who was the author of almost all that it has to boast.

The population of Madrid falls very far short of 200,000. It contains 146 Churches, 33 monasteries, 29 Convents of Nuns and 2 theatres.

The situation is not ill chosen and it would have a good appearance from without were its vicinity more cultivated and adorned. It is surrounded by a low wall interrupted frequently by houses and other buildings, there are no buildings without the walls, so desolate is the neighbouring country that you may lean your back against the very wall of the city and look over a tract of 20, or 30 miles without seeing a tree, a shrub, a habitation or a human being; so that if a stranger were placed in the situation I speak of, he would imagine himself in the deserts of Asia or Africa, or any where but within a yard of the Capital of a great kingdom. This however cannot be said of the North west side of the city where the palace is situated, and from which the view is lively and agreeable. The ground there is high and the view extends for some miles up a valley enlivened with trees and the glittering waters of the river Manzanares; the view being bounded by the Guadarama mountains.

The interior of the City does not answer a foreigner's expectations of a Capital; there are three wide and handsome streets, but there is not one regularly built, the houses being of all sizes, shapes and colours. There are likewise two or three Squares but they are undeserving of any description.

The Custom House and the post office are both very handsome buildings.

The churches are generally rich and handsome inside, but few of them present anything remarkable on the outside.

The Royal Palace situated on the north west part of the city is a large and beautiful building of white stone, and contains many splendid suites of apartments; the paintings are numerous and excellent, forming a fine collection of the Italian and Spanish schools.

The Palace of the buen retiro has been completely destroyed by the French; in the gardens of this palace is the famous statue of Philip IV.

The Royal armoury is very well deserving of a visit. It contains many magnificent suits of armour of the different Spanish Monarchs, of the horses, etc ancient swords, sabres, lances, shields, sadles [sic], etc.

Amongst the armour is that which Charles V wore in his expedition to Tunis, 2 beautiful suits of Philip II and Philip III of Fernando Catolico and his Queen Isabella and another of El Rey Chico, the last King of Granada. This I should be inclined to doubt. I believe the Moors did not use full suits of armour; it does not seem Moorish workmanship; and being of ordinary size, it is strange its wearer should have been surnamed Zogoybi or the little. Amongst the shields are two of exquisite workmanship in steel and gold, with numerous figures and devices.

Amongst the swords I looked with particular interest on those pointed out to have belonged to Don Pelayo, the Cid, Roldan Bernardo del Carpio and other Spanish heroes, one [of] Gonsalvo de Cordova, of Fernando Catolico; But the French have carried away what the Spaniards showed to Foreigners with the greatest triumph, that is the sword of Francis I the rival and prisoner of Charles V. There are many Moorish and Damascus sabres, the handles and sheaths of some of which are covered with gold and precious stones. Amongst the former they show that of El Rey Chico, amongst the latter some taken in the battle of Lepanto.

Next to the Armoury, the Park of Artillery is most deserving of attention. Here are to be seen excellent models of all the various kinds of fortifications; modes of attacking a city, of fortifying it; models of the principal fortresses in the Spanish dominions, and two famous ones of Cadiz and Fort Figueras, that of Cadiz is of immense size, occupying the greater part of a large room. Every house is exact, and from a gallery above the model every one may trace the way through the different streets and squares to his own habitation. It is certainly an astonishing performance; it was made by order of Count O'Reilly when Governor of that city. There is in the same room with the model another very admirable one of Gibraltar … The Cabinet of Natural History is open twice a week for the public. The minerological collection is rather showy than extensive or complete. It contains some magnificent specimens of Gold and silver from the mines of America, of sulphur from Concil, of Rock Chrystal and precious stones as well as a fine collection of the marbles of Spain. The greatest curiosity in the whole cabinet is the skeleton of a Mamoth perfectly preserved, every bone and even the claws being entire. It does not stand much higher than an Elephant, but the length of the backbone and the feet is astonishing as well as the enormous size and thickness of all the bones. There are besides some serpents from 20, to 25 feet long.

The Prado of Madrid is the public walk within the walls, about a mile long and shaded by 5, or 6 rows of Elms.

The Delicias is another public walk like the Prado, but outside the walls of the city; on Sundays and feast days these walks are crowded with all ranks of people and they certainly furnish one of the greatest amusements Madrid has to boast.

There is perhaps no Capital where a stranger can find so little to amuse himself as in Madrid; in London he may loiter away months in looking into the shop windows, but there is scarcely one handsome shop in this city and certainly not one that you would ever enter unless compelled by necessity. Had it not been for the good society in which we were during our stay, our time would indeed have passed very tediously in Madrid.

Bull Feasts

During our stay in Madrid we had several opportunities of attending these celebrated spectacles, perhaps the most magnificent and most bloody which have been displayed since the spectacles of the Amphitheatre amongst the Romans.

Charles III sensible of the injurious effects of these amusements on the morals and industry of his subjects, and on Agriculture, made several regulations limiting the number of the Bull Feasts, and the number of victims. In 1805 Charles IV abolished them altogether. But as Ferdinand is willing that no improvement shall take place in the nation he governs, or that where improvement shall have taken place, it shall all be undone again, at the same time that he restored the Friars and Inquisition, restored likewise the Bull Feasts, at which he is almost always a spectator.

The Amphitheatre for the exposition of these fights is just without the walls of the city. It contains about 15,000 people, and the arena is about 100 yards diameter. This is surrounded by a barrier about six feet high for the men to jump over when pursued by the Bull, and behind there is another barrier still higher before the seats for the spectator commence. The plaza, as the amphitheatre is called, is generally full two hours before the business begins, which is as follows.

The trumpet sounds and two Alcaldes on horseback accoutred in the ancient Spanish dress make their appearance, and ask permission of the Governor to have a Bull feast. This being granted the public crier advances to the middle of the plaza and is met by five other Alcaldes on foot likewise in the old Spanish dress, to whom he proclaims the Feast, and this being done, they retire. One of the mounted Alcaldes then rides out of the plaza and returns followed by the Picadores or horsemen who have to attack the bull. In the morning they are only two in number, in the afternoon three. Their entry into the plaza is a most beautiful and striking sight. Their dress is the most elegant and splendid that can be imagined. They have a large white hat with a rim 8, or 10 inches wide, like those worn by the peasantry of Andalusia, and a short jacket of coloured silk, covered with gold and silver tassels; their waistcoat the same; and their leathern breeches are stuffed with wool or some such material to defend them from the horns of the Bull and to prevent their legs from being crushed when they fall under the horse. When they have made their obeisance to the Governor a long lance is given to each and they take their station near the door where [the] Bull is to come out, standing one behind another at a distance of 20 paces. At the same instant spring into the plaza a number of people on foot arrayed from head to foot in a light dress of richly coloured silk, like that of the Picadores, covered with gold and silver lace and tassels. The only arms these men carry is a cloak of coloured silk; one of them places himself near each of the horsemen to call away the Bull in case of an overthrow.

However noisy and clamorous the Spectators may have been till this moment, a complete stillness pervades the place when all is prepared for action, and even he who can see man and horse dashed to the ground without the slightest emotion, feels his heart beat when this silence is broken by the trumpet, the well known signal for turning out the Bull. If the Bull is a courageous one, it flies at the first horse, and the Picador with the greatest skill and coolness receives it on the point of the lance and throws it off past his horse's head. It springs on the other horses, and being turned in like manner, launches out into the plaza, whilst the picadores gallop round in the opposite direction to meet it again in front. The Bull, finding himself wounded at every charge he makes at the horse, soon turns shy and begins to pursue the men; and the excellence of a Bull is estimated by the number of times he attacks the horse, or in the technical language by the number of lances he takes. When they find that he will no longer run at the Picadores, these retire and those on foot, called the Chulos run up to the Bull, and as he makes his thrust at them, stick short barbed darts into his neck, which makes him run and jump up and down the place, bellowing with pain and rage. The first time you see these darts put in, you think it the most dangerous operation of all and are astonished that every man is not killed as he has absolutely to extend his arms over the very horns of the enraged animal; but the placing of these darts (Bandilleros) is in fact the securist part of the fight and accidents very rarely happen. When the bull is wearied with his exertions of trying to shake off the Banderillos and chasing his persecutors; the trumpet sounds again and the Matador, or man whose office it is to kill the Bull, makes his appearance armed [with] a red cloak and a long straight sword. He tries two or three times whether the Bull runs boldly at his cloak; and then as the furious animal rushes forward he plunges his sword up to the hilt in its neck and saves himself by skipping aside at the moment he makes his stroke. The sword is well place[d], he staggers, runs a little way, and kneels down, when a person behind despatches him in an instant by stabbing him between the horns with a short knife. This is the regular career of the bull, but it is varied in some degree by the nature of the animal itself, and is diversified by the dangerous predicaments, the accidents and narrow escapes of the various actors. If the Bull is cowardly and wont run at the horses, they stick into his neck fine banderillos which go off as soon as they pierce his flesh, fizzing and making reports as loud as pistols. His rage then amounts to madness and he runs and jumps in such a furious manner that he is soon spent and easily dispatched by the Matador. In the height of his fury the men continue placing fresh Banderillos with a dexterity that is truly astonishing. Some of the bulls, though but few will run at the horses as often as opposed to them, till they drop with fatigue or almost expire with the wounds of the lances. Other Bulls will do nothing else but jump over the barrier. I saw one Bull do this eight times, once after it had been stabbed by the Matador, and the last time with the sword up to the hilt in its neck. Another I saw clear the first barrier and the intervening space between the first and the second, being stopped only in his leap by the cords of the second barrier which fortunately threw him back or he would have got amongst the people. And a third I saw spring diagonally over the back of one of the horses and over the barrier at a single leap without touching either the one or the other in the slightest degree with his feet. The Chulos sometimes fall before the face of the bull, but his companions are always ready with their cloaks to draw off the attention of the animal. The Matadores have often very narrow escapes. I have repeatedly seen them thrown against the barrier by the Bull; one I saw struck on the knee by the point of his horn, and the best among them wounded in the hand and have his waistcoat unbuttoned by the animal as he attempted to kill him.

But of all engaged in the fight, the Picadors are those exposed to the greatest danger, and never a day passes without there happening some very narrow escapes and many dreadful falls. The horse caught upon the horns of the Bull is often completely turned over upon its rider in such a way, you think he must be crushed to death, and he is frequently very severely injured, being often unable to rise for some minutes and not infrequently carried out of the amphitheatre to the surgeon who always attends on these occaisions [sic]. Perhaps nothing so powerfully displays the force of habit as the total indifference evident in all the spectators to the most bloody scenes of this barbarous sport. The women as well as the men seem to take peculiar relish in the most horrible and disgusting scenes,& indeed appear to have little pleasure in the common occurrences of the fight. These all have witnessed so often that they completely cease to make any impression whatever. Nothing delights the multitude so much as to see the Bull stand alone in the arena having killed every horse and disabled every Picador, and put to flight all the Chulos; the plaza then rings with the shouts of thousands who applaud the animal as they would an excellent actor. It might be supposed from the nature of the entertainment that frightful spectacles must frequently be presented to the eye; and those which actually do take place surpass even the worst imagination could have pictured. The horse commonly receives his first wounds in his flanks, when the bowels instantly gush out; his rider continues spurring him on to attack the Bull, though his entrails are dragging along the ground, and he keeps tearing them to pieces with his feet. Sometimes the horn of the bull penetrates the breast of the horse which the[n] presents a truly melancholy sight; it begins to turn round and round without moving from the spot, till it falls with loss of blood. If the wounds are not mortal, the horse is taken out and they are sewed up, and he is introduced again into the Plaza. Sometimes when man and horse have been dashed to the ground, the horse getting up with the bandage over its eyes, a thing always done when the animal fears to meet the Bull, he gallops off in an agony of pain and dashes out his brains against the barrier. Few horses will face the Bull without a bandage, after having been once gored, but some will meet him with steadiness without a blind though wounded again and again. Where a horse is this courageous, the dangers both to himself and rider are much diminished for a timid horse wheeling round is taken in flank, and one good horse is said to outlast four bad ones. At the same moment I once saw both Picadors carried senseless out of the Plaza; one of their horses gored to death by the Bull and the other, wounded and blindfolded, dash his head against the barrier and fall dead on the spot. The calmness, courage and intrepidity of the men is most extraordinary, and doubtless these qualifications and their fidelity in assisting one another in danger, are the principal reasons why fatal accidents in these sports are so rare. Never a single fight passes without the Picadores meeting with the most terrible overthrows and the Bull as constantly gores his horse under which he is lying; yet I never saw but one Picador absolutely wounded with the horn of the Bull; he was gored under the arm, in that manner dragged along the ground and he very narrowly escaped with his life. The last man killed in the Plaza of Madrid was the famous Pepe Illo,[10] a matador who with his own hand had dispatched in the amphitheatre upwards of three

---

[10] Pepe Illo was the most famous matador of his time. Goya depicted him in action and also at the point of death in two plates of his celebrated series of etchings called the 'Tauromaquia'.

thousand Bulls. He was a very small man, the bull he had to kill was a very large one and death was mutually given and received. But, after all, the number of fatal accidents is not in any proportion to that of miraculous escapes. These Bull Feasts occur in Madrid once a fortnight, in the Spring and Autumn 18 in the year; the fight occupies two hours in the morning and two in the afternoon; the number of Bulls killed in every feast, fourteen, when the king is present 15, and on very great occasions 16. On an average as many horses are killed as Bulls, that is every Bull is said to kill its horse; but this of course varies according to the quality of the bulls. I never saw less than 10, fall, once 15, once 17 once 22 and the last time 27 horses perished on the horns of the bull. Sometimes a single bull kills 10 or 12, but this is rare. We may form some idea from this destruction of life in a single amphitheatre in a single day; how great a slaughter must take place in all all [sic] Spain in the course of a whole year, or the reign of a single monarch.

The expence of the Bull Feasts is very great and no trifling sum is requisite to pay for such a number of Bulls and Horses, and the wages of the men, of whom the Picadores and Matadores receive from 200, to 300 dollars each, and the Chulos in proportion. The receipts of the plaza, are however not only sufficient to meet such an expence but commonly there is a considerable overplus, arising from entirely from [sic] the seats and this goes to the support of a hospital. The receipts sometimes amount to £1000, or, 1200, and yet sometimes the expence is so great as to leave nothing for the Hospital. The price of a seat is one shilling to 5, or 6, according to the situation; and those in the sun are only half the price of those in the shade, the one charged 12 rials in the morning is charged 24 in the afternoon, and so vice versa.

The first Bull fight I attended made me nervous, sick and unwell, not only that day but the two successive ones. What induced me to go a second time to this spectacle and what excuse to make for so doing, I cannot easily understand; the principal reason certainly was that time hung so heavy on my hands at least during the day, that to do or see anything was no small relief and pleasure, and even if it had been attended with some personal danger the pleasure would not have been less, since the excitement would have been increased. I never once left the amphitheatre with so much eagerness for the sport as I had entered it; on the contrary, I never went out with the wish of attending again. But time went on, the day came round, I walked with pleasure and alacrity and when the trumpet sounded, I was always to be seen in my place.

August 1st

We had reckoned at the time of leaving Cadiz that our business in Madrid might detain us a month, but at most not above six weeks; and that concluded, we meant to proceed to Valencia, Barcelona, thence Leghorn or Genoa, and return home by Switzerland and the Rhine, or through France and Holland, if the state of things permitted. During the first two months of our residence in Madrid, not being over anxious to proceed homewards and passing our time agreeably enough in the parties and Balls of our numerous friends; I felt happy and contented. Towards the end of two months I became satisfied [i.e. sated?] with the gay and dissipated life of the Court, our business seemed drawing towards a speedy conclusion, and we daily expected to quit Madrid and set out for Italy and England, an event I looked forward with more eager anxiety than to any other of life. In the course of June, after having been delayed from day to day for some time, we fixed the hour for our departure; we took out our passports, and sent our servant Francisco with all our clothes except such as we wanted on the journey, forward to Barcelona determining to follow him the day but one after. The day arrived and our journey was put off; the next the same thing happened and the next, and so on till August already overtook us in Madrid. The extreme mortification I suffered at each fresh disappointment was more than I can describe, and more I hope than I shall ever again experience. If the kind attention of our friends and great public news, could have made me happy, I should have been so during the latter part of my stay in Madrid; but when uneasy in our own minds, we are unable to enjoy the most agreeable concurrence of external circumstances.

At Seville on our way to Madrid the first intelligence of the landing of Napoleon, reached us. On arriving at Madrid we heard of his being in possession of Paris. As might naturally be expected, this event threw a great gloom over our diplomatic Friends; the fortunes of many of whom were ultimately connected with the fate of Louis,[11] and of all with that of their particular sovereigns. This gloom continued for some time, and alarm was raised to its height of the two first Bulleteens [sic] from France giving an account, first of the discomfiture and then of defeat of the Prussian army; it being considered impossible for the English army to face the enemy alone. The joy then occasioned by Bonapartes own Bulleteen of the Battle of Waterloo[12] may readily be imagined; so far exceeding the most sanguine expectations and even wishes.

We received the joyful inteligence in the morning and soon after had a note from Sir Henry Wellesley requesting us to dine with him and drink his Brother the Duke of Wellingtons health. We went according, and found the party, with the exception only of ourselves, very select. It consisted of the different Ambassadors and Ministers, the Duke de Bourbon, the Grand Inquisitor, the Pope's Nuncio and a few Spanish Generals. The joy which pervaded the whole party was very great; toast followed toast in bumper glasses, and most of the party

[11] Louis XVIII, the restored Bourbon King of France (1814–24), was briefly deposed by the restoration of Napoleon between 20 March and 22 June 1815.

[12] The Battle of Waterloo: 18th June 1815. It would be interesting to know how long it took for the news of Wellington's victory to reach Madrid.

turned out on the Prado a tolerably merry plight.

Sir Henry Wellesley soon after gave a grand Ball to which we were also invited. King Ferdinand, all the Grandees of Spain, the Ambassadors Ministers and all illustrious foreigners there in Madrid, were among the numerous guests. The Ball was given in a magnificent but temporary building in Sir Henry's garden, which was itself lighted up with colored lamps; the whole being finished in a splendid and Princely manner. The King, his Uncle and his brother, sat in state Chairs at the top of the dance, and every couple before leading down made his majesty a low bow. Between the dances he walked about conversing with and bowing to the Company. The supper table was very magnificent indeed; the King and two Infantas sat at the top of the table, and there was room sufficient for all the Ladies to sit down and the Gentlemen stood behind them to amuse and attend upon them. Lady Hunter and her daughters placed themselves under my protection, and as they sat only a few places from the King I had a good opportunity of observing his Majesty's evolutions. The ladies had soon done and, tired, and hungry, we were impatient to partake of the good things before us, but we waited long in vain, for Ferdinand continued eating and drinking for above an hour and a half and then came the toasts; his Catholic M. [Majesty], his Britannic M., the Duke of Wellington, etc. etc. At last the departure of his majesty released us; the Ladies rose, we took their places, cleared the table and returned to the Ballroom where dancing continued till four oclock, then handing the Hunters to their carriage, we returned to our lodgings.

Parties at the English, Swedish and Dutch Ministers, made us sometimes forget for an hour, our inexpressible desire of quitting Madrid; sometimes we invited our German Friends to spend the evening in playing at Chess; sometimes the theatre amused us for an hour or two. But our principal dependence was on our female friends at the Consul General's. We went there at all times of the day and staid as long as inclination prompted; in the evenings we often found them alone, and passed it in pleasant chat, or at the Piana forte [sic]. We more frequently however found a few friends and sometimes a large party. After returning from one of these when we had met a singular mix of people of different nations, we were induced to write down the names of those present before they might slip from our memory. The names were these.

Cardinal		The Pope's Nuncio
Sir H. Wellesley	}	
Mr C. Vaughan		English Embassy
Prince Laval		
Count Montmorenci	}	
Count D'Agoult		French Emb[y]
Count de Coux		

Baron Taticheff
Baroness d[itt]o
Mons'r de Severin
Mons'r Bobliboff
} Russian Emb^y

Baron Werther
Baroness Werther
} Prussian Emb^y

Mons Genot
Madame do
} Austrian Emb^y

Count la Gardie
Mons'r de Rook
} Swedish Emb

Chevalier de Souza
Madame do
} Portugueze Emb

Mons'r Cambier
Madame do
2 Madamoiselles do
Mons'r Eldevir
} Dutch Emb

Mons'r Hugo
Prince de Leon
Conte d'Osmond
Madame Haurie
Mademoiselle do
} Sicilian Embassy

General O'Neill
Genl. Sir John Downie
Colonel Downie
Colonel Campbell
Duchess of Ossuna
Duke of Abrantes
Ducthess of do
Duke and Duchess of Frias
Marquis of Villafranca
Marchioness of Santa Cruz
Marchioness of Mosse
Marquesita of ditto
Marquis de Saluchi

Mons'r Bourbon de Thionville
Mons'r de Thionville
Sir John Hunter
Lady Hunter
Miss Hunters
Mr Ellis M.P.
Miss Ellis
Miss Palmer
Mr Ellis Jun[r]
Lady Hervey
Lord Howard
Sir James Duff Gordon M.P.
Lady Gordon
I. Hodgson and R. Greg

In this party not uncommonly numerous were individuals of no less than 19 nations, viz.

English
Scotch
Irish
Russian
Prussian
Polish
Bavarian
Danish
Swedish
Dutch
Flemish
Austrian
French
Spanish
Portugueze
Genoese
Florentine
Neapolitan
Sicilian

19 Nations

August 3rd

Mr Thomas Kinder, with whom we became acquainted the day after reaching Madrid, had consented to accompany us in our tour through Italy and Switzerland. But finding ourselves detained so long in Madrid we all resolved to return straight to England the moment we found ourselves released. Kinder at last became impatient with our repeated delays and resolved to set out for Bilboa that very night. I determined instantly not to lose the opportunity and told him if he would stay till the following night I would accompany him. I then went to I. Hodgson and told him that he had kept me in daily expectation of departing for upwards of two months; that if he would give me any positive assurance that he would leave Madrid in a fortnight, or even in a month I would willingly stay, that I could not live on expectation any longer, and that if not I must leave Madrid the following night with Kinder. After some demur the whole was arranged that night, and I began to prepare for my departure.

August 4th

A Friar, having been convicted some days before of murdering a young woman whom he suspected of being unfaithful to him, had been, contrary to the common opinion been [sic] sentenced to death. I myself much doubted of the execution being put in effect, and determined to convince myself by seing [sic]. I accordingly went to the place and stood boiling in the sun for near two hours. He appeared in the usual manner mounted on an ass with a small Cross in his hand and a large one carried before him. The people in general seemed well behaved and serious. I waited to see him in such a situation as to preclude the probability of a reprieve, and then turning my back on the mournful scene went to take leave of my numerous friends. The Hunters seemed surprised and sorry at my sudden departure, and I could not but feel much in taking leave of those to whom I owed so much, but I cannot pretend to say that the joy of leaving Madrid did not predominate over the sorrow of leaving such kind and attentive friends.

I returned to my lodgings in the afternoon, packed up the few effects which remained to me after the large detachment sent to Barcelona. Our German friends drank tea with us, and the horses coming to the door, Kinder and I took leave, mounted our saddles and with joy embittered only by leaving behind the companion of my travels, I galloped through the streets [of] Madrid. Kinder followed me and passing out by the northern gate of the City we soon found ourselves in the open country. It was 8 o'clock when we quitted Madrid and there being no moon we were soon involved in darkness; we continued however at the gallop, nor checked our pace till we reached the end of the stage, then mounting fresh horses crossed in darkness the gloomy wilds of the Soma Sierra.

Instead of cooling breezes during the night, the wind wherever there was any, was the blast from a furnace. As day broke we reached an old Moorish town called Burtriago where we got a little refreshment, that is a cup of Chocolate. Towards 9 oclock the sun became so insufferably hot that we were compelled to stay at a small hamlet amongst the hills, distant about 80 miles from Madrid; which notwithstanding the unavoidable delays that must arise in night travelling, particularly where roads are bad or where there are no roads at all, we accomplished in 13 hours. We got a few hours sleep and some dinner here, and when the sun was fairly sunk below the horizon we again mounted our horses, and proceeded over wild, open country without any road; which added to the darkness made us much afraid of a fall. Our fears were not without foundation for [at] the second stage, having mounted a high heavy horse I found it stumble so often as to keep me in constant alarm. With the fatigue of the former night, I fell fast asleep, although my horse still continued at the gallop. In this state I was awakened by one of the most violent shocks I ever received; in crossing some deep sand the horse came down with such violence that I was thrown off head first, and my head completely shot into the sand; the horse then falling on me pushed me as it were through the sand wh^c filled my ears, mouth and hair. I got up again as well as [I] was able, I thought if my nose was not carried off with the blow, at least all my front teeth were knocked out; but to my extreme astonishment, though sadly scratched and bruised, I found my nose and teeth in their place; and taking courage I mounted again and proceeded. Not long after Kinder got a fall, though not so serious a one; had mine happened anywhere but on the very spot where it did, it would most unquestionably have cost me my life.

Kinder not being quite well, we had to rest for half an hour at different places, and did not reach Burgos until 2 o'clock the following day, the distance being about 90 miles from our sleeping place. Having advanced farther north, and the wind being from a Cold quarter we were enabled to proceed on our journey notwithstanding the sun; and here for the first time for some months I experienced the sensation not of chillness, but of coolness. Having got some refreshment we went out to look about the town, and although somewhat fatigued saw the Cathedral, and afterwards climbed up the Castle hill,[13] which so long had baffled the valour of our troops and the skill of their Commander. Burgos has a fine appearance from a distance embosomed among mountains and standing in a beautiful valley, which particularly pleased us after the dull, uninteresting country we had passed between that and Madrid. The Cathedral is principally remarkable of two two [sic] towers done in stone net work, of singular height and beauty, the magnificence of the carving within and the elegance of its lantern tower. In elegant simplicity it appeared to me inferior to that of Segovia, in outside show, to that of Toledo.

With the exception of a few good houses facing the river, Burgos is a dirty, ill-looking city, presenting in every street the most evident symptoms of poverty and decay. It has no manufactures, and is principally supported by the passing of the wool carriers, this being the place appointed for all duties to be paid on that article. Burgos is not a walled town; it was in possession of the English all the time during the siege of the Citadel. The place which resisted so effectually so effectually [sic] the efforts of our troops, was the ancient Castle, situateed on an insulated hill commanding the city. The hill itself the French had cut into a regular fortification, and defended with these tremendous trenches and mounds, and thus strong in itself and so strengthened it might forever have defied the attacks of the bravest and most numerous army. After scaling the walls [of] Badajoz, however, we cannot wonder at Lord Wellington thinking everything within the possibility of his troops.

Fatigued, and having been up for two successive nights and riding 180 miles, we were not sorry to get into a tolerable bed, such as I had not seen in any posada in Spain.

August 7th

Kinder continuing unwell we could not get away from Burgos till neer [sic] noon, and then mounting our horses we reached a small town about dark, and Kinder still being unwell, and the necessity of travelling by night having now ceased, we determined to put up there for the night.

August 8th

We were on horseback before sunrise; and still travelling on along a barren and uninteresting country, we came about 8 o'clock to a most remarkable pass in the mountains called Pam Corvo, where the rocks over hang the road in a most extraordinary and frightful manner. Leaving this behind us, we instantly found ourselves in a completely different country, variegated with hill and dale, symptoms of woods, and and green fields, and my pleasure at seeing these once again was great indeed. Everything proclaimed our approach to the frontiers of Biscay, even a change of climate, for it threatened rain, a singular phenomenon in this season in Castile.

In two hours more we reached Miranda on the Ebro, here a river as large at the Trent at Nottingham. At Miranda we quitted the post road and consequently post Horses, and hired therefore a couple of mules to carry us to Orduña, about 40 miles farther. Violent rain came on which detained us till noon. We then, proceeding quietly on our sober animals, had leisure to enjoy the views, for the country continually improved; the number of brooks, meadows and trees calling forcibly to my mind the sweet vallies of England, which I now thought to myself I should soon enjoy. After ascending for some hours a chain of mountains we reached the summit about evening, where one of the most enchanting scenes I ever witnessed opened on our view. At the bottom of the precipitous descent of the hills on which we stood lay the circular valley of Orduña, surrounded by mountains so steep and high as seemingly preclude all egress; the whole valley was green to perfection, beautifully wooded, and white cottages scattered in every direction, on the banks of the numerous rivulets. The city of Orduña stood

[13] Wellington had failed to dislodge the French from the castle in 1812.

in the centre.

We stood gazing for a long time at the beautiful, and to us novel scene, and should have gazed longer, if a tremendous thunder cloud, that had long been threatening had not burst in the instant over our heads. We therefore descended hastily by an angular road that is carried down the almost perpendicular side of the mountain. The storm was so violent we were compelled to seek shelter. But soon abating we reached Orduña by evening.

August 9th

... proceeding along a pretty stream of water, well lined with wood, cottages, covered with vines, and neat Gardens, we reached Bilboa about noon and went immediately to the house of my Cousin George Warre the Consul. He was in England but We met a kind reception from Mr. John Bayley who took us to his house in the country pleasantly situated on the river at a distance of about 2 miles from Bilboa.

If any people in Spain, or even in the world, can pretend to pre- eminence in love of liberty and independence, it is the Biscayans, for they have continued free from time immemorial, and perceived the use of their ancient language till the present time notwithstanding the successive invasions and conquests of the kingdom of which they constitute but an insignificant portion.

Their language, a branch of the ancient Celtic, formerly spoken over the greater part of Europe, has remained uncorrupted by, the Latin, Gothic, Moorish and Spanish tongues; and though most of the Common people understand Spanish, they always converse with one another in Basque. In like manner their country has remained unsubdued by the Carthagenians, Romans, Goths and Moors, and the King of Spain is only Lord of Biscay. He is unable either to levy taxes, impose customs and duties, or raise soldiers in Biscay which is governed by a kind of council elected by the people. It was amongst the mountains of this Province that the valiant Don Pelayo and his successors baffled all the attempts at invasion made by the victorious infidels. There are few families in Biscaya that do not claim an illustrious descent, and over the doors of almost all the cottages, on an immense stone, are engraved the arms of the noble family who reside there.

Bilboa is a small neat town infinitely cleaner than most of the Spanish towns. The streets are narrow, paved with coloured stones placed in the shape of diamonds, squares etc, and least [sic] this order should be deranged, no carts are allowed in the streets, but everything is carried on small triangular sledges. Bilboa is situated at the bottom of [a] deep narrow valley; its distance from the sea is about six miles. The river is in some places very shallow, and even with the aid of the tide, vessels that draw more than 7 feet of water cannot reach the town. Vessels generally unload in a village at about 2 miles from Bilboa, called Portagalette. The name of the river is Biscayan, and I never met any who could pronounce it.

The whole course of the river from Bilboa to the sea is extremely beautiful, the woods and hills being crowded with neat white cottages and country houses. We had now already been a week at Bilboa, anxiously waiting for a vessel for England, and none promising a speedy departure, we both wished extremely to go by way of France, though the accounts from that quarter were by no means favorable for attempting to pass that way; but my orders not to do so were of such a positive nature, I could not think of disobeying them. We were however relieved of our embarrassment one morning by the intelligence that a little Cutter, the Horatio, from Guernsey, was just arrived with a small cargo of wheat, and might easily be induced to turn again and touch at any port in the south of England.

We immediately went down to the port and found the vessel so small, to all appearance a mere boat, that thinking [it] imprudent to risk ourselves in so small a thing across the terrible Bay of Biscay, that [we] almost gave up at once all idea of engaging a passage in it. We however went on board, and found everything so complete, and the Captain willing to sail in two days, we could not resist the thought of being in England so soon. We at once arranged with the Captain who positively engaged to sail on the morning of the 19th.

The Horatio was probably the smallest vessel that had crossed the Bay of Biscay; its burthen was only 26 tons or one third or fourth of the tonnage of a common Flat on our canals. It was built at Plymouth as a pleasure boat, and as admirable a piece of workmanship as can be imagined. Its crew consisted of the Captain, two men and a boy, a sufficient complement for so small a vessel.

August 19th 1815

We walked down to the mouth of the river at an early hour and found there our vessel waiting. The wind was unfortunately exactly a head and the Pilot Boat obstinately refused to take us across the bar which is here shallow and dangerous. We waited [until] the afternoon, when we hoped that with full tide we should be able to prevail with the Pilot. Between bribery and entreaty we succeeded, and bidding a joyful adieu to the country where I had so long resided, I soon looked back on Spain [no] more, but fixed my eyes on the horizon, beyond whose dark line lay the country from which I had long been parted. The clouds gathering darkly around and the gloomy appearance of the sky portended a storm, but neither the fear of this, the contrary wind, nor the pain of sea-sickness which owing to the roughness of the waves, soon came over me, prevented [me] from enjoying by anticipation the pleasure I was soon to experience. Mr Kinder though an old sailor who had twice crossed the Equator, was also sick and by mutual consent we adjourned to our births [sic] for the night.

August 20th Sunday

I passed an uncomfortable night, dosing [sic] between fits of sickness. On enquiring after the wind I learnt it was favorable but light, carrying us gently on, at a rate 2, or 3 miles an hour. I went on deck and found the sea as calm as the surface of a sheltered lake, and I staid there till towards noon, when the sun became so hot as to be insufferable on deck.

In the evening the wind rose high and the sea began to swell, which increased all night, and the next morning the gale blew so hard as to make us feel rather uneasy for in so small a vessel with not above 12 inches between our face and the deep, every wave that broke over us made a tremendous noise.

The gale continued with unabated violence during that night and the following day, the 22nd, during all which time we both were very ill, and obliged to keep below, with the dead lights on as we were almost as much under the water as above; and indeed with every precaution the water could not be kept out of the Cabin.

August the 23rd

The storm was rather abated in the morning and we flattered ourselves had spent its violence. The wind had continued most of the time to blow from the North West, a direction which would [have] prevented a square rigged vessel from making any way; but ours being a cutter, and an admirable sailer, had got on pretty well, and we now found ourselves about 60 miles South of the English Channel.

Our hopes had been vain the storm soon came on with greater violence than ever, as night drew on it increased, and we had the most dangerous part of our voyage immediately before us; namely the passage from the Bay of Biscay into the English Channel, where the meeting of contrary tides and currents in rough weather is always to be dreaded. We were all on board uneasy as night approached; what rendered it still more alarming was, that our vessel was so very small, and the waves so high that we were necessarily obliged to carry more sail than was safe in order to keep it steady in the water, and prevent it being rolled completely over by violence of the sea. About midnight the Captain came down to say that we were then entering the Channel, and if all went on well with the first light of the morning we should see the shores of England, and reach Plymouth towards noon. This was indeed pleasing intelligence, but in the mean time, we had enough to occupy our thoughts. We were tossed about backwards forwards and sideways at the mercy of the waves, which instantly broke over the deck with a frightful noise, and made every plank vibrate. Sometimes, after a very heavy sea had struck us with a crash like thunder, so perfect a silence ensued that for an instant we knew not whether we were afloat or already embosomed in the waters, and even a second wave was welcome music to our ears.

At length, notwithstanding the noise and motion I fell asleep and when I woke, day had already dawned, the sea was quite calm, we were sailing swiftly but gently before the wind, and the shores of England were in view. Kinder was already on deck; I soon followed him, and we contratulated [sic] one another on our release from Spain and Spaniards and the prospect of again breathing the unpolluted air of freedom in our native country. About two o'clock we entered Plymouth harbour and the beautiful grounds of Mount Edgecombe engaged our sole attention. We landed shortly after without any trouble from the Custom House, no one suspecting our little vessel to have come from such a distance. My joy on setting my feet once again on English ground I cannot express: but it might have been greater had I been more capable of enjoying myself; but having eaten scarcely anything since leaving Bilboa, and nothing at all for two days but a little brandy and water, having suffered for so much from sickness, I was so weak as scarcely to be able to walk to the inn.

After getting a basin of broth I proceeded to wash, shave and dress, all which I had been unable to do since leaving Bilboa. That being done We sat down to a good beef stakes [sic] and ale, luxuries to which we had been total strangers for nearly 12 months. We walked out afterwards, and everything seemed as strange and new to me as if I had never been in the country before, and I could not help continual astonishment at seeing everybody look so like Englishmen and hearing everyone speak English.

August 25th

All coaches and public conveyances being occupied by the sailors, lately paid off, we took a chaise and reached Exeter that night, the rain and fog being so thick, we could not see beyond the Hedges.

August 26th

We went on the top of the Coach to Bath. In the whole course of my life I never enjoyed a day so much. The mode of travelling was new to me, the beauty of the surrounding country; the exquisite greenness of the fields, the neatness of the hedges, cleanliness of the cottages, magnificence of the Inns, and above all the roses which bloomed on the cheeks of my countrywomen; delighted me more than words can express, and for no title in the world would I have exchanged that of Englishman. The day was very fine and all complained of heat except Kinder and myself.

We reached Bath in the evening, and put up at the house of a friend of Kinder's.

August 27th Sunday

There was no Coach for the North and I willing enough staid the day at Bath. My Aunt Greg, being from home I took my abode at the Percivals, who gave me a very kind reception. I was truly happy to find myself once more in a Christian country, to see the sabbath kept as it ought to be, and once more to attend divine worship myself. With the single exception of that one morning at Gibraltar, I had not been in a church since I was in this same part of the country on my way down to Falmouth 11 months before.

August 28th

Taking leave of Kinder I set off by an early Coach to Birmingham. The beautiful Vale of Rodborough, which had pleased me so much before, seemed as much improved by abscence as everything else.

August the 29th

Proceeding by an early Coach I reached Congleton in good time; from this place to Wilmslow, I well knew the road, and my heart beat with joy at beholding those scenes which raised a thousand agreeable associations in my memory, and promised future happiness.

At Wilmslow I met my Sisters Marianne and Hannah, it being the third time they had come to meet me. We soon reached Quarry Bank and I there completed a journey from which I have derived some benefit; in which mingled with much enjoyment I experienced my share of pain and unhappiness, and from which I hope to receive as much pleasure hereafter, as I did from its various scenes and events when actually passing.*

* See the additional note about this journal on p. 250.

TRAVELS IN FRANCE, SWITZERLAND, ITALY AND GREECE AND THE OTTOMAN EMPIRE IN 1817

Introduction

> A man who has not been in Italy, is always conscious of an inferiority, for not hav-
> ing seen what is expected a man should see. The grand object of travelling is to
> see the shores of the Mediterranean.
>
> Dr Samuel Johnson

On 2nd January 1817, Robert Hyde Greg left London to go to Europe. He was to travel to those cities and countries associated with the Grand Tour made by the sons of the aristocracy in the seventeenth and eighteenth centuries. While business interests no doubt had to be dealt with at some points on the tour, cultural interests seem to have been of much greater significance.

It took him four days to reach Paris. An indefatigable sightseer, he rambled all over the city during the three weeks that he spent there, visiting churches, museums and palaces, carefully noting down everything that he saw. His evenings were usually spent in theatres or at private soirées. This was rather a different Paris from the one we know today. It was yet to be transformed into a splendid city with wide boulevards worthy of the Second Empire of Napoleon III by Baron Haussman, but there was plenty for Greg to see in 1817.

He was impressed by the contents of the Louvre, and went to the trouble of listing the numbers of pictures by various artists. He wrote enthusiastically about a visit to Versailles which he greatly admired, and applauded the action of Louis XVIII in "fitting up the Palace" again, saying "who that had such a place would not do the same and if Versailles falls to ruin would not Europe have lost one of its brightest monuments?"

Despite the fact that Britain and France had so recently been at war for the better part of twenty years, there is no evidence in the journal that Greg encountered any hostility from French people when travelling in France.

After Paris he made for Geneva and Chambery to travel through the Alps by way of the Mont Cenis Pass into Italy. The journey, in February, was both exciting and alarming. Part of it had to be by sledge through the spectacular mountain scenery. He wrote to his mother:

> The path was never more than eight feet wide, often not six and very much in-
> clined ... our driver however, far from being alarmed either for himself or for his
> precious charges, kept nodding off all the way, only opening his eyes to flog his

horse or when a fog told him we were out of track...[1]

Italy in 1817 was a mere "geographical expression" in the words of Prince Metternich, for the country was yet to be united under a single government. In Turin, Greg noted that the King of Piedmont-Sardinia kept his court there, but there is no other reference to the various states of Italy or the political conditions there. In Spain he had had plenty of time in which to observe the effects of the restored monarchy of Ferdinand VII. In Italy, like most tourists, he was far too busy sightseeing to concern himself with politics. Once in Florence, and then in Rome, confronted by the embarras de richesses of those cities, he dutifully tried to see everything of importance and methodically noted down places visited, things seen, encounters with fellow travellers – this church, that arch, ceremonial gates and ruined colonnades, paintings and sculptures. In Rome he went to religious services in St Peter's, the Pantheon and the Sistine Chapel, where he noted that, "Michaelangelo's Last Judgement is black and unintelligible". His attitude to Catholicism was more tolerant when he was in Italy, than when he was in Spain.

The quality of his writings changed once he reached Naples. The diary entries are longer and more detailed than those of the earlier part of the journey. He was obviously excited by what he saw of the classical remains in the vicinity of the city. The reader really shares his fascination and terror when he visited Avernus, and his wonder at the Greek Temples rising majestically from the plain at Paestum.

Pompeii and Herculaneum, newly discovered in the eighteenth century, were explored. In Pompeii he noted: "There is a foolish order of the Government to prevent anyone drawing, but I took a few sketches by stealth".

There had been an eruption of Vesuvius in 1794 and the volcano was still active, spewing out rocks from time to time. This did not deter tourists from ascending it and peering into the crater as Greg did on two occasions.

It was in Naples on Thursday 14th April that the most momentous event of the tour took place. Greg briefly noted that he was: "introduced to the Prince of Homburg[2] and fixed with his Highness a tour in Greece". Fortunately, in the archives of Quarry Bank Mill there is an unpublished letter to his mother which provides details about the meeting and the Prince himself.

Naples – Tuesday 22nd (April 1817)

My Dear Mother

I was uncertain with respect to my intentions of visiting Greece instead of making my tour in Sicily as I formerly proposed when Mr Ramsay and the Prussian Consul Mr Daget (?) introduced me to his Highness the Prince of Hesse Homburg. The Prince said he was going to make a short excursion into Greece, and proposed being absent two months, and if that my plans could be made to agree with his, he should be charmed to have me for his companion. He was going on an economical system, should take only one servant and meant to be in the North of Italy in July. What could I say, what could any one say in such a situation, but I shall feel myself exceedingly happy in having such a companion for such a journey... I understand his Highness is connected with the Royal family of Prussia.

[Marginal note:] The Prince is own cousin [sic] to the King of Prussia, and his Sister is married to one of the King's Brothers. He is General in the Prussian Army and was wounded at Liepsic [sic] where he commanded a division of the Allied army.

He is a tall thin man in his person and of very obliging manners, speaks French but indifferently though more fluently than I do, and as far as I can yet judge he is not of very brilliant talents or particularly well prepared for the journey, but it is a sudden thing with him as with me also. His major domo assures me that he is a quiet regular person and will not lead me into any mischief whatever. The Prince carries letters of introduction which I could not have obtained – and in many cases his title will be a passport where I would have found none. I shall however endeavour to make myself as independent as possible providing myself with all things which I think may be useful or necessary. I will write as frequently as opportunities occur, these are irregular but I believe not infrequent...

Greg must have been a personable young man who could be relied on to be well organised and willing to accept responsibility. He was an experienced traveller, accustomed to coping with all kinds of conditions. He was not merely a travelling companion for the Prince, but was an efficient personal assistant who organised transport and accommodation in the various places they visited. He quite clearly relished the preferential treatment that he enjoyed as the travelling companion of a royal personage. As an ordinary traveller this would have been

[1] This and other letters of Greg to his mother are in the National Trust archive at Quarry Bank.

[2] The Prince of Hesse Homburg was Prince Louis William (1770–1839), second son of Frederick V (1748–1820), ruler of Hesse Homburg, a tiny principality near Frankfurt on Main. He was a direct descendent of Frederick II (1633–1708), the 'Prince of Homburg' immortalised by Heinrich von Kleist's famous play, and the opera by Hans Werner Henze (1960). He and his brothers and sister were linked by marriage to other European royal families. His elder brother married a daughter of King George III of England, and his sister married a brother of King Frederick William III of Prussia. His own marriage in 1804 to Princess Amalie of Nassau-Ussingen ended in divorce a year later. He fought and was wounded in the Battle of Leipsig in 1813. He was 47 when he met Robert Hyde Greg in Naples. In 1829 he succeeded his elder brother Frederick VI Joseph as ruler of Hesse Homburg. He died in 1839, to be succeeded in turn by three other brothers, the last of whom died childless in 1866, when Hesse Homburg became extinct as a separate state, absorbed into Prussia. (We are indebted to Dr Jarl Kremeier for this information.)

denied him.

After Naples had been left behind and Apulia crossed, the Prince and Greg arrived in Bari where, once the news of the arrival of a prince had spread around the town, all the local grandees came in full ceremonial dress, bowing and scraping to greet them and the whole city was agog. Everywhere they went they were followed by large crowds anxious to catch a glimpse of them. The whole episode was at once touching and comic, and ultimately tiring and embarrassing.

Eventually they arrived in Greece. This was the age of Philhellenism. Greg felt obliged to apologise for not responding in the right kind of way when he first set foot on the Greek mainland. He confided to his journal that he had to admit that he was so busy making arrangements for their overnight accommodation that he quite forgot that he was actually in Greece. Later, on leaving Athens, he made amends by spending two hours at the Parthenon "mourning over the enchanting ruins ... On my way home I cast a thousand, long, lingering looks to the Acropolis and Parthenon and temple of Theseus & thanked the kind fortune which had led me to the shores of Attica".

Greece at this time was still part of the Ottoman Empire that stretched from the shores of North Africa to the borders of Hungary. Everything might have seemed tranquil and pleasant to Greg and the Prince, but, beneath the surface, grievances against the Turkish administration were producing tensions which would erupt into the Greek War of Independence which began a mere four years after Greg's tour. The places that he visited saw some of the most appalling atrocities perpetrated in the history of warfare. Most, if not all, of the people who welcomed the Prince and Greg on their journey must have been slaughtered in the most horrendous series of revenge killings. Both Greeks and Turks were guilty of truly dreadful treatment of their opponents: men, women, children and tiny babies were massacred. It was said that afterwards not a Turk remained in the Peloponesus or a Greek on Chios or in Smyrna. Greg was lucky, for no hint of what was to come affected his pleasure in the tour.

After Greece the travellers went across the sea to Asia Minor, the site of Troy, the Sea of Marmora and ultimately to Constantinople. Travelling conditions in the Ottoman Empire were much like those of Spain. While private houses were sometimes available for their accommodation, outside towns and cities the travellers had to stay in *khans*, which resembled the *posadas* and *ventas* of Spain. These provided nothing more than bare walls and an open space for travellers, their animals, and baggage. Travel was on horseback or primitive carts. On the Black Sea, the Prince and Greg were rowed across the waters so progress was very slow. Food had to be taken on journeys as none was available in the *khans*. The heat was frequently intolerable and one of the party was badly affected by this as they rode towards Troy.

But the great city of Constantinople surpassed anything that Greg had ever

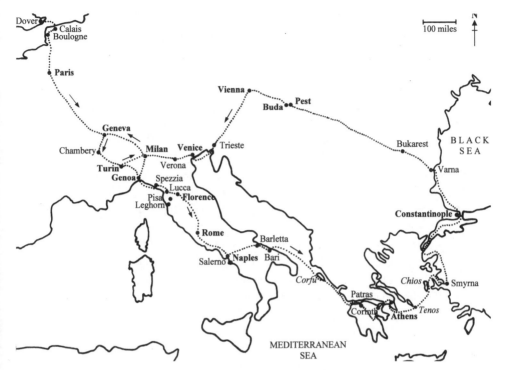

Robert Hyde Greg's travels in France, Italy, Greece and Turkey in 1817.

seen. It was, for him, the fairyland of the Arabian Nights. His pleasure in what he saw was enormous and he relished with undisguised delight the privileges that he enjoyed in the company of the Prince. He saw the Sultan and his palace and even the harem; he visited a mosque; attended a review of Turkish artillery and went to Fêtes Champetres on the shores of the Bosphorus. He loved the exotic food, the music, the long-stemmed pipes, the dancing and the sheer glamour of it all.

From Constantinople to Buda and Pest, travel was endured rather than enjoyed. Then, there was Vienna, the capital city of the Habsburg Empire, a handsome city as Greg put it, but comparatively modest in comparison with the grandiose buildings and the Ringstrasse of later developments under the Emperor Franz Joseph.

Having taken farewell of the Prince of Homburg, Greg journeyed to Trieste, which reminded him of Cadiz, and then to Venice, where he encountered customs officers on the Lido who delayed his entrance to the city by several hours. Customs officers were the bane of his life on his travels abroad. He detested their petty behaviour and delight in delaying travellers. Above all, he was scandalised by their shameless touting for bribes.

He spent a fortnight in Venice, no longer under the Doges but now under

191

Austrian control, of course. Then he travelled through Northern Italy. In Milan he visited the cathedral where "Napoleon did more than had been done 200 years before, but much remains to be done ..." He went to see the fresco of the 'Last Supper' by Leonardo da Vinci: "It is in a miserable state, the water from above having trickled all over it". In Genoa he enjoyed the hospitality of friends and then it was time to make his way back into France.

The journal stops abruptly at Geneva. We know that his mother was taken seriously ill at this time, and it is possible that he was summoned home and had to curtail his journey. What is definitely known is that on his return to England Robert Hyde Greg went into partnership with his father and had to start work as Manager of Quarry Bank Mill. There would probably have been little spare time for travel writing.

Later in life, as a married man, he took his family abroad with him to countries such as Switzerland, Austria and Germany. His daughter Caroline produced a series of watercolours, which show some of the places that they enjoyed visiting. If there are more of the travel journals they have yet to be discovered.

1817 January 2nd Thursday

Left London at 6 o'clock in the evening. Coach stopped 2 hours at Canterbury. Reached Dover at 9 o'clock next morning. Had barely time to pass the Luggage and get a hearty breakfast. They gave me no trouble at the Customs House. Got on board at 9½ and under weigh by 10 o'clock. View of the castle and cliffs of Dover very fine. Reached Calais in 2 hours and twenty minutes. Wind strong and sea rather rough. Everybody sick myself included, tho' not much. Put up at the Hotel Bourbon, good accommodation.

Jany. 4th

at 11 o'clock set off in the diligence. My companions, Sir Richard Levygige, Mr Haliday, Mrs Cooke and two Frenchmen. Dreadful storm of wind and rain. 4 hours in going 11 miles. Dined at Boulogne at 5 o'clock.

Jany. 5th

Breakfast at Abeville at 6 o'clock. Joined there by Mrs Dalrymple an English lady. Dined at Amiens. Mrs D. very ill and obliged to leave her at Breteuil, where we arrived at 8 o'clock and lay down till midnight, when we set off.

6th Jan^{y.}

Breakfast at Clermont. Country pretty and well wooded to Paris, where we arrived at 4 o'clock and in dreadful rain. Found my cousin, R. Batt in the Hotel de Mirabeau Rue de la Paix. The fatigue of travelling in the diligence is very great – dined at the table d'hôte.

7th Jan^{y.}

Spent the morning rambling over the city the Thulleries [sic] gardens etc. Dined at Mr Callaghan's and played at "vingt-une" in the evening with a party of French ladies. Left at 12½pm.

Jany. 8th

Walked along the quays to the <u>Jardin des Plantes</u> and from the alpine region of the Gardens had a most enchanting view of Paris and the neighbouring country. The <u>Cabinet d'Histoire Naturelle</u> was not open. Returned by St Genievre [sic] deservedly ranked amongst the finest of the Parisian buildings. The Portico and interior of admirable architecture, the order Corinthian. The exterior is heavy, and the Dome not half the size of St Pauls, is yet too large for the building. The <u>Eglise de Supplice</u> [sic] is a heavy crumbling and unmeaning edifice. In the evening went to the Theatre François; <u>Talma</u> played Egiste in the tragedy of <u>Agamemnon</u>. I admired as much as any actor I ever saw and he left all his fellow players at an infinite distance. The farce "<u>Monsr. Poncennae</u>" by Moliere was well played. The Theatre is the most sombre, and one of the shabbiest I ever was in.

Jany. 9th

Went to the <u>Montaignes Russes</u> about two miles out of Paris. In the evening went to the Theatre François saw <u>Mademoiselle Mars</u> in the "Misanthrope" and in the "<u>Comedie du jeu d'hazard</u>". Her acting in the part of Silvia surpassed anything I have ever witnessed. I was enchanted with her sweet voice and infinite variety of expression.

Jany. 10th

Called on Mr Ord and Monsieur Gautier and went afterwards to the <u>Monumens Francois</u> [sic] with which I was much pleased. The monuments of Cardinal Richelieu and Mazarin are amongst the finest, but that which covers the ashes of <u>Eloise and Abelard</u> is the most interesting. There are also some good statues and busts of the principal kings and great men of France. Spent the evening looking about the Cafés, Gaming houses and various scenes of the Palais Royal.

January 11th

Set off in good time to <u>Versailles</u>, fog too thick to see the country. The interior of the Palace very magnificent, nothing to be seen but paintings, mirrors, gold and the richest marbles, all lavished with incredible profusion. <u>The Gallerie de Glace</u> is almost a unique for richness and beauty. The grand Façade which looks toward the Gardens defies the power of language to do it justice, the extent is truly astonishing, the beauty enchanting, nor can it be regarded with[out] admiration and wonder. It would injure it to compare it with any building or range of buildings in Paris, nor in my opinion, is Paris so well worth seeing as Versailles. Everything is on the same magnificent scale, the walks, ponds and fountains among; the latter the '<u>Bains d'Apollo</u>' is prominent and worthy of a visit from Paris. The walks are crowded with beautiful marble vases and fine statues. The trees are high. The woman who has charge of the immense <u>Orangery</u> has served in her present situation during the reign of Louis XV, XVI, the republic, Napoleon, Louis XVIII, Napoleon and Louis again. The King is again fitting up the Palace; he is blamed for it, but who that had such a place would not do the same and if Versailles falls to ruin would not Europe have lost one of its brightest monuments?

(Theatre Vaudeville in the evening).

Jany. 12th

Walked about the <u>Champs Elyseés, Place Louis Quinze</u> and Thuileries Gardens. In my opinion the most striking view about Paris is from the <u>Pont Louis XV</u>. Went in the evening to a <u>soirée</u> at Mrs Callaghan's, rather stupid party.

Jany. 13th

Walked to see the Catacombs, distant an hour and half from my hotel, out of the Barriere d'Enfer. Descent into them near 60 feet. There are it is said 2,060,000 skulls visible. Saw one or two that had been trepanned. The[y] still continue to work at the excavations altho' sufficiently large for generations.

Dined at Madame Gautier to whom I brought a letter of introduction from Dr Roget.[3] I was most hospitably received and entertained. Monsr. G took me in the evening to the Opéra Comique. The plays were La Journée des Avantures, etc.

Jany. 14th

Went into the Louvre now open for the first time for many months. The Gallery is now fitted up in an admirable style and the pictures better arranged than they were before. They are arranged in Schools. I was much disappointed in the paintings of Rubens taken from the Luxembourg. The French and Dutch and Flemish good and numerous. I admired extremely the paintings of Vernet, Le Sueur, Rembrandt, Gerard Dow, Vanderwerf, Ostade and Teniers. I had not time to examine well the Italian school.

Among the paintings there are:

by				
	Poussin	32	Guercini	12
	Le Sueur	42	Guido	23
	Claude	10	L. da Vinci	9
	Vernet	30	Murillo	5
	Gerard Dow	11	P. Veronese	10
	Vandike	17	Raphael	14
	Rembrandt	15	Titian	22
	Rubens	42	Salr. Rosa	5
	Teniers	14		
	Wouverman	12		
	Albani	17		
	A. Carracci	24		
	Corregio	3		
	Dominiquin	14		

Went in the evening to the Theatre François and saw two highly amusing pieces, "Les Chateaux d'Espagne" and "Les Etourdes".

Jany. 15th

Monsieur Gautier called according to promise and took me in his carriage to the Sorbonne to see 2 of the chef d'oeuvres of David, "Leonidas" and "Les Sabines",

---

3   Dr Peter Mark Roget – physician in Manchester and later in London. He was a friend of the Greg family and is famous for compiling *Roget's Thesaurus*.

two of his last productions. The anatomy of his figures is considered as perfect, but his colouring is bad, and though all his figures are correct in their light and shade, all parts of his pictures being equally light. It seems as if he had copied a number of statues and placed them all on the same canvas without any relation one to another. The[re] is also a want of unity and simplicity in the conception and grouping of his figures and the trivial parts are so highly finished and brightly coloured as to call off the attention from the more important, according to Sir J. Reynolds a great fault, and not known in the old Schools.

We went afterward to the Luxembourg. All the paintings are moved excepting two chef d'oeuvres of David, the "Judgement of Brutus" and "Les Horaces" which have the same excellence and the same faults as the two others. The Chambre of Lords in the same Palais is chaste, handsome and comfortable.

Being a stormy night, staid at home.

Jany. 16th

Rainy morning and not being able to go far, spent the day at [the] Louvre. In the evening went to the Theatre François to see Fleuris and Mademoiselle Mars perform in the "Femme Savantes" and "La Nièce Supposée". Mars played "Henriette" and "Eugenie" and displayed great talent, she was truly enchanting. Fleuris too was admirable.

January 17th

Rainy morning. Dined [at] a small family party at Mad^e. Gautier's. In the evening met with a chapter of accidents. I wished to go to the Opera François but told the coachman by mistake the Opera Italienne, which was shut up and on recognising my mistake, the coachman made another and set me down at the theatre where I had to pay double for a ticket, could get no seat, found out where I was too late to rectify it, and the play concluded a few moments after.

January 18th

Went with Mr Vogel to see the "Cabinet d'histoire Naturale" at the Jardin des Plants. We arrived too late to examine the Minerals thoroughly, but they seem to be much superior to our collections at the British Museum. The Gold and Silver specimens, especially the former, are most magnificent, superior I think to those in the Madrid Cabinet. The coppers too were very rich. For the number, beauty and fine state of preservation of the birds and butterflies I should think this collection is unrivalled, at least I never saw anything to be compared with it. Went in the evening to the Theatre Francois saw Mad.^lle Mars and Fleuris in the "Coquette Corrigée", as much pleased as usual.

January 19th

Took a walk down the Seine as far as the Bridge of Jena, crossed it into the

Champs de Mars, passed the Ecole Militaire and returned to the Thuilleries by the Hospital of Invalids [sic]. Rainy afternoon. Went to a Soireé at Mr Callaghans' in the evening.

January 20th
Walked up the Seine and round the city by the Boulevards. All theatres shut in the evening.

January 21st
Walked down the Seine on the South side and then about the Thuilleries, afterwards to the Bibliotheque Royal with Mons. Gautier. The theatres not being open staid at home.

January 22nd
Monsieur G having procured me a ticket for the Chambre de Deputés. I went early to stand 3 or 4 hours, unfortunately an election of a president prevented any debate. The room is handsome and a semi circle like the Chamber of Peers in the Luxembourg. On returning found I. Hodgson. Went together to the Theatre de'Odéon, where in the "Auberge de Calais" we saw an excellent caricature of my Lord Anglois's entrance among the French.

January 23rd
Breakfasted with I.H. and went to the Place Royale formerly the residence of the first French Nobility now the worst part of Paris. We then went to see the great Elephant of Bonaparte, 40 feet high without the Castle which is 14, the length is 45 feet. It was to be cast in Bronze. By the Pont Austerlitz we went to the Jardin de Plants then to Halle de Vins which it is said contains 200,000 Barrels. The Gobelins we found shut, but saw Notre Dame, extremely rich outside, plain inside, with Corinthian pillars supporting Gothic arches. We were too late to get our passports; called on Madame Gautier but did not find her at home. Dined at a Restaurant and went to "Theatre François" to see Madam.^{lle} Mars and Fleury in "Le Tartuffe" and Madame de Sevigny, admired them as much as ever.

January 24th
Went to procure passports from our Ambassador. Afterwards to the Bibliotheque Royale. Saw the models of the Alps including the country round Geneva and the passes of the Simplon, Mont St Gothard and St Bernard. Spent the afternoon at the Louvre. Went in the evening to the Opera Francoise. The theatre is the handsomest in Paris, but far inferior to the London ones. The scenery is uncommonly good. The two pieces, "Panurge" and "Paul et Virginie". The former a grand opera and ballet, the latter a Pantomime and ballet well acted and almost as affecting

as the story. There was a ballet called the "Pas Russe" something in the style of the Bolero which is a <u>dance</u>, the French and Italian Ballets are nothing but a collection of <u>steps</u>.

January 25th

Went to the <u>Gobelines</u> [sic] or Manufactory of tapistry. At the distance of a few feet it is impossible to distinguish the tapestry from a fine painting and they can imitate anything and to any degree of exactness.

January 26th Sunday

At 7 o'clock in the morning set out in the Diligence for Geneva, it passes by Auxerre, Avallon and Dijon. Slept at the later place on Tuesday night and reached Dole at Wednesday at noon. Changed our conveyance and were put into a most miserable machine cramping every way and not on springs. Towards evening began to ascend the mountains and at 6 o'clock next morning **January 30th** found ourselves in the regions of frost and snow. We continued to ascend and the road being frozen and dangerous walked to the little village of Morais situated at the foot of the Jura Chain. There we continued to ascend on foot for 6 miles amidst most magnificent scenery till we reached Hautuise, a small village at a great elevation, beyond which all is ice and snow. Here we mounted a sledge drawn by two horses and travelled smoothly and rapidly along the edges of precipice for 6 or 8 miles. We walked on the summit and then after sunset saw Mont Blanc still glittering in its beams. A descent of two hours brought us to Gex, where we again took the Diligence and reached Geneva at 11 o'clock.

January 31st

Called on Mr Fazy who walked about with us all morning. Dined with him and spent the evening at Mr Martin's.

February 1st

Set off at 4 o'clock in the morning per Diligence to Chambery, Capital of Savoy. Had no trouble at the Custom House. The ride [through] the Savoyard vallies enchanting. Reached Chambery at 9 o'clock and found the Turin Diligence gone which compelled us to wait 3 days.

February 2nd and 3rd

Walked about the town and environs. The situation is fine and the mountains equal any I ever saw, I think even those of Granada.

February 4th – Tuesday

Climbed to the summit of several of the neighbouring hills, the grandeur and singularity of the mountains cannot be surpassed any more than the romantic and [?] appearance of the vallies, the weather equal to our fine summer days.

February 5th

At 3 o'clock in the morning set out in the Diligence. Breakfast at Aigubelle. Weather broke and hills and vallies were covered with Snow. Stopped a few hours at night at St Michel at the foot of the Alps.

February 6th

Off at 2 o'clock by moonlight along a frozen road and through terrific passes. Breakfasted at Lansleburg at the foot of Mont Cenis. Began the ascent at 2 o'clock in a covered sledge or trunk. Reached the summit at 4, the descent rapid, precipitous and dangerous. Reached Susa at the foot of the mountains at 8 in the evening. The summit of Mount Cenis at Post house is 6260 high, the rocks about 3000 higher. A fine day doubtless but frightful wind on descending.

February 7th

Off at 4 o'clock, a charming day welcomed us to Italy. Crossed a cultivated plain and reached Turin at noon. Called on Messrs Sassieri and Dutoit. Walked about the city and environs, and to the top of the observatory whence is a magnificent view of the Alps and country round. The King of Sardinia and Piedmont now holds his court at Turin.

February 8th

Set out for Genoa in the Diligence. Crossed a highly cultivated irrigated plain to Alessandria which we reached at about 7 having set out at 4 o'clock in the morning.

February 9th

Were off again 4 – and kept waiting an hour at the gate by some fools who pretended an order from the King. 2 miles farther entered the fatal plain of Marengo.[4] At ten well among the Appenines and soon commenced the descent of the Bochetta, one of the highest, it is said 5000 feet. The heat was annoying and no snow on the summit. The descent long, rough and precipitous. Reached Genoa at 5 o'clock in the evening.

February 10th

Called on Messrs Drago and Walsh and Mr De La Rue. Mrs W Walked about with us all morning. Went to the Church Carignoli; red plaster and white marble do not agree especially when the former predominates.

[4]   Napoleon's army defeated the Austrians at the Battle of Marengo in 1800.

February 11th
Went to the Palazzo Durazzo, some good paintings. Spent the morning in the Porto Franco.

February 12th
Went to the Palazzo Sera, nothing to be seen but one splendid Saloon, gold and mirrors. Spent the morning in the Porto Franco. Dined at Mr Drago's a very pleasant family. Spoke Italian before dinner, French at dinner. Went with Mr Walsh in the evening to the Opera. The house large but not handsome. The performance pretty good. The ballet "Timour the Tartar".

February 13th
The weather being favourable, we arranged with the captain of a felucca bound to Leghorn to sail at 4 o'clock. Went to see the <u>Cathedral</u>. Nothing very remarkable inside or out. <u>In the church of St Ambrose</u> rich in marbles and gilding, I saw one admirable Guido and two Rubens. The church of <u>Annunciata</u> is the richest interior I have yet seen, the Corinthian pillars of red and white marble beautiful. The Senate room is very handsome, adorned with statues of the heroes and paintings of the military achievements of Genoa. From the summit of the Carignano Church I had a much finer view when I ascended before. I went afterwards to the <u>Albergo de Poveri</u>, an institution for the acceptance of Orphans and one of the best of the kind. There were 1200 children at present. An admirable Relievo of Michel Angelo is the principal attraction of strangers. Got under weigh about 5 o'clock and had a charming view of Genoa and the Appenines.

February 14th
At 6 o'clock in the morning found ourselves with contrary wind off Levano 35 miles from Genoa. Obliged to return to Sestri and remain there all night.

February 15th
Took mules and set off at 7 o'clock in company with an Abbé of Lucca and a native of Spezzia. Our road lay entirely in the bosom of the Appenines. We did not reach <u>Spezzia</u> until two hours after sunset. Took a carriage forward 8 miles to <u>Sarzana</u> where we arrived at one o'clock in the morning.

February 16th
Accompanied by the Abbé set out in a post carriage and passing through a beautiful country or rather garden reached <u>Lucca</u> early in the evening.

February 17th
Off from Lucca at 11 o'clock and reached <u>Florence</u> at 9 in the evening, passing

through <u>Pescia</u>, <u>Pistoia</u> and <u>Prato</u>. The country being all the way a perfect garden.

February 18th

The last day of the Carnival. Walked about the city in the morning, then the <u>Lung Arno de Mezzo Giorno</u> or public walk. Afterwards the Corso where all the Nobility and Gentry were collected, &, in the evening went to a Public mask[ed] Ball at the theatre, where we were much amused. The principal beauties of all three places were English.

February 19th [to Friday 28th]

Attended to our business. During the 10 days spent at Florence having no acquaintance and the theatres being shut, our evenings were generally spent at home, that is in very comfortable lodgings in the Piazzo Ste Maria di Novella. Our amusements during the day were visiting the Gallery of Paintings, the churches, or walking about the enchanting environs of the beautiful city of which too much perhaps cannot be said. The Val d'Arno is as famous in modern times as Tempe in the Antient. In the <u>Gallery</u>, I spent some hours every day and my enjoyment increased [each] time I entered it. In the <u>Tribune</u>, besides the chef d'oeuvres of all the famous painters, are the Venus di Medicis, the Jeune Appolon, the Rotateur, the Faun and the Wrestlers. In the Church of <u>Sta Croce</u> I regarded with great delight and reverence the tombs of <u>Galileo</u>, <u>Michael Angelo</u>, <u>Alfieri</u> and some other names known to the whole world as well as to Italy. The tombs of the Medicis, the work of M. Angelo in the <u>Church of St Lorenzo</u> claim more than one visit and those of Politian and Mirandola in <u>St Marco</u> must not be forgotten. The <u>Chapel of the Medicis</u> is the richest in marbles I have yet seen. The finest walks and those I visited oftenest were the hill of Bellosguardo, Convent on Mount Olivet, the Poggio Imperiale, the Convent of St Miniato etc. Fiesole is yet more interesting from its antiquity and commanding situation. The <u>Villa Careggi</u>, the country house of Lorenzo di Medicis and in a chamber in which he died is doubly attractive from that circumstance and the fine situation.

The <u>Ponte Trinita</u> of 3 arches over the Arno is the handsomest bridge I have seen. The arch between Gothic and circular.

March 1st – Saturday

Set out early in a Calesa for Pisa where we arrived in the evening after running the gauntlet thro' a number of Rascals resolved to cheat us and having knives drawn for 3 pence. Good inn in the Lung Arno.

March 2nd

Much shocked to hear of the death of Mr Horner for whom we brought letters.

Spent the morning in the Cathedral and Campo Santo. The famous Tower leans 14 feet out of the perpendicular. Found Monsr Archard and his family setting out for Rome. Spent the evening with Mrs Drew and family, 3 sisters, 2 daughters and almost the first English I had spoken to since leaving home.

March 3rd
Went on early to Leghorn. Dined with Mr and Mrs Routh and went to the theatre in the evening.

March 4th
Dined with Mr and Mrs Ulrics and went to the theatre in the evening with T. Pares, Welsh and Green who had joined us that morning.

March 5th
Went to see the burial ground of Protestant strangers. Dined with Messrs Grant and Pillars. In Leghorn there is nothing to see and we attended to nothing but business, that done we proceeded early.

March 6th
... and breakfast with Pares etc at Pisa. Went on all together to Lucca and then to the hot Baths 15 m further and returned to Lucca.

March 7th
Rained hard. Returned all to Florence. Arrived late.

March 8th
Walked to San Miniato, the Casino etc. Dined with T.P. and his party.

March 9th
Saw the <u>Pitti Palace</u>. The collection of paintings excellent. One Michel Angelo, 8 Raphaels of which one, the Madonna della Sedia pleased me more than any painting I ever saw in my life. Titians also fine.

March 10th
Set off for Vallumbrosa on horseback in company with Tom Pares etc. Reached it two hours before dark, saw the sunset from the summit of the mountains in the sea, &, being only one bed, we all slept over a blazing fire.

March 11th
Off at seven and reached Florence to breakfast at 1 o'clock.

March 12th

Set out for Rome at 6 o'clock in company with a Prima Donna &. passing through the Val d'Arno superiore, stopped for the night at Levane 30 miles from Florence.

March 13th

Proceeded through rich cultivated vallies to Carnuscia 34 miles, visited on the road Cortona and saw the sunset from its walls over the lake of Trasimenes.

March 14th

Road lay along the side of the lake, country woody and beautiful. Between the villages of Borghetto and Passignano passed over the ground and the fatal stream where [H]Annibal defeated the Romans. At the same place, entered the Papal territory. Reached Perugia in time to look through its desolate streets, how can they be otherwise containing 48 convents, 70 churches and 10,000 inhabitants. 40 miles.

March 15th

Country beautiful, passed through the charming Valle Spoleta, left Assisi and Spello on the left and the sources of the Clitumnus on the right. Reached Spoleto, beautifully situated among green and rocky hills at sunset. Joined three other parties going to Rome and travelling in the same manner.

March 16th

Passed Monte Somma near 4000 feet high. At Terni staid a few hours to see the famous falls of the Velino,[5] the only falls which have not disappointed me, they surpassed my expectations. We stopped again to visit the ruined Bridge of Augustus at Narni, an ancient town magnificently situated and commanding a fine view of the Val di Narni and snowy Apennines which rise here to an elevation of 8 or 9,000 feet. The scenery of Terni and Narni in their kind are unrivalled. Slept at Nene a Post house.

March 17th

Soon entered the Campagna of Roma, desert but woody in these parts. Passed Civita Castellana supposed by some to be the ancient Veii. At Nepi which contains a few beggars within the immense extent of its ancient walls we were disappointed of our breakfast and were obliged to go on to Nepi [sic] where we slept.

---

[5] The Falls of Vellino are the Cascata delle Marmore, an artificial cascade created by the Roman Consul Marius Curius Dentalus when he dammed the River Velino and diverted its waters to prevent the adjoining land from becoming a swamp.

March 18th

Crossed the remaining part of the dreary Campagna and entered Rome about Midday. After breakfast went to St Peters and afterwards into the Museum of the Vatican where night surprised us gazing on the Apollo which I preferred to the Venus.

March 19th

Went to the Pantheon to hear High Mass. Then to the Capitol, Forum, Temple of Peace and Coliseum, and returned by the Fountain of Trevi and Forum Trajanum.

March 20th

Went to the Campidoglio. The Antinous and the Dying Gladiator, the most interesting statues. The collection of paintings not first rate, the Sybils of Dominchino and Guercino the most remarkable. But the first objects of interest are the Rostral Pillar and the Wolf of Bronze struck with lightening on the death of Caesar. A fine bronze bust of J. Caesar, and another of Brutus are in the same apartment. The Campidoglio is totally unworthy the genius of M. Angelo. Went afterwards to the Vatican, the collection of everything extensive and excellent except the paintings wh$^{c.}$ are few in number but all chef d'oeuvres. The famous Transfiguration affected me as it might and I felt its merit. Canova's Perseus is admirable but should be considered as a copy of the Apollo, it is, in fact little more. We afterwards spent some time in St Peters wh$^{c.}$ improves and indeed grows every time it is entered. The front is however nothing but the front of a Gigantic house. I went in the evening to a large party at the Duke Torlonia's. Met there Mr and Mrs D. Gaskell,[6] Monsr Achard and Mr Coxe an Edinburgh acquaintance.

March 21st

Passed through the forum by the Temples of Concord, Jupiter Stator etc to the Baths of Titus, thence to St John Lateran, St Croce, Temple of Venus and Cupid, Porta Maggiore, Temple of Minerva Medica, Gallieno's Arch, St^a Maria Maggiore and Monte Cavallo. In the afternoon went through the worst parts of Rome and spent the evening at Mr Gaskells.

March 22nd

Rained most violently. In the afternoon went to St Peters.

March 23rd

Went to attend an English service in the forum of Trajan, but having mistaken the hour walked in the rain 3 miles to St Peters and attended Mass in the Sistine Chapel where was the Pope with all the Cardinals. Michelangelo's Last Judgement is black and unintelligible. Spent some hours in the Museum and afterwards went to that of the Capitol. Walked in the evening round the Pallatine Hill to the Coliseum and spent an hour there. Drank tea at Mr Gaskells.

March 24th

Visited the Ponte Rotto, house of Pontius Pilate, Temple of Fortuna Virilis, Temple of Vesta, Portico of Octavia, Theatre of Marcellus, Arch of the Four Fountains, Cloaca Maxima, Mont Palatine, Palace of the Caesars, Baths of Livia, Church of San Gregorio, where are rival paintings of Guido and Dominichino. In the afternoon went to the beautiful public walk which overhangs the city and Porta del Popolo and spent the evening in the gardens of the Villa Borghese.

March 25th

Went to the baths of Diocletian, now a church belonging to a convent of Carthusians. Afterwards out of the Porta Salara and visited the villa Albano, some good statues but nothing extraordinary in anything.

March 26th

Went to the Coliseum, then to St Peters, through the Sacristy where there is nothing to see, thro' the vaults where repose the remains of most of the early Popes, and then to the Tomb of the Apostles Peter and Paul. The Priest showed us round as if a wild bear show. The head of St Peter is in the Church of St John of Lateran and half of the body of St Paul in the Church of that Saint fuori della porta. We afterwards ascended the Dome. The view is extraordinary for it towers far above the 7 Hills, and every building in the city is distinguishable. I ascended the ball and leaned on the Cross, though the wind was strong, and afterwards went inside the ball which may be done without difficulty. Went afterwards to the Manufacture of Mosaic, a picture of middling size takes 20 years to finish is worth £2000 and upwards. Tomb of Augustus is turned into an amphitheatre. Went in the evening with the Gaskells to a musical party at Signor Rufinis.

March 27th

Went to the Farnese Palace, everything removed to Naples. To the Palazzo, some few good paintings, the most interesting object is the Colossal statue of Pom-

---

[6] Not the family of Mrs Elizabeth Gaskell the famous novelist. She was born in 1810, and married the Reverend William Gaskell in 1832. She first visited Rome in 1857. It is possible, though not certain, however, that the Gaskells mentioned in this journal were related to the family of the Reverend William Gaskell and like him, came from the Warrington area in Cheshire.

pey, at the foot of which Caesar is said to have fallen. The sculpture is very fine. Found the Guistinicani palace, shut, and so went to the Palazzo Doria where are many fine paintings of A. Carracci, Gaspar Poussin and Titian also many Guidos and 4 or 5 Claudes. Spent the evening at Torlonia's, Duke of Bracciano, English innumerable [sic]. Met Monsr Achard and Mon^{sr} and Me Constant and their two daughters, Mr and Mrs Gaskell and their two daughters and Miss Pilkington.

March 28th

Torlonia's servants sent for 5 Pauls,[7] a usual custom here. Ascended the tower of the Campidoglio and had a most magnificent view. Went to the Tarpeian Rock, over Mount Aventine, by the Pyramid of Caius Cestius out of the Porta Ostiense and visited St Pauls Church, remarkable only for 24 beautiful corinthian pillars taken from the Tomb of [H]Adrian and some other fine antique columns. Returned by the Tiber, Temple Vesta, Fortuna Viriles etc.

March 29th

Set out at 6 o'clock to Tivoli. Stopped to look at the lake of Tartarus and the stream of the Solfaterra which smells the same and as strong as the Harrogate waters. The whole country round is formed of layers of calcareous and sulphureous depositions. At the distance of four miles from Tivoli we alighted to examine the Remains of [H]Adrian's villa which cover a hill 7 miles in circumference. The ruins being of brick are not magnificent but from the foliage are very picturesque. In the ruins of the Naumachia[8] we were fortunate in meeting among other things that surprised us Mr and Mrs G and Miss P and so we joined parties for the day and returned to Rome in Company. The day was charming and the temples of the Sybil and Vesta, the villas of Maecenas, Catullus etc. and the famous falls gave us much delight. The latter though more classic and better known are far inferior to Terni, this I expected for nothing can surpass those. We reached Rome by the Porta Lorenzo and Baths of Diocletian about 8 o'clock.

March 30th – Sunday

Engaged with a man to take us to Naples on the 4th of April. Went to the Capitol for 2 hours and then to attend the English service in the Forum of Trajan. The Congregation large and of course respectable. Went to St Peters and the Vatican. Walked on the Trinita del Monte at Sunset and afterwards by a bright moonlight went to the Roman Forum, passed the Arches of Severus, Titus and Constantine, the Temples of Concord, Jupiter tonans, Jupiter Stator, Faustina, the Temples of Peace and of the Sun to the Coliseum. This ought never to be seen but by moonlight, it is strikingly beautiful, grand, sublime and affecting. The ruined Palace of the Caesars, of Nero's Golden House and the Aqueduct between the Palatine and Caelian Hills add both to the scenery and interest. I think upon the whole it is the sublimest scene I have ever witnessed.

March 31st

Passed between the Palatine and Aventine Mounts and by the Therme of Cara-calla to the tomb of the Scipios. Then under the Arch of Drusus out of the Porta Sebastiana, to the Campo di Anibale, Temple of Dio Ridiculo, Grotto of Egeria, the Church of St Stephen, remarkable only for being the entrance into the Cat-acombs. These are not worth seeing, being nothing to see. We then visited the Circus, temples etc of Caracalla and the tomb of Cecilia Metella. Temple of Bac-chus. The day enchanting but hot. At night took our friends to a conversazione and visited the Pantheon by a bright moonlight.

April 1st

Went to the palladium, Temple of Remus, Le Sette Sale,[9] and St Pietro in Vini-colo where the attraction is a great Moses of Michael Angelo, the arms of which struck me much. Went afterwards to the Studio of Terwalsen[10] in which we thought we observed more marks of Genius than in Canova's though his statues are not so well finished. Saw the excellent mosaic of Paestum for which Louis 1,000 are demanded. Drank tea with the Gaskells.

April 2nd

Went to the Sistine Chapel to hear the Miserere, sent back because not full drest, returned, got in, and found the immense crowd inside composed almost entirely of English and too much noise and bustle to hear the Music well. The Miserere the only good part. Went afterwards into the Museum with the Gaskells to see the statues by torchlight. The effect very fine. The Lacoon appeared to most ad-vantage, but I was most struck with the difference between Canova's Perseus and the Apollo a difference more perceptible than by day. Indeed the excellence of a statue cannot be so well judged of by daylight as torchlight. The muscles are seen perfectly.

---

[7] The '5 Pauls' is an intriguing but baffling expression and we would welcome an ex-planation. A paul was a small obsolete Italian coin.

[8] The Naumachia was an area that could be flooded for mock sea battles – very popu-lar Roman entertainments.

[9] Le Sette Sale is an enormous vaulted structure built as a reservoir for the Baths of Tra-jan. It is near the Church of San Pietro in Vincolo.

[10] 'Terwalson' was the Danish sculptor Thorwaldson.

April 3rd

Went to receive the benediction of the Pope.[11] He was very ill and infirm and I was much disappointed in the ceremony. All ceremonies of this kind disappoint. Went again in the evening to the Sistine Chapel to hear the Miserere, a great crowd, but got in. Found the Gaskells and afterwards entered St Peter's to see the famous cross of fire suspended from the Dome. The effect would have been fine and striking had we never heard of it, but too much has been said. The lights and shades on the Dome were certainly sublime but the whole affair was inferior to the holy week at Seville. On coming out the moon showed the front, the colonnades and fountains to great advantage. Drank tea with the Gaskells and took leave.

April 4th

Set out per vettura, passed through the Foro Romano as the sun rose. Reached Albano by 11. Visited the Lake, Castle Gandalfo and the outlet for the waters. Reached Veletre at 4 o'clock and proceeded no farther.

April 5th

Off at one o'clock, cold extreme. When the sun rose found ourselves on the Pontine marshes. Reached Terracina at 12 o'clock and 6 miles farther entered the Neapolitan dominions. Reached Mola at 8½.

April 6th

Set out at 2 o'clock, reached Capua at noon and entered Naples in the dusk of the evening; the weather on the journey fine but a strong north wind made it cold.

April 7th

Called [on] some of our friends but found none at home being [a] feast day. Ascended to the Carthusian Convent for the view and returned through the town and along the shore. Spent the day looking through the City. Went at night to the theatre of San Carlo considered the finest in Europe. It is more splendid and larger than our London ones though not more elegant.

April 8th

Set out at an early hour to Pompeii, distant 15 miles. The ride very interesting along the shore and at the foot of Vesuvius, over the various streams of Lava. Passed through Torre del Greco, half buried in the eruption of 1794. The most interesting part of Pompeii are the streets and private houses; temples and Basilicas are seen elsewhere. There are about 50 men now employed and continue discovering. On returning visited Herculaneum. Not much to see as all is darkness and one excavation filled up with the soil taken from the new one. Nothing has now been done for 40 years. Pompeii has been destroyed by loose ashes. Herculaneum by a tufa now extremely hard, and 70 feet deep – Nothing is now in the museums but some paintings. In execution these are daubs, but the design elegant and great spirit and freedom in the drawing. Everything but the paintings are removed to Naples.

April 9th

Spent the morning in the Custom House. At two went to the Grotto of Pausilipo, then to Virgil's tomb. Ascended the hill and walked round the promontory almost to Nisida. Saw a fine sunset over Ischia and Baia, and the view of Naples and Vesuvius on our return was magnificent. We reached home about 8. A column of smoke above 1,000 feet high rose from the volcano and as the weather was doubtful though the evening fine we determined to ascend immediately. Set out with that intention at 11 in the evening, but the horses would not leave Naples, and after many attempts we got out and walked 6 miles to Portici. In a few minutes found Guides and Ciceroni and commenced the ascent on asses at 12½ o'clock. We reached the hermitage by 2¼. The night was so dark we were obliged to have torches the whole way and the constant flame and repeated eruptions of burning stones from the crater were seen to great advantage. At the foot of the great cone we left our asses and commenced the ascent extremely difficult from the steepness and the softness of the ashes. In about 3 quarters of an hour we arrived at the bottom of the two small cones, each formed by the ashes of its respective crater. We here sat down in a hollow out of which ascended hot air, to watch the eruption and wait for day. When day broke we found ourselves wrapt in clouds. We visited the stream of Lava and saw it oozing out of [the] side of the mountain, found the heat very great both to the face and feet. The clouds clearing away for a few minutes, discovered a most magnificent view of the bay, Naples, all the islands and promontories and of the Calabrian mountains, but in an instant all disappeared. We reached the hermitage again about 7 o'clock and Portici at 8½ – Vesuvius was more than one half lost in clouds, and rain soon came on and continued all day.

April 11th

Rained all day; went in the evening to the theatre Nuova.

---

[11] Pope Pius VII signed the Concordat with Napoleon I in 1801. It was he who was summoned to the coronation of Napoleon as Emperor of the French in 1805, only to see Napoleon crown himself. From 1809 to 1814 he was imprisoned by Napoleon in Savoy.

April 12th

Went to the Studio or Museum.[12] The collection of Statues consists of the famous Farnesian and those found at Herculaneum and Pompeii. The Farnesian Hercules, the Flora colossal, the Venus, which Canova has almost <u>copied</u> in his famous Venus of the Pitti Palace, a Juno and some Gladiators were those which struck me most; of those from Herculaneum I remarked some Muses, and the two statues of the Roman Consuls found in the Amphitheatre, with some others in bronze. Two equestrian statues of the Balbi Father and Son, Proconsuls of Herculaneum are also remarkable. The former had the misfortune to have his head carried off by an English cannon ball about 12 years ago, fired by a Frigate which entered the bay unexpectedly. The King was at dinner in the same Palace, for it stood formerly at Portici. The Paintings which are but just returned from their long sojourn at Palermo are some of them very interesting, 3 or 4 admirable Raphaels, some Titians and other excellent paintings. The original sketch of Michael Angelo's Last Judgement, finished by Venusti. The Plans of the temples of Paestum and other ruins are well executed in cork. The collection of Vases, dishes etc, generally distinguished by us by the names of Pompeii and Herculaneum were none of them found in those towns, but all in tombs and those all Grecian scattered in various parts of Southern Italy. The process of unrolling the <u>Papyri</u> is wonderfully tedious. Many however have been done, more remain and these cannot be distinguished from lumps of Charcoal. One Latin poem has been found, the rest Greek, and the most important of these the writings of Epicurus. They publish them as they proceed, two volumes are out and several others will soon be published. They have a Latin translation at the side.

Went to the San Carlo in the evening.

April 13th

Went up to the Capo del Monte where stands an ugly old Palace in a noble situation. Near it is the observatory commenced on a beautiful plan by Murat, the view from it of the bay, Mount Vesuvius and the city is wonderfully fine. Went over the hill till we found ourselves in the Capua road. This walk presents a succession of magnificent views that cannot be surpassed. Dined and spent the evening at Mr Routh's.

April 14th

Ascended the hill of the Certosa Convent and went through the Castle of St Elmo, the views from both fine. While in the Castle snow fell, and the wind was bitter cold. To San Carlo in the even[g.]

April 15th

Went to pay a second visit to the statues and paintings of the Studio. Rainy day. To the Theatre Nuovo.

April 16th

Through the Grotto of Posilippo and Pozzuoli to Cuma[e], this was the first settlement of the Greeks in Italy, it is now an immense plain of foundations. On a
high rock stood the castle and some temples, and below we found the real Sybil's
Grotto mentioned by Virgil.[13] From Cuma[e] we proceeded to the Lago Fusaro,
said to be the Acheron of the poets, now a Royal Fishpond. The Styx the[y] call
a dirty brook which runs into this lake. We walked from here over the hill to the
famous shore of Baiae; the whole coast is nothing but a mass of Ruins dignified
by mighty remains; some are seen under the water, and all overhang it. Here are
seen the ruins of the Temples of Diana and Mercury both circular like temple of
Minerva Medica and the Pantheon at Rome. That of Mercury has only a small
piece wanting in the Dome, and there is the strongest and most extraordinary
echo I have ever heard. The adjoining temple of Venus is octagonal, with the remains of many buildings behind. Here we embarked and passing a thousand
ruins stopped at the Stufe di Nerone sweating baths. We accompanied our guide
along a narrow passage in the rock, in some parts almost too steep to stand, and
filled with the hottest steam. Arrived at the farther end we found a well of boiling water, and having brought some with us in a few minutes boiled a couple of
Eggs. Though stripped, the perspiration ran in streams down our faces. But few
travellers go to the well, and no wonder for on coming out we looked as if we had
been boiled alive. From the Stufe we proceeded to the Lake of Avernus evidently
the crater of a volcano. The Lucrine lake is dwindled to a pond and its place supplied by Monte Nuova a hill 500 feet high which in one night rose from the bottom of the lake. This happened about 300 years since. Here it was that Aeneas
descended into the infernal regions; we followed the same subterranean passage now miscalled the Sybil's cave which is the one at Cuma[e]. We rode a long
way on mens backs through the dark passages half filled with water, but came to
nothing at last but the place where all had fallen in. We returned to our boat and
sailed to the promontory of Misenus covered with the remains of a thousand villas. We went through some large arched caverns, made for a cistern to supply the
Roman Fleet with fresh water. From the summit of this high promontory we had
an enchanting view of Baiae, Ischia, Procida, and all the neighbouring coasts. We
proceeded then through the Bay of Misenus which formerly contained the
Roman fleet and from which the Elder Pliny sailed to observe Mount Vesuvius,
and landed in the Elysian Fields. These are orchards and vineyards, interspersed
with ancient tombstones. Our guide on returning pointed out the spot where
Agrippina Mother of Nero was killed. This is probably a mistake and it is certain

---

[12]   The Studio or Museum collection he describes is now in the Archaeological Museum
       of Naples.

[13]   Virgil, *The Aeneid*, Book vi.

that what they call her tomb is not a tomb at all. We now stretched across the Bay, passed the remains of the Mole called Caligula's and landed at Pozzuolo. Here we visited the noble ruins of a temple of Jupiter Serapis and the trifling ones of a temple of Neptune. The remains of the Coliseum are considerable. The Cathedral is part of a palace of Augustus, and about a quarter of a mile on the Avernus side of the town are the ruins of Ciceros Academia. Solfatara is a most singular spot distant about a mile. It is the crater of a volcano crusted over, if stamped upon it sound hollow, and sulphurous fumes rise from many orifices. This chrystalizes and is collected. Returned through the grotto of Posilipo. it was quite dark and came on a storm of rain. It is needless to note that this is too much for one days work, the first day should finish with Cumae and the second embrace Misenus.

Thursday 17th
Was introduced to the Prince of Homburg[14] and fixed with his Highness a tour in Greece.

April 18th
Called again on the Prince and fixed the 30th for our departure.
    At 4 o'clock I. Hodgson left me.

April 19th
Called on the Marquis de Berio to whom I had a letter of introduction, but found him just gone to Genoa. Mrs Falconet I found was in the country. I followed her there and met with a very civil reception from her and her daughter the Countess of Pertolis. Their house commands one of the finest views about Naples.

April 21st
Being a fine day devoted it to Pompeii and saw many things I had missed before. There is a foolish order of the Government to prevent anyone drawing, but I took a few sketches by stealth.

April 25th
Being the first fine day of some time I devoted a second visit to Vesuvius. I set out from Naples at about 2 p.m. At the Hermitage found a party [of] English amongst whom [were] two lovely girls. At the summit saw a new stream of Lava and many eruptions of stones; ran round the edge of one of the craters and saw it to the bottom. Got away in time to avoid a great eruption of stones. From the summit I had an enchanting view of the country and coast as far as Terracina, all lighted by the setting sun. The moon shone bright before reaching the bottom.

April 26th

Set out early and passing Pompeii, arrived at Salerno about noon. Passed Nocera de'Pagani and La Cava the country beautiful, and the mountains magnificent. The bay and town of Salerno much resemble Naples, and are inferior only in classic interest. Reached Eboli 16 miles farther about sunset, the country still beautiful and the wood finer than general in Italy.

April 27th

A dark grey misty morning, off by sunrise to Paestum distant 14 miles. The road lies over an uncultivated plain. I was more struck with these ruins rising majestic on the desolate coast, than with any I ever saw excepting the Coliseum. The largest temple that of Neptune wants little but the roof. The two others retain their pillars and cornice nothing more. The proportions of all the parts are the double of what they sh$^{d.}$ be according to the rules of Architecture, yet they do not seem disproportioned. Paestum is amply worth a visit from Naples, so is Salerno. The country the whole way is beautiful and interesting. Slept at Salerno, there in time for a ramble.

Naples 28th

Arrived in the afternoon in hard rain.

April 29th

Called on his Highness to make final arrangements. Called on Mrs Falconet to bid goodbye.

April 30th

After having finished all business I took a walk upon the Chaia[15] to bid adieu to Naples and its bay, it was a lovely evening and the scene lighted up first by the setting sun and then by a full moon. At midnight I went to the Bureau des Diligences and was soon joined by his Highness.

May 1st

At daybreak found ourselves at the foot of the Appenines, here very high and covered with snow, for about 40 miles from Naples, the country is picturesque, cultivated and mountainous. Stopped all night at a miserable inn at Ariano, a town situated on the summit of a high, barren hill surrounded by other bare brown hills and resembled much a Spanish scene. This town is about 60 from Naples and 80 miles from Bari. 140 miles in all.

[14] See the Introduction for information about the Prince of Hesse Homburg.

[15] The Chaia is an important thoroughfare in Naples.

May 2nd

Off from Ariano at 4 o'clock and after a few miles of mountains entered a plain which extends to Barletta, Bari and all the coast of the Adriatic. This plain is mostly uncultivated, entirely so in the neighbourhood of Cerignola. The only objects visible or interesting was the plain of Canne[16] on the right and the Gulf and Promontory of Maupedona on the left. Reached Barletta as the moon rose magnificently from the sea, and passing along the coast we arrived at Bari at sunrise.

May 3rd

His Highness went to lye down and I to enquire for a vessel for Corfu. We went out together to see the town and old Castle now a prison. The English Vice-Consul accompanied us. I had sent for him in mistake. The news spread of the arrival of a Prince. The Intendente of the Province sent to offer his palace and ask us to dine. Whilst in the Castle, the Governor came [in] full dress bowing and scraping, another great man met us cap in hand in the square, and two officers sent to attend us. The people thinking we were nothing less than Kings pursued us, and the whole city was agog. Our luggage was instantly removed to our chambers in the Palace, and the principal nobility invited to meet us. Among the latter the Duke of Casa Massima, whose son was also present had been seized by a famous band of robbers who infest the country, kept with for 24 days till his father ransomed him for 2,000 ducats and has now only been returned one week. During that time the robbers 32 in number maintained 5 engagements with troops of the line once 600 strong. In one of these the young Duke received a ball through his hat. A General[17] and Colonel also dined with us had an engagement of 2 hours with the same band of 32, they were 60 strong, the General had his horse killed under him. The Colonel is still a cripple from the wound he received in his left arm and the men were compelled to retreat.

After dinner the Mayor and corporation came to pay their respects to his highness and then the Archbishop and two Cardinals. The Prince made the siesta a plea for retiring and I followed him.

May 4th

An expedition was planned for going to Noya, distant about 9 miles and at 8 o'clock all was prepared. In mounting his horse the Intendente Prince Carpece Turlo pulled the bridle of his horse too hard, it reared, fell back almost dead upon the pavement carrying with it the Prince of H. Homburg, and giving the Intendente two dreadful blows on his head. The latter remaining in the hands of the surgeons, we proceeding on our expedition, the Prince in a carriage, I and General Roth on horseback. We passed through a rich cultivated countryside though perfectly plain to Noya. This little place was infected with the plague last year and a cordon drawn round it for 10 months. 800 persons died but it did not spread. A deputation of the principal inhabitants met us to <u>salute the Prince</u>. The bells rang and guns fired and the same was repeated in another little town through which we passed in returning. We dined with General Roth. He was 7 years in Sicily during the war without the possibility of learning whether his wife was alive or dead. We walked out after followed by an immense crowd of people. In the evening had a large musical party in the Intendente's Palace.

May 5th

Engaged all morning in making preparations for our voyage whilst some priests took his highness to show him the body of San Nicolas. Dined with Signor Viuste who was hospitable to excess. About 6 o'clock took leave of Prince Turlo and attended by all our friends and many hundred people went to the mole and embarked. The sun was just setting over the beautiful plain of Bari and I bid a lingering adieu to Italy thinking that probably it was the last time I should ever behold it. Sat talking with the Prince for some time of our reception at Bari and then having disposed of Signor Viuste's immense dinner, I went below. The wind continuing strong and favourable the next day at noon brought us to the coast of Albania, but the evening proving contrary and also during the night we made no progress.

May 7th

[S]ailed quietly into Corfu[18] and arrived about noon; by the efforts of General Maitland and the Prince's name instead of 8 days quarantine we were let off with half a one. And next day –

May 8th

at 9 o'clock we were set at liberty. General M. was just setting out for Malta. We dined with him at 3 o'clock and saw him off in the Frigate. He gave us both lodgings in his own house in the Castle, appointed a vessel to carry us to Corinth or Patras and left us in charge to Colonel Stuart second in command. Ascended the signal tower and had a most magnificent view of the surrounding sea and mountains. Drank tea at Colonel Travers and had the band of music playing all evening under the windows.

[16] Hannibal routed the Roman army at the Battle of Cannae in the 2nd Punic War.

[17] Note on the opposite page of the manuscript: 'General Roth who commanded the Sicilian troops under Lt. W. Bentinck. Colonel Zurmer [?] taken prisoner by Lt. Cochrane in Spain.'

[18] Corfu and the other Ionian Islands were administered by the British government under the terms of the settlement of Europe made by the Congress of Vienna in 1815. The Protectorate lasted until 1863.

May 9th

Walked out some miles into the country which is a sort of fairyland. Dined at Colonel Stuart's and spent the evening.

The Chamber of Deputies consists of 40 persons, Corfu sends seven. The population of all the islands is about 200,000, that of Corfu alone 50,000. The present garrison consists of 3000 English and 500 Albanians.

May 10th

Busy in making preparations for our journey. At noon saw Colonel Hankey sail with 3 deputies and the new constitution for London. Dined with Teutoki [?], President of the Chamber of Deputies. Sailed ourselves about sunset in a beautiful little gunboat of Colonel Robinson's.

May 11th

Calms and contrary winds but the views of the Albanian coast extremely fine. At sunset off Paxos.

May 12th

At 3 o'clock in the morning a gale of wind coming on we were forced into the little port of Paxos. Went on shore to look through the island, which is nothing but a limestone rock covered with olive trees. The only export is oil, in good years amounting £30,000, as that of Corfu does £1,000,000 in good years. It grows little or no corn and wine only for 2 months consumption. The inhabitants amounting to 4,000 are well dressed and good looking, the little town is neat and picturesque. Paxos sends 3 or 4 members to the Chamber of Deputies. There is a small fort which defends the port, which is small but deep and secure. The garrison consists only of 20 men; the Commandant or Capo de Governo is Captain Williams.

May 13th

Sailed at 8 o'clock and were carried along by a gentle breeze. With some difficulty made St. Maura by sunset. Cast anchor almost on the spot where the battle of Actium[19] was fought. The view of the Albanian mountains from this place is uncommonly striking.

May 14th

Admiral Penrose's vessel was lying at a little distance from shore. We had seen him at Corfu, and he called upon us at 6 o'clock to take us to the town in his launch. We followed him after an invitation from Colonel Ross, Capo de Governo, to accompany him in an expedition to a distant part of the island. Found the Colonel and his lady, the Admiral and his three daughters with some others sat down to a comfortable English breakfast. I joined them no small pleasure being an unexpected treat. Set off in two boats, to a beautiful bay on the south of the island, and afterwards a ramble in the neighbourhood found a splendid dinner spread out under a plane tree of immense size in a spot surrounded with rocks and large myrtles and commanding an interesting view. Never was a party better satisfyed with their cheer or more reason to be so. We returned to our boats with no small regret. I walked the last 5 miles to see the site of the ancient town of Leucadia, placed on the eastern side of the island. There are the foundations of 2 temples to be seen but nothing more. Stᵃ· Maura, the ancient Leucadia, is rather a peninsula than an island, for boats cannot pass between it and the mainland. It contains about 18,000 inhabitants. The number of troops is about 200 English with some few Albanians. It sends 4 or 5 deputies. The export is oil, but little corn or wine is grown and this island is generally not so well wooded or so rich as the others. Sailed an hour after sunset. Wind contrary.

May 15th
Calm and thick fog, which cleared up towards evening and enabled us to see the famous promontory or lover's leap rendered famous by the name of Sappho.
　　Reached the harbour of Ithaca two hours after sunset.

May 16th
The Capo di Governo Major Temple waited on the Prince betimes. Went on shore and walked through the town, like all the others neat and clean. The inhabitants amount to 9,000, of which 1,000 are sailors. The principal export is red wine and currants. The hills are as sterile as in ancient times. The garrison consists of about 100 men. There is a small fort to command the entrance into the harbour which is very spacious deep and secure. Went afterwards to the Castle of Ulysses, the ascent most laborious, but the view fine. The ruins are very small. Many tombs have been lately opened in this hill and gold coins and ornaments found to a great value. Sailed from Ithaca about 3 o'clock.

May 17th
Found ourselves at no great distance from Patras, but the wind from the gulph [sic] of Lepanto was so very strong we had the greatest difficulty to beat up by 6 o'clock in the evening. I immediately went on shore, found the Consul absent at Trannina, but his deputy Mr Barthold offered us lodgings at the Consul's House.

---

[19]　Battle of Actium: 31 B.C. Naval battle in which the forces of Mark Antony were defeated by those of Octavian – the heir of Julius Caesar. The battle effectively ended the civil war and the Roman republic leaving Octavian all powerful, soon to take the title of Augustus.

Immediately returned accompanied by 4 Janissaries[20] to <u>bring</u> his <u>Highness</u> ashore. We found comfortable rooms and a good cup of tea to refresh us after our voyage and welcome us to the Classic shores of Greece. So much for first impressions. When the body is not at ease, the mind is not open to Classic or sentimental impressions. I had been seven days at sea, without taking off my clothes, for aboard there were no beds. I had made a short dinner for our provisions were finished and the gale of wind for several hours previous had made me rather sick. I came on shore not knowing whether I should find a lodging for the night, and on account of quarantine I could not return to the vessel. These were the considerations which occupied my mind on landing, and it was not until returning to the shore after having secured lodgings at the Consul's, that I even remembered that I was in Greece. I am not ashamed to own this for I know that all in similar circumstances would experience, whatever they might acknowledge, the same that I have done.

May 18th

Walked out with Mr Barthold to the famous Cypress mentioned by Pausanius, it is certainly of great age and as it has 27 feet circumference, and the cypress is one of the trees of slowest growth. The country round Patras is green and picturesque, the mountains especially on the north of the gulph magnificent, and the town has a very good appearance from every quarter. The streets are narrow, dirty and almost impassable even for horses. The only trade is currants of which a vast quantity are annually exported. The only antiquities are some trifling remains of a temple, seeming Roman.

May the 19th

Commenced our journey in the Peloponesus at about 6 o'clock and crossing the high mountains behind Patras reached about noon a Khan or country inn. Here we found a large party of Greeks, men and women sitting under a tree, we joined their party and they soon offered us coffee and part of their dinner whc. we accepted. They were on their way to a famous convent to celebrate the feast of St John. We saw also many other parties on the road for the same purpose. Here we entered into the Ancient Arcadia and passed through many beautiful vallies and rocky dells worthy [of] the reputation they have enjoyed for so many ages. Among these may be mentioned that of Gourzourmitza, which takes its name from that of a small town distant 2 hours from Calavrita. Here we were to stay the night, Calavrita; we arrived about an hour after sunset. The Greek for whom we had a letter, was absent, and his wife had not courage to let Franks[21] into the house during her husband's absence. We were still in the street not knowing whither to go when a servant came to offer us a house for the night. We found excellent accommodations, and the moment we were seated on the sofa, the only piece of furniture in these parts, a domestic splendidly dressed brought us each a long pipe, 6 feet or more in length, and afterwards Coffee. He always laid his hand on his breast when he offered us anything, this is the common mode of Salutation in Greece. They soon after brought us a good supper, and then laid a mattrass on the floor for our beds.

May 20th

The horses did not come of three hours after the time ordered, and whilst waiting for them, the lady of the house came to pay her compliments to us; her manners gentle and agreeable, and of good appearance. She said her husband was absent with the Pacha of Tripolitza, that he was governor of ye town, and had also a hundred villages under his command; she remained about half an hour, and returned again to take leave. This days journey to a Khan 8 hours distant both from Tripolitza and Calavrita lay entirely among the high mountains of Arcadia, but the country not so pretty as the day before. We rested for an hour on the banks of a small brook during the heat of the day, and reached the Khan at Sunset; a Khan never offers anything but bare walls, never either chair or table. We sat down in the open gallery, a universal luxury in the houses here, and finding three Turks who seemed inclined to be very civil we fell into conversation, and found that one of them had been an officer in the Turkish army in the affair of Jaffer.[22] He saved himself by jumping into the sea, he said that more than 6,000 were shot by Bonaparte. The Prince assured me that Napoleon had related circumstance to him, himself, said the number was the same as that mentioned by the Turk and that his reason for doing it was that they had broken their parole, and that he had no means of transporting them.

We slept on our sacks filled with straw and a portmanteau made a good pillow.[23]

[20] The Janissaries were the elite military corps of the Ottoman Empire. Originally recruited from Christian youths who were trained to become fanatical Moslems, they became a formidable body in palace politics. Resentment at Janissary oppression within the Empire and an incipient rising by them led to their total liquidation in 1826. An angry mob, backed by the Sultan, attacked their barracks and massacred between 6,000 and 10,000 of them.

[21] 'Franks' is the name used by the Turks to denote persons of Western European origin, i.e. foreigners (see Greg's explanation under May 22nd).

[22] The Affair of Jaffer was a notorious stain on the reputation of Napoleon's army. In 1799 he personally led 13,000 troops into Syria to pre-empt a Turkish attack on his army in Egypt. His troops quickly overcame Turkish resistance in Jaffa and then perpetrated the most appalling atrocities on the defenders and civilians alike; 2,000 Turkish troops were bayoneted when trying to surrender and Napoleon ordered the execution of a further 3,000 who had surrendered.

[23] 'saddle' seemingly overwritten with 'pillow'.

May 21st

We were off by daylight, and stopped to rest among the ruins of Mantinca, 3 hours distant from Tripolitza. The foundations of the walls visible all round the town, and also some trifling remains of the theatre. The Plain of Tripolitza, and the approach to this Capital of the Morea, is triste and desolate, there not being a single tree. The interior is a wretched village. All the good houses are in small courts, and towards the street there is nothing but hovels and bare walls. We arrived about 2 o'clock. We cd [sic] not have horses without an order from the Pacha, and for that we were obliged to make him a visit. He could not receive us till the following morning. Almost the only trade of this place is in ornamenting pistols and knives etc which are generally covered with wrought silver.

May 22nd

Passing through the guards we were ushered into the room of the prime Minister of the Pacha, and here we remained, smoking, drinking Coffee, and talking till the Pacha was ready. That being announced we were conducted into a handsome Saloon lined with domestics, and took our seats on two chairs prepared purposely for the Franks, as all are named who wear tight breeches. The Pacha soon appeared with a numerous company who the moment he had taken his seat, bowed their heads in the oriental manner and uttered a loud cry. Pipes 8 feet long were then brought us, then Coffee, then excellent marmalade,[24] after that Sherbet, and the scene concluded by offering us incense and sprinkling us with holy water. These two last ceremonies are only dispensed to persons of high rank, and I am indebted for them to my companion. This Pacha is a great favorite of the Grand Seigneur;[25] he has been viceroy in Constantinople, and by his manners it is easy to perceive he has had much intercourse with Europeans. After a short conversation we parted. At 4 o'clock we got off and by a most difficult descent reached of the pretty valley of Agathamlo in the territory of Argos, four hours distance from Tripolitza, and 4 from Argos. We passed the night in a Khan in the same valley.

May 23rd

Before setting out we heard that three English were sleeping at another Khan just by. We found Mr Evans, Pigon and Capt. Sotherby. For the former I had a letter. We breakfast with them and then first learn that the plague had broken out in Negropont, and that we might possibly find some difficulty in entering Athens. The view of the plain and bays of Argos on descending the mountains is pretty. Reached the town about noon, and found good lodgings in the House of one of the Primates. A deputation of the Primates came to pay their respects to his highness. In the evening walked out to see the country and some remains of a temple, almost the only antiquity.

May 24th

Could not find horses and were obliged to remain till the next day. Returned the visit of the Primates and were treated in the usual manner both among Greeks and Turks, viz. Pipes Coffee, and sweetmeats. Walked about the town and country. Argos is a much better city than Tripolitza; like all the other towns the houses and small gardens are surrounded with miserable mud walls. There is some manufacture of calicoes and hair cloths, but all carried on in private houses.

May 25th

Rose at 3 o'clock and with great difficulty got horses by 7. Nauplea or Napoli di Romanie is distant from Argos two hours, thence to the ancient city of Tyrrinthe ½ hour. We left these to the right, and took the route of Corinth. At two hours distant from Argos, we visited the ancient city of Mycene destroyed more than 2000 years since. The treasure of Atrius, alias tomb of Agamemnon and the ancient Gateway of the Cyclopean fortress are well worth se[e]ing. From thence 2 hours more brought us to Nemea; of this city not a vestige remains, but three Doric columns of the temple of Jupiter standing alone in a desert plain. 5 hours more brought us to Corinth. Found good lodgings in the house of a Primate, where were two Gentlemen one English the other Hungarian, going also to Athens. The environs of Corinth are beautiful. The Temple of Jupiter is perhaps the most ancient of Greece, the proportions almost the same as those of Paestum.

May 26th

to Megara 12 hours. The ride across the isthmus is very fine and the view of the Acro – Corinth rising among the mountains and between the two seas is most magnificent. Reached Megara at sunset. It is a miserable town but, most singular, being exactly another Pompeii; I should have fancied myself in the streets of the latter place. Lodged in the best house, but slept on a stone floor. The plain, mountains, the sea and the Island of Salamis make an interesting and beautiful landscape.

---

24 'Marmalade' is presumably sweetmeats made by boiling fruit such as quinces or oranges with sugar or honey, to produce a thick paste, which, after being spread on a flat surface and cooled, could be cut into pieces.

25 'The Grand Seigneur' is the Sultan. At this time he was Mahmud II (1808–39). He destroyed the Janissaries in 1826 and reasserted the absolute power of the Sultanate but could not prevent Serbia and Greece securing their independence from the Ottoman Empire.

May 27th

To Athens 8 hours. 4 to Eleusis where we stopped to rest; a wretched village, but extensive foundations of the ancient city, and remains of many great columns of the famous temple of Ceres. Found there 2 English. Proceeded along the via sacra to Athens. The first view from the mountains of the plain, city, Acropolis and Mount Hymettus is singularly striking, displaying an elegance and gaiety combined with magnificence, forming a singular contrast to the mournful approach to Rome. We entered Athens at 4 o'clock, and found comfortable lodgings prepared for us. We went out instantly to the temple of Theseus, almost entire to this day. Hence we passed to the temple of Adrian without the walls one of the finest monuments of Athens. Returned by the temple of Jupiter Olympico, in the Bazar.

May 28th

Ascended the Acropolis. Payed our compliments to the Governor and met with the usual treatment, but had to make him a present of 2 Zequins,[27] in return for which he sent us each a carnation. Close to the Governors, stands the Parthenon or famous temple of Minerva lovely in its ruins. It is made of Pentilic marble, white as snow inside, but tarnished without. Afterwards visited the temple of Panderosa and Erectheus and other curiosities of the Acropolis. The Propylus is sadly mangled.

Called on Monsieur Fauvel, the French Consul, an amiable, well informed man, a Frenchman of the old school. Called on Lusieri, Lord Elgin's Agent; he is a comple[te] Italian. In the evening called again on Monsr. Fauvel, who being a good antiquarian, accompanied us again to the Acropolis, to explain everything we did not understand.

May 29th

Called on Lusieri[28] and saw his drawings which are most admirable both for likeness and execution; at present they are only in pencil, or in ink, but if he lives long enough he will colour them. He accompanied us [to] the temple of [H]adrian the ancient stadia and different small but interesting remains to the South of the city. In the evening Monsr Fauvel accompanied us to the temple of Theseus, and then without the modern walls, and showed us the foundations of the Pynx where the assembly of the people was, and those of the court of Areopagus.

May 30th

Accompanied by the two gentlemen we met at Corinth, we set out early to Mount Pentele, distant 3 hours, to see the famous quarries whence the Athenians got the marble for the temples and statues. 3 hours more brought us to the plain of Marathon. Here we visited the field of Battle, trophies tombs etc. The mountains and Bay are very beautiful, the view also of the island of Eubea, and many others of the Archipelago was also interesting. We slept in a little hovel on the field of battle, and setting out at 4 o'clock reached Athens at noon. In the evening called on the English Consul and then on Monsr. Fauvel, who made another excursion with us.

June 1st
Rose early and spent all the morning sketching. Spent the evening with M. Fauvel.

June 2nd
Went round the city and Acropolis, called on Lusieri, Fauvel and English Consul. In the evening visited the Ports of Phalerus, Munychia and Pireus.

June 3rd
We went out to search for the Academia, could not find it; called on Fauvel. Dined with Lusieri, Messrs Curtis, Wittingham, Anderson, Cunningham and Finch, Englishmen were there.

June 4th
Made a successful search for the Academia and the tomb of Pericles. Called on the English Consul. In the evening Messrs. C. and W. gave a ball being the King's birthday. A number of Greek ladies were there and some Smyrniste Italians. The music was miserable and one tune served for dances Greek, Turk and English. The Greeks have only two or three dances, and those slow and monotonous. After two Greek dances, English country dances followed, and then waltzing; then we took our part in the Greek dances. We afterwards attempted a German Cotillion, but what thro' want of knowledge, want of language to explain, and want of music it did not succeed. The 10 supper dances, I had for my partner Lord Byrons Maid of Athens.[29] The supper was better than could be expected, we had various bumper toasts, sung "God save the King" and then followed some beautiful Greek and Italian songs. Dancing recommenced, and I made my escape with difficulty at 5 o'clock in the morning.

---

[27] Zequins or Sequins were small gold coins. The name was derived from the Italian *Zecchina*, another name for a Venetian ducat.

[28] Lusieri was Lord Elgin's Italian agent, who had supervised the removal of the marble sculptures from the Parthenon between 1801 and 1810. In 1817 he loaded two more ships with an assortment of vases, gravestones and other antiquities from other sites.

[29] A reference to Byron's lyrical poem written in 1810. The Maid was probably a twelve-year-old girl, daughter of the widow of a former British Consul. She would have been about nineteen when Greg encountered her.

June 5th

Went to the Parthenon and spent two hours mourning over the enchanting ruins. Called to bid adieu to Mr Lusieri and Fauvel, to my fair partners and my countrymen. At 5 o'clock, a sweet southern evening, I bid adieu to Athens and made [sic] continued my way in silence to the port of Pireus. On my way I cast a thousand, longing, lingering looks to the Acropolis and Parthenon and temple of Theseus and thanked the kind fortune which had led me to the shores of Attica. Our companions Mr Culmer a Hungarian, and Mr Hamborough not being yet arrived, the Prince and I wandered for a long time on the sea coast. At ten we embarked on a good schooner, which we had sent for from the Island of Hydra.[30]

Continuation of the tour[31]

June 6th

In the morning found ourselves halfway between Pireus and the Island of Egina. Landed at Egina to see the temple of Jupiter, the morning being very hot and the temple on the summit of a mountain, all my companions declined and I went alone. It is of the Doric order and 25 columns remain standing. Embarked again at ten and reached Cape Colonna or Sounion at sunset. Landed to see the remains of the temple situated on the promontory. It is of the Doric order of Pentilic marble perfectly white and 16 or 17 columns remain standing.

June 7

A gale of wind driving the night obliged us to put into a little port in the Island of Zia, anciently Cers, here we remained all day.

June 8

sailed at sunrise and obliged by contrary winds to put into Tenos. This little town neat and well built, is inhabited only by Greeks and Franks. The inhabitants have the privilege of building steeples and using bells.

June 9th

Calms and contrary winds and made but little way. Saw almost all the Islands of the Southern Archipelago, even to the mountains of Crete.

June 10th

Fine wind. Saw the distant mountains of Chio[s] and of Asia, and at sunset landed for a few minutes on the coast of Chio[s].

June 11th

at noon landed at Chio[s] a large and flourishing city. The great export is Gum Mastic. Sailed again at two o'clock. At sunset entered the Gulf of Smyrna.[32]

June 12th

A fine strong north wind carried us rapidly down the gulf and we reached Smyrna at sunset. An hour after we went on shore we welcomed each other to the coast of Asia and in the Hotel of the Franks, found better lodging than we had seen since leaving Corfu.

June 13th

Called on the different Consuls and persons to whom we had letters. Found that the plague was in at the villages and that a journey of one day to visit the ruins of Ephesus which we had intended to have done would be unsafe. Resolved our departure for tomorrow. With the greatest difficulty prevailed on my companions to take the route of Troy and the Dardanelles in preference to the direct one.

Smyrna is the most commercial town of the Levant, 30 or 40 English vessels amongst others, are usually freighted here. The principal exports are Cotton and drugs. Of 80,000 bales of Cotton annually grown here 50,000 are exported. Manufactured goods and Iron, tin etc are the imports. Of cotton twist the consumption is about £100,000, low numbers 20 to 30 water, 30 to 36 crude.

June 14th

Went out at 5 o'clock to see the town and ascended the Hill to see an old deserted Fortress. The view thence of the sea and valley of Smyrna is enchanting, the latter exactly resembles some of our charming English scenery, so green and so well wooded. Returned through the Bazaar and the centre of the town, the streets are narrow and dirty as in all Turkish towns, but the houses picturesque and prettily painted. Went into a mosque almost finished but not consecrated, the work tasty [sic] and well done. The afternoon prepared for our departure; we formed a cavalcade of 15 horses, one for Janissary, 3 for the postillions, 4 for the luggage and 3 for our servants and four for ourselves, the Prince, Baron Kulmer, Mr Hamborough and myself. An hour before sunset we set out being obliged to travel by night to avoid the heat. The noise made by so great a caravan brought all Smyrna to the windows. After crossing the plain we entered the mountains, and found much difficulty in the rocky and precipitous paths, there being no moon. We stopped half an hour at a little coffee house distant 4 or 5 hours from Smyrna; at sunrise we entered the great plain of Magnesia, and an hour after the city itself, nobly situated at the foot of a rocky mountain. This city was represented to us as larger than Smyrna. This is incorrect, the latter contains more

[30] Volume 1of the manuscript ends here.

[31] Volume 2 of the manuscript begins with this heading.

[32] Smyrna is now Izmir.

than 100,000 inhabitants. Magnesia, I should think not more than 20,000. We stopped at a miserable Khan or Caravansara and took our sleep on the bare floor.

June 15th

An hour before sunset we again commenced our journey. We crossed the rich but almost desert plain of Magnesia. It is watered and often overflowed by a large River, the ancient Hermus, the modern name being Turkish it is impossible either to pronounce or remember it. We again entered the mountains and continued our route with difficulty and some risk owing to the badness of the road or track. Our luggage horses fell frequently, and Mr H falling asleep, came to the ground twice. We were told that Bergamo whither we were going was distant from Magnesia only 12 hours, in reality the distance is 24. Towards dawn the Postillions refused to proceed and the Janissary to rest in the woods after beating the Postillions, the latter prevailed, but in half an hour we lost our way and were obliged to seek some village. To our dismay we found that we had still 10 or 12 hours to Bergamo and being quite overcome with fatigue we threw ourselves from our horses on the ground and fell asleep. Our servants in the meantime made a fire and prepared coffee and an hour after we awoke to breakfast. We then proceeded through woods and mountains exposed to the rays of a burning sun till noon when we stopped to rest the horses for a couple of hours, after which we again set out and at 5 o'clock entered the plain of Bergamo, beautiful as that of Magnesia and almost equally desert. Both plains and mountains whether cultivated or not are covered with rich verdure and abundance of wood and in this respect form a striking contrast, to the extreme, and almost unvaried sterility of the Peloponesus. At 8 o'clock we entered Bergamo, excessively fatigued, having been on horseback 24 hours out of 28 and scarcely eaten anything. We found a Khan of the better sort, that is larger. They are all alike in one thing: they offer nothing to the traveller but floor and bare walls, chairs, table or eatables are out of the question.

June 17th [sic, should be 16th]

Baron Kulmer, either from the heat and fatigue, or malaria of the preceeding day, awoke with a violent fever and was unable to stir out. Bergamo, the ancient Pergamus one of the first Asiatic names which occur in Roman History, presents many antiquities, though the only one mentioned by the many travellers with whom we had conversed is an antique vase of beautiful workmanship. For this therefore we enquired and a Greek came to conduct us to it. It is of white marble about 5½ feet in diameter and 5 high. The figures have been much abused, the execution is spirited, but they are not well finished, the subject seems to be a horse race. For this vase some English travellers have offered as high as £1000 but the owner a Turk is not willing to part with it, it was found filled with Zequins and he imagines if he sells the vase some ill luck will happen to him.

It is situated in the Baths of the Turkish women of whom several being there when we arrived, they very civilly, not to keep us waiting, returned into the Sholatory [?] or sweating bath, the heat of which is extreme. Before we had well examined the vase we received a message from the ladies saying they were in chemise, and that the heat was so great they must come out, and that therefore they requested us to depart. Our guide said that there were other things, and conducted us to some considerable remains, amongst which was a magnificent arch of Roman architecture, which on closer examination we found was the entrance of an immense Theatre, the outline of which was distinctly perceptible. He said if we would walk a mile farther he would show us something much finer. We followed him out of the town and behind the hill, in the centre of a steep valley we found a ruin, for size, solidity and excellence of masonry a rival of the Coliseum itself. I instantly recognised a Naumachia and from the nature of the arena and arches beneath it was probably used for nothing else. From the simplicity of the building and want of all ornament, it is probably of a date anterior to the Coliseum. Many of the arches stand entire without another stone to support them. The work is Roman, probably built for some Rich Proconsul. Our guide wished to conduct us to the top of a very high hill which overhangs the Town, where is situated a great Turkish fortification and about which we also perceived the remains of Roman walls, but the heat was so great we should have been imprudent to have attempted the ascent. In the same Valley which contained the Naumachia we found another very considerable ruin, the foundations of which stand to great distance but what the building had been we could not guess. Along the summit of the hills we saw also a great aqueduct almost entire of Roman work and which evidently supplied the Castle with water. We visited afterwards some vaults which being much in the style of the Sette Sale and Baths of Titus at Rome I concluded to have been destined for similar purpose. Another work of considerable excellence and also Roman is the covered archway which conducts a large stream or torrent under the town. We found immense quantities of broken columns, blocks of marble and huge squared stones, which attest the former magnificence of the place. The few Remains of statues which we were shown were Grecian. The situation of Bergamo is fine and commands a charming view of the plain and surrounding mountains. We returned to the Khan at noon well pleased with our ramble.

June 17

A little before sunset we were on horseback, and we instantly plunged into the mountains. In about two hours Baron Kulmer became so extremely ill as to be unable to proceed. Being at the summit of a high mountain with a path so narrow that a man a and horse could not stand abreast we begged him to make an effort to reach some village, but in vain, he threw himself off from horseback on the bare rock, and it was impossible to move him. Finding this we unloaded the horses, made him a bed and laid there till morning. We made a fire but the Janissary apprehensive lest it should attract people or perhaps set the wood on fire, which indeed it was near doing, made us put it out.

June 18th

The view which opened to us at sunrise of wood, mountain and valley was most magnificent. We set out meaning to breakfast at a village distant 3 or 4 hours, but having gone 3, and finding it still 3 farther, we stopped in a beautiful spot covered with oaks and huge masses of rocks, made a fire and boiled our coffee. We set off again in pursuit of this village which not only fled as we advanced, but seemed to gain ground upon us, for after going the 3 hours, they told us it was yet four farther on. We rested an hour and then proceeded and after 5 hours more among the mountains towards the sea shore, and reached at last this ignum fatuus,[33] it was a miserable hamlet and though the poor invalid would willingly have rested there and we were all excessively wearied, our Janissary persuaded us on to another farther to Cremer a considerable village situated on the Gulf of Adrymitti. Here we were happy to enter a miserable Khan wh^{c.} we reached late in the evening.

June 19th

In the morning we walked about the village leaving poor Kulmer still very ill in the Khan. In the evening however he lost his fever and was well enough to proceed to Adrymitti distant 2 hours from Cremer. The heat was still great when we set out being 92 degrees of Farenheit, but as our way lay almost entirely among woods of olives and gardens we were not much incommoded. We reached Adrymitti in time to look through the town and environs both which are extremely picturesque. On our return a Greek who had good lodgings in a corner of the Khan, offered them to us and another a native of Corfu, fearing that some Franks were arrived came and joined our party. He was physician to the Vayvode[34] and had lately made the voyage of Arabia, Egypt and Palestine. We sat chatting with him till a late hour and then stretched ourselves on the ground for a short rest.

June 20th

Rose at 1½ o'clock and were off at 2. Our route lay through the plain of Adrymitti, a perfect desert and yet a paradise. The trees were the fig, the olive, the Pomegranate and the vine which grew around wild and luxuriant, and the air was scented with the sweetest perfumes. Our course lay along the sea shore on quitting the plain, on the right lay a beautiful chain of hills like the Apennines, covered with olives and Pine Trees. We rested near a small Khan to breakfast, and under the large Pine to dine. About an hour before sunset we quitted the shore and entered the mountains and arrived soon after at the little village of Chipney. There being no Khan we were quartered on a Greek. To avoid the immense quantity of vermin in all the houses which renders sleep almost out of the question Mr H and myself always slept out of doors, and here we did the same.

June 21st

Off at three o'clock and soon after entered a beautiful valley much resembling Matlock. Our Janissary now demanded if we wished to see some antiquities which he said were on another route, but not out of our way. From the description and direction I knew them to be the ruins of Alexander Troias, but was aware they lay many hours from our route, however as I wished to see them I said nothing to my companions. We continued our route without rest till 11 o'clock when we arrived at the little village of Tryzik when our Janissary expected to find the ruins but we were informed that they lay 4 hours distant in another direction, and so finished our excursion to Alexander Troias. Having breakfasted and rested a couple of hours we again set out, and after riding 5 hours we reached the village of Inide. Here we passed the night in a Khan where we were devoured with fleas. At three o'clock we were on horseback and after skirting the Menderi for near four hours, with occasional views of Mount Ida, we arrived at Bournabachi, a considerable village situated on the rising ground which bounds the plains of Troy. We did not enter the village but descended on the plain, made our fire at a fountain under some large trees and what with a good appetite, the pleasure of finding ourselves in such classic ground, and so near the end of our journey, we made a merry and hearty breakfast. As to remains, the site itself of ancient Troy[35] was unknown 2000 years ago. Were I to hazard a conjection I should say the city stood not on the plain, but either on, or at the foot of one of the hills, for such is the situation of all the ancient towns of Greece and Asia Minor of the same date with Troy. The view before reaching Bournabachi of the plains of Troy, the Dardanelles, the Thracian Chersonetus (?) and the Islands in the north of the Egean Sea, is extremely beautiful. From Chipney to the Dardanelles one might think the country was a part of England. We reached the town of the Dardanelles towards sunset, and put up with a miserable lodging at a Khan. We were all extremely fatigued having been 8 days on the journey, during which time we had

[33] 'Ignum fatuus' should be ignis fatuus – will o'the wisp.

[34] A vayvode was a Turkish governor.

[35] Some time after this tour, Robert Hyde Greg wrote an article on "The Site of Troy", which he presented to the Literary and Philosophical Society of Manchester. It was published in No. 9 of the *Proceedings of the Manchester Literary and Philosophical Society*, pp. 151–224.

never sat down or lay down but on the floor or the ground, eat [sic] but little, and though we generally arrived an hour after sunset, yet as three hours were necessary for cooking we got but little sleep, and during that time I never had my boots off.

June 23rd

A whole synagogue of Jewish Consuls came to torment us at our toilet and breakfast. The only Christian Consul is the Imperial one, who has a comfortable house on the sea shore where we spent the day.

Having hired a rowboat of 8 oars, the wind at this season being always contrary, we set out at sunset and past [sic] by the light of a bright moon, the Capes of Abydos and Sestos and the tower of Hero. The Turks have lately constructed here 2 new forts.

June 24th

Towards 9 o'clock the wind being too strong to proceed we went on shore to the little village of Galata on the spot where the famous battle of Egos Potomos was lost by the Athenians. Lampsacus opposite on [the] Asiatic coast still retains its ancient name.

Off again at 5 o'clock and reached Gallipoli at 8, here we spent an hour in a Coffee house on the shore and again set out.

June 25th

In the morning found we had made little way, went on shore as usual to breakfast being unable to cook aboard. Supped on the sands by the light of the moon.

June 26th

A thunderstorm came on with the first rain we had seen since leaving Naples. Reached Rhodosto with difficulty in the evening and staid there 2 or 3 hours, it is a large city and here the route from Salonica joins that of Gallipoli. Off at midnight.

June 27th

Made considerable progress during the night, and stopped to breakfast at Heraclea, a small village about 11 o'clock. Set out again at two and did not stop till the following morning.

June 28th

When after a hasty breakfast we again put to sea, and towards noon came in sight of the thousand domes and minarets of Constantinople. The shores of the Dardanelles and Sea of Marmora are flat, bare and uninteresting. Here they begin to change into the most beautiful scenery in the world, and the views which opened upon us on entering Constantinople,[36] surpass all I have yet seen, and realise all the fairyland of the Arabian tales. It was nearly dusk before we could get on shore and were most happy to find a good hotel we were both fatigued and hungry having passed two days with nothing to eat or drink but a cup or two of Coffee, and 5 days without lying down, our boat being too small.

June 29th

Sunday, walked about almost a day infinitely amused with the variety of figures physiognomies and dresses and with the most magnificent views the universe can display. At night a dreadful thunderstorm. The Prince and I went to another Hotel.

June 30th

Called on Mr Black of the House of Niven Kerr and Co for whom I had a letter of credit. On return found the Minister of Prussia ready to accompany the Prince on an excursion. Took a boat together and went to Eaux Douces, a country house of the Grand Seigneur situated in a Romantic valley with trees of a size and richness of foliage that would grace an English park. We then called on Mr Frere, Chargé d' Affaires for England. Returned home and dined and afterwards received the visits of some of the Ministers who came to pay their respects to the Prince.

July 1st

Sallied forth with his Highness crossed the water and landed at Constantinople, visited the principal Mosques of Stª Sophia, Sultan Solyman, Sultan Achmet etc. We could not enter farther then the courtyards or Cloister but got a hasty glympse [sic] of the interior. All admission has been forbidden since the Russian Embassy about a year since drew down the vengeance of some fanatics by their indecorous behaviour. Visited the Mint, all the machinery is worked by men; it is much better than I expected, but the manner of rolling the metal is so defective that accident only can make two pieces of the same weight. In the ancient Hippodrome of Constantine, we found his obelisk once covered with Corinthian brass and supported on a single block of marble 10 feet square. Also the obelisk of Theodosius a single block of Egyptian granite like those at Rome. Between them is the singular bronze screw said to have once supported the tripod of Delphi. The tour of Honorius and an aqueduct, and a singular place underground supported by an infinity of marble columns and which they call a cistern, are

---

[36] Constantinople is Istanbul: people in Western Europe referred to the city by its original name – the city of the Emperor Constantine – long after the Turks captured it in 1453 and renamed it.

other antiquities which we visited. We also spent some time in the Sublime Court which something resembled Westminster Hall. The great Hall is crowded with lawyers, the smaller courts of Justice open into it. Here the grand Vizier hears causes twice a week.

We concluded our excursion by ascending a very high tower in the principal barracks of the Janissaries, whence is a most magnificent view of the city and suburbs. Returned home fatigued, took a late dinner with Mr Black, met there the Bennets who are just setting out on a tour to Jerusalem.

July 2nd

The Prussian Minister waited on the Prince to accompany him to Constantinople; we crossed the water and the city from end to end, to the sea and then made the circuit of the walls to the river. The walls of Constantinople still stand and may rather be said to want repair, than be in a state of ruin. They are triple, the two inward ones the highest and both flanked with towers at every 100 paces. They are overgrown with ivy, and the fosses with large trees making the most picturesque ruins possible. The Greek arms are still over one gate, the Porta aurea still exists, but stripped of its ornaments, but we regarded with the greatest interest the Gate by which the city was taken. The breach is well defined by the modern Turkish repairs and the adjoining ruins are in the state to which they were reduced that fatal day. Not far distant stands the ancient palace of Belisarius.

July 3rd

Thursday. Set out early with the Prussian Minster and Russian Ambassador Baron Strogonoff to the Eaux douces, a country palace of the Grand Seigneur to see a review of Turkish Artillery. It was better conducted than we expected, with the cannon they hit the mark repeatedly, with the bombs being more difficult, not once. The General instead of being on horseback, was seated on a carpet under the shade of [a] tree smoking, with a black slave on his knees before him singing romances. The Baron knew him and we took our seat at his side. As a great favor, afterwards we were admitted not only to see the palace but even the most secret chambers of the Harem. I found here the luxuries and beauties we read of in the Arabian tales.

As a still greater favor we were admitted into the mosque, neat simple and beautiful and in form and decoration the same as all the others of Constantinople. There is a pulpit the same as in our churches.

July 4th

Took a boat and sailed along the enchanting shores of the Bosphorus. Crossed to Scutari the suburb on the Asiatic side of the water and saw the Grand Seigneur go to Mosque and return again to embark. He is a man of about 35 years of age, good looking and with a long black beard. The dress of some of the Guards was magnificent, white pelisses, shalls of Cashmere for their belts, and golden arms. We afterwards took horses and rode to the summit of a hill a few miles distant, which commands a view on every side. That towards the interior of Asia [is] perfectly barren, that towards Constantinople I think is the most beautiful and striking I have ever seen. We returned to our boat and passing under the walls of the Seraglio returned to our quarter of Pera. In the evening took a delightful ramble through the Champs des Morts, so called because [it is] covered with burial mounds. The views from this side are extremely picturesque. The Barracks there are a splendid Palace, as indeed most of the others of Constantinople.

July 5th

The Prince and Prussian Minister went to pay a visit to the Rus Affendi, Minister of Foreign affairs, they were received in the same manner as we had been by the Pacha of Tripolitzia. I was unfortunately prevented from going by the arrangements for our departure. These completed I bid adieu to Constantinople about noon, and proceeded by water to Bujuctary an enchanting village situated near the embouchure of the Bosphorus into the Black Sea and where all the Corps Diplomatique resort to spend the summer months, as well as the first Greek families of Constantinople. The Prince had promised to spend two or three days with the Prussian Minister before taking his departure and of course we found rooms prepared for us in his house. We dined at Baron Strogonoff's, and met there all the Ministers and a constellation of elegant ladies, wives and daughters of the same. After dinner we found boats and the Janissaries of the Minister ready to convey us to the opposite side of the Bosphorus where the Baron had made preparations for a splendid Fête Champetre. The place chosen was a beautiful green valley shut in with hills and opening only to water and shaded with oriental planes of immense size. One of these which I measured was between 40 and 50 feet in circumference, nor have I any reason for supposing it the largest. A wide circle was traced out, corded off and a tent pitched in the centre where a handsome entertainment was prepared. In a short time crowds collected from both sides, a great number of Turkish Greek and Armenian women arrived and sat down, some on the grass, some on rich carpets, outside the circle. The rest of the circle was filled up [with] Turkish Grandees and groups of Greek families and all seated on the ground crossed legged à la Turc. Beyond these and under the shade of the Plane trees were numerous parties of peasants, who ran from all sides attracted by the illuminations. Waltzing commenced, and the European figures within and various groups without made the most singular and interesting scene I have ever witnessed. When the sun set, innumerable torches were lighted all round the circle, which supplied its place. We amused ourselves sometimes dancing, sometimes walking round to gaze at the singular groups which encompassed us, talking or trying to talk with the women of whom many Turks as well as Greeks were of the first distinction. They were not particularly reserved but quite ready to commence a conversation especially if introduced by a cake or a cup of coffee. This amusing and novel entertainment lasted till past ten, when we returned to our boats, immense bonfires were then lighted on the opposite side of the water to guide us back to Europe and we again assembled in the Baron's Palace to take refreshments after our voyage.

July 6th
Rose at 4 o'clock, took a boat and rowed to the middle of the Bosphorus to make a sketch of Bujuctary, then landed on the Asiatic side and walked towards the Black sea, returned at 10 o'clock. The Prussian Minister gave a dinner to the other Ambassadors, and in the evening we assembled in the house of the Austrian Ambassador.

July 7th
Baron de Sturmer gave us a dinner, or Fête Champetre in another beautiful valley on the Asiatic shore, and we afterwards rowed halfway to Constantinople to see once more the enchanting scenes which the Bosphorus presents. At nine we returned to Bujucdere, and at 10 to Baron de Senft's where after a comfortable cup of tea and hearty adieu to the Baron and his amiable wife, we embarked on a small row boat which was to convey us to Varna on the Black Sea. The boat was the same as the one from the Dardanelles, with this exception that as in the former we could not lie down, so in this one we could not sit up, nor stand up, and I know not which is most fatiguing.

July 8th
Found ourselves only at the embouchure of the Bosphorus, and the wind being contrary were compelled to remain there all day.

July 9
sailed at sunrise, light winds, but good way during the night and breakfasted at Caracorvina next morning.

July 10
Reached the little village of Agathopolis and slept there for a couple of hours, off again at midnight, but having contrary winds.

July 11
towards sunset put into Gopolis a considerable village where we staid a few hours. Off again at midnight and by next morning

July 12th had crossed the Gulf of Burgas.

July 13th

At sunrise entered the bay of Varna and landed soon after, took coffee in a coffee house on the shore, and our Firman[37] procured us lodgings in an empty house. The voyage from the Bosphorus is most uninteresting, the country a desert plain, the coast low and rocky, and covered with the remains of Shipwrecked vessels. Varna is one of the most important fortresses of Turkey, strong by nature, but ill fortify'd and now totally out of repair. It has been twice taken by the Russians but with loss. It requires a Garrison of 10,000 men to defend it.

July 14th

At sunrise quitted Varna in Turkish Arabahs, or covered carts, the most abominable jolting things, and I have never been so fatigued, or suffered so much in my life. The country for about 20 miles beyond Varna, along a chain of lakes is pretty enough, but after that flat, no wood, and thinly peopled. Towards evening our postillions drove us into a kind of marsh where there was good grass for the horses, and took them out without saying a word, and on demanding a reason they said we must pass the night there. About midnight however we set out.

July 15th

Stopped two hours to breakfast, again 2 hours in the middle of the day and passed the night as before. The country still uninteresting and desert and we passed only through one town.

July 16th

At noon we came in sight of the mighty Danube, and an hour after reached the city of Kutshuk on its banks. After having walked about for an hour or two we crossed the river to Georgius and found lodgings, miserable indeed and swarming with vermin but welcome being positively worn out with the fatigue of the horrid Arabahs. Off early next morning.

July 17th

in a small open cart, and after an hour crossing a river we entered Wallachia,[38] and hailed once more a Christian country. It is however a Principality governed by a Prince appointed by the Porte,[39] he must however be Greek. There are no Turks to be seen. 2 leagues from Georgius brought us to the Post establishments.

The posting in Wallachia is tolerably cheap 10 paras, or 2 pence per league

[37] A firman was a written authorisation in an official letter from the Turkish government.

[38] Wallachia joined with Moldavia in 1862 to become the autonomous principality of Rumania whose full independence from the Ottoman Empire was recognised in 1877.

[39] 'The Porte' is the government of the Ottoman Empire. The name was derived from La Sublime Porte, the main gate into the Sultan's palace.

for each horse and as each person takes 4, it is 8^d per league. For your domestic, and for your luggage you pay the same, that is in all 2 shillings or 8^d per mile. In our train we had 29 horses – This is when the £ is worth P.30 Turk. From Bukarest to the frontier we had 8 horses but it cost us not a para, as the Prince Carreggah gave us an order to take as many as we liked. To the Postillions we paid 6^d or 7^d per post of 10 or 12 miles.[40]

& we proceeded in small carts drawn by 4 horses, each one having a cart to himself. On the 12 leagues to Bukarest I rode 9 on horseback but found the heat too great. The country is flat, uninteresting and little cultivated, the villages few and miserable, the language a corrupted dialect of the Latin. The first view of Bukarest, with a thousand white picturesque towers peeping out of the trees is singularly beautiful and striking. We reached the House of the Austrian Consul at 3 o'clock, and found an excellent dinner and good lodgings prepared for us.

July 18th
Looked through the town, where the mixture of all kinds of dresses, European and Oriental, is very amusing. Hessian boots peeping out of Turkish breeches and Turkish boots from under the petticoats of Greek ladies. Dined at the Austrian Consul's, went afterwards to the promenade à voitures returned to tea, and in the evening went to pay our respects to the Prince Carregah, the King of Wallachia. The Princess, his wife, and his daughter and son-in-law were the only ones present. The Prince in all but his religion is a complete Turk, he is obliged to be so, or the Grand Seigneur cuts off his head.

Pipes ten feet long were brought for the two Princes, none for me, this is the etiquette of Turkey: had I gone alone I should not have been denied one, they however gave me coffee with the rest. Prince Carreggah speaks French quite well and from his conversation seems perfectly acquainted with what is going on in Europe. His brother is Dragoman to the Sultan. Returned to the Consul's to tea.

July 19th
Called on Mr Wilkinson the English consul a Smyrniste by birth. Dined again at the Aust. Consul's. We went out afterwards to a country house of the Princess Marigolo. Beautifully fitted in semi oriental style, among the engravings found the scene out of Tom Jones the same as at the little inn at Disley.

July 20th
Sunday. Dined at our accustomed table and met there the Russian and English Consuls and some others. Went out afterwards to the promenade en voiture, which is in the open plain which surrounds Bucarest. Returned to the Consul's and staid with our hospitable friends till midnight.

July 21st

Set out in a covered cart which we had purchased, drawn by 8 horses. It had no springs and consequently shook intolerably. Came on hard rain and we with difficulty reached a miserable post house at Pitestia small town distant about 6 posts (3 leagues each) from Bucarest. After about an hour we received a pressing invitation from a Boyar or Greek Noble to come to his house, and we waded half a mile in the rain to get to it. Found a comfortable neat house consisting of three rooms, one for the men, one for the women and another for the servants. Our host a good merry man but as we could [not] speak a single word to one another we did not profit much from his conversation. We had a good supper set before us and all eat out of the dishes, plates being used to catch what may fall from the mouth. They do the same in Turkey with this improvement that all eat with the fingers. Felt cold for the first time since leaving Naples. Slept soundly on the sofa, our hosts on the floor.

July 22nd

Off early. First post is almost at the foot of the mountains which separate Wallachia and Transylvania; from this place to Georgevo on the Danube is a perfect plain. At the next post I mounted on horseback, the road being so bad and full of quagmires as to be next to impassable. The scenery in the mountains very picturesque. Staid for the night in a small village where the Prince who slept out of doors and I in were alike devoured by fleas.

July 23rd

Off at six o'clock. I as usual on horseback. The road so bad that even I had extreme difficulty in passing almost all the wooden bridges, carried away, or broken down or wanting a plank or two, and our horses often slipt through. The scenery still beautiful, about 4 o'clock crossed the Alt and about 2 hours more brought us to the guard of Austrian soldiers on the frontiers. Here we bid an adieu, and in all probability an eternal one to the Turkish dominions. A mile beyond is Rothenthurn a small neat village, charmingly situated on the banks of the Alt and shut in by lofty mountains. Here we stopped at the door of a comfortable cottage our abode during the quarantine. It was however destitute of furniture and the floor continued to be our bed. A letter from the Governor of Hermanstadt, let us off with five days enforcement, counting the day of our arrival.

July 24th, 25th, 26th

Continued in prison, the Director came however every evening [to] take us out

---

[40] The whole of this paragraph is a side-note.

and give us a little exercise, he was much alarmed if we approached within 5 or 6 feet of him. We had several heavy showers every day.

July 27th

Towards evening a crowd of Physicians and fumigators entered our apartment, and after a smokey ordeal of a quarter of an hour, they said to our great joy, Gentlemen you may go about your business. I instantly took advantage of my new acquired freedom, and made a delightful ramble through the rocks and woods of Rothenthurn Pass.

July 28th

Set out early with 4 horses instead of 8, and stopping half an hour to breakfast with [the] hospitable Colonel who commands on the frontier, we reached Hermanstadt to an early dinner. It is a considerable and neat town, and the principal Place of Transylvania. We proceeded in the afternoon the horses being everywhere in the fields we were much detained, and were obliged to go on all night which is exceedingly fatiguing in a cart. The 1st evening we reached Michenbach, the second Dobra the 3rd Lugosh, and the morning of the 4th day **31st July** arrived at Temeswar,[41] where we remained a few hours to repose. To this Place the country being flat and unenclosed is not picturesque yet is everywhere cultivated and not uninteresting. The villages numerous and composed of neat white houses. The language, Wallach, and Hungarian, but there being vast numbers of Saxons established in the country for many centuries, who have retained their language laws and religion, German is also much spoken. Latin is the polite language of Hungary, spoken in the national assembly; the laws are written in it, and public business transacted, and even advertisements are often seen printed in that language. Hence many of the people are acquainted with it. I asked at one of the little inns what language they spoke there, and was answered Latin Wallach and Hungarian, at another they replied Hungarian, German and Roman. If this latter meant latin, or Wallach, a corrupt dialect of the latin I could not learn. From Temeswar to the banks of the Danube which we reach[ed] one stage before Bude is a perfect unvaried, uninteresting, and almost boundless plain. The only objects which break the dull line of the horizon, are houses, cornstacks, and hay cocks and even sometimes bullrushes and reeds were sufficient to do it. Where there are no marshes and pools of water which recur continually, it is however cultivated, and villages occur every 5 or 6 miles. We reach'd Bude[42] the evening of the

August 2nd

passed Pest, and the Danube and stopped at the Good fortune in the fortress of Ofen.[43] The Prince went immediately to see his Brother the Hereditary Prince,[44]

Governor of Bude. He was unluckily absent, for having heard that a caravan was arrived at Belgrade, he concluded it must be us and went immediately to give us the meeting he had been gone only two days. The Prince therefore agreed to accompany me to Vienna. We instantly removed ourselves and chatels to the Palace of the Governor.

August 3rd

The Prince being engaged in paying and receiving visits, I went to look through the town and churches, which latter have as little pretensions to architecture without as to simplicity within. They are however clean neat and commodious, and a decency and propriety prevail which one rarely sees in the churches of Italy, Spain and Portugal. In this respect they resemble our Catholic chaples [sic] in England. The religion of Hungary is Catholic, but there are many protestants, and all sects are tolerated.

Bude is composed of two, three or four distinct towns. The new city of Pest is handsome and well built, containing perhaps 30,000 souls; it occupies the north bank of the Danube, and is connected with Ofen the city on the South by a bridge of boats. The river is as wide as the Thames at London Bridge. Ofen is composed of the fortress or ancient Turkish city, and the new town on the banks of the Danube and surrounding hills, which may perhaps have a population of 50,000. The city remained in possession of the Turks above 200 years, and was taken by the famous Prince Eugene. The situation is uncommonly fine, and its appearance from some points can scarcely be excelled by that of any city. The Prince dined with the Archduke Ferdinand, and I alone. In the evening he took me to the Opera, (Cinderella). The house is large and elegant but exceedingly dark, there being only 6 small single lamps in the body of the house and the stage lamps were not seen being let down as in other theatres only to represent night.

August 4th

Rode with the Prince to the new Observatory situated on a high rock which overhangs the Danube. The Professor was very civil, of what country he was I know not but he carried on the conversation in Italian. The instruments seem good, but

---

[41] Temeswar is now Timisoara in Rumania.

[42] Buda and Pest were two separate cities until 1873.

[43] Ofen was the German name for Buda. German settlers were invited to repopulate Buda by King Bela IV after 1242 when the Mongol army which had attacked and destroyed both Buda and Pest, retreated.

[44] The Hereditary Prince is Frederick Joseph (1769–1829) who fought at the Battle of Leipsig (1813), and was married in 1818 to Princess Elizabeth, daughter of King George III of Great Britain. He succeeded his father as ruler of Hesse Homburg in 1820.

few, the building on the best principle. The Prince again dined with the Arch-duke.

August 5th

Took a ramble with the Prince through the streets and churches of Pest. At 6 o'clock went to a review of the Hungarian and Italian troops, the former are un-questionably the finest looking soldiers I have ever seen. The uniform white jacket, tight pantaloons and small boots, and Granadeer [sic] caps. The Emperor of Austria has always on foot 30,000 Hungarian troops, which regiments must be recruited in Hungary. If the Emperor, in time of war, wants more troops they can be granted only by the Parliament. I was mounted on a fine Grey charger of the Hereditary Prince's, which had made 7 campaigns and on which he was wounded in the battle of Leipzick.[45] It of course stood the fire of the artillery tol-erably well. Returned home late.

August 6th

Rambled through Pest and the neighbourhood. The Prince dined at home and took me in the evening to the Opera (Lodoiska).

August 7th

Set our early for Vienna, still in our cart. The country after leaving Bude is flat and uninteresting, but the villages, all neat and picturesque. Got a short night's rest in the fortified town of Baab. Reached Pressburg the second Capital of Hungary about noon.

August 8th

The appearance from a distance is imposing; we crossed the Danube in a singu-lar kind of swing ferryboat, the only one of the sort I have seen, and the princi-pal [sic] of which I could not perfectly comprehend.

Pressburg[46] has a dull dead appearance within. The Emperor is here crowned King of Hungary. He is obliged at the conclusion to gallop upon an el-evated platform on the banks of the river, giving four cuts with a sabre, in all di-rections, swearing to defend Hungary from all enemies. At one stage further, Hambourg a beautiful town, we quitted Hungary and entered into Austria. The Banks of the Danube from Hambourg to Vienna are remarkably fine, a succession of views strongly resembling that from Richmond Hill. We entered Vienna by midnight and put up at the Crown of Hungary.

August 9th

Walked out with the Prince, entered the fine old Gothic Cathedral, of rich work without, and impressive gloominess, and magnificence within. Gothic architec-ture is unquestionably the best adapted to Churches, and religious effect. After dinner the Prince took me to call on his brother Prince Philip[47] L. [Lieutenant] General in the Austrian service, an agreeable clever man. In the afternoon took a ramble together and in the evening went to the theatre.

Walked about Vienna and the neighbourhood, certainly a handsome city, though the streets too narrow, at least within the walls. The Palace is an insignificant building, and few have any architectural pretensions though in a neat and chaste style.

Prince Philip dined with us, and we went together to the Pantomime in the evening.

August 10th

Amused myself as usual rambling about. Prince Philip took us to dine with General O'Reilly,[48] an old emigrant Irishman who stands high in rank and honour at the Austrian Court. He left England in disgust 50 years ago, and has nearly forgotten his native language. Met there a small party of friends. Rainy evening, but my kind companions not withstanding took me again to the Pantomime.

August 12th

Made preparations for the prosecution of my journey. Prince Philip again dined with us, and afterwards took us in his carriage to the Royal Palace of Schonbrun. The gardens are fine, from the summerhouse we had a magnificent view of the city, environs, and country round to an immense extent, with the battlefields of Aspern and Wagram. In the former the regiment of Prince P. brought him 460 French Officers, prisoners, in the latter it was nearly destroyed. This is the Palace that the young Napoleon[49] inhabits. Few if any are allowed to see him, and now

45 The Battle of Leipzick (Leipsig) in 1813 was the so-called Battle of the Nations, where Napoleon was defeated by the armies of the Fourth Coalition and as a result was forced to abdicate and be exiled to Elba in 1814.

46 Pressburg is now Bratislava, capital of Slovakia.

47 Prince Philip is Philip Augustus (1779–1846), who fought at the Battle of Leipsig 1813, married in 1818, and succeeded his brother, Louis William (the Prince with whom Greg travelled), in 1839 as ruler of Hesse Homburg until his death in 1846.

48 Count Andrew O'Reilly (1740–1852): an Austrian Field-Marshal of Irish origin who fought in wars under Maria Theresa and Joseph II before taking part in the struggle against Napoleon. As Governor of Vienna he was forced to surrender the city to Napoleon in 1809 after a short bombardment. The rest of his life was spent in retirement in Vienna.

49 The Young Napoleon was the son of Napoleon I and his second wife Marie Louise (daughter of the Emperor of Austria). Born in 1811 he was called the 'King of Rome'. In 1817 when Greg saw him he was effectively orphaned, his father living out his days on St Helena and his mother enjoying her new life as Duchess of Parma. Loyal Bonapartists called him Napoleon II though he never used this title. He became known as the Duke of Reichstadt. He died in 1832.

no one knows how to call him as his titles are withdrawn. He is a beautiful and engaging child which both my companions regretted, and shook their heads when they spoke of him. He was then walking with his tutor on the terrace but I could see nothing but the top of his bonnet. Returned home late and bid adieu to Prince Philip who had shown me every attention during my short stay at Vienna. Half an hour after I took an affectionate farewell to my kind companion Prince Louis William; it was with the sincerest regret; during three months and a half that our journey lasted he treated me always with a kindness, interest and affection which could not have been greater had I been his son. He was well informed, and full of anecdote, was always cheerful and contented, and never lost his good humour amid the greatest fatigues and privations. To his agreeable company, and to his valuable introductions in all the places we visited, I owe more than half the pleasure of a delightful tour. One thing however he certainly owes to me, as well as Baron Kulmer and Hamborough, and that is, having seen Troy; this is no trifle, and he confessed his obligation to me very strongly in one of our last conversations.

August 13th

At 7 o'clock put myself in a post carriage with Christophe, our Greek servant, and away we went. Being exceedingly impatient to get to Venice[50] and receive some intelligence from [sic, unspecifed, home?], and the German Postillions being intolerably slow I continued my course night and day to Trieste 450 miles and arrived having not stopped half an hour on the road, in four days and three nights, at 12 pm.

August 15th

rather fatigued and hungry.

August 16th

Having no introduction to anyone rambled through the town and environs. The town is regularly built, clean, busy and flourishing, it reminded much of Cadiz. Sailed in a small boat with 13 miscelaneous [sic] passengers about 8 in the evening. Dreadfully flea bitten during the night.

August [17th]

Light winds in the morning, breeze in the evening, reached the Custom House at Lido about midnight.

August 18th

Danced attendance three hours and then had our trunks ransacked to the last rag. Scarcely got half a mile before other C[ustom] H[ouse] Harpies bore down on us again, ransacked the vessel found a piece of Nankeen, took one of the passengers into custody and detained us scandalously. The Health Office detained us another hour and a half, and thus though half starved the day before, were we kept 5 hours without a breakfast of which we stood in so much need. Called on the Vice Consul Mr Scott, grieved to find my letters not arrived. Dined with Mr Scott.

August 19th

Saw the <u>Grimani Palace</u>. Some few good Statues and paintings. Among the former the statue of M. Agrippa from the Pantheon, and that of a Greek Orator were the most remarkable.

In the Church of <u>San Paolo and Giovanni</u> is an admirable painting of Titian.

In the <u>Belle Arte</u> are some fine paintings Bassano, Tintoret and Titian and a beautiful statue of Cannovas, A Muse in a Chair. Dined with Mr Scott and in the evening accompanied him in a Gondola, to an Armenian Convent[51] which occupies a small island on the Laguna. It is an interesting establishmt [sic]. The Friars are all from Constantinople or from farther East. The evening was very fine and the view of Venice the sea and the Alps was striking and magnificent.

August 20

The Architecture of the churches of San Giorgo Maggiore, and Redentore by Palladio, is the best, I have seen in Italy. In La Salute there are some indifferent paintings of Titian and Sasso Ferrato.

Dined with Mr Scott who took me in the evening to a conversazione at Signora Bensoni's.[52] If all Venetian Cons. resemble this which I am assured they do, they are stupid things.

August 21st

Saw the Manfreni Palace. Some very good paintings among many inferior. Dined with Mr Scott. With him took a Gondola to the Lido, a public walk; return to Venice by the light of the moon.

---

[50] Venice was occupied by Napoleon's troops in 1797 when the Venetian Republic and the office of the Doge were abolished. The city and hinterland were ceded to Austria later in that year, but were recovered by France in 1805. In 1815 the whole of Venetia was returned to the Austrian Empire and remained under Austrian control until 1866 when it was incorporated into the Kingdom of United Italy after Austria's defeat by Prussia in the Austro-Prussian War.

[51] The Armenian Convent is on the island of San Lazzaro. Lord Byron spent some time there, learning Armenian and compiling an Armenian dictionary or grammar (opinions differ as to which it was).

[52] Signora Bensoni was one of Lord Byron's lady friends in Venice during the riotous time he spent there in 1816–17.

August 22nd

Went to visit the Arsenal an immense fabric now totally deserted, not a thing touched since the French quitted it. Of 7 first rate, and 8 frigates, only 3 frigates are complete. The construction is reckoned excellent. They are built under cover. The Armoury presents some curious old pieces of armour and ancient arms, immense two handed swords, and among some droll pieces of artillery a leather Mortar. Dined with Mr Scott and met there a Mr Ruden.

August 23rd

Went into the Ducal Palace, a most singular scene semi-oriental, semi-Gothic building. Some good paintings of various glorious circumstances in Venetian history. Dined with Mr Scott, and walked till dark in the public Gardens.

August 24th

Took a gondola with Mr Scott and went to the island of Torcello about five miles, it was there that the original settlers first took refuge from the ravages of Atila [sic]. There is a singular old Cathedral, some of the windows, have stone shutters which I believe cannot be seen elsewhere. Dined with Mr Scott, and went with him to the public gardens to see some bad fireworks.

August 25th

Went again to the Ducal Palace, saw the ancient Senate room, and numbers of good paintings representing the glorious actions of the republic. Ascended the steeple of San Mark's Church which is of astonishing height, and the view from the summit very striking. The ascent is by an inclined plane like the Giralda at Seville. Dined with Mr Scott and took leave.

August 26th

half an hour after midnight went to Diligence office and being too early I took a ramble along the great canal to the Rialto, where I remained some time admiring the singular scene by the light of a full moon. I then entered a Gondola with some other passengers, and we glided smoothly along among the once magnificent palaces of Venice. A gentle breeze carried us quickly over the Laguna, and in an hour's time I once more set my feet on the main land of Italy. Here we entered the Diligence, and reached Padua about day break. Padua is a poor looking place, no good buildings, and nothing interesting. At Vicenza we staid about two hours, which gave me time to run hastily to see the palaces, churches, and Olympic Theatre of Palladio. He unquestionably had more idea of good Architecture Architecture [sic, repeated] than any Italian architectur [sic] and for this reason he consulted the ancients more than his fancy. I do not believe he would have defaced the Rock of the Capitol, with the miserable building Michael Angelo has placed there. We arrived at Verona rather late and I had scarcely light enough to see the ancient Roman Theatre.

August 27th

Off at 3 o'clock at Peschiera, crossed the Mincio, and entered the Milanese. Had some fine views of the Lago di Garda. We passed through Brescia, and reach[ed] Milan about 2 o'clock in the morning of

August 28th

& made my way to a comfortable bed at the Hotel di Europa. Looked through the town, went to the Arena built by Napoleon on the plan of the Ancient. It is both Hippodrome and Naumachia, but not quite finished. There is a portico of eight granite columns, in a very good style. Walked thence round the walls to the Arch of the Samplon. It is not half finished, though almost all the marble is ready worked and might be erected at a trifling expence. The whole is of marble, corinthian architecture, and in much better taste than the triumphal arch at Paris. I went afterwards to see the famous Lords Supper of Leonardo da Vinci's. It is in a miserable state the water from above having trickled all over it. In the evening went to the famous Theatre of the Scala, the greatest in Europe, though in richness and ornament far inferior to the San Carlo at Naples.

August the 29th

Ascended the tower of the Cathedral, whence is a striking view of the gardens of Italy, the Alps and the Appenines. The building is as highly finished, and as well worth seeing above as below. It is all of white marble, which in the new parts, for example almost the whole point, is of a dazzling brightness. The number of ornaments is perhaps too great, and that is the reason that after so many centuries it remains unfinished. Napoleon did more than had been done 200 years before, but much remains to do for they told me that when all was complete there would be among other trifles 11,000 statues. It certainly deserves the reputation it enjoys, though I much doubt its being equal to York Minster. In other countries the people as much overprize their monuments as we undervalue ours. Went in the evening to the Concano Theatre.

August 30th and 31st

Looked about the town etc etc and went to the grand Promenade being Sunday.

September 1st

At 5 o'clock off in the diligence. Passed through Pavia, and crossed the Po by a large bridge of Boats. Reached Novi late in the evening. Novi is at the foot of the mountains, and there the rich garden which extends from Venice thither ceases.

Sept 2nd

The road through the mountains very bad. Crossed the Borghetta a second time and reached Genoa about 4 in the afternoon. After ablutions and dinner I went to call on Mr Drago, and found him and his agreeable family in the grotto taking the fresco. After being so long accustomed to strange faces and strange places, how sweet it is to see, what we have seen before.

Sept 3rd

Spent the morning in the Porto Franco, dined with Mr Drago at 3 o'clock and amused myself with the ladies in the garden till ten.

Sept 4th, and 5, and 6

Ditto, ditto, ditto, except that each day was more agreeably spent that the pre-ceeding one.

Sept 7 Sunday

Went out into the country to at [sic] Mr Dover, a Swiss family, and an agreeable one. Mrs D. who has been about a year married, is one of the handsomest and most enchanting women I ever saw –

Whilst the Gentlemen were preparing some fireworks, I took a long ramble with the ladies among the gardens and vineyards which surrounded the house. Returned to Genoa at a late hour.

Sept 8th

Being again jour de fête, and no work to be done, Mr Drago and his family took me to dine and opened the day at his brother's, distant some miles from Genoa on the sea coast. There was a pretty large party, but I am now so accustomed to Italian society that nothing strikes me as singular, and I almost cease to make my remarks, indeed I but just observed that the Gentlemen all sat at table without coat, waistcoat or neckcloth, and some with their shirt sleeves tucked up above the elbow. The heat of the weather was some excuse for what we should consider as an indecency. As Mrs Drago however was not a Mrs Dover, neither in beauty or character, Monday was not so agreeably spent as Sunday. In the evening went to see the Doria Gardens, which gave me much pleasure inasmuch as they are á l'Angloise. Returned late to Genoa.

Sept 9th

Spent the morning arranging my affairs, dined with Mr Drago, and staid till a late hour. With more regret than I can express did I bid adieu to this kind, delightful, excellent family, from my own I could not have received more, from no other have I received so much attention, and such warm marks of affection.

Sept 10th

at midnight set out in a monster of a diligence. Walked over the Appenines the Brochetta being a frightful road, and gained an hour on the diligence. Slept at Alessandria.

Sept 11

after 3 or 4 hours sleep, off again at 3 o'clock as usual; and reached Turin at 5. The country most beautiful and the views of the Alps magnificent.

Sept 12 and 13

Remained at Turin.

Sept 14

Set out in the diligence at 3 in the morning and slept at Novara; I met tolerably pleasant company in the diligence for the very first time, amongst others was an intelligent Greek of Saio (ant. Chio).

Sept 15

off again at 2 o'clock and reached Milan at 1 P.M. I had not been half an hour arrived before I had secured a place in Baron de Crud's carriage to Geneva.

Septr 16

Remained at Milan.

— 17

Set out with the Monsr. Le Baron, and at noon reached the Marquis d'Alberini's where we dined. We set out again the same evening, and travelling all night found ourselves in hard rain on the banks of the Lago Maggiore at day break. The weather continuing very bad, we continued our route, but were compelled to stop at Domodosola.

Sept 19th

The weather something better. The number of English on the road so great that the horses were almost killed, and we walked on foot from Tzel to Brig about 11 leagues, arriving before the carriage. I found my companion one of the most pleasing, amiable, excellent, well informed men I have ever met with.

Septr 20th

Continued our journey slowly along le Vallais, on account of the horses. Reachd the frontiers of Savoy at sunset and Geneva next morning at 9 o'clock.

Sept 21st – Sunday

Went to English chapel. Service admirably read, and the music of the Organ affecting; I never experienced more fully the power of that art. Went out to Mr Fazy's country house and passed the evening agreeably with him and his family.

Septr 22nd

Dined at Fazy's. Called on Mons. Achard, spent the evening with Fazy and a small company of friends.

Sept 23rd

Set out at 6 o'clock in the Chamouny diligence, and at 8 in the evening reached St Martin. It rained hard all day.

Septr 24th

Still bad weather, notwithstanding I walked to Chamouny, visiting on the way the Glacier of Bussous. This is 7 hours good hard walking.

Septr 25th

Most beautiful morning. At 7 o'clock set off with Mr Hammond to ascend the montanvert, 5550 feet above the sea. Accomplished this in 2 hours and spent some time in examining the mountains and the wonderful mer de Glace. In descending we visited the source of the River Arveron, which runs out of Glacier de Bois. I rested half an hour and then proceeded by the mountain of Prarion, nearly as high as the montanvert, to the Baths of St Gervais. This is a most enchanting route, infinitely preferable to the common one; it is 5 or 6 good hours walking from Charmouny and I arrived tired at 8 o'clock.

Sept 26th

Still on foot, 2 hours to St Martin, 3 to Cluse, 3 to Bonneville which I reached much fatigued at 5 o'clock.

Septr 27th

Set out again at 4, and walked to Geneva, 5 hours. After breakfast I walked out of town 3 miles to call on Baron Crud, who showed me every civility and made me stay [to] dinner though inconvenient to me. His wife and two daughters are polished and amiable. Returned home late.

September 28th[53]

---

[53] Here the journal ends. The text is left incomplete.

ROBERT HYDE GREG IN LATER LIFE

Having joined his father's firm in 1817, Greg spent the rest of his working life as a textile manufacturer. He was the most efficient and successful of the Greg brothers in controlling the affairs of the firm, which at the time of his father's death in 1834, was one of the largest spinning and weaving concerns in the country. Robert Hyde Greg became one of the leading Manchester manufacturers in the first half of the nineteenth century.

In 1824 he married Mary Phillips, whose brother Mark was one of the first Members of Parliament for Manchester after the great Reform Bill in 1832. Greg himself represented the city from 1839 to 1841, supporting the Anti-Corn-Law League and Free Trade.

Robert Hyde Greg had the reputation of being a prudent and highly efficient businessman with a meticulous command of detail as far as the affairs of his firm were concerned. Very hard working, he was a perfectionist and expected the highest standards from others. As an employer, he provided good living and working conditions by the standards of his day – Styal was a model village – and in return he demanded hard work and obedience from his employees. He was both paternalistic and exacting in his attitude to his workforce who remembered him as a "very reserved person".

A man of wide and deep interests, he was an active member of Manchester's intellectual society, supporting such organisations as the Manchester Literary and Philosophical Society, the Manchester Royal Institution and the Geographical and Geological Societies of the city. He helped to found the Manchester Mechanics Institute, which became the University of Manchester Institute of Science and Technology (now part of Manchester University) and was an early member of the Society for the Preservation of Ancient Footpaths.

As a landowner, he was interested in new methods of farming and arboriculture.

Robert Hyde Greg died on 21st February 1875.

ADDITIONAL NOTES

Ian Robertson, authority on early British travellers to Spain, considers that Robert Hyde Greg's Spanish journal is an unusual (perhaps unique) survival from a period when Spain was not considered to be a safe place in which to travel.

Greg was familiar with the accounts of their travels by Henry Swinbourne (published in 1779), J. F. Bourgoing (1789) and Robert Semple (1807). Other travellers such as Edward Clarke and Joseph Baretti (friend of Dr Johnson), Richard Twiss and Major William Dalrymple also wrote about their journeys before the Peninsular War (1809–1814).

Spain during this war, and the years immediately following it, was no place for the ordinary traveller, and only letters and military memoirs of various kinds survive from this period.

So Greg's journal provides an interesting link between the pre-war writings and those of later visitors to Spain, who only started to venture there again in the 1830s. The most important of these were George Borrow (author of *The Bible in Spain*) and the most notable hispanophile of the nineteenth century, Richard Ford, who spent three years living in Andalucia and travelling elsewhere in Spain some fifteen years after Robert Hyde Greg's tour. His *Handbook for Travellers in Spain* and *Gatherings in Spain* were first published in the 1840s.

ISAAC HODGSON

Isaac Hodgson, the travelling companion of Robert Hyde Greg, was his cousin. His mother, Elizabeth Lightbody, was the sister of Robert's mother Hannah. He became the business partner of Samuel Greg in 1813. The Spanish government of Ferdinand VII imposed very heavy customs duties on foreign imports. A large consignment of cotton goods from the firm of Samuel Greg and Co. was confiscated in Cadiz. Isaac failed in 1815 to secure their release and the firm consequently suffered very heavy losses. Isaac was ruined, retired from the partnership, and had to hand over his spinning mill at Caton near Lancaster to Samuel Greg as part payment of his losses. He later started a business in Liverpool to trade with Brazil, which was successful. After this he became a managing partner in Pare's Bank in Leicester. He died in 1861.

NOTE ON QUARRY BANK MILL

Five generations of Gregs entered the family business. The handsome, brick-built Quarry Bank Mill, in its beautiful setting in the Bollin Valley, together with the estate which includes the village of Styal with its workers' houses, school, shop and church, and the Apprentice House, where pauper child workers lived in the early part of the nineteenth century, now belong to the National Trust. The whole complex was donated to the Trust by the late Alec Greg in 1939. Production by the firm ceased in 1959.

The Mill has been fully restored, and working demonstrations of the various processes in textile production are given to visitors. The Mill produces cotton cloth which is sold in the museum shop. It is one of the most important and interesting industrial museums in Britain.

Quarry Bank House, built by Samuel Greg for his family, was sold separately from the estate and was privately owned and occupied until late in 2006 when the National trust was able to purchase it from the owner, thus reuniting the Greg family home with the Mill.

INDEX OF PEOPLE AND PLACES

The index is confined to people and places. Greg was not always consistent, however, in the spelling of names, and alternative spellings found in the text are given where necessary. It is possible that he spelt names as he heard them, especially in the Ottoman Empire. References to notes (indicated by n. or nn.) are included where appropriate. Illustrations are indexed as 'Pl.' or 'Pls'.

Xenil, River (see Genil)
Xeres (Jerez de la Frontera), 140, 142

York Minster, 245

Zia or Cers, Island of, 224
Zurmer (?), Colonel, 215: n. 17

1. Quarry Bank Mill from the Mill Meadow. Photograph © Caroline Hill, The National Trust.

2. Stirling Castle and the Vale of Menteith, from Vol. 1 of *A Journey from Edinburgh Through Parts of North Britain* (1811) by Alexander Campbell. Reproduced courtesy of the John Rylands Library, University of Manchester.

Sketched on the Spot by Alex.r Campbell

3. Fingal's Cave in Staffa, from *A Tour of Scotland and Voyage to the Hebrides* (1772) by Thomas Pennant. Reproduced courtesy of the John Rylands Library, University of Manchester.

4. 'A View of Falmouth and Places Adjacent', an engraving by R. Polard published in June 1806 by H. Mitchell of Falmouth. Reproduced courtesy of the Falmouth Art Gallery.

5 (opposite). Aqueduct of Alcantara, from *Sketches of Country Character and Costumes in Portugal and Spain* by the Rev. William Bradford (1809), reproduced courtesy of the John Rylands Library, University of Manchester.

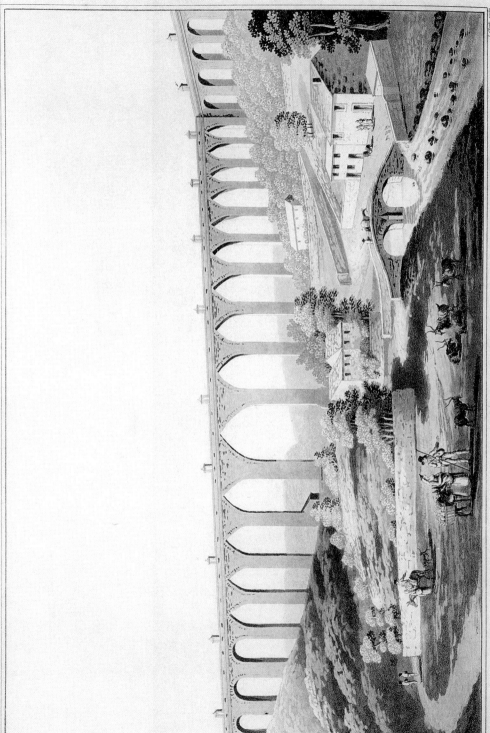

AQUEDUCT OF ALCANTARA.

CINTRA.

6. Cintra, from *Sketches of Country Character and Costumes in Portugal and Spain* by the Rev. William Bradford (1809), reproduced courtesy of the John Rylands Library, University of Manchester.

The carriage in which we travelled from Lisbon to Badajos

The man and his mules taken from the inside of the Calisa.

7. 'The Carriage in which we travelled from Lisbon to Badajoz' and 'The Man and his Mules taken from the inside of the Calisa', both from the Sketchbook of Robert Hyde Greg. © Quarrry Bank Mill, The National Trust.

8. The Venta at Bencasim in c.1813, from *Views in Spain* (1824) by Edward Hawke Locker. Rreproduced courtesy of Ian Robertson.

9 (opposite). Greg's manuscript of the first page of the second volume of the journal of travels in the Iberian Peninsula.

Journey from Seville to Granada, Malaga,
Gibraltar, Tangiers, Tetuan, Ceuta, & Cadiz.

January 4th. At mid day I repaired to the
Posada del Lobo, and the main body of our
Caravan I found had already departed. I &
the head Muleteer were not long in following
them, and we left Seville by the Gate of Carmona.
The first two miles of the road lay along the acqueduct of Carmona, and soon after we entered
on the great plain by which Seville is on every
side surrounded. My equipment
was not particular, either for expedition,
or for making a great show; I had an ass
provided me, which, besides an enormous pack
saddle, carried a week's provision, two or three
sacks and baskets, my prog and wallets, together with a number odd things, and I seated myself as I could on the top of this heap
of baggage, riding backwards, or forwards,
or sideways, according to inclination, or the
convenience of conversing with my companions. At a short distance from the city I saw
a man's leg nailed to a piece of wood, I was
told that it belonged to a man who had

12. One of the pillars of the Court of Lions, from the journal.

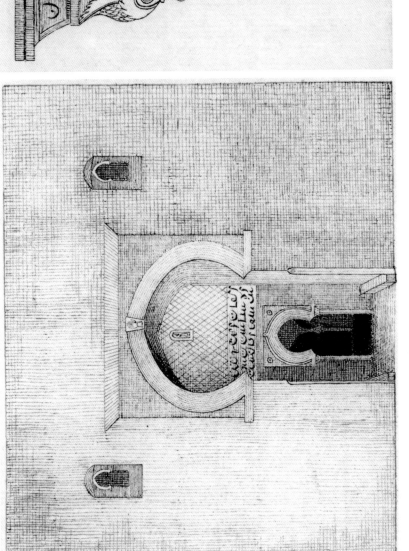

11. The principal entrance to the Alhambra, from the manuscript of the journal.

10 (opposite). The Alhambra, from the sketchbook of Robert Hyde greg. © Quarry Bank Mill, the National Trust.

13. Moorish Castle and Cathedral of Malaga, visited by Greg on January 28th 1815. From the sketchbook of Robert Hyde Greg, © Quarry Bank Mill, The National Trust.

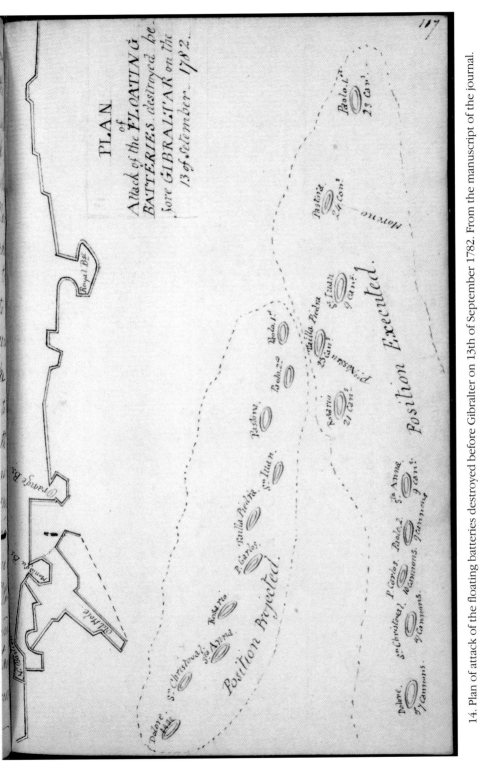

117

PLAN
of
Attack of the FLOATING
BATTERIES destroyed be-
fore GIBRALTAR on the
13 of September 1782.

Royal Bʸ.

Orange Bʸ.

Montue Bʸ.

Old Mole

Position Projected.

Dolore
Talla

Sᵗ Christoval
Sᵗᵃ Anna

Rosario

P. Carlos
Talla Piedra

Sᵗ Ilidm.

Pastora.

Paolo.2ᵈ

Paolo.1ᵗ

Position Executed.

Dolore.
5 Cannons.

Sᵗ Christoval.
Wannens.
4 Cannons.

P.Carlos
4 Cannons.

Paolo.2.
Sᵗᵃ Anna.
9 cans.

Rosario
21 cans.

Sᵗ Ilidm.

Talla Piedra
23 cans.

Sᵗ Ivan.
9 cans.

Pastora
24 cans.

Moreno

Paolo.1ᵗ
23 cans.

14. Plan of attack of the floating batteries destroyed before Gibralter on 13th of September 1782. From the manuscript of the journal.

15. View of the tops of houses at Tetuan, February 12th, 1815. From the sketchbook of Robert Hyde Greg. © Quarry Bank Mill, The National Trust.

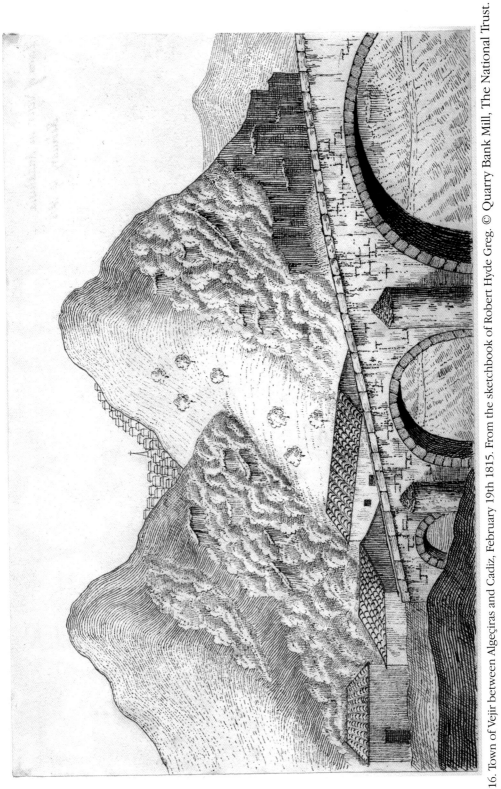

16. Town of Vejir between Algeçiras and Cadiz, February 19th 1815. From the sketchbook of Robert Hyde Greg. © Quarry Bank Mill, The National Trust.

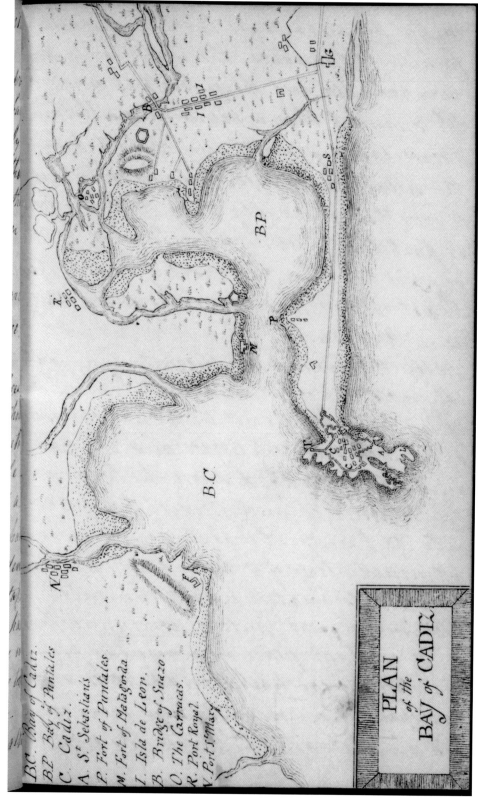

B.C. Bay of Cadiz.
B.P. Bay of Puntales.
C. Cadiz.
A. St Sebastian's
P. Fort of Puntales.
M. Fort of Matagorda
I. Isla de Leon.
B. Bridge of Suazo.
O. The Carracas.
R. Port Royal.
V. Port St Mary

PLAN
of the
BAY of CADIZ

17. Plan of the Bay of Cadiz. From the manuscript of the journals.

18. Eastern front of the Escorial Palace, May 13th, 1815. From the sketchbook of Robert Hyde Greg. © Quarry Bank Mill, The National Trust.

19. Southern front of the Alcazar of Segovia. From the sketchbook of Robert Hyde Greg. © Quarry Bank Mill, The National Trust.

20. Toledo, from *A Picturesque Tour through Spain* by Henry Swinburne (1806). Reproduced courtesy of the John Rylands Library, University of Manchester.

Le Prado à Madrid.

Prévost anet. Sculpsit.

21. Le Prado à Madrid, from *L'Espagne et le Portugal* by M. Breton (1815), reproduced courtesy of the John Rylands Library, University of Manchester.

22. Pepe Illo making the Pass of the 'Recorte'. Etching from *La Tauromaquia* by Henry Swinburne (1806). Reproduced courtesy of the John Rylands Library, University of Manchester.1

23. The Pass of Pancorbo, by Genaro Perez Villaamil, from *España artística y monumental* (1842–4), courtesy of Ian Robertson.

24. Miranda del Ebro, from *A Picturesque Tour through Spain*, by Henry Swinburne (1806). Reproduced courtesy of the John Rylands Library, University of Manchester.

25. Chateau des Tuileries, Vue du Jardin, from the *Nouveau Plan de Paris* (1822). Reproduced courtesy of the John Rylands Library, University of Manchester.

26. Paris Digilence, from *The Stranger in France, or; A Tour from Devonshire to Paris*, by Sir John Carr (London, 1814).
Reproduced courtesy of the John Rylands Library, University of Manchester.

27. Chambery (February 1817), from the Robert Hyde Greg Sketchbook, courtesy of Mrs Kitty Gore.

PLATE 8

Drawn by E.F. Batty.

London, Published June 1820 by Rodwell & Martin, New Bond Street.

Engraved by Chas Heath & J. Lewis.

28. Genoa, from *Italian Scenery from Drawings made in Italy in 1817*, by Elizabeth Frances Batty.
Reproduced courtesy of the John Rylands Library, University of Manchester.

29. Florence: a View of the Ponte Trinita, from *Italian Scenery from Drawings made in Italy in 1817*, by Elizabeth Frances Batty. Reproduced courtesy of the John Rylands Library, University of Manchester.

London, Published Dec.ʳ 1,1818 by Rodwell & Martin, New Bond Street.

30. Rome from the Palatine Hill, from *Italian Scenery from Drawings made in Italy in 1817*, by Elizabeth Frances Batty. Reproduced courtesy of the John Rylands Library, University of Manchester.

31. The Coliseum in Rome, from *Italian Scenery from Drawings made in Italy in 1817*, by Elizabeth Frances Batty. Reproduced courtesy of the John Rylands Library, University of Manchester.

32. The Eruption of Vesuvius, from *Campi Phlegraei*, by William Hamilton (1779). Reproduced courtesy of the John Rylands Library, University of Manchester.

Drawn by E.F.Batty.

London, Published Aug.1, 1819, by Rodwell & Martin, New Bond Street.

Engraved by G.Cooke.

33. Lake Avernus, from *Italian Scenery from Drawings made in Italy in 1817*, by Elizabeth Frances Batty. Reproduced courtesy of the John Rylands Library, University of Manchester.

34. A Street in Pompeii, from the sketchbook of Robert Hyde Greg.
© Quarry Bank Mill, the National Trust.

Drawn by E. F. Batty.　　　　London, Published Oct.ʳ 1, 1819, by Rodwell & Martin, New Bond Street.　　　　Engraved by Sam.ˡ Mitan.

35. The View from the Chiaia (Naples), from *Italian Scenery from Drawings made in Italy in 1817*, by Elizabeth Frances Batty. Reproduced courtesy of the John Rylands Library, University of Manchester.

Ithaca - May 16th

36. Ithaca on May 16th 1817, from the sketchbook of Robert Hyde Greg.
© Quarry Bank Mill, the National Trust.

House of a Greek Primate --
Argos
24/M

37. The House of a Greek Primate at Argos, May 24th 1817, from the sketchbook of Robert Hyde Greg.
© Quarry Bank Mill, the National Trust.

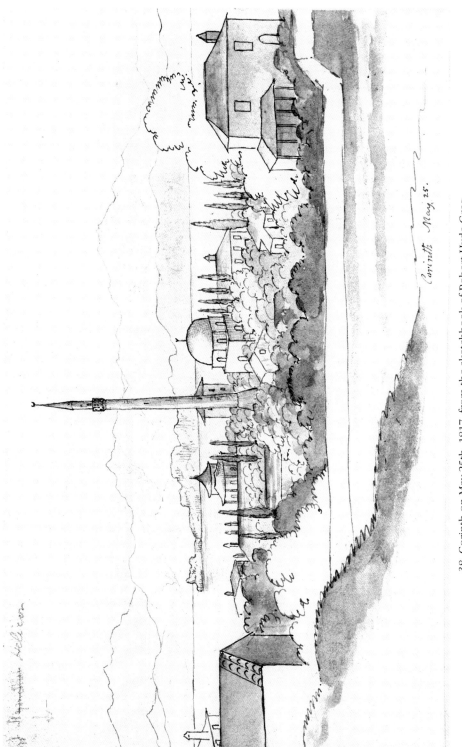

38. Corinth on May 25th, 1817, from the sketchbook of Robert Hyde Greg.
© Quarry Bank Mill, the National Trust.

Acropolis from Sarillo

June 1st

39. The Acropolis (May 1817), from the Robert Hyde Greg sketchbook, reproduced courtesy of Mrs Kitty Gore.

40. The Parthenon and Erechtheion, from *Views in Greece* (1821), by Edward Dodwell. Reproduced courtesy of the John Rylands Library, University of Manchester.

41. The Temple of Jupiter Panhellenius on the Island of Aegina, from *Views in Greece* (1821), by Edward Dodwell. Reproduced courtesy of the John Rylands Library, University of Manchester.

W. Turner delt.

London, Published by I. Murray, 1820.

I. Clark Sculpt.

42. The Mode of Travelling in Turkey, from Journal of a Tour in the Levant, by William Turner Esq. (London, 1820). Reproduced courtesy of the Skilliter Centre for Ottoman Studies, Newnham College, Cambridge.

43. Subaltern Officer of the Janisseries, from *Costumes of Turkey, Picturesque Representations of the Dress and Manners of the Turks* (London, 1814). Reproduced courtesy of the Skilliter Centre for Ottoman Studies, Newnham College, Cambridge.

44 (opposite). A Public Khan, from *Beauties of the Bosphorus, by Miss Pardoe, from Original Drawings by William H. Bartlett* (London, 1838). Reproduced courtesy of the Skilliter Centre for Ottoman Studies, Newnham College, Cambridge.

45. Bujuctory, on July 6 1817. From the Robert Hyde Greg sketchbook. Reproduced courtesy of Mrs Kitty Gore.

Drawn by Capt. Frankland.

Pub. by H. Crltham. London. 1838.

Engraved by J. Clark.

46. The Bosphorus from the Giant's Mountain. From *The Beauties of the Bosphorus by Miss Pardoe, from Original Drawings by William H. Bartlett* (London, 1838). Reproduced courtesy of the Skilliter Centre for Ottoman Studies, Newnham College, Cambridge.

47. A Sultana or Kaddin, from *Costumes of Turkey. Representations of the Dress and Manners of the Turks* (London, 1814). Reproduced courtesy of the Skilliter Centre for Ottoman Studies, Newnham College, Cambridge.

48. Moorish Barracks, with entrance by the Black Sea, from the Robert Hyde Greg Sketchbook, reproduced courtesy of Mrs Kitty Gore.

W. Turner del.^t

I. Clark sculp.^t

London, Published by I. Murray, 1820.

49. A Turkish Arabah, from *Journal of a Tour in the Levant* by William Turner (London, 1820).
Reproduced courtesy of the Skilliter Centre for Ottoman Studies, Newnham College, Cambridge.

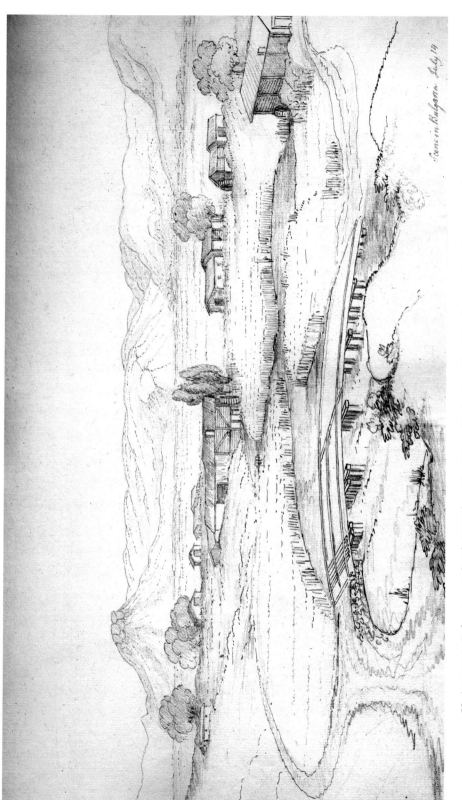

Scene in Bulgaria. July 14

50. A scene in Bulgaria on July 14, 1817, from the Robert Hyde Greg Sketchbook, reproduced courtesy of Mrs Kitty Gore.

Printed by Engelmann&Co

51. A posting in Wallachia, with a Janissary Tartar, from *Narrative of a Journey from Constantinople to England*, by the Rev. R. Walsh (1728). Reproduced courtesy of the Skilliter Centre for Ottoman Studies, Newnham College, Cambridge.

52. The Archbishop's Palace in Bucharest, July 19, 1817, from the Robert Hyde Greg Sketchbook, reproduced courtesy of Mrs Kitty Gore.

53. Kingen on July 23, 1817, from the Robert Hyde Greg Sketchbook, reproduced courtesy of Mrs Kitty Gore.

54. Rothenthurn in the Carpathian Mountains, the view from Greg's quarantine on July 27, 1817, from the Robert Hyde Greg Sketchbook, reproduced courtesy of Mrs Kitty Gore.

Frontier Guard House

55. The Frontier Guard House of Transylvania, July 27, 1817, from the Robert Hyde Greg Sketchbook, reproduced courtesy of Mrs Kitty Gore.

Torre Rotta

Ancient frontier between Wallachia & Transylvania.

Transilva July 28. 1817

56. Torre Rotta, an ancient frontier point between Wallachia and Transylvania, on July 28, 1817, from the Robert Hyde Greg Sketchbook, reproduced courtesy of Mrs Kitty Gore.

57. An Hungarian village, August 7, 1817, from the Robert Hyde Greg Sketchbook, reproduced courtesy of Mrs Kitty Gore.

Printed by Engelmann. & Co.

58. A Saxon Peasant of the Reformed Church in Transylvania, from *Narrative of a Journey from Constantinople to England* by the Rev. R. Walsh (1728). Reproduced courtesy of the Skilliter Centre for Ottoman Studies, Newnham College, Cambridge.

59. Buda in August 1817, from the Robert Hyde Greg Sketchbook, reproduced courtesy of Mrs Kitty Gore.

Drawn by E.F. Batty.

PL. 9.

London. Published June 1, 1819 by Rodwell & Martin, New Bond Street.

Engraved by Saml Mitan.

60. Venice, from *Italian Scenery from Drawings made in Italy in 1817* by Elizabeth Frances Batty. Reproduced courtesy of the John Ryalnds Library, University of Manchester.

62. Robert Hyde Greg at the time of his marriage in 1824. © Mrs Katharine Walker.

61 (left). Quarry Bank House, built by Samuel Greg for his family.
Photograph © Caroline Hill and the National Trust.